LIVING ART

INDONESIAN ARTISTS ENGAGE POLITICS, SOCIETY AND HISTORY

LIVING ART

INDONESIAN ARTISTS ENGAGE POLITICS, SOCIETY AND HISTORY

EDITED BY ELLY KENT, VIRGINIA HOOKER AND CAROLINE TURNER

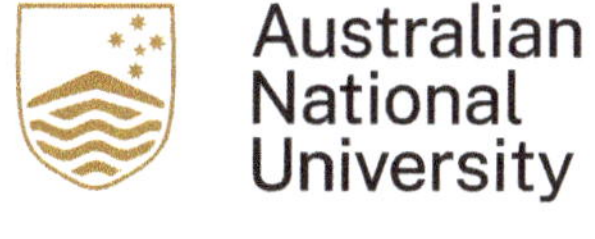

ANU PRESS

ASIAN STUDIES SERIES MONOGRAPH 17

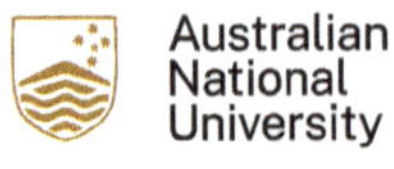

Published by ANU Press
The Australian National University
Canberra ACT 2600, Australia
Email: anupress@anu.edu.au

Available to download for free at press.anu.edu.au

ISBN (print): 9781760464929
ISBN (online): 9781760464936

WorldCat (print): 1344222452
WorldCat (online): 1344222529

DOI: 10.22459/LA.2022

Cover design and layout by ANU Press.

Cover image: Tita Salina (b. 1973), South Sumatra, *1001st Island – The Most Sustainable Island in Archipelago*, 2015.

This book is published under the aegis of the Asian Studies Editorial Board of ANU Press.

Contents

Acknowledgements

We thank Professor Will Christie, former head of the Humanities Research Centre (HRC) at The Australian National University (ANU), and the HRC for its generous support of the 2019 conference 'Contemporary Worlds: Indonesian Art', which was the genesis of this book. The conference was a joint project of the HRC and the National Gallery of Australia (NGA) and was also supported by the School of Art and Design, ANU, and the Indonesia Institute, ANU. We extend our thanks to these institutions, our co-conveners, the speakers and others who assisted with the conference. The conference conveners were Elly Kent, Virginia Hooker, Caroline Turner, David Williams, Chaitanya Sambrani and Rohan Nicol from ANU; Carol Cains and Jaklyn Babington from the NGA; and Christine Clark.

Professor Craig Reynolds, chair of ANU Press's Asian Studies Series, offered ongoing support for the book and encouraged us more than we can express. Thank you, Craig.

We extend our thanks to our copyeditor, Dr Rani Kerin, for her very careful and thoughtful editing of the manuscript as well as to the highly skilled publishing team at ANU Press for their meticulous work producing and designing this book, especially manager Ben Wilson, former deputy manager Emily Tinker, production editor Elouise Ball and designer Teresa Prowse.

The editors express their special thanks to Professor Robert Cribb for providing the maps for the book. We were blessed to have an internationally famous cartographer prepare the meticulous maps of Indonesia. We are also grateful to Dr Maxine McArthur, who advised on the Timeline and Glossary.

The editors gratefully acknowledge a grant from the ANU College of Asia and the Pacific to fund the copyediting of this book; a grant from the ANU College of Arts and Social Sciences for an international conference keynote; and support from the Indonesia Institute, ANU, for an online webinar in 2021.

The editors express their particular thanks to the authors in this book for their individual contributions that make this volume such a strong collection of essays: FX Harsono, T. K. Sabapathy, Jim Supangkat, Alia Swastika and Wulan Dirgantoro. We are immensely grateful to the family of Sanento Yuliman, especially his children Danuh Tyas and Puja Anindita, for their generous permission to publish Dr Kent's translation of his work, and for their trust in the process. We are privileged to have their support for this publication.

Our sincere thanks to the anonymous reviewers for their invaluable feedback.

Our profound gratitude to each of the artists whose art is illustrated and their families, as well as the institutions, individuals, copyright owners, collectors and others who helped us with research, provided images and gave permission to reproduce images of their artworks.

Artists

We wish to thank the following artists: Nindityo Adipurnomo, Siti Adiyati, Dyan Anggraini, Irwan Ahmett, Zico Albaiquni, Arahmaiani, Cheo Chai-Hiang, Dadang Christanto, Heri Dono, FX Harsono, Iswanto Hartono, Yusuf Susilo Hartono, Mella Jaarsma, Jompet Kuswidananto, Moelyono, Patriot Mukmin, I Made 'Bayak' Muliana, Mangku Muriati, Eko Nugroho, A. D. Pirous, Rangga Purbaya, Nency Dwi Ratna, Karina Roosvita, Tita Salina, Tisna Sanjaya, Dolorosa Sinaga, Marintan Sirait, the late Srihadi Soedarsono, the late Hildawati Soemantri, Studio Malya, Dede Eri Supria, Yaya Sung, Agus Suwage, Taring Padi Collective, Titarubi (Rubiati Puspitasari) and Tintin Wulia.

Families and Other Copyright Holders

Our most sincere and grateful thanks to the following (listed by year of artist's birth):

- Kartika Affandi, for permission to reproduce artworks by her late father, Affandi
- S. Sudjojono Center, and especially Maya Sudjojono, its director, for permission to reproduce works by the late S. Sudjojono

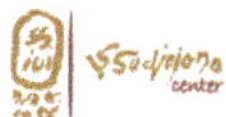

- Ravi Ahmad Salim, for artworks by his late father, Ahmad Sadali
- Adwi Prasetya Yogananta and family, for permission to use the work of their late father, Amri Yahya
- Taufik Riantoso, for the late Umi Dachlan
- Konfir Kabo.

Institutions

We wish to thank the British Library, Art Gallery of South Australia (AGSA), Galeri Nasional Indonesia, Indonesian Visual Art Archive, National Gallery of Australia, Museum and Gallery of the Northern Territory (MAGNT), Queensland Art Gallery | Gallery of Modern Art (QAGOMA), and National Gallery Singapore.

Galleries, Artist Representatives and Artists' Studios

We also wish to thank the Aboriginal Artists Agency Ltd (for the late Minimini Mamarika), Edwin's Gallery (for Ahmad Sadali), Jakarta and Serambi Pirous Studio Gallery, Bandung (for Pirous), Somalaing Studio (for Dolorosa Sinaga), Studio Kalahan (for Heri Dono), Jan Manton Gallery Brisbane and Nancy Sever Gallery Canberra (for Dadang Christanto), and the Cemeti Institute for Art and Society.

Individuals

We are most grateful to all those who kindly assisted us with both the conference and the book. We extend our special thanks to curators Carol Cains and Jaklyn Babington; Nick Mitzevich, director; and the executive team at the NGA, Bianca Winataputri and Eliza Williams; as well as many other staff at the NGA. We also acknowledge Kirsten Paisley, former deputy director of the NGA, and Dr Mikala Tai, former director, Gallery 4A, for their major roles in developing the conference collaboration between the NGA and ANU.

We extend our sincere thanks to the many other individuals who have assisted us: the director and staff of the Galeri Nasional Indonesia and especially curator Bayu Genia Krishbie; Hardiwan Prayogo and Dwe Rachmanto, Indonesian Visual Art Archive; Jim Supangkat; T. K. Sabapathy; Emeritus Professor David Williams; Dr Chaitanya Sambrani; Christine Clark; the staff at QAGOMA, especially Chris Saines, director, and the executive team, curators, publications and library staff, particularly Judy Gunning and Cathy Pemble-Smith; Rusty Kelty and Antonietta Itropico of AGSA, as well as the director of AGSA, Rhana Devenport; Dr James Bennett and Rebekah Raymond of MAGNT; Professor Will Christie; Professor Paul Pickering, Research School of Humanities and the Arts; Professor Ed Aspinall, director, ANU Indonesia Institute, and board members; our fellow conference conveners acknowledged by name above as well as all the speakers at the conference.

We would especially like to thank colleagues who assisted our research, including Professor David Elliott, Emeritus Professor Pat Hoffie, Dr Jennifer Lindsay, the late Neil Manton, Professor Jen Webb, Dr Michelle Antoinette, Dr Alison Carroll, Dr Zara Stanhope and Dr Zhang Lansheng. For help with images we gratefully acknowledge Anthony Wallis of the Aboriginal Artists Agency Ltd; staff of the National Art Gallery Singapore, especially Malyanah Manap; Agni Saraswati, manager of Studio Kalahan; Edwin Rahardjo of Edwin's Gallery Jakarta; Professor Kenneth M. George for his photograph of the work of A. D. Pirous; Sasha from Serambi Pirous Studio Gallery; Nancy Sever; Cut Nurkemala Muliani for her image of Tisna Sanjaya in performance; Nia Fliam for assistance with the image by Amri Yahya; Ismail from *Tempo* and *Tempo* magazine; and Mark Sherwood and Ariel Budianto for their photographs.

Webinar

The webinar in 2021, supported by the Indonesia Institute, ANU, underpins the Epilogue. The editors are particularly grateful to the speakers: Dr Anissa Rahadiningtyas, Arham Rahman, I Made 'Bayak' Muliana, Alia Swastika and Karina Roosvita, and the discussant, Dr Wulan Dirgantoro.

***

Our very special thanks to our fellow editors and our families.

Dr Kent is grateful for the support of a Visiting Fellowship in the Centre for Art History and Art Theory, School of Art and Design, ANU, and for support from colleagues there and in the Department of Political and Social Change, ANU College of Asia and the Pacific. Dr Kent also thanks colleagues at the Institute of Technology, Bandung's Faculty of Art and Design, especially Dr Rikrik Kusmara; the Kunci Cultural Studies Centre in Yogyakarta, Yogyakarta Biennale Foundation; Jatiwangi Arts Factory; Sanggar Bangun Budaya; Tlatah Bocah; Joglo Jago; Indonesian Visual Art Archive; Cemeti; Hendro Wiyanto; and many others who are not mentioned here but who provided invaluable insight and inspiration for this research, which was supported by an Endeavour Prime Minister's Australia–Asia Postgraduate Award.

Dr Turner acknowledges and thanks the Australian Research Council for their support of research undertaken on the ARC grants 'Art and Human Rights' (DP 0452961: Turner, Webb, Hoffie and Neale) and 'The Rise of New Cultural Networks in Asia' (DP1096041: Turner and Antoinette). In addition, her research was informed by her curatorial work on the Queensland Art Gallery's Asia Pacific Triennial exhibitions in 1993, 1996 and 1999.

The editors express their special acknowledgement and personal appreciation for the support and friendship of the late Margaret Williams. Over her long association with the School of Art, ANU, Margaret welcomed numerous visiting artists and scholars, many of them mentioned in this book. Her kindnesses remain with us. Vale, Margaret Williams.

Introduction

Elly Kent, Virginia Hooker and Caroline Turner

In pre-pandemic 2019, when it was possible to organise international art exhibitions, the National Gallery of Australia (NGA) curated and presented an exhibition of contemporary Indonesian art to show the diversity and richness of art in new millennium Indonesia. *Contemporary Worlds: Indonesia* was the first major survey of post-1998 Indonesian art seen in Australia and a significant number of the works were acquired for the national collection.[1] The genesis of this book was a scholarly international conference organised to complement the NGA exhibition by the Humanities Research Centre at The Australian National University (ANU), working in partnership with the NGA.[2] The three editors of

1 The exhibition, 21 June – 27 October 2019, presented the work of over 20 contemporary Indonesian artists from 1998 to the present in a variety of media. See NGA, 'Contemporary Worlds Indonesia', accessed 16 March 2021, nga.gov.au/contemporaryworlds/. See also Jaklyn Babington and Carol Cains, *Contemporary Worlds: Indonesia* (Canberra: National Gallery of Australia, 2019), exhibition catalogue published in English and Indonesian. Writers for the catalogue included NGA curators Carol Cains and Jaklyn Babington as well as art scholars Alia Swastika, Enin Suprianto, Elly Kent, Chaitanya Sambrani and Caroline Turner. Artists represented in the exhibition were: FX Harsono, Mella Jaarsma, Eko Nugroho, Garin Nugroho, I Made Wiguna Valasara, Agus Suwage, Tromarama, Duto Hardono, Entang Wiharso, Melati Suryodarmo, Handiwirman Saputra, I Gusti Ayu Kadek Murniasih, Yudha 'Fehung' Kusuma Putera, Uji 'Hahan' Handoko Eko Saputro, Zico Albaiquni, Faisal Habibi, Jompet Kuswidananto, Albert Yonathan Setyawan, Julian Abraham 'Togar', Tita Salina, Octora, Akiq AW, Adi 'Uma Gumma' Kusuma, Tisna Sanjaya. The exhibition concentrated on contemporary art, but Indonesia has a rich history of traditional art forms and court arts long admired in the West. The NGA's collection includes one of the world's largest collections of Southeast Asian traditional textiles.

2 The conference, entitled 'Contemporary Worlds: Indonesian Art', was held on 24 June 2019 and was a joint project of the Humanities Research Centre, The Australian National University (ANU) and the National Gallery of Australia (NGA) and was also supported by ANU School of Art and Design and ANU Indonesia Institute. Conference conveners: Elly Kent, Virginia Hooker, Caroline Turner, David Williams, Chaitanya Sambrani, Rohan Nicol (ANU); Carol Cains, Jaklyn Babington (NGA); Christine Clark (National Portrait Gallery of Australia, NPG). The conference

the book were among the conference conveners. The conference was intended to provide a broad scholarly context for Indonesian art and had a much wider historical time frame than the NGA exhibition. It reflected new research on themes in Indonesian modern art that echoed the dramatic social and political changes of the nation's political history: Indonesia under Dutch colonial rule, the pre-independence period of the 1930s and early 1940s, Japanese occupation during the Pacific War, independence under President Sukarno (1945–65), the New Order of President Suharto (1966–98) and the period of Reformasi (1998–present).[3] The book adopts the same time frame as the conference to explore new perspectives on Indonesia's modern and contemporary art, with a focus on art from the 1930s to the present. It is intended as a contribution to Indonesian art history and art historiography as well as to the emerging scholarly discourse on modern and contemporary art in Southeast Asia and Asia more generally in terms of both national and regional art histories.[4]

---

was open to the public as well as to art specialists and scholars, students and journalists. Interest in both the exhibition and conference reflects a long Australian commitment to the culture of Indonesia. Indonesian contemporary art has been shown in a variety of exhibitions in Australia since the Artists' Regional Exchange exhibitions in Perth in the late 1980s and the Asia Pacific Triennial exhibitions at the Queensland Art Gallery beginning in 1993 (see Chapter 7). All state galleries and territories in Australia have significant collections of contemporary Asian art, including Indonesian art. Other exhibitions held in Australia have included *AWAS! Recent Art from Indonesia*, 1999, which travelled throughout Australia and overseas; *Crossing Boundaries: Bali: A Window to Twentieth-Century Indonesian Art* (2002); and *Crescent Moon: Islamic Art and Civilisation in Southeast Asia, Bulan Sabit: Seni dan Peradaban Islam di Asia Tenggara* (2005), organised by the Art Gallery of South Australia and NGA. The most recent major exhibition was in 2014: *Masters of Modern Indonesian Portraiture*, consisting of 35 works from the independence generation to the present, from the Galeri Nasional Indonesia organised by the NPG and the Galeri Nasional Indonesia.

3 This historical context is outlined in Chapter 1. Indonesia declared independence from Dutch rule in 1945 and fought a war for that independence that officially ended in 1949. Indonesia's first president, Sukarno, was replaced in 1966 by the New Order of President Suharto. Since 1998 there have been five presidents of Indonesia.

4 See discussion on Indonesia's art history below and 'Art Historiographical Introduction to Important Sources and Selected Further Reading on Modern and Contemporary Asian Art' (Appendices, this volume) for the broader context of Southeast Asian and Asian art histories.

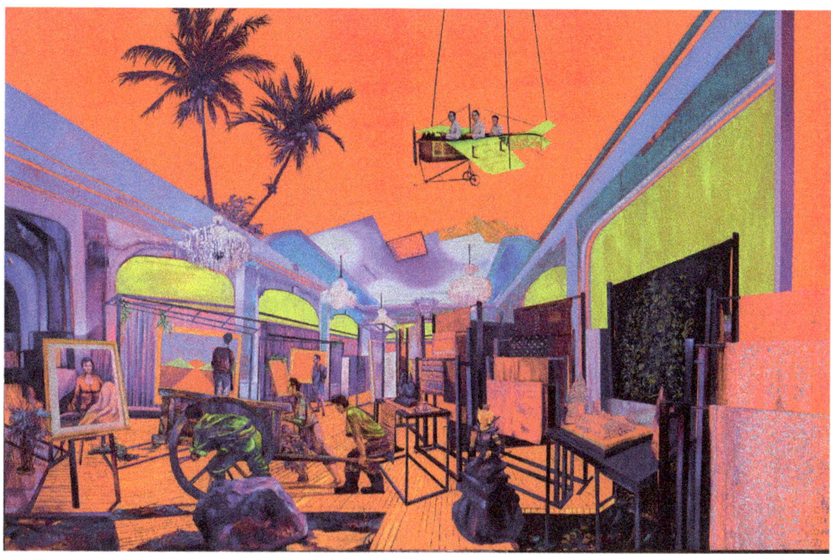

Figure 0.1: Zico Albaiquni (b. 1987), Bandung, West Java, *Ladies and Gentlemen! Kami Present, Ibu Pertiwi!* 2018.

Oil and synthetic polymer on canvas. Shown in the exhibition *Contemporary Worlds: Indonesia*, 2019. Image courtesy the artist. The painting, as the NGA catalogue text by Tarun Nagesh notes, borrows its title from leading artist of the independence generation S. Sudjojono's 1965 painting *Kami present, Ibu Pertiwi* (*Stand Guard for Our Motherland*) (see Figure 0.7). There may also be allusions to the nineteenth-century painter, Raden Saleh.[5] The image is based on the traditional Indonesian textiles greatly admired in the West in the 2018 *Festival couleurs d'Indonésie* exhibition in Paris. Three Javanese men in a plane fly past.

The title of this book, *Living Art: Indonesian Artists Engage Politics, Society and History*,[6] takes its wording in part from the concept put forward by artists from the pre-independence era of the 1930s and 1940s to express the essential nexus they believed existed between art and everyday life.[7] Indonesia's foremost art historian of the late twentieth century, Sanento

5 Tarun Nagesh, 'Zico Albaiquni', in *Contemporary Worlds: Indonesia*, 75.

6 The title of this book, *Living Art: Indonesian Artists Engage Politics, Society and History*, is not intended to suggest that all artists were producing art that was, or is, overtly political in subject or activist in intent. However, because artists are necessarily part of human society, their work, we argue, has a connection with life in those societies even if their art is an individual aesthetic or spiritual journey.

7 See Kent, Chapter 2 (this volume). The term 'everyday' (*sehari-hari*), or variations thereof, appears often in writing by Indonesian artists and theorists. Sanento Yuliman and J. Supangkat, 'Seni Rupa Sehari-Hari', in *Seni Rupa Baru Proyek 1: Pasaraya Dunia Fantasi* [New art project 1: Fantasy world supermarket], ed. J. Supangkat (Jakarta: Gramedia, 1987), 14–18. For an earlier iteration, see independence-era artist Sudjojono's insistence that Indonesian artists address 'our daily life', quoted in translation in Claire Holt, *Art in Indonesia: Continuities and Change* (Ithaca, NY: Cornell University Press, 1967), 195–96.

Yuliman (1941–1992), writing from the perspective of the mid-1970s, stated his strong belief that '[n]ew Indonesian Art cannot wholly be understood without locating it in the context of the larger framework of Indonesian society and culture' and the 'whole force of history'.[8] Our objective in putting together the essays in this book has been to accept Yuliman's challenge to locate Indonesia's modern and contemporary art in that framework, as elaborated and discussed in Chapter 1 and throughout the essays in the book. In exploring the nature of the connection between art and society in Indonesia in its sociopolitical and historical environments and circumstances, in an extended time frame and through the art produced by a wide range of practitioners, *Living Art* seeks to place Indonesian art of the second part of the twentieth and early twenty-first centuries in a broad historical continuum.

To anchor the book in Indonesian views and voices that have shaped Indonesian art theory, the editors have selected three primary sources by key figures who helped define the parameters of an Indonesian art history in the late twentieth century. These provide both the 'backbone' of the book and examples of Indonesian reflective writing about art that have shaped and continue to shape how many Indonesians envisage the intersections between art and society.

The first of these primary source essays, Chapter 3, documenting the emergence of modern art in Indonesia, was written in 1976 by leading Indonesian art historian Sanento Yuliman, and, like much of his work, was not previously available in English. Translated for this book by Elly Kent, it establishes a continuity of discourses across Indonesian art history that Yuliman believed was only interrupted by the advent of a streak of anti-lyricism emergent in the mid-1970s. The second primary source document, Chapter 6, is an essay published in 1993 by Jim Supangkat, the pre-eminent Indonesian curator of the late twentieth century, writing about the development of modern and contemporary art in Indonesia for an international readership at a time when Indonesian contemporary artists were connecting with the contemporary international art world. Supangkat makes the critical point that modern art can, and has, developed in different ways in different countries, including in Indonesia. The essay

8 Sanento Yuliman, Chapter 3 (this volume). Further, M. Agus Burhan writes that 'the study of the history of visual arts concerns not only the various documents and the visual facts, but also the sociocultural contexts'. M. A. Burhan, J. Suyono and U. Hartati, *Masterpieces of the Indonesia National Gallery* (Jakarta: Galeri Nasional Indonesia, 2012).

contributes to an evolving discourse on modernism in Asia. The third essay, Chapter 10, is a very personal text by FX Harsono looking back over the course of his nearly 50-year artistic career. One of Indonesia's most respected contemporary artists, Harsono was at the forefront of artistic resistance to the Suharto regime and remains a highly influential artist and art theorist. The essay was delivered as a keynote lecture in 2019 as part of the ANU conference. These three primary source documents add significantly to the book, bringing together Indonesian perspectives on the art history of the art of their country by three key protagonists writing at pivotal moments of transformation in Indonesian history and art history.

Under our overarching theme of 'Living Art', a number of major sub-themes are analysed in chapters in this volume that present new research by both established and emerging scholars. These include artistic ideologies developed in the pre-independence era of the 1930s and 1940s and established in the new nation as expounded by Elly Kent in Chapter 2; the link between aesthetics and art inspired by Islam and individual social and ethical responsibility as analysed by Virginia Hooker in Chapter 4; the challenges confronting women artists under the New Order, the subject of Chapter 8 by Alia Swastika; the responses of post-1998 artists to the silenced histories of events, such as the killings in 1965–66 when President Suharto came to power, as discussed by Wulan Dirgantoro in Chapter 9; and the commitment by so many Indonesian artists to the role of the artist as one with a particular responsibility to their society as elucidated by FX Harsono in Chapter 10. The second half of the twentieth century was a period in Southeast Asia when artists challenged older conventions of art and a new Indonesian art history was in formation in the context of an emerging global art, as analysed by Sanento Yuliman, T. K. Sabapathy, Jim Supangkat, Caroline Turner and FX Harsono in Chapters 3, 5, 6, 7 and 10. Issues of identity in the new Indonesian nation, both collective and personal, encompassing political, ethnic, gender, religious and regional identity, are examined throughout the book.[9]

9 Indonesia is a diverse nation geographically, ethnically, spiritually and culturally, with a population in 2021 of approximately 277 million.

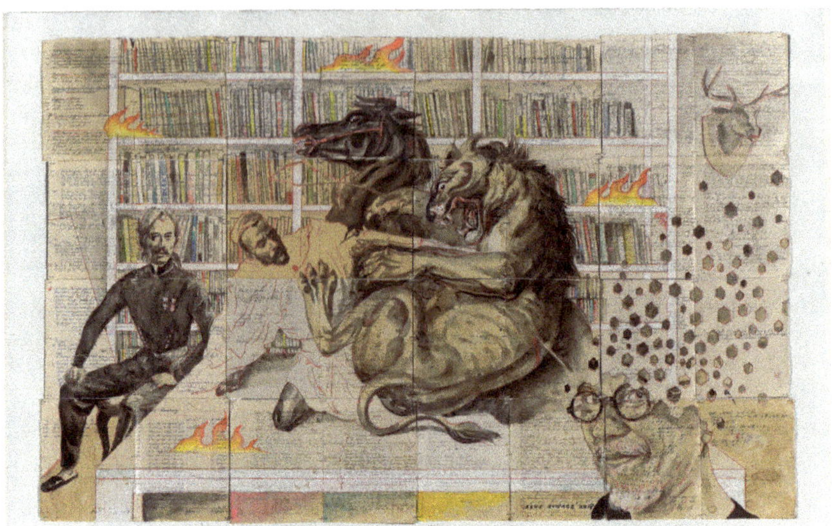

Figure 0.2: Agus Suwage (b. 1959), Purworejo Central Java, Indonesia, *Fragmen Pustaka* #2 after Raden Saleh, 2018.

Drawing in graphite, watercolour, ink and tobacco juice over handwritten text in pen and black and blue ink on 16 found notebooks. 84.8 (H) x 131.0 (W) cm (image); 94.0 (H) x 143.2 (W) cm (sheet, irregular); 1.8 (D) cm (board); 97.0 (H) x 135.5 (W) x 6.5 (D) cm (frame). Shown in the exhibition *Contemporary Worlds: Indonesia*, 2019. Collection: National Gallery of Australia. Purchased 2018 (2018.757). Image courtesy NGA. Permission: the artist. In this work, Suwage references the nineteenth-century Javanese painter Raden Saleh.

Living Art in the Context of Indonesian Art Historiography

As Chapters 1 and 2 indicate, Indonesian artists and writers engaged in an often intense and passionate discourse—what Jim Supangkat describes as 'theoretical cultural debate' on the directions of art and culture—especially in the decade leading to and after the declaration of independence from Dutch rule in 1945. Sanento Yuliman, discussed in-depth by Elly Kent in Chapter 2, was one of the first Indonesians to obtain a doctorate in art history overseas, gaining his degree in Paris in 1981. In her chapter in this volume, Kent analyses the artistic ideology that Yuliman identified across Indonesian art history, and the propensity of this ideology to break down the oppositional thinking that had characterised the cultural and artistic discourses previously used to describe Indonesian art. Yuliman's text on Indonesian art history, published as a book by the Jakarta Arts Council in 1976, is a seminal contribution to Indonesian art history, which was, at the time, a nascent discipline inside Indonesia. However, there are certainly others who are recognised as contributing at an earlier time to establishing an art historical narrative. These include the artist and critic Kusnadi[10] and Claire Holt, from Cornell University.[11]

A definitive art historiography of modern Indonesian art is still to emerge, but most writers agree on two key artists, born nearly exactly 100 years apart, who can be seen as inaugurating Indonesian modern art. They are the nineteenth-century Javanese aristocrat Raden Saleh (c. 1811–1880), who gained a great reputation in the courts of Europe,[12] and S. Sudjojono (1913–1986). Sudjojono was one of the most influential artists and art theorists of the independence generation in Indonesia, identified with the emergence of a national consciousness in art and often called the father of Indonesian modern art. Raden Saleh and Sudjojono were depicted together on the cover of a special issue of *Tempo* (Time) magazine in 1976 devoted to a significant exhibition of Indonesian art held that year entitled *A Hundred Years of Indonesian Art* (Seabad Seni Rupa Indonesia).[13]

---

10 Sidharta suggests that Kusnadi established the narratives for Indonesian art, a task he says was continued by Claire Holt and other scholars including Sudarmadji (Soedarmadji Damais). Amir Sidharta, 'Art Archives and the Exhibition-Based Approach of Art', *NOW! JAKARTA*, 24 May 2019, nowjakarta.co.id/art-and-culture/arts/art-archives-and-the-exhibition-based-approach-of-art-history. Kusnadi was involved in the curation of the 1976 exhibition, *A Hundred Years of Indonesian Art* [Seabad Seni Rupa Indonesia] (discussed below), and wrote for the Gate Foundation catalogue for their exhibition in the Netherlands in 1993, along with Soedarso SP and Jim Supangkat. Other early writers on art are Noto Soeroto (c. 1888–1951), a Javanese prince, poet and journalist; Kartini (Raden Ajeng Kartini) (1879–1904) (see Figure 6.5); and Oei Sian Yok (1926–2000), writing for the *Star* newspaper in the late 1950s and early 1960s. See Brigitta Isabella, 'Oei Sian Yok', *Southeast of Now* 4, no. 2 (October 2020): 285–309, doi.org/10.1353/sen.2020.0013, which includes translations of her art writing.

11 Claire Holt was born in Latvia in 1901 and became a journalist in the US, travelling to Indonesia in the 1930s. Her major book, *Art in Indonesia: Continuities and Change*, published in 1967, was a groundbreaking publication in English on both performing and visual arts. See Cornell University Library, 'The Claire Holt Papers', accessed 2 January 2021, rmc.library.cornell.edu/holt/.

12 Werner Kraus has called Raden Saleh's 1857 painting about the arrest of Prince Diponegoro, a Javanese aristocrat who had fought the Dutch for years in the Java wars, an example of 'proto-nationalist' modernism. See Werner Kraus, 'Raden Saleh's Interpretation of the Arrest of Diponegoro: An Example of Indonesian "Proto-Nationalist" Modernism', *Archipel* 69 (2005): 259–94, doi.org/10.3406/arch.2005.3934. See Chapter 1 (this volume), Figure 1.4, and a discussion of this work in footnote 105 in that chapter.

13 The exhibition's management was led by Yoop Ave, the head of the Presidential Palace, and Soedarmadji Damais, adviser to the Jakarta Arts Board. Their advisory team included Zaini, Soedjojono (Sudjojono), Sudarso and Basuki Abdullah, while a selection committee included Kusnadi, Sumarjo, Alex Papadimitriou, Fadjar Sidik and Suparto. Works from both the Presidential Palace Collection and private collections (notably that of Adam Malik, who would soon become Suharto's vice-president) were included. As the inaugural exhibition at the newly established *Balai Seni Rupa Jakarta* (Jakarta Art Center, later the Museum of Fine Arts and Ceramics), it was opened by President Suharto. Ajip Rosidi, 'Pameran Seabad Senirupa Indonesia (1876–1976)', *Budaya Jaya*, no. 101 (1976): 577–83.

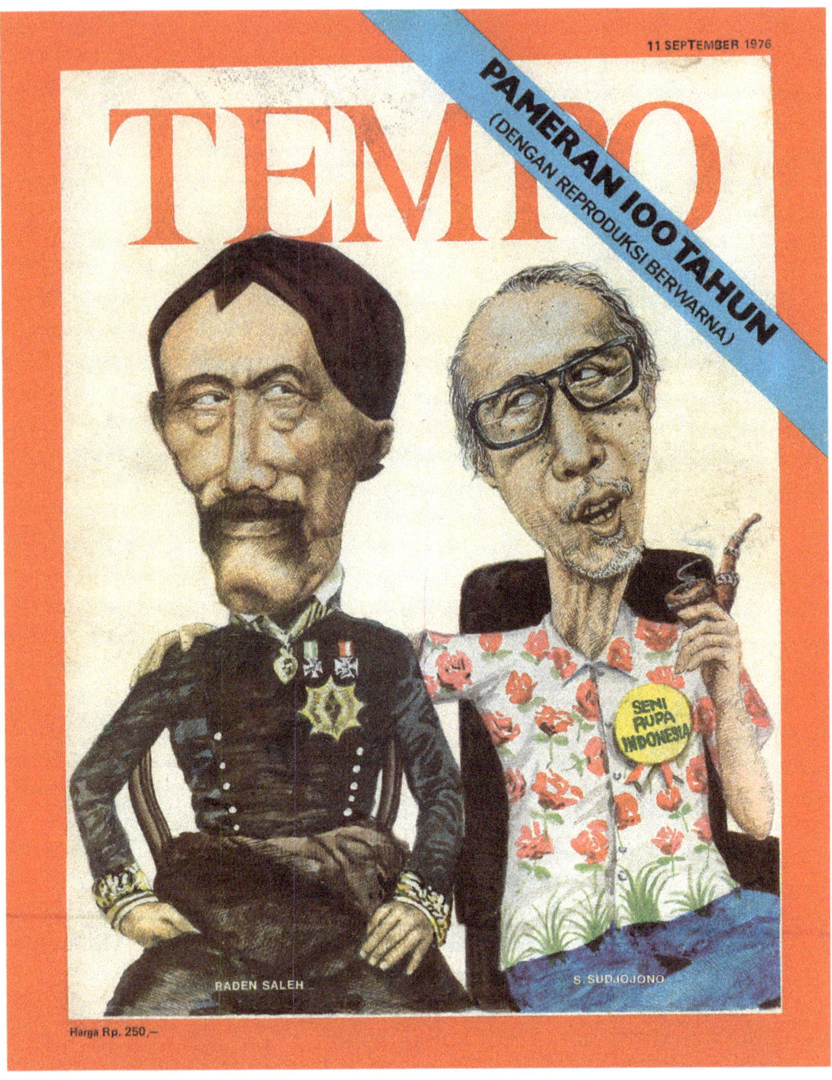

Figure 0.3: The cover of a 1976 issue of *Tempo* (Time) magazine featuring a cartoon-like illustration of Raden Saleh and S. Sudjojono (Edisi 11 September 1976).

The issue includes illustrations from an exhibition in the same year commemorating 100 years of Indonesian art. Image courtesy datatempo.co/Majalah TEMPO.

Sanento Yuliman begins his 1976 analysis of Indonesian painting in his essay in this volume with Raden Saleh, 'a legendary figure for most Indonesian painters in subsequent generations', and emphasises the role of the artists of the independence movement in the 1930s and

1940s led by Sudjojono.[14] Jim Supangkat also begins his 1993 essay on modern art in this book with Raden Saleh and calls the later period of the independence movement against Dutch colonial rule of the 1930s 'the spring of Indonesian modern art'.[15] The focus on Raden Saleh and Sudjojono as critical innovators and trailblazers has continued in John Clark's monumental new book on Asian modernism published in 2021.[16]

A parallel but distinct form of modernism developed in Bali, born out of substantially different circumstances.[17] Yuliman points out that painting traditions have been maintained in Bali for centuries through living Balinese–Hindu religious practices of painting on cloth, paper and lontar palm.[18] In the 1920s, the influx of Western tourists, changes to illustrated educational resources in primary schools and the arrival of photography introduced through advertising presented new ways of image making.[19] In the 1930s, anthropologists Gregory Bateson and Margaret Mead commissioned over 1,000 drawings and paintings to support their research into the Balinese character; the later publication by Hildred Geertz, *Images of Power: Balinese Paintings Made for Gregory Bateson and Margaret Mead* documents this project.[20] With Cokorodo Raka Sukawati of the Ubud royal family and other local painters, European artists then residing in Bali, Walter Spies and Rudolf Bonnet, founded the Pita Maha Arts Society in 1936. This was used as a vehicle to promote Balinese painting in

---

14 See Yuliman, Chapter 3 (this volume).

15 See Jim Supangkat, Chapter 6 (this volume).

16 John Clark's major monograph, *Modern Asian Art* (Sydney: Craftsman House, 1998), was the first in his series of seminal publications on modern Asian art. His newest publication, *The Asian Modern*, is published by the National Gallery, Singapore (2021). In the latter work, Clark discussed only three key Indonesian artists: Raden Saleh, Sudjojono and FX Harsono. Clark quotes Saleh's description of himself as between 'two worlds' (p. 51) and states that Saleh was somewhat isolated by the Dutch and Javanese on his return to Java (p. 54). Clark's treatment of Sudjojono is particularly interesting. He points out his limited access to art training in Indonesia and that he did not go abroad to study in his formative years. He did, however, have access to modern art works brought to Indonesia in exhibitions by European residents such as the Regnault family, including works by artists such as Van Gogh. The circulation of information on modern art helped lead to the foundation of PERSAGI, which is discussed in Chapter 2 (this volume) (p. 223). For images of the artist's work, see S. Sudjojono Center, [Home], accessed 2 September 2021, ssudjojonocenter.com/; Digital Archive of Indonesian Contemporary Art, 'Sudjojono', accessed 2 September 2021, archive.ivaa-online.org/pelakuseni/s-sudjojono.

17 Ellen Kent, 'Entanglement: Individual and Participatory Art Practice in Indonesia' (PhD diss., The Australian National University, 2016), 42–43, doi.org/10.25911/5d5146060c32c.

18 Sanento Yuliman, 'Seni Lukis di Indonesia: Persoalan-Persoalannya, dulu dan sekarang (Budaya Djawa, Dec 1970)', in *Dua Seni Rupa, Sepilihan Tulisan Sanento Yuliman*, ed. Hasan Asikin (Jakarta: Yayasan Kalam, 2001).

19 Hildred Geertz, *Images of Power: Balinese Paintings Made for Gregory Bateson and Margaret Mead* (Honolulu: University of Hawai'i Press, 1994), 10.

20 Geertz, *Images of Power*, 1.

Indonesia and abroad, and as a measure of control over the aesthetic form of emerging practice.[21] However, Vickers notes that '[t]he complexity of relationships between "traditional" and "modern" and "Indonesian" and "Balinese" means that there is no single process of development from local tradition to national modernism'.[22]

Part of what is at stake in identifying the precursors of modern art in Indonesia is the role of the artist in Indonesian society. The impact of various geopolitical movements in the twentieth century—such as decolonisation, World War II and the Japanese occupation, and the rise of communism—and artists' involvement in these movements, had distinct impacts on aesthetic and discursive developments in modernism, as explored in Chapter 1. Artists responded accordingly and Sudjojono expressed a clear concept of what artists' responsibilities to society and their own creative practices should be. As discussed further by Kent (Chapter 2) and Yuliman (Chapter 3), Sudjojono implored Indonesian artists to observe, internalise and express the reality of everyday life for ordinary Indonesians through their paintings, a process he called the 'visible soul' (*jiwa ketok*).[23] In response to Dutch art critic J. Hopman's comment that an Indonesian art had yet to emerge, Sudjojono wrote:

> About the future of Indonesian art, we as Indonesians are quite capable of deciding for ourselves. Since the Dutch colonial era, in the era of PERSAGI [Persatuan Ahli Gambar Indonesia/ Indonesian Picture-Makers' Association], we already know where we will be taking our Indonesian art.[24]

---

21 Debate continues over the influence that Spies, and especially Bonnet, exercised over Balinese painters. See Geertz, *Images of Power*, and Christopher Hill, *Survival and Change: Three Generations of Balinese Painters* (Canberra: Pandanus Books, 2006), 46.

22 Adrian Vickers, 'Bali's Place in Indonesian Art', in *Crossing Boundaries—Bali: A Window to 20th Century Indonesian Art* (Melbourne: Asia Society AustralAsia Centre, 2002), 22.

23 S. Sudjojono, 'Seni Loekis Kesenian dan Seniman' [Painting, art and artists], Penerbit Indonesia Sekarang, Yogyakarta, 1946, 11.

24 S. Sudjojono, '"We Know Where We Will Be Taking Indonesian Art", 1948', trans. Brigitta Isabella, *Southeast of Now: Directions in Contemporary and Modern Art in Asia* 1, no. 2 (October 2017): 159–64, doi.org/10.1353/sen.2017.0017. The text was first published in *Revolusioner Magazine*. Sudjojono continued:

> We will not blame our European colleagues for their mistakes. We will honour them, for they have worked sincerely, even sacrificing their lives for a great aspiration. We will use their works as a landmark, like a shipwreck in the ocean, of our people's struggle in this world and in our revolution in Indonesia, not only to enable artists to become artistic, but also to make the whole society become artistic, to become artistically conscious as Indonesia was before [in the past].

In 'Seni Lukis di Indonesia: Persoalan-Persoalannya, Dulu dan Sekarang' (Painting in Indonesia: Issues past and present) Yuliman contended that the modernism that dominated discourses in the first quarter century of independence was rooted in 'a broader reality, changes in society and culture that are occurring in Indonesia and the rest of the world'; in other words, modernisation.[25] He identified three main stances in this modernism: the artist as the centre of creative energy; the autonomy of art (especially from political influence); and the embrace of all art traditions, rather than categorisation by culture. These gave rise to what Claire Holt called the 'great debate' of 1935, the *Polemik Kebudayaan* (Cultural Polemic) that consumed those working in literature and the arts.[26] Most prominently, writer and intellectual Takdir Alisjahbana argued that Indonesians should seek equality by cultivating 'Western' individualism and materialism, while the poet Sanoesi Pane urged a syncretic approach based on the superiority of the East.[27] Yuliman distilled this debate into two questions: How can modern art that is focused on the individual artist be of use, benefit or meaning to broader society? How can art drawn from the treasury of the world's art still base itself on the territory and interests of the nation? Yuliman deconstructed these questions, linking them back to one social factor: that modern art in Indonesia appeared in the midst of living art traditions that retained important social functions for ordinary citizens.[28] It cannot go unremarked, however, that emancipatory modernist art discourses nonetheless failed to address the fate of those most oppressed in Indonesia's (post-)feudalist, postcolonial context: women. The absence, and even the erasure, of women artists is evident throughout Indonesian art history. Some of the work to redress this has begun and, in Chapter 8, Alia Swastika makes an important contribution to that project.[29]

25 Yuliman, 'Seni Lukis di Indonesia', 70–71.

26 The term is borrowed from Holt, *Art in Indonesia: Continuities and Change*, 211–54.

27 For further descriptions and analysis of this cultural polemic, see ibid.; Antariksa, *Tuan Tanah Kawin Muda* (Yogyakarta: Yayasan Seni Cemeti, 2005), 5–6; Yustiono, 'Seni Rupa Kontemporar Indonesia dan Era Asia Pacific', *Jurnal Seni Rupa* 2 (1995): 57–62.

28 Similar arguments have been made around art practice in India, see Kalpathi Ganpathi Subramanyan, *The Living Tradition: Perspectives on Modern Indian Art* (Calcutta: Seagull Books, 1987).

29 An interesting analysis of the way the art world in Indonesia mimicked its former colonial masters is presented in Heidi Arbuckle, 'Performing Emiria Sunassa: Reframing the Female Subject in Post/colonial Indonesia' (PhD diss., University of Melbourne, 2011). Arbuckle's dissertation provides an invaluable exploration of the absence and erasure of women from artistic discourse in Indonesian art history. See also Carla Bianpoen, Farah Wardani and Wulan Dirgantoro, *Indonesian Women Artists: The Curtain Opens* (Yayasan Senirupa Indonesia, 2007).

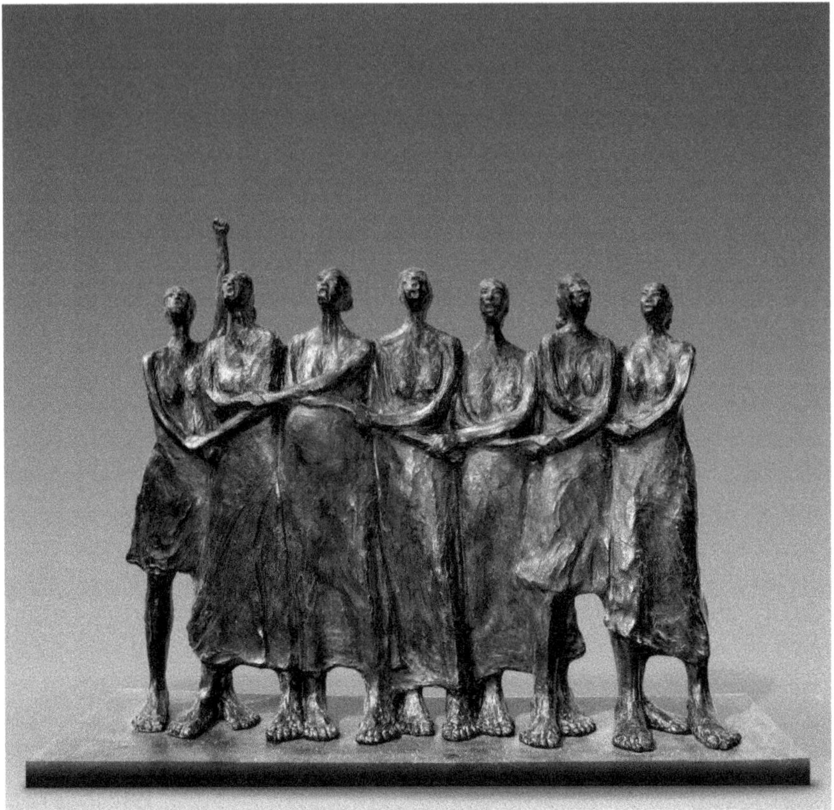

Figure 0.4: Dolorosa Sinaga (b. 1953), North Sumatra, *Solidaritas* (*Solidarity*), 2000.

Bronze and copper plating, 110 x 43 x 83 cm. Image and permission courtesy the artist.[30]

30 One of Indonesia's most distinguished artists, Dolorosa Sinaga, is also a senior art academic who has been involved in issues related to social justice for many years. She graduated from the Jakarta Arts Institute in 1977 and also studied at St Martin's School of Art, London. See the discussion of her art under the New Order by Alia Swastika in Chapter 8 (this volume) and illustrations of her sculptures in Chapters 1 and 8. See also 'Dolorosa Sinaga Indonesian Sculptor with a Social Conscience. Part II: From Social Comment to Social Conscience', *Independent Observer*, 26 November 2020, accessed 7 November 2021, observerid.com/dolorosa-sinaga-indonesian-sculptor-with-a-social-conscience-part-ii-from-social-comment-to-social-conscience/. The artist has written a text for this work. Part of her description reads:

> The lump of clay in my hands immediately turns into seven figures of women standing together side by side hand in hand interlocking expressing the chain of [the] human … their bodies glued together creating a concrete wall, massive and powerful that can never be demolished … one is pregnant … symbolises the newborn generation will continue to bear the spirit to fight all crimes against humanity.

Text in email communication sent by the artist to the editors, 28 September 2021.

After the war for independence was won, and Indonesia's status as a nation was finally recognised internationally in 1949, Sudjojono's 1946 treatise *Seni Loekis, Kesenian dan Seniman* (Painting, art and artists) continued to be influential. But, as discussed in Chapter 1, some of the most detailed discussions of the social, political and cultural contexts in Indonesia during the *Orde Lama* (Old Order)—the period of President Sukarno's leadership from 1945 to the mid-1960s—related to literature, but are also relevant (and often linked) to visual arts practice. These debates and declarations on the shaping of Indonesian culture give evidence that the development of originary art discourses, drawn from endogenous and exogenous sources, was a strong feature in Indonesia's first three decades. The importance of these originary discourses in postcolonial nations like Indonesia has been noted by Clark, who draws attention to their role in voicing (possibly pre-existing) 'parallel or alternative modernities'.[31]

Other manifestos began to emerge and many publications on art within Indonesia continued to be underpinned by ideological positions. The apparent polarities of the *Polemik Kebudayaan* were assuaged in the 1945 Constitution, which emphasised a national culture built on indigenous traditions and enriched by foreign cultures, oriented to national unity and civilisational progress.[32] But the construct of the *Polemik Kebudayaan* contributed to a pendulum of dominant art discourses, swinging largely on political terms. This allowed different art practices (politically engaged or 'apolitical' art) visibility, depending on the prevailing power structure and the interests that served it.[33]

Many critics and scholars alike have perpetuated these paradigms. In 1967, Claire Holt positioned Yogyakarta as the centre of 'Indonesianism', while Bandung stood for the 'purely aesthetic' and international.[34] Thirty years later, Kenneth George described the 'personal experiments' of Bandung artists as 'cool intellectualism' in contrast to Yogyakartan artists' 'exuberant

31 John Clark, 'The Worlding of the Asian Modern', in *Contemporary Asian Art and Exhibitions: Connectivities and World-Making*, ed. Michelle Antoinette and Caroline Turner (Canberra: ANU Press, 2014), 67–88, doi.org/10.22459/CAAE.11.2014.04.

32 Virginia Matheson Hooker, 'Expression: Creativity despite Constraint', in *Indonesia beyond Suharto: Polity, Economy, Society, Transition*, ed. Donald K. Emmerson (New York: M.E. Sharpe, Asia Society, 1999).

33 Kent, 'Entanglement: Individual and Participatory Art Practice in Indonesia', 39–40.

34 Holt, *Art in Indonesia: Continuities and Change*, 252.

… embrace of the people'.[35] However, Sanento Yuliman described these oppositional constructions as the 'myth of the "Yogya camp" and "Bandung camp" established by older artists, formulated first by Trisno Sumardjo and consecrated by Claire Holt' and then extinguished by the advent of Gerakan Seni Rupa Baru Indonesia (GSRBI, later GSRB) also known as the Indonesian New Art Movement, later the New Art Movement.[36]

In 1967, Claire Holt published her English language study *Art in Indonesia: Continuities and Change*, which covered Indonesian art, including the performing arts, from its earliest beginnings.[37] Holt, who had studied Indonesian culture from the 1930s, stressed the contexts for art and, as an academic at Cornell University, helped found in the 1950s the Cornell Modern Indonesia Project. Her book was divided into three parts: 'The Heritage', 'Living Traditions' and 'Modern Art'. It was a groundbreaking introduction to Indonesian visual and performing arts for international readers and remains highly influential.

As the pendulum of art discourses swung away from the left in the late sixties, abstraction and decorative arts gained prominence, not least because of the New Order government's depoliticisation policy. However, this did not mean disengagement from social and collective engagement. Brita Miklouho-Maklai traced the history of socially engaged art from Lekra through to the early 1980s in her book *Exposing Society's Wounds, Some Aspects of Contemporary Art since 1966,* showing how, in the mid-1970s, room emerged for veiled critique from contemporary artists, just as a new generation was emerging and reacting to the attitudes of senior artists and the conditions of wider society.[38]

35 George subsequently stresses Holt's 'acute observation' that Yogyakartan artists are focused on the social significance of the artwork, but also quotes the pamphlet essay accompanying the *Eleven Bandung Artists* exhibition of 1966, which declares the artwork to be 'an experiment created by an artist as a response to life'. Kenneth M. George, 'Some Things That Have Happened to *The Sun after September 1965*: Politics and the Interpretation of an Indonesian Painting', *Comparative Studies in Society and History* 39, no. 4 (1997): 617, doi.org/10.1017/S001041750002082X.

36 Sanento Yuliman, 'Kemana Semangat Muda (date unknown)', in *Dua Seni Rupa: Sepilihan Tulisan Sanento Yuliman*, ed. Hasan Asikin (Jakarta: Yayasan Kalam, 2001), 148.

37 Holt, *Art in Indonesia: Continuities and Change*. Her papers and digital collection of images held at Cornell is a rich resource for scholars. Other libraries in the US also have important collections related to her extensive research, for example, the New York Public Library for the Performing Arts.

38 Brita Miklouho-Maklai, *Exposing Society's Wounds, Some Aspects of Contemporary Art since 1966* (Adelaide: Flinders University of South Australia, 1991), 21.

Three artists' groups from that period have received the most attention: Desember Hitam (Black December), GSRBI and PIPA (Kepribadian Apa/What Identity). These three movements all arose out of young art school students or practising artists who were frustrated by the dominance of decorative art. Major and minor exhibitions over the following decade, and the texts associated with them—exhibition catalogues but also opinion pieces and reviews published in magazines, journals and newspapers—became the site of a struggle between the 'stagnant' establishment and an emerging contemporary strain. Many of these texts were published in widely circulated newspapers such as *Kedaulatan Rakyat* (The people's sovereignty) and *Tempo,* contributing to a growing body of documented discourse between artists, intellectuals and writers.[39]

In their essay for GSRBI's 1987 exhibition *Pasar Raya Dunia Fantasi* (Fantasy world supermarket) catalogue, Supangkat and Yuliman reflected that what remained from earlier work was 'a manifestation of exploration, opposition to elitism and revitalizing pluralism in fine art through practices of art in every day life'. Arief Budiman's contribution to the same catalogue read the re-emergence of the debate around Indonesian art's orientation as proof that the national culture was still in a state of indecision.[40] The influence of GSRB artists and Yuliman's writing have remained strong in Indonesia over the decades since the 1970s; however, a dearth of translations has led to a disjuncture between the complex development of contemporary art in Indonesia and how it is interpreted on the international stage.

A number of books published during the 1990s and later, such as Supangkat's *Indonesian Modern Art and Beyond* (1997), and exhibition catalogues provided knowledge of Indonesian contemporary art, particularly for international audiences, as discussed by Turner in

39 For more on the series of renegade exhibitions see ibid. and Kent, 'Entanglement: Individual and Participatory Art Practice in Indonesia'. The 'establishment' exhibitions included the annual *Pameran Besar Seni Lukis Indonesia* [Grand exhibition of Indonesian painting], which changed to the Jakarta Biennale from 1975, and others such as the *Pameran Seni Lukis Dunia Perminyakan* [Paintings of the world of petroleum], which was sponsored by the state-owned oil and gas company.

40 Arief Budiman, 'Menduniawikan Nilai Estetika yang Sakral' in Sanento Yuliman et al., *Pasar Raya Dunia Fantasi*, ed. Taman Ismail Marzuki and Gerakan Seni Rupa Baru (Jakarta, 1987), 23–25.

Chapter 7.[41] Art exhibitions have always been, and continue to be, significant sites for art historical formation. A guide to the publications of institutions and catalogues from a number of important exhibitions can be found in the 'Art Historiographical Introduction to Important Sources and Selected Further Reading on Modern and Contemporary Asian Art' in this volume.[42] The essays in this book help situate the discussion of artists in new discourses, presenting updated research on key topics. Especially in the years since 1998, much new scholarship, including on what art historian Anissa Rahadiningtyas calls new approaches in art historical writing to locate and fill 'absences and erasures' in that art history, has emerged.[43] This book contributes to filling gaps in some of those disregarded areas, including art by women artists (Chapter 8 by Alia Swastika) and Islam-inspired art (Chapter 4 by Virginia Hooker). Three further areas that have attracted special interest in recent years and to which this book contributes new insights are the broader Southeast Asian art context as analysed in relation to the 1970s by T. K. Sabapathy in Chapter 5; the role of Indonesian artists of Chinese descent (a focus in particular of Chapter 10 by FX Harsono, himself Chinese-Indonesian); and responses by artists of the new millennium to events such as the mass killings in 1965–66 (discussed by Wulan Dirgantoro in Chapter 9).

The role of archives in collecting and preserving documentary material is now a major focus of Indonesian art and art history and the three important primary sources reproduced here are a part of the emphasis of

41 Jim Supangkat, *Indonesian Modern Art and Beyond* (Jakarta: Yayasan Seni Rupa Indonesia/The Indonesian Fine Arts Foundation in association with the Museum Universitas Pelita Harapan and Edwin's Gallery, 1997). Exhibition catalogues for international exhibitions such as the Asia Pacific Triennial exhibitions from 1993, and Asia Society New York's *Traditions/Tensions* exhibition 1996, as well as catalogues from the Fukuoka Museum of Art, Japan, and Japan Foundation Asian exhibitions played a major role for audiences outside Indonesia gaining knowledge of Indonesian art. Other important publications from the 1990s were Astri Wright, *Soul, Spirit, and Mountain: Preoccupations of Contemporary Indonesian Painters* (Kuala Lumpur: Oxford University Press, 1994); *Indonesische Moderne Kunst, Indonesian Modern Art, Indonesian Painting since 1945* (Amsterdam: Gate Foundation, 1993), catalogue of an exhibition in 1993. See Chapter 7 (this volume), which discusses international exhibitions in which Indonesian artists participated, and 'Art Historiographical Introduction to Important Sources and Selected Further Reading on Modern and Contemporary Asian Art' (this volume).

42 Indonesia lacked significant national art infrastructure for contemporary art for many years, the gap being filled by artist-run initiatives such as Cemeti Art House, founded in 1988. See Christine Clark, 'Distinctive Voices: Artist-Initiated Spaces and Projects', in *Art and Social Change: Contemporary Art in Asia and the Pacific*, ed. Caroline Turner (Canberra: Pandanus Press, 2005), 554–68. The opening of a national gallery (Galeri Nasional) in Indonesia in 1999 was extremely important as was the advent of new private museums, such as The Museum of Modern and Contemporary Art in Nusantara (MACAN) in 2017.

43 Anissa Rahadiningtyas, quoted in 'Epilogue' (this volume).

contemporary scholarship on original documents. The Cemeti Gallery (later Cemeti Art House) was founded in 1988 by artists Nindityo Adipurnomo and Mella Jaarsma. They also developed an archive of Indonesian art and ephemera from the gallery's inception, initially called the Cemeti Art Foundation and now the Indonesian Visual Art Archive.[44] New directions in historical research and art practice continue to emerge and some of these are described in the Epilogue to this book.

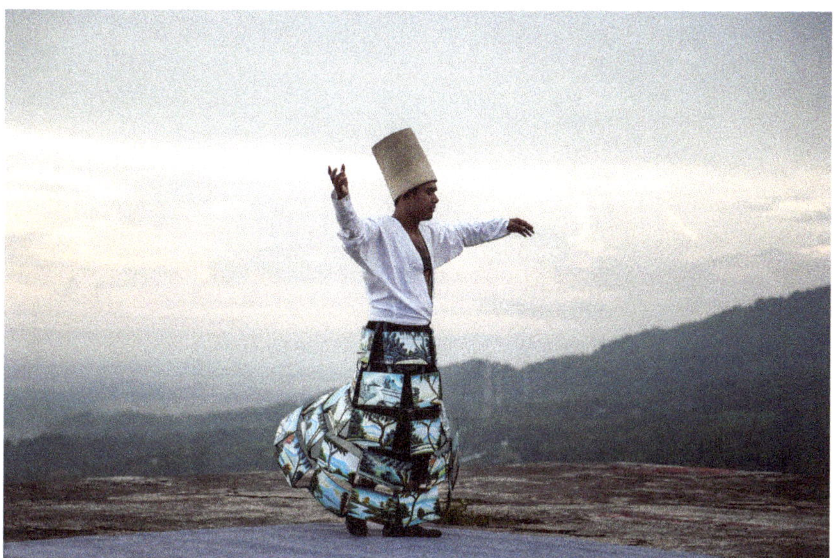

Figure 0.5: Mella Jaarsma (b. 1960), the Netherlands, *The Landscaper*, 2013.

Still from a single-channel video: 3:40 minutes. Costume: wood, paint, iron and leather; colour, sound. Wooden panels carved by Pengho and painted by Anex. Photograph by Mie Cornoedus. Collection: National Gallery of Australia. Shown in the exhibition *Contemporary Worlds: Indonesia*, 2019. Image courtesy the artist. The artwork refers to the history of the colonial era when a major mail road constructed by the Dutch with Indonesian corvée labour was completed at the cost of many local lives. The costume of the Sufi dancer has images from the *Mooi Indië* (Beautiful Indies) artistic style of Dutch and Indonesian landscape painters from the early twentieth century—paintings seen by later Indonesian independence generation artists as an exotic and colonial construction. The costume was made at a workshop in West Java with local artists.

44 Anna Mariana, Erie Setiawan, Galatia Puspa Sani Nugroho, Gde Putra, Hafiz Rancajale, Helly Minarti, Joned Suryatmoko, et al., *Arsipelago: Archival Work & Archiving Art & Culture in Indonesia* (Indonesian Visual Art Archive, 2014).

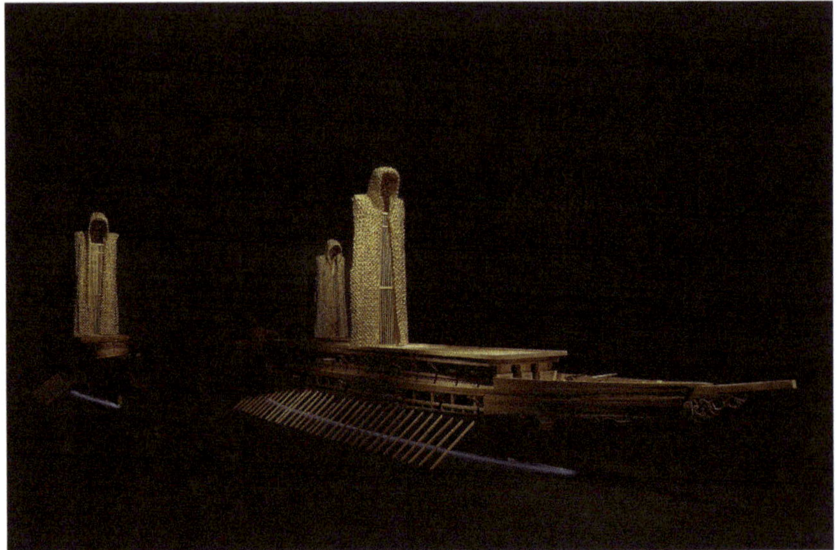

Figure 0.6: Titarubi (Rubiati Puspitasari) (b. 1968), Bandung, West Java, *History Repeats Itself*, 2016.

Gold-plated nutmegs, copper-plated wood, nickel-plated wood, burnt wood, sampan, wood, aluminium, copper, soil, light and nutmeg perfume. Installation at the 2016 Singapore Biennale. Image courtesy the artist. In this complex work there are suggestions of both Indonesia's important maritime past and colonial history. Rulers in peninsular Malaya and North Sumatra (Aceh) were locked in naval warfare for control over the Straits of Melaka, especially during the sixteenth and seventeenth centuries (see Map 1). Aceh enjoyed a period of prosperity during the seventeenth century under the rule of four queens when commerce was said to flourish. Titarubi especially suggests the dark side of colonial history in the seventeenth century when the English and Dutch fought over a monopoly of the lucrative spice trade. Nutmegs grown on the Banda islands were then worth as much as gold in Europe. The Dutch commander of the Dutch East India Company in the early seventeenth century, Jan Pieterszoon Coen, is notorious for massacring and enslaving the local inhabitants of the spice islands.[45]

This section of the Introduction describes the particular contributions of each chapter to the book's thematic concerns.

Chapter 1 provides an essential overview of Indonesian history and society and breaks new ground by drawing on essays, poems, novels and journalism, as well as art, to describe the political and cultural

45 Titarubi, one of Indonesia's leading artists, studied ceramics in Bandung in the late 1980s and is an interdisciplinary artist working across different media, including performance, music and theatre, as well as being the co-founder and co-director of iCAN (Indonesian Contemporary Art Network). See Chapter 1 for a discussion of her work with Suara Ibu Peduli (Voice of Concerned Mothers) under the New Order. See also 'Timeline of Selected Indonesian Historical Events' (Appendices, this volume).

context in which art was and is created. It endeavours to draw on what Indonesians say about themselves rather than what is said about them.[46] The chapter explores significant influences on the development of the independence movement, the impact of decolonisation and occupation on the new nation's identity, and political and economic upheavals across the decades. Importantly, it pays attention to the violent shift away from the Old Order and provides examples of the effect this had on Indonesia's artists, as well as the strategies they created to resist and criticise many of the New Order's policies. The chapter concludes with new millennial interest in reinterpreting Indonesia's earlier history and new engagements with the political and religious landscape. Chapter 1 sets the stage for the analytical interweaving of art and the context in which it exists in Indonesia that follows throughout the book, demonstrating how Indonesian artists respond to, resist and engage with the historical, political and social world they are embedded in.

Chapter 2 investigates some key ideologies that have permeated both artistic and social practices across Indonesia's national history, and their role in defining particular roles for artists—roles that artists have embraced, resisted, extolled and critiqued in different periods and contexts of Indonesia's history. Elly Kent draws on extensive new research based on Indonesian language sources that she has collected and translated, and the theoretical frameworks and analyses within these. Drawing on writing produced by Indonesian artists, theorists and historians, Kent explores an ongoing concern that art should be connected with society through examinations of four particular manifestations of 'living traditions' that have resonated across Indonesian art history to the present day. She demonstrates that many contemporary artists in Indonesia draw on and respond to ideas—long-embedded in Indonesian art—that conjoin individualist creativity and specific social responsibilities for artists. Kent builds on Yuliman's concept of a continuing artistic ideology to situate contemporary artists in continuity with established discourses of modern Indonesian art but underlines that these discourses are not received uncritically and remain part of an ongoing dialectic with those from other disciplines, cultures and places.

46 From at least the 1930s, study clubs, artists collectives, conferences, radio broadcasts, journals, newspapers and magazines (and more recently the internet) provided forums for Indonesians to consider, debate and hone ideas about their society, culture, politics and history.

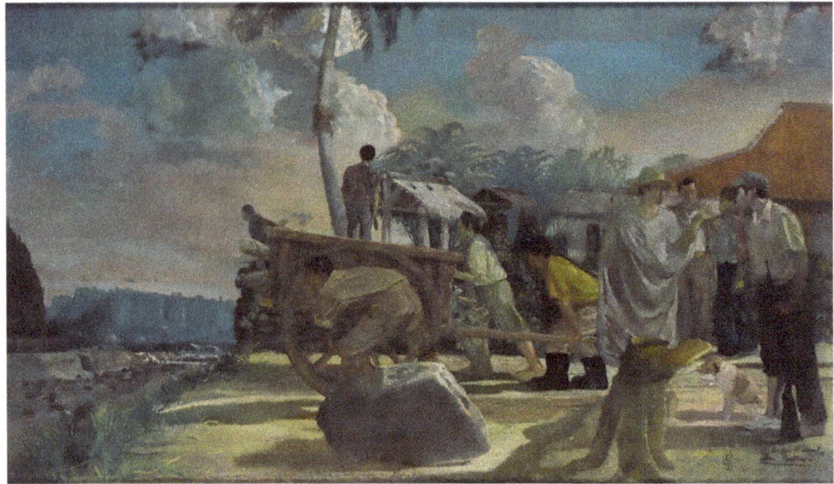

Figure 0.7: S. Sudjojono, *Kami Present, Ibu Pertiwi* (*Stand Guard for Our Motherland*), 1965.

Oil on canvas, 176 x 300 cm. Collection: National Gallery Singapore. Permission courtesy the S. Sudjojono Center, Indonesia.[47]

In **Chapter 3** Yuliman's own writing is given centre stage, in an English language translation of his groundbreaking 1976 essay *Seni Lukis Indonesia Baru* (New Indonesian Painting). Yuliman's essay describing the genesis of Indonesian art's encounters with modernity, and the distinct conditions that influenced its particular manifestation, was originally published as a book by the Jakarta Arts Council[48] and has since been reproduced in various Indonesian language publications. It came at the same time that emerging Indonesian artists were exploring new mediums and ideas and establishing a distinctly contemporary, and cosmopolitan, trajectory for their practices. Yuliman was deeply involved in this movement, and this was especially evident in his contributions to the formation of GSRB. In this text, Yuliman traces the history of Indonesian art from Raden Saleh through to the tumultuous 1970s, applying the tools of an art historian to the field by identifying and analysing three distinct periods and various tendencies within these periods. He ends with a critique of the new tendency to 'anti-lyricism' that he sees emerging in the artists of his own milieu, who are now the senior practitioners in an established and

47 Although the painting was done in 1965, scholars suggest it draws on Sudjojono's involvement in the independence struggle against the Dutch and his sketches done in the late 1940s.

48 Sanento Yuliman, *Seni Lukis Indonesia Baru: Sebuah Pengantar/Oleh Sanento Yuliman* (Jakarta: Dewan Kesenian Jakarta, 1976).

globally recognised art scene. As a contemporary of FX Harsono, Jim Supangkat (who is also a contributor to this book), Siti Adiyati, Nanik Mirna, Dadang Christanto, Hardi, Nyoman Nuarta and Dede Eri Supria, Yuliman's significance in the development and, perhaps more importantly, the understanding of Indonesian art history cannot be overstated. The inclusion of this essay in translation represents one of the most important contributions this book makes to the broader understanding of that history outside of Indonesia, by providing a window into a formative period in the generation of new art knowledge in Indonesia.

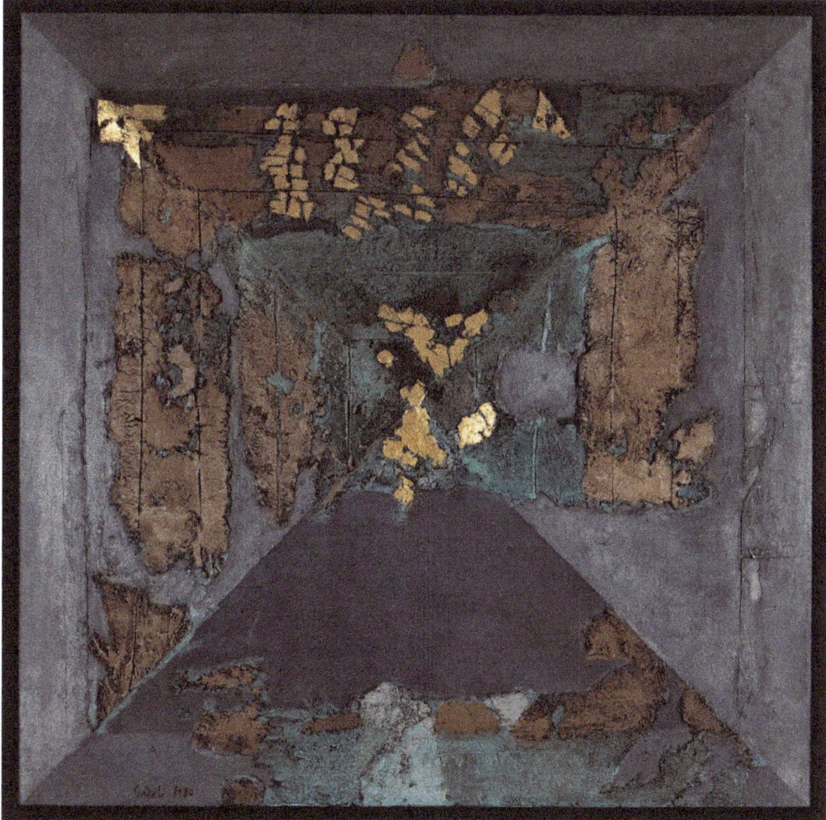

Figure 0.8: Ahmad (Achmad) Sadali (1924–1987), West Java, *Gunungan Emas* (*The Golden Mountain*), 1980.

Oil, wood, canvas, 80 x 80 cm. Collection: Galeri Nasional Indonesia. Image courtesy Galeri Nasional Indonesia and Ravi Ahmad Salim.[49]

49 See Chapter 4 (this volume) for a discussion of Sadali's art.

In **Chapter 4** Virginia Hooker brings to the fore Indonesian art by the significant, but under-recognised, number of artists who have chosen to base their art on Quranic foundations. 'Islam-inspired art', as Indonesians call it, has been largely unexplored by Western historians of Indonesian art although its main exponents are respected and revered within Indonesia, Islamic Southeast Asia and the Middle East.[50] During the heady years of the 1950s in newly independent Indonesia, the heated debates between groups of Indonesians about the form their 'national' culture would take included vocal contributions from Muslim intellectuals, writers, artists and students about how Islam could contribute to that national culture. Virginia Hooker explains the Quranic basis for Islam-inspired art and analyses the artistic ideologies of four well-known artists: Ahmad Sadali (1924–1987), A. D. Pirous (b. 1932), Tisna Sanjaya (b. 1958) and Arahmaiani Feisal (b. 1961). She argues that their choice to frame their art within Islam is also a choice to combine ethics with aesthetics, a position Sanjaya imprints on his installation and Arahmaiani preserves in video recordings of her collaborative works. In taking this position, Hooker argues, they develop a conscious style of 'visual language' that engages not only with Islam but also with ethical issues that face all Indonesians in their daily lives. Arahmaiani's recordings extend the impact of her projects across time and borders.

In **Chapter 5** the book expands its focus to the broader Southeast Asia region in which Indonesia has played and continues to play a significant role. Singaporean T. K Sabapathy is one of Southeast Asia's most distinguished art historians and his essay is a revised version of the keynote lecture he gave at the ANU conference. For more than 40 years Sabapathy has been deeply engaged with the need to develop regional perspectives and to link the modern and contemporary art of Southeast Asia to its rich and varied artistic traditions.[51] In this essay, Sabapathy explores the emergence of the idea of the contemporary in Southeast Asian art, as distinguished from the modern, pinpointing the 1970s as a moment of change, and a time in which regional collaborations began to expand the field of artists' practice. He does this through a discussion of exhibitions and texts and with a focus on a number of key artists: FX Harsono in Indonesia, Redza Piyadasa and Sulaiman Esa in Malaysia, and Cheo Chai-Hiang in Singapore. He points to parallels in their artistic experiments

50 As described briefly in Chapter 1 (this volume).

51 An example being the influence of temple architecture from Java on developments at Angkor Wat. He notes that, for centuries, artists in Southeast Asia transformed imported artistic styles and developed their own art.

in the decade of the 1970s, which can also be seen in the work of other artists such as those in the Philippines in the early 1970s. Sabapathy notes, however, that:

> [I]nitiatives for advancing the contemporary spring from the make-up of individuals or collectives and their worldviews; from historical factors particular to specific locations and to living in them, and not from a single, identifiable wellspring or from interconnected resources within the region of Southeast Asia.

Sabapathy's essay in this book provides an important perspective on the broader historical and cultural scene in which the development of Indonesian contemporary art is played out.

In **Chapter 6** the editors have selected another historical perspective that helps to situate modern and contemporary art developments in Indonesia. Jim Supangkat, Indonesia's foremost curatorial voice in the late twentieth century, presents an overview of Indonesian art to the early 1990s.[52] Supangkat originally wrote the piece in 1993 for publication in the book *Tradition and Change: Contemporary Art of Asia and the Pacific*.[53] The essay is thus written primarily for an international audience, and it was the first introduction for many English-speaking art scholars and artists to developments in Indonesia written by an Indonesian scholar. Supangkat traces the evolution of modern and contemporary art in Indonesia, pointing out that modern art grew out of Western art practice rather than traditional forms. As he puts it, 'modern art in developing countries could thus be seen to have both an international and a national identity'. Supangkat also addresses key issues in Indonesian art such as the influence of traditional art, regional differences and the rise of an art market. Critically, he examines the complex transition from modern to contemporary art between the 1970s and 1990s, beginning with the GSRB in 1975, of which he was a key participant and founder, and the significance of expanding international contacts that were to help change the visibility, and to some extent the direction, of contemporary Indonesian art in the 1990s.

---

52 For a discussion of Supangkat's curatorial career see Patrick D. Flores, *Past Peripheral: Curation in Southeast Asia* (NUS Museum, National University of Singapore, 2009).

53 Jim Supangkat, 'A Brief History of Indonesian Modern Art', in *Tradition and Change: Contemporary Art of Asia and the Pacific*, ed. Caroline Turner (Brisbane: University of Queensland Press, 1993), 47–57. *Tradition and Change* was the first volume in English to survey artists across Asia and the Pacific and one of the first to put forward the necessity of exploring parallel art histories through the voices of scholars from those countries.

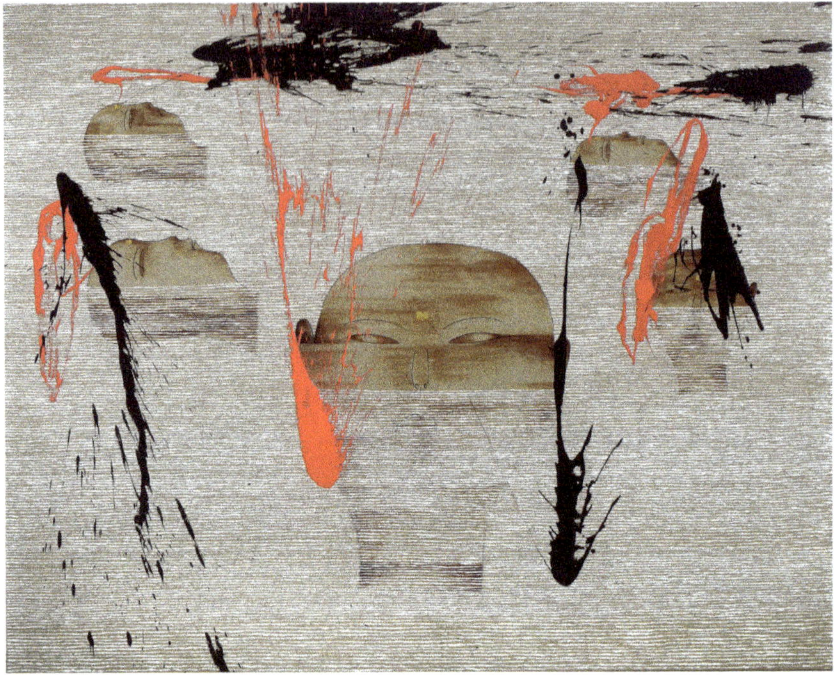

Figure 0.9: Dadang Christanto (b. 1957), Java, *The Water Flows Far Away*, River Series, 2009.

Painting. Image courtesy the artist and Jan Manton Gallery, Brisbane. The work refers to the bodies seen floating down the Brantas River in the Indonesian killings of 1965–66.

Sabapathy and Supangkat's texts move the book from the setting of a distinctly Indonesian modernism into the sphere of the global contemporary. In **Chapter 7** Caroline Turner examines the art of four post-independence generation Indonesian artists: FX Harsono, Heri Dono, Dadang Christanto and Arahmaiani Feisal. They were (and remain) influential innovators in Indonesian contemporary art and were also among the Indonesian artists most exhibited internationally during the 1990s. They are thus examples of artists whose work has been recognised both in Indonesia and internationally. Turner's analysis of key works by these four artists and the responses to them by viewers at exhibitions outside as well as within Indonesia, reveals that the issues addressed by those works have meanings that transcend place and respond to the local and global issues of our times. She also argues that these artists not only 'joined the new global art world in formation in the 1990s but also contributed to reshaping its discourses and redefining contemporary art for a new century in transcultural contexts'. Turner's chapter in this book provides important case studies that reveal how Indonesian artists responded to the ways in which geopolitical change gave rise to a new global art world in the 1990s.

The 1990s also represented a decade of rapid social change in Indonesia, as discontent grew among those most marginalised by the New Order. In **Chapter 8** Alia Swastika examines the neglected role of women artists under that regime, during which 'it seemed that women's voices were systematically silenced'.[54] Swastika has undertaken extensive research on this subject for a book currently only available in Indonesian. In this essay she argues that, two decades after the reform period ushered in by the New Order's fall, women artists still struggle with a systemic lack of recognition and opportunity. Swastika looks in particular at how New Order gender policies influenced the artistic practices of five women artists: Siti Adiyati, a prominent artist who played significant roles in Kelompok Lima (The Bandung Group of Five), *Pernyataan Desember Hitam* (Black December Statement) and GSRB; Hildawati Soemantri, who 'dedicates her life to tertiary education and was the first Indonesian female to be awarded a doctoral degree in art history'; Dyan Anggraini, who 'works in the bureaucracy of the culture sector'; Dolorosa Sinaga, 'a lecturer and activist'; and Mangku Muriati, 'a priestess' who 'serves in the temple'.

In **Chapter 9** Wulan Dirgantoro looks at another legacy of the New Order's methods of suppression and silencing. Examining the work of artists who continue to express the trauma linked to the mass killings of that era, she reveals the 'complex entanglements' between 'testimony, trauma and [artistic] representation'.[55] Dirgantoro provides an overview of the visual strategies developed by artists from the 1990s to remember the past in the present and then extends this study into works by the current generation of artists who, in the post–New Order reform period, have been able to access records that were previously hidden or suppressed.

54 She comments:

> Critics, such as Sanento Yuliman, Bambang Bujono, Kusnadi, and Soedarmadji did indeed write about female artists who displayed interesting artistic ideas through their works, but the numbers were not significant compared to the male artists.

55 Dirgantoro, Chapter 9 (this volume).

In her search for methodologies to 'examine the representation of historical violence and trauma in Indonesian history', Dirgantoro applies Ernst van Alphen's analytical approach to visual representations of the horrors of the Holocaust to contemporary Indonesian representations of the atrocities of 1965–66. Dirgantoro extends her research to works by second- and third-generation descendants of survivors and finds even greater diversity in the methods they choose as framing techniques for their works, including what she terms 'the forensic imagination'. Dirgantoro's conclusion, that 'meaningful and imaginative remembering is necessary for a survivor to move beyond crisis, and the process of remembrance is not an individual but also a social process', brings us back to the core theme of this book, how living art is engaged with politics, society and history.

In **Chapter 10** the book presents the autobiographical account of an artist whose life span has extended across almost the full length of the Indonesian nation, and who has played significant roles in the formation of contemporary art, in building theoretical frameworks for the analysis of Indonesian art history and in the education of successive generations of emerging artists. FX Harsono's chapter was originally presented as a keynote lecture at the ANU conference in 2019. It presents not just an outline of his nationally and internationally acclaimed artistic career, but a portrait of Indonesian history, society and art over 50 years in the context of crisis and change in Indonesia. Renowned for his commitment to social justice, Harsono's art has explored environmental degradation, and social and institutionalised violence and racism from personal, familial and collective perspectives. He was awarded the international Joseph Balestier Award for Freedom of Art in 2015. The chapter is a testament for future generations as much as an examination of past events and is an important primary source for understanding Indonesian art.

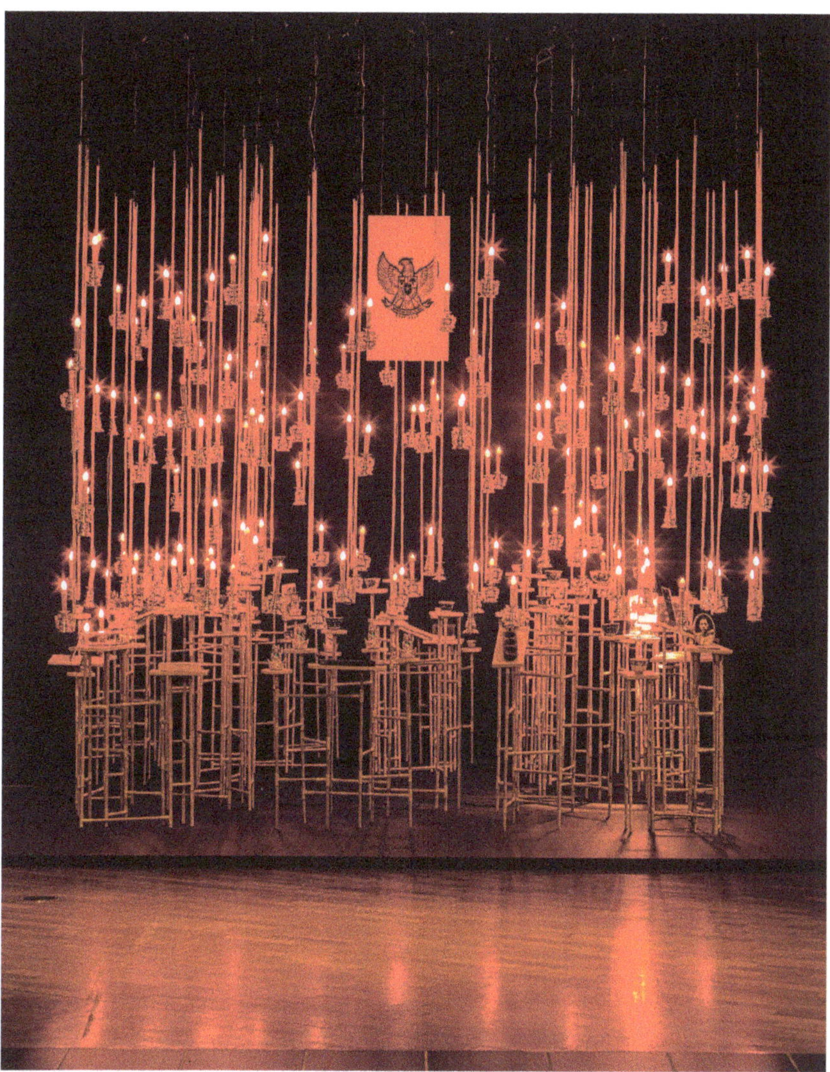

Figure 0.10: FX Harsono (b. 1949), East Java, *Gazing on Collective Memory*, 2016.

Wood, found objects, books, ceramic bowls, wooden butter mould, wooden cookie mould, metal spoons, 3D digital prints, framed photographs and electric candle lights. 300.0 (H) x 220.0 (W) x 220.0 (D) cm (overall). Shown in the exhibition *Contemporary Worlds: Indonesia*, 2019. Collection: National Gallery of Australia. Purchased 2018. © FX Harsono. 2018.755.A-GJ. Image courtesy NGA. Permission: the artist.

The last chapter of this book, the **Epilogue**, draws in part on a virtual discussion held via webinar in March 2021, in which artists and writers from the generation of Indonesians who have built their careers in the twenty-first century discussed the future of Indonesian art and art history in the new millennium, and Indonesia's expanding role in new regional and global art histories now under construction. Contributors from across the spectrum of Indonesian artistic practice were invited to reflect on five themes and their challenges for future practice: curatorial practice and its contribution to intellectual debate on the national and international stage, art history/historiography and its contribution to understandings of the role of art in broader Indonesian history, artistic and curatorial practice outside the major centres, interdisciplinary collaboration in experimental and research-based art, pedagogy and politics in artistic practice, and the emergence of new directions within old discourses in Indonesia and also globally. Art historian Anissa Rahadiningtyas spoke about art history and collaborative research and practice, identifying 'absences and erasures' as a key site for future art historical work, while Karina Roosvita looked at the continuing importance of art projects that create safe spaces to address gender and sexuality. The expansion of contemporary art curatorship beyond centres in Java and Bali and into other provinces, a project currently making significant progress, was addressed by curators Arham Rahman and Alia Swastika, and Balinese activist-artist, I Made 'Bayak' Muliani. Bayak, as well as Swastika, identified an increasing urgency for art and curatorial practice to lead conversations and action on threatened environments and climate change.

The responses of artists in Indonesia to the current COVID-19 pandemic, as explained in the Epilogue of this book, remind us how many Indonesian artists still see connection with their communities and the task of keeping hope alive for those communities as part of the role of an artist. As suggested in Chapter 1 and throughout this book:

> If there is any one theme that emerges from an overview of 'artistic ideologies' it is this: nothing is out of bounds, ideas come from any time and place, the status quo is there to be contested, injustice must be challenged and diversity respected and valued.

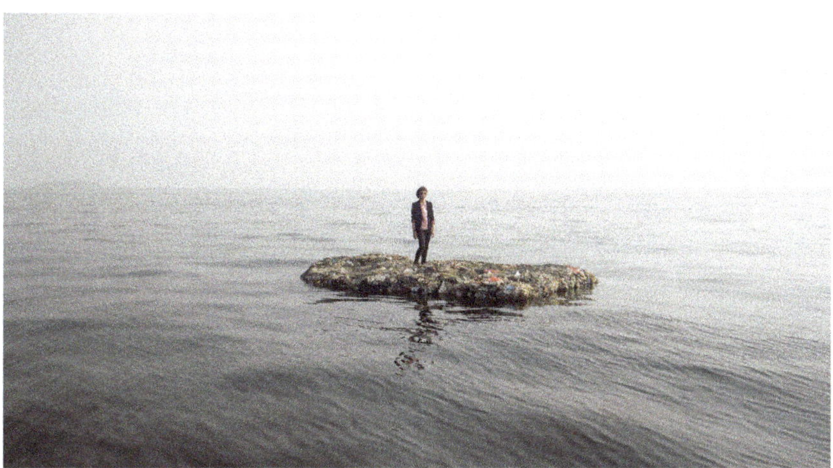

Figure 0.11: Tita Salina (b. 1973), South Sumatra, *1001st Island – The Most Sustainable Island in Archipelago*, 2015.

Plastic waste, fishing net, rope, floats, bamboo, LED lights and oil barrels. Single-channel video: 14:11 minutes, colour, sound. Image courtesy the artist. Shown in the exhibition *Contemporary Worlds: Indonesia*, 2019. The raft is built from plastic waste from Jakarta in Indonesia but the theme is pollution and threats to the environment in Indonesia and globally.[56]

56 See Carol Cains, 'Tita Salina', Contemporary Worlds Indonesia, accessed 10 May 2022, digital.nga.gov.au/archive/contemporaryworlds/artists.cfm%3Fartistirn=50074.html. The video can be viewed on YouTube (youtu.be/mWcr9OwmEzw).

1

Contextualising Art in Indonesia's History, Society and Politics

Elly Kent, Virginia Hooker and Caroline Turner

In 1985 Goenawan Mohamad, Indonesia's internationally recognised journalist and philosopher, wrote: 'It is art that helps us to revive our crushed feelings. It attacks habit'.[1] This succinct description of the impact of an event at Taman Ismail Marzuki,[2] Jakarta's first arts centre, conveyed Mohamad's tribute to the power of the arts to touch individuals deeply and to provoke change. He concluded his piece with the caution that liberty is a prerequisite for the arts to flourish and that he could not guarantee that prerequisite in Indonesia at that time. He celebrated the power of the arts but linked their wellbeing to Indonesia's political condition. Mohamad was founder and editor of Indonesia's respected weekly journal *Tempo* (Time) in 1971 to which he contributed a weekly column that fearlessly evaluated Indonesia's politics, society and culture in direct and indirect ways.[3] His editorial policy ensured all the arts, but especially visual art,

---

1 Goenawan Mohamad (b. 1941), *Sidelines: Writings from Tempo: Indonesia's Banned Magazine*, trans. Jennifer Lindsay (South Melbourne: Hyland House in association with Monash Asia Institute, Monash University 1994), 94.

2 Known by its acronym 'TIM', it was founded in 1968 by Jakarta's governor and remains a major venue for art exhibitions and cultural events.

3 For example, see Goenawan Mohamad, *In Other Words: Forty Years of Essays*, trans. Jennifer Lindsay (University of New South Wales: NewSouth, 2015).

were reviewed regularly in *Tempo*. This not only kept his wide readership across the archipelago informed, but also nurtured writing about the arts and made it possible for individuals to develop as professional art critics.

Goenawan Mohamad is a writer and this book is about visual art, but his words can be compared with the visual images of Indonesia's artists, and, indeed, in Indonesia, the connections between artists and writers are strong and the boundaries are permeable. Most writers are not artists, but many artists were and are also writers. As examples in this chapter illustrate, from the 1930s they shared many of the same concerns—they read the same publications and signed petitions and declarations that publicly stated their positions. They appreciated and criticised each other's work. In essence, they inhabited the same intellectual landscape. So what kinds of worlds did and do these individuals inhabit? From where did they draw the experiences, emotions, inspirations and motivations that are reflected in their works? To provide a direct experience of the worlds of the artists and writers, this chapter includes quotations from essays, poems and prose, as well as works of art, to show the shared dedication to common concerns and the personal interaction that enriched both.

There is no linear progression in the thinking and ideologies of these individuals. Their successors weighed up their arguments, rejecting many and adopting and developing others. The New Order government of Suharto, Indonesia's second president (1966–1998), tried to enforce an ideology of art and culture that contributed to the nation. But his concept of what that meant was contested by Indonesian writers and artists who themselves held no single ideology, as the chapters in this book clearly illustrate. If there is any one theme that emerges from an overview of 'artistic ideologies' it is this: nothing is out of bounds, ideas come from any time and place, the status quo is there to be contested, injustice must be challenged, and diversity respected and valued.

Writing in 1969, Dr Sanento Yuliman (1941–1992), arguably Indonesia's premier art theorist, expressed it like this:

> If there was a framework that proposed clear and detailed characteristics of Indonesian-ness, a proud trademark of Indonesian painting, there would still be artists who would deliberately deviate from it, just to prove that they can be different … But why one framework? Why not several frameworks, why

> not many? Is it not possible that Indonesia contains rich and unknown facets and concerns, increasing numbers of facets and concerns, including those that are mutually oppositional?[4]

He also wrote:

> Like art in general, Indonesia's new art, which has grown in Indonesia, cannot be wholly understood without locating it in the context of the larger framework of Indonesian society and culture. In other words, without locating it within the whole force of history.[5]

The sociopolitical and historical overview that follows unfolds chronologically. It is compiled with hindsight and written in the new millennium with access to records and materials that were not available to many of the Indonesian actors of the time. As well, knowledge of Indonesia's past is a work in progress and is still incomplete. Interpretations of the past change over time in response to new material as well as changing fashions in historiographical and artistic ideologies. Two examples demonstrate this. First, recent reassessments of the contribution of nineteenth-century Javanese painter Raden Saleh to Indonesian art and the responses to that new understanding in contemporary art. Second, the changing nature of artistic responses to the events and consequences of the extreme violence that accompanied the extermination of the Communist Party of Indonesia (PKI) and the rise of General Suharto, as described in Wulan Dirgantoro's contribution to this book (Chapter 9).

The Region, Its Peoples, Monuments and 'Living Traditions'

Broadly speaking, the Republic of Indonesia occupies the territory previously ruled by the Netherlands under the name of the Netherlands East Indies. Located at the centre of monsoons that brought trade vessels

4 Translation by Dr Elly Kent, from 'Sanento Yuliman, Mencari Indonesia Dalan Seni Lukis Indonesia' [Sanento Yuliman seeking Indonesia in Indonesian painting], in *Dua Seni Rupa: Sepilihan Tulisan Sanento Yuliman* [Two arts: Selected writings of Sanento Yuliman], ed. Asikin Hasan (Jakarta: Yayasan Kalam, 2001), 67, first published in *Budaya Djaya*, November 1969. The quote appears in Elly Kent, 'Looking for Indonesia in Contemporary Art', in *Contemporary Worlds: Indonesia*, Jaklyn Babington and Carol Cains (Canberra: National Gallery of Australia, 2019), 23.

5 Sanento Yuliman, 'Seni Lukis Baru Indonesia' (1976), translated in this volume as Chapter 3: 'New Indonesian Painting'.

from both sides of the globe to and from its coasts, it is the largest archipelago in the world, with over 13,000 islands that spread across the equator (see Map 1). Its current population of over 270 million is unevenly spread across its 6,000 inhabited islands, with Java, Madura, Bali, Sulawesi and Sumatra home to the majority. The peoples of Eastern Indonesia have been in contact with the indigenous peoples of the Torres Straits and northern Australia for centuries and share elements of their historical cultures.

For the past 2,000 years at least, foreigners have been encouraged to settle in the Malayo-Indonesian archipelago under the protection of local rulers. Many inter-married with local populations, establishing communities that adopted or respected local cultures. The Chinese and Indian presence is centuries old and Arabs from several regions in the Middle East traded, married local wives and spread Islam, with results we shall see below.

Ethnic diversity is one of the classic descriptions of Indonesia, but the number of ethnic groups depends on the criteria used for classification. Estimates range from at least 100 to 1,000. In the 2000 population census of Indonesia's 30 provinces, single ethnic groups were dominant in only seven provinces. The remaining 23 provinces had mixed or very mixed populations. A breakdown of figures reveals that the major ethnic groups of Java, that is Javanese, Sundanese (West Java), Madurese, Betawi (the local inhabitants of Batavia/Jakarta), Bantenese and Cirebon people together make up 65 per cent of Indonesia's population.[6] The Republic officially recognises six religions: Islam, Protestantism, Catholicism, Hinduism, Buddhism and Confucianism. Indonesia has the largest Muslim population in the world, with about 88 per cent of the population acknowledging Islam as their religion. It is important to acknowledge that, in many areas of contemporary Indonesia, urban or rural, life is fragile and maternal and child mortality remains higher than it should be. In these circumstances, belief in the power of supernatural forces is strong, regardless of religious faith, and that power is reflected in traditional ceremonies and in the arts, including in the work of some contemporary artists.[7]

6 See Ian Chalmers, *Indonesia: An Introduction to Contemporary Traditions* (South Melbourne: Oxford University Press, 2006), 41–42.

7 Robert Cribb gives a concise survey of Indonesian history in his 'Nation: Making Indonesia', in *Indonesia beyond Suharto: Polity, Economy, Society, Transition*, ed. Donald K. Emmerson (Armonk: M.E. Sharpe, 1999), 3–38.

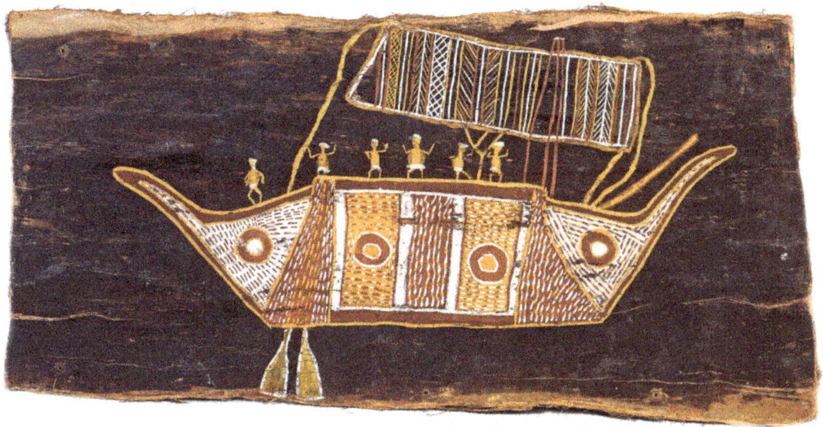

Figure 1.1: Minimini Mamarika (1904–1972), Anindilyakwa people, Northern Territory, Mitjunga, *Malay Prau*, 1948, Umbakumba, Groote Eylandt, Northern Territory.

Earth pigments on eucalyptus bark, 43.7 x 86.0 cm (irreg). Gift of Charles P. Mountford, 1960, Art Gallery of South Australia, Adelaide. © estate of the artist. Permission: Aboriginal Artists Agency Ltd. From the eighteenth century until the twentieth, peoples from Sulawesi and Eastern Indonesia sailed to northern Australia to collect trepang (*bêche de mer*), an item prized by the Chinese. Local indigenous people helped collect, then boil and dry it on local beaches. Material exchanges must have taken place to maintain the seasonal relationship. Records of the contact in the form of rock art and bark paintings are not uncommon.[8]

The stunning natural beauty of the Indonesian archipelago has been celebrated for centuries and exploited by modern tourism. Dolmens and menhirs from distant prehistoric times and the remains of monumental stone temples from the eighth and ninth century CE, particularly those of the Buddhist stupa Borobudur[9] and the Hindu temples at Prambanan in Central Java, testify to well-organised and flourishing centres of regional wealth and culture (see Map 2).[10] Nowadays, evidence of the scale and

8 See further James Bennett and Russell Kelty, *Treasure Ships: Art in the Age of Spices* (Adelaide: Art Gallery of South Australia, 2014), 309, cat. no. 191, note by Elle Freak.

9 Srihadi Soedarsono (1931–2022), one of Indonesia's best loved painters, painted Candi Borobudur in his 'lyrical expressionist' style, which conveys both spirituality and tranquillity (see Chapter 6, this volume). For further details of his life, see Yuliman, Chapter 3 (this volume); *Masterpieces of the National Gallery of Indonesia* (Jakarta: Galeri Nasional Indonesia, 2014), 198–99.

10 There is evidence of paintings on cloth and paper from sixteenth-century Java. See Claire Holt, *Art in Indonesia: Continuities and Change* (Ithaca and New York: Cornell University Press, 1967), 191. Beautifully illuminated manuscripts copied in royal courts across the archipelago have survived from as early as the seventeenth and eighteenth centuries. See Ann Kumar and John H. McGlynn, *Illuminations: The Writing Traditions of Indonesia* (New York: Weatherhill, Inc., in cooperation with the Lontar Foundation, 1996). Figure 1.5 in this chapter shows an illuminated Quran from early nineteenth-century Aceh.

complexity of pre-modern Indonesian cultures can be viewed either at the sites themselves or in Indonesia's National Museum, but until the 1950s during Sukarno's presidency, they were not widely known outside Dutch scholarly circles.[11]

After Indonesian independence, the (now) world heritage monuments together with 'living traditions' of dance, music, shadow theatre, oral narratives and poetry, weaving, wax-resist and tie-dyed textiles, embroidery, jewellery, metalwork (gold, silver, damascened kris), carving, sculpture, architecture, complex ceremonial events, religious ceremonies, shamanism and specialist cuisines were recognised as expressions of national culture.

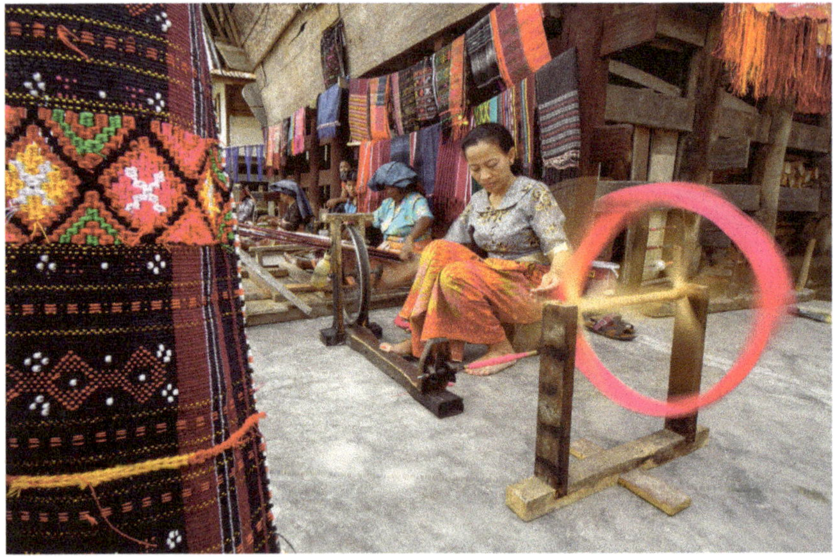

Figure 1.2: Traditional Batak tailors making ulos (traditional cloth of the Batak people) in Huta Raja village, North Sumatra, Indonesia.

The cloths are used in ceremonies related to significant events such as weddings, births and deaths; traditionally woven by women, different motifs and compositions have specific meanings and functions. In the background, cloths hang on a building in the vernacular Batak architectural style. Photograph by Maula039 on Wikimedia Commons (CC BY-SA 4.0) (see Map 3).

11 The majority of Indonesians learned about their own antiquity only after information became available in Indonesian texts (after 1945) or they visited the theme park Taman Mini Indonesia Indah (Beautiful Indonesia in Miniature Park) in Jakarta after it was opened by its patron, Ibu Tien Suharto, in 1975. See a description of the park in Virginia Matheson Hooker, 'Expression: Creativity despite Restraint', in Emmerson, *Indonesia beyond Suharto,* 265–68.

To summarise: the physical landscape of Indonesia has been shaped for millennia by the forces of nature. Earthquakes, tsunamis and volcanic eruptions have swallowed villages and destroyed towns. Powerful floods and landslides have changed (and continue to change) the course of rivers, resulting in severe siltation of coastlines. Small islands come and go, and roads and rail tracks wash away, making travel by water the most efficient means of transport in many places. Since the end of the New Order (1998), political parties regularly change allegiances and new coalitions form and dissolve. As in all nations, competition for power enables opportunities for corruption. Despite all that, or perhaps because of it, during the new millennium—after electoral reforms and voter education—Indonesia has had one of the highest voter participation rates in the world and its elections have been reported by outside observers to have been well run. In such a vast nation with a diverse and massive population, that is a noteworthy achievement.

Life as 'a Native' in the Netherlands East Indies

The Portuguese and English left their mark in the archipelago, but it was the Dutch in the mid-nineteenth century who placed their presence on a more formal footing and gradually extended their authority over most of what is now modern Indonesia.[12] Before that time, the Dutch presence was dependent on treaties and contracts established with individual local rulers, who then felt free to call in Dutch firepower to use against each other. By the early twentieth century, the Dutch ruled through a Dutch governor-general in Batavia (Jakarta) with layers of bureaucracy descending through Dutch administrators who were spread across the archipelago. They, in turn, devolved power to local elites, many of whom were highly corrupt and abused their authority over their fellow 'natives'.

12 Dutch contact with the indigenous peoples of the archipelago began in the early seventeenth century; however, to avoid the expenses associated with direct administration, the Dutch operated through a private monopolistic trading company (Vereenigde Oost-Indische Compagnie, VOC) until it went bankrupt in the early nineteenth century. Reluctantly, the king of the Netherlands assumed power over the VOC's former territories, which became overseas possessions of the Netherlands. For the complexities of the laws operating under the Dutch, see Peter Burns, 'The Netherlands East Indies: Colonial Legal Policy and the Definitions of Law', in *Laws of South-East Asia,* Volume II, ed. M. B. Hooker (Singapore: Butterworth & Co, 1988), 148–292.

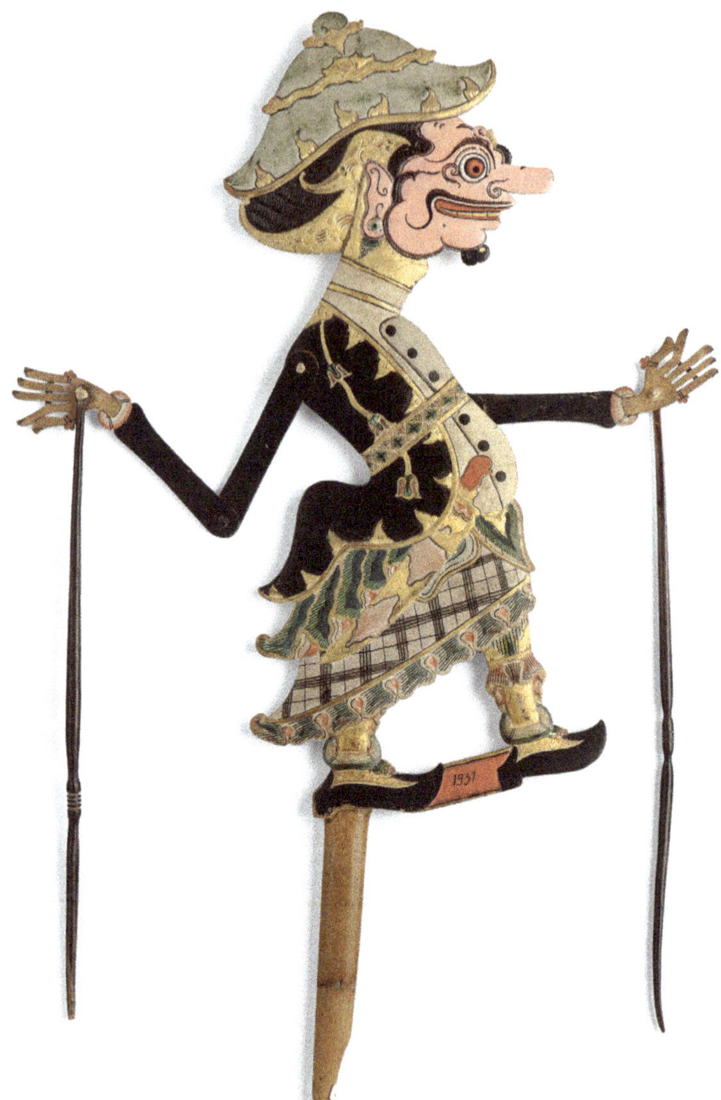

Figure 1.3: Indonesia, rod puppet (*wayang klitik*), churlish courtier, 1931, Central Java.

Wood, leather, pigment, gold leaf, 53.0 cm (figure including handle). D'Auvergne Boxall Bequest Fund 2013, Art Gallery of South Australia, Adelaide. This puppet is not one of the characters from the Indian epics that provide the plots for the episodes of the Javanese shadow theatre; rather, it is a parody of a member of the Javanese elite who implemented Dutch colonial policy in Java.[13]

13 For further details see Bennett and Kelty, *Treasure Ships*, 167.

Under Dutch colonial law, the peoples of the archipelago were divided into a hierarchy of Europeans (including Japanese), 'Foreign Orientals' (including Chinese and Arabs) and 'Natives'. The Dutch offered members of the local elites the opportunity to attend Dutch-run schools and colleges to train as professionals, doctors, lawyers and engineers. The cream of these elites might be sent to the Netherlands for tertiary education. After their return to their homeland, some from that very privileged group organised their fellows into social organisations that 'played a major role in shaping modern Indonesian social and political history'.[14] These non-government movements were particularly active during the repressive years of the 1970s–90s.

The first 'Indonesian' we know of to study Western-style painting was Raden Saleh Syarif Bustaman (1811–1880), who is now widely regarded as the founder of Indonesian art. In his essay entitled 'New Indonesian Painting' (see Chapter 3), Yuliman begins his survey with Raden Saleh, identifying him as 'the first Indonesian painter to take up new techniques and styles and also—in association with this—a new aesthetic'. Raden Saleh studied and painted in Europe between 1830 and 1851, spoke Dutch, French, German and English, was appointed royal painter to the king of the Netherlands and honoured with titles by the German princes for whom he painted. On his return to Java he continued to paint but his works were held in the collections of those who commissioned them and were rarely available for public viewing. A full appreciation of Raden Saleh was to come more than a century after his death when archival material was discovered in Europe that led to a reappraisal of all Raden Saleh's work, as described at the end of this chapter.

14 Frederick Bunnell, 'Community Participation, Indigenous Ideology, Activist Politics: Indonesian NGOs in the 1990s', in *Making Indonesia: Essays on Modern Indonesia in Honor of George McT. Kahin*, ed. Daniel S. Lev and Ruth McVey (Cornell University, Ithaca, New York: Southeast Asia Program 1996), 180–81, doi.org/10.7591/9781501719370-011.

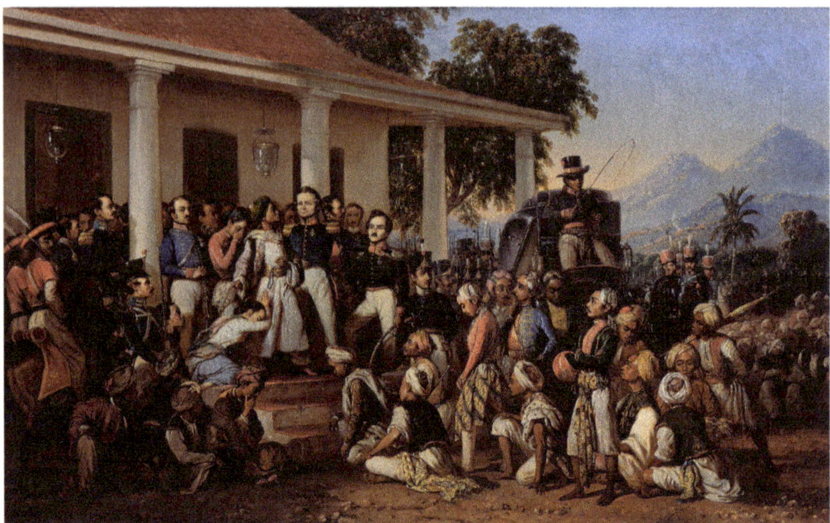

Figure 1.4: Raden Saleh (1811–1880), Central Java, *The Arrest of Prince Diponegoro* (*Penangkapan Pangeran Diponegoro*), 1857.

Oil on canvas, 112 x 179 cm. Collection: Presidential Palace Indonesia. The painting depicts Dutch General de Kock and his forces arresting Javanese noble Pangeran (Prince) Diponegoro in 1830, thus ending his five-year insurrection against the Dutch known as the Java War. Public domain.

One of the most compelling accounts of life under Dutch rule in the early twentieth century is given in a set of four historical novels written by one of Indonesia's best-known authors, Pramoedya Ananta Toer (1925–2006). Drawing on archival materials from the early twentieth century—newspapers, Sino-Malay literature, Dutch reports—the 'Buru quartet' describes the humiliations and legal discrimination endured by 'natives' in Dutch colonial society.[15] The quartet also describes the early stages of Indonesian nationalism and the strength and intelligence of the indigenous population, particularly its main female character.

15 As a prominent member of Lekra (Institute of People's Culture), Pramoedya was arrested in 1965 and exiled to the prison island of Buru. Between 1965 and his release in 1979, he composed the novels. The priceless archival materials on which they were based were destroyed at the time of Pramoedya's arrest in 1965. See further, Pramoedya Ananta Toer, *This Earth of Mankind*, trans. Max Lane (Ringwood, Victoria: Penguin Books, 1982), v–x.

Finding a Language: Proto-Nationalist Activities, 1920s–42

The colonial Dutch administrators are described as 'probably unique among European colonial powers in limiting the access which the native subjects had to the language of their masters'.[16] The Dutch believed their non-elite indigenous populations should remain as native as possible and 'they should be only very selectively touched by the achievements of Western culture'.[17] Goenawan Mohamad points out that the Dutch policy of severely restricting access to their language as a means of communication across the archipelago actually encouraged 'the natives' to find an alternative. Mohamad notes that by late 1925 there were at least 200 newspapers in the colony, and most used Malay as their medium. Malay soon became a symbol of an archipelago-wide movement for freedom from Dutch rule.[18] In 1928, this was formalised at a mass meeting of representatives of youth organisations. They took an oath, the *Sumpah Pemuda* (Youth Pledge) swearing to work for one language, one land, one people. The concept of a new nation, Indonesia, free of Dutch rule, had been publicly declared and the date of the oath is celebrated every year throughout Indonesia.

The significance of this acceptance of one national language cannot be overestimated. It enabled any Indonesian, whatever their status, ethnicity or gender, to understand the speeches of nationalist leaders; read the daily news, publications of clubs and organisations, books or translations from foreign languages; and join organisations anywhere in the archipelago. Writers whose mother tongue was not Malay (and that was overwhelmingly the population of Java) had to experiment with developing a style appropriate to writing about social change, the main

16 See Goenawan Mohamad, 'Forgetting: Poetry and the Nation, a Motif in Indonesian Literary Modernism after 1945', in *Clearing a Space: Postcolonial Readings of Modern Indonesian Literature*, ed. Keith Foulcher and Tony Day (Leiden: KITLV Press, 2002), 186. Mohamad gives the figure of 0.3 per cent of 'the natives'—who made up 97 per cent of the population in 1930—having minimal knowledge of Dutch.

17 Ibid., 186, quoting Hendrik Maier.

18 Ibid., 187.

theme of the new literature. Artists were also experimenting with style and subject and both writers and artists were trying to connect with new audiences of readers and viewers.[19]

Writing about the 1930s, Yuliman describes it as the period when 'a new art that took the form of individual expression' and 'shifted the centre of creative energy from society to the individual' was occurring. These characteristics were apparent, he says, in the literary movement Pujangga Baru (New Poets) in 1933, the art group PERSAGI around 1937 and, 'to some extent', in the Balinese art movement Pita Maha in 1934.[20]

Sudjojono, a founding member of PERSAGI (Persatuan Ahli Gambar Indonesia/Association of Indonesian Draughtsmen) became one of Indonesia's most influential and revered artists and art theorists.[21] In an earlier article (1970), Yuliman noted:

> Sudjojono's view of painting as 'the visible soul' implies that painting is not a copy of what is visible externally, but rather making visible what is hidden in the soul.

He went on to argue that 'the development of Indonesian painting since *Persagi* has prepared the ideas and sensibilities … for the emergence of abstract paintings'.[22] The concept of 'the visible soul' is further explored by Elly Kent in Chapter 2 and, from a different perspective, in Ahmad Sadali's Islam-based philosophy and abstract art described in Chapter 4.

Life for Muslims

Islamic religious education had been available to the indigenous peoples of the archipelago since the first conversions to Islam around the fourteenth century, or even earlier. Local mosques and religious schools taught the

---

19 As described, for example, by Benedict Anderson, *Imagined Communities: Reflections on the Origin and Spread of Nationalism* (Norfolk: Verso Editions and NLB, 1983), although Anderson does not include artists in his study.

20 Sanento Yuliman, 'Seni Lukis Di Indonesia: Persoalan-Persoalannya, Dulu Dan Sekarang' [Painting in Indonesia: Issues, past and present], in *Dua Seni Rupa, Sepilihan Tulisan Sanento Yuliman*, ed. Hasan Asikin, trans. Elly Kent (Jakarta: Yayasan Kalam, 2001), 71, first published in *Budaya Djawa*, December 1970. On *Pita Maha*, see Holt, *Art in Indonesia*; Astri Wright, *Soul, Spirit, and Mountain: Preoccupations of Contemporary Indonesian Painters* (Kuala Lumpur: Oxford University Press, 1994). Both these books are now classic texts on Indonesian art and are essential reading for an appreciation of the complexities and richness of that art.

21 See further Chapter 3 (this volume) where Yuliman describes his work and theories.

22 Yuliman, 'Seni Lukis Di Indonesia'.

basics of Islam and Quranic Arabic and promising scholars travelled to the holy cities of Mecca and Medina to study and mix with believers from across the Muslim world, establishing links between the holy land and Southeast Asia.[23] In the late nineteenth century, Southeast Asian Muslims also visited Egypt, where the very influential modernist scholar Muhammad Abduh (1849–1905) was writing and teaching about how to live as a Muslim in the contemporary world. His approach was to select the best from the West and from it learn how to strengthen Islam.

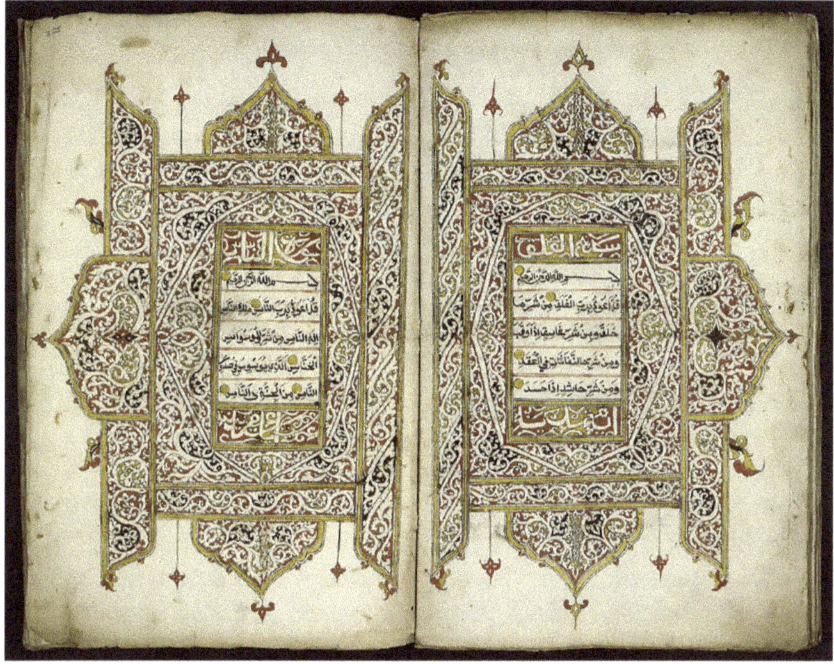

Figure 1.5: Illuminated frames decorating opening pages of a Quran from Aceh, c. 1820s.

British Library. Public domain.[24]

23 See further Azyumardi Azra, *The Origins of Islamic Reformism in Southeast Asia: Networks of Malay Indonesian and Middle Eastern Ulama in the Seventeenth and Eighteenth Centuries* (Crows Nest NSW: Allen & Unwin, 2004), doi.org/10.1163/9789004488199.

24 The manuscript has been digitised and is viewable at the British Library, accessed 16 September 2021, www.bl.uk/manuscripts/Viewer.aspx?ref=or_16915_f002v. Annabel Gallop, lead curator Southeast Asia at the British Library, provides a technical description of the manuscript, 'Three Qur'an Manuscripts from Aceh in the British Library', British Library, Asian and African Studies Blog, 14 June 2021, blogs.bl.uk/asian-and-african/2021/06/three-quran-manuscripts-from-aceh-in-the-british-library.html.

Muhammad Abduh and his followers advocated education for all Muslims, including women, and, through a publication delivered throughout the Netherlands East Indies, interested Muslims could learn more about Islam in the contemporary world. Groups of modern-minded individuals met in study groups to discuss how to spread this new understanding of Islam. In 1912, a new organisation named Muhammadiyah was founded in Yogyakarta and its very active women's wing was established in 1916. Muhammadiyah's current membership is about 30 million, with branches in every province of Indonesia. It is respected for its practical activities in education (founding kindergartens, schools, universities) and medicine (establishing hospitals).

In response to this modern-minded and forward-looking form of Islam, the traditional Islamic scholars of Java were moved to form their own organisation, Nahdlatul Ulama (Revival of the Religious Scholars) in 1926. Known as NU, and with well over 40 million members, it is the world's largest Muslim mass social organisation. Particularly strong in Central and East Java, it respects local attitudes to indigenous, popular folk beliefs and has maintained sites of pilgrimage to graves of so-called saints of Java.[25]

NU has maintained and developed the Javanese traditional style of Islamic teaching conducted in *pesantren* (Islamic boarding schools and colleges), which still attract millions of students—women and men. Abdurrahman Wahid, who became Indonesia's fourth president, was educated in the *pesantren* system, as were many leading Indonesians, including artists, writers, journalists, entrepreneurs and intellectuals. Learning to recite the Quran is a duty and an act of piety with specialist training required to learn the exacting science and art of Arabic calligraphy.[26] The visual and creative aspects of Arabic calligraphy, as well as its spiritual significance, have also provided a wellspring for many Indonesian artists, from early modern painters through to contemporary artists. The moral and ethical philosophies embedded in the faith have also underpinned the aesthetic paths pursued by many artists working across fields as diverse as traditional calligraphic practices, abstract painting and community engagement, as Hooker explores in Chapter 4.

25 See the readable and authoritative study on this topic by George Quinn, *Bandit Saints of Java* (Leicestershire: Monsoon Books Ltd, 2019).

26 For further details on the teaching of Quranic calligraphy in contemporary Indonesia see Virginia Hooker, '"By the Pen!": Spreading *'ilm* in Indonesia through Quranic Calligraphy', in *'Ilm: Science, Religion and Art in Islam*, ed. Samer Akkach (Adelaide: University of Adelaide Press, 2019), 81–97, doi.org/10.20851/ilm-1-05.

Japanese Rule, 1942–45

In 1941 Japan attacked US forces at Pearl Harbor, landed forces in northern Malaya and started the Pacific War. By 1942, Japan controlled all of Southeast Asia, gaining access to its raw materials and populations, which were then directed to supporting its war effort. In the Netherlands East Indies, Europeans were interned, and the indigenous peoples witnessed the reversal of European fortunes and status at the hands of an Asian people. The compulsory requisition of crops and the shortage of labour to tend the land resulted in widespread famines, particularly in 1944 and 1945. Indonesia at this time has been described as 'a land of extreme hardship, inflation, shortages, profiteering, corruption, black markets and death'.[27] To win over the indigenous population, the Japanese said they would support the independence movement and assist with preparations for full independence. Writing about this period, Goenawan Mohamad described the Japanese occupation of the archipelago as very difficult for all its inhabitants, and for 'intellectuals and people of the arts it was a time of hard choices'.[28]

The Japanese established a cultural centre to attract Indonesian intellectuals and artists to support the Japanese cause, suggesting that a Japanese victory would lead to Indonesia's independence. While ostensibly supporting Japanese propaganda, many of the Indonesians were able to use radio broadcasts, their writings and art to communicate subtle anti-Japanese messages to their fellow Indonesians. In his essay 'New Indonesian Painting' (see Chapter 3), Yuliman refers to the cultural centre, Keimin Bunka Shidoso, established by the Japanese and lists the Indonesian painters who began to emerge at this time. Many later became leading artists in the post-independence period.[29]

---

27 See M. C. Ricklefs, *A History of Modern Indonesia since c. 1200* (Houndmills, Basingstoke: Palgrave, 2001), 249.

28 Mohamad, 'Forgetting', 195.

29 In 2002, even though speaking to a Japanese audience, Goenawan Mohamad made the point that, during their occupation of Asian countries, including Indonesia, Japan was under the illusion that it could redefine relationships between Asia and the West. See Goenawan Mohamad, 'Indonesia's Asia', *Asia in Transition: Representation and Identity*, Japan Foundation 30th Anniversary International Symposium 2002 (Tokyo: Japan Foundation, 2002), 269.

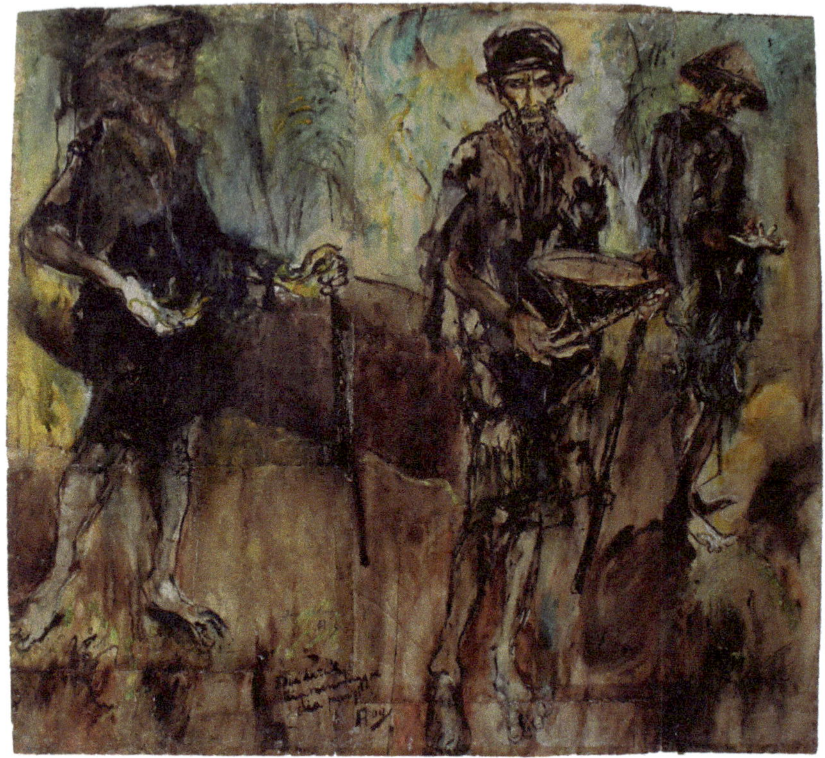

Figure 1.6: Affandi (1907–1990), West Java, *He Comes, Waits and Goes*, 1944.

Watercolour on paper, 117 x 126 cm. Collection: Affandi Museum. Image courtesy Kartika Affandi and the Affandi Museum.

The young poet Chairil Anwar (1922–1949) is an example of what could be achieved by using Japanese support to achieve nationalist ends. His background also reflected that of many of his peers. Of Minangkabau descent, but born in Medan (North Sumatra), he moved to Java (like so many of his generation) to participate in the more cosmopolitan atmosphere. He seized any opportunity to publish his poetry and spread his views on the future of the arts in an independent Indonesia.[30] In two of his radio broadcasts in 1943 (for Japanese propaganda purposes),

30 Unless otherwise indicated, information on Chairil Anwar is taken from Mohamad, 'Forgetting', 195.

he emphasised that '[conscious] thought plays a very important part in [the creation of] *seni yang tingkatnya tinggi* (art of a high standard)'. He did not support 'the results of improvisational art'.[31]

During the Japanese occupation, Chairil made a radio broadcast (republished in 1949) entitled '*Membuat Sajak, Melihat Lukisan*' (Making verse, seeing paintings) in which he compared poetry and visual art.[32] Although the materials are quite different, he said, the form and content may be compared. He considered artists superior to poets because poets work with language in an intuitive way and it is the subject of the poem that is of the utmost importance. Artists can work on any subject but what they convey must be determined by the strength of their emotions. A painting of a pair of old shoes can be as 'good' as a vase of flowers if it arouses emotion in the viewer.[33]

Chairil Anwar was in close contact with many of the artists of his generation and Mochtar Apin (1923–1994) painted his portrait in 1947.[34] Chairil dedicated one of his poems to the painter Affandi (1910–1990), a doyen of modern Indonesian art, and they were later to write and sign a common declaration of universal humanism.[35] But they differed over the relationship between an individual and his or her fellows. As the late Professor A. Teeuw, Dutch scholar of Indonesian literature expressed it: 'For Chairil, human dignity was contained and expressed in the individual; for Affandi, humanity is achieved by man as a social creature acting in harmony with his environment'.[36]

In contemporary Indonesia, Chairil Anwar's name is known to all school children as the writer of the poem *Aku* (I or me, 1943), a defiant celebration of personal freedom without constraint or inhibition. Its passion and emotion would have been lauded by his contemporary,

---

31 Goenawan Mohamad and John H. McGlynn, '*Pasemon*: On Allusion and Illusions', *Manoa* 18, no. 1 (2006): 79, doi.org/10.1353/man.2006.0033.

32 H. B. Jassin, *Chairil Anwar Pelopor Angkatan 45* (Djakarta: Gunung Agung, 1968), 150–51.

33 Jassin, *Chairil Anwar*, 150.

34 The portrait is reproduced in A. Teeuw, *Modern Indonesian Literature*, Volume I (The Hague: Martinus Nijhoff, 1979), opposite 135.

35 Comparing Affandi and fellow artist Basuki Abdullah, Chairil concluded that '*Affandi hidup lebih dalam dan benar*' [Affandi lives more deeply and truly], quoted in Teeuw, *Modern Indonesian Literature*, 125 (original emphasis). See Yuliman's description of Affandi and his work in Chapter 3.

36 Quoted in Anthony H. Johns, *Cultural Options and the Role of Tradition: A Collection of Essays on Modern Indonesian and Malaysian Literature* (Canberra: Faculty of Asian Studies in association with The Australian National University Press, 1979), 47.

the artist and theorist Sudjojono, who was urging his fellow artists to paint with feeling, as described in Chapter 3. Translated from Indonesian, Chairil's poem reads:

> I
> When my time comes
> I don't want anyone to mourn
> Not even you
>
> No need for sobbing
>
> I am a wild creature
> Cut loose from its fellows
>
> Let bullets pierce my hide
> I will keep raging, kicking
>
> I will run, bearing the wounds and poison
> Run
> Until the pain has gone
>
> And I won't give a damn
> I want to live a thousand years more.[37]

Independence and Its Aftermath, 1945–55

Sukarno declared the birth of the Republic of Indonesia on 17 August 1945, immediately after World War II and the Pacific War ended with the surrender of Japan. In the eyes of the Netherlands, however, Indonesia (then 'the Netherlands East Indies') remained its colony. The Dutch returned to their 'colony' in 1945, thus initiating five years of violent and bloody armed conflict regarded as Indonesia's war of independence. Hostilities ended in late 1949 and the United Nations recognised Indonesia's sovereignty in 1950.

The new nation was stronger in theory than in reality. It had been ruled as one entity only for a short period by the Netherlands (Aceh was only finally 'subdued' in 1912) and for an even shorter period by the Japanese. There were no laws, and the founding fathers (no mothers) took advice

37 Text from Jassin, *Chairil Anwar*, 33, trans. Virginia Hooker. See Mohamad, *Sidelines: Writings from Tempo*, 12–13, for a discussion of the significance of the first-person pronoun title.

on a constitution that strove for humanitarian ideals and an ideology of five lofty principles known as Pancasila,[38] which were the touchstone and inspiration for a new nation.

Enshrined in Article 32 of the 1945 *Constitution of Indonesia* is the statement that the government will develop a national culture as an expression of the personality and vitality of all the peoples of Indonesia.[39] Article 32 has been taken seriously by all governments of Indonesia and, with some more recent amendments, remains the foundation of official policies and funding of 'Indonesian culture'. 'Culture' has usually been administered with education in a combined Ministry of Education and Culture.

The greatest challenge for the new Republic, then and now, is constructing and then maintaining a physically and ideologically unified nation. Almost as if they were taking turns, exclusivist Islam and socialism have vied to become the ideological underpinning of the state, at the expense of democracy as expressed in the constitution. The 1950s was a period of experimentation with democracy, foreign policy (non-alignment was the final choice) and economic management. Artists and writers were also debating their visions for the new nation.

Debating a 'National Culture', 1950–65

Asrul Sani (1927–2004) has been described as the writer who 'recorded more fully than any other writer of the time the collision of ideas that characterized intellectual and creative life' in Indonesia during the late 1940s and early 1950s. He described Jakarta during this period as 'a place where values "crash against each other" … and people find "an arena" of new Indonesian cultural values and a new Indonesian life'.[40]

In this atmosphere, a group of writers and two artists formulated and published one of the most quoted declarations of the purpose of art and culture in the new nation. In 1946, soon after the bloody, armed conflict of revolution against the Dutch had begun, Chairil Anwar pushed for

38 Literally, 'the Five Principles': Belief in One God, National Unity, Indonesian Democracy, Humanitarianism and Social Justice.
39 See Virginia Matheson Hooker, 'Introduction', in *Culture and Society in New Order Indonesia*, ed. Virginia Matheson Hooker (Kuala Lumpur: Oxford University Press 1993), 4.
40 Mohamad, 'Forgetting', 198.

the formation of a group called 'Artists of Independence'. Between them, the group published a literary supplement *Gelanggang* (Forum) that came out with the political weekly *Siasat* (Investigation). Chairil Anwar died of typhus in April 1949, but he had already worked with members of the Gelanggang group to formulate a statement of their vision for a cultural revolution to abandon obsolete values to make way for the new ones that would inspire Indonesia's national culture. It was published as *Surat Kepercayaan Gelanggang* (Gelanggang document of beliefs) in October 1950.[41]

The aims and tone of the Gelanggang document set the benchmark for other cultural statements and manifestos that were to come. The document is expressed in seven concise paragraphs and begins:

> We are the legitimate heirs of world culture, and we will perpetuate this culture in our own way. We were born from the ranks of ordinary people, and for us, the concept of 'the people' signifies a jumbled hodge-podge from which new, robust worlds are born.

Another paragraph declares:

> Indonesian culture is established through the unity of a great variety of catalysts, of voices coming from all corners of the world and then hurled back in the form of our own voices. We will oppose all attempts to restrict or obstruct a proper examination of values.

The final paragraph describes the relationship between artists and society: 'Our appreciation of the surrounding conditions (society) is that of people who acknowledge the reciprocity of influences between society and the artist'.[42]

A recent collection of essays entitled *Heirs to World Culture: Being Indonesian 1950–1965* analysed Indonesia's cultural history during those years of the new Republic. The essays reveal the complexity and fluidity of the period and also 'an overriding common commitment to the future, to the nation, to Indonesian culture and what it might be'.[43] In her opening

41 Based on Mohamad, 'Forgetting', 202–03, in which a full English translation, as well as the original Indonesian, is given.

42 Translation quoted from Mohamad, 'Forgetting', 202–03.

43 Jennifer Lindsay, 'Heirs to World Culture 1950–1965: An Introduction', in *Heirs to World Culture: Being Indonesian 1950–1965*, ed. Jennifer Lindsay and Maya H. T. Liem (Leiden: KITLV Press, 2012), 6, doi.org/10.26530/OAPEN_403204.

chapter, Jennifer Lindsay describes the sense of excitement about the final international recognition of the new Republic of Indonesia in 1950 and the frequency with which the words '*baru*' (new) and '*lahir*' (birth) are used in writings of the time. She states: 'To be Indonesian in 1950 was to be modern'.[44] She summarises the period in this way:

> This was a time when Indonesia's cultural mobility and cosmopolitanism mean that people with very different agendas and points of view could interact with the outside world and each other in a vibrant and vigorous way.[45]

Lindsay identifies '[t]he inter-relationship between Indonesia's cultural traffic abroad and developments at home during the 1950–65 period' as an essential part of the forging of the new nation and its national culture.[46] Riding this wave of excitement, artists, writers and cultural groups left Indonesia to travel the world, sometimes as official representatives of 'Indonesian culture', to experience at first hand the international cultures they had been reading about and discussing. The painters Affandi and Mochtar Apin were overseas for several years or more and others accepted scholarships to study abroad. They went to China, Europe and the US, and some joined the Colombo Plan to come to Australia.[47] Chapter 7 describes the travels of the next generation of artists.

Art for the People, from the Left

While some Indonesians were able to travel abroad, they were a tiny minority. For the vast majority of new Indonesian citizens during the post-revolution years, political life was volatile and unstable. The new and independent Republic was centrally governed from Jakarta and the majority of its politicians had rejected an Islam-based nation-state. For these and other reasons, some local, there were armed rebellions in parts of Sumatra, Sulawesi and West Java. It was a hazardous time for the new nation and Sukarno held it together with rhetoric and risky politics.

44 Ibid., 15.

45 Ibid., 23.

46 Ibid., 7.

47 See also the detailed analysis of Brigitta Isabella, 'The Politics of Friendship: Modern Art in Indonesia's Cultural Diplomacy, 1950–65', in *Ambitious Alignments: New Histories of Southeast Asian Art, 1945–1990*, ed. Stephen H. Whiteman, Sarena Abdullah, Yvonne Low and Phoebe Scott (Singapore: Power Publications and National Gallery Singapore, 2018), 83–105.

The Gelanggang document was conceived in the heady days of the revolution but not published until October 1950. On 17 August that year, Independence Day, a group of 15 'cultural workers' (not members of the Gelanggang group) met to form a new cultural group, Lembaga Kebudayaan Rakyat (Institute of People's Culture) known by its acronym 'Lekra' and to endorse its statement of purpose entitled *Mukadimah* (Manifesto). Also present at the inauguration were two leaders of the PKI, a fact used later to assert that Lekra was a branch of the PKI.[48]

Foulcher places the *Mukadimah* in the broader cultural history of Indonesia to show how its proponents rejected the culture of Indonesia's ruling elite (of the late 1940s) and accused them of pursuing the same colonial culture as the Dutch. The *Mukadimah* stated that the aims of the revolution had not been achieved and that the Indonesian people remained oppressed. To maintain their own position, the Indonesian 'ruling class' perpetuated 'an anti-People, feudal and imperialistic culture' that the members of Lekra would replace with 'a people's culture'. For that to happen, Indonesia needed to establish a popular democracy as the basis for the Indonesian state. Indonesian cultural renewal would rest on nationalism, anti-imperialism and social equality.[49]

In 1955, Lekra revised the *Mukadimah* with more emphasis on 'people-oriented' (*kerakyatan*) art and supporting a diversity of styles and forms, provided they 'are faithful to the truth' and strive for 'the utmost artistic beauty'. Foulcher points out that many of the 'great names' of Indonesian painting were associated with Lekra from the mid to late 1950s (and even into the early 1960s), painters including Affandi, Basuki Resobowo, Sudjojono, Henk Ngantung and Hendra Gunawan.[50] At its first national conference in 1959, Lekra resolved on a practice to bring 'cultural workers' even closer to the people, through going to villages, living with the inhabitants and working with them. Further details are given by Elly Kent in Chapter 2.

48 See Keith Foulcher's pathbreaking study of Lekra, *Social Commitment in Literature and the Arts: The Indonesian 'Institute of People's Culture' 1950–1965* (Monash University: Centre of Southeast Asian Studies, 1986), 17–18. His study remains the basic source for material about Lekra and its members. See also Chapter 3 (this volume), in which Yuliman repeats the common misunderstanding—promoted by the New Order government—that Lekra was a branch of the Indonesian Communist Party. Yuliman points out that *not* all artists who joined Lekra followed its prescriptions on appropriate artistic styles.

49 Based on Foulcher, *Social Commitment*, 18–19.

50 Ibid., 30, 41–42.

At the national political level, in 1959–60 Sukarno dissolved parliament and imposed what he termed 'Guided Democracy'. He engaged in anti-Western rhetoric and behaviour, alarming the West during the tense period of the Cold War.[51] In response to Sukarno's own 1959 manifesto for national life (MANIPOL[52]), a group of anti-Lekra intellectuals (with whom Yuliman was sympathetic) published their own *Manifes Kebudayaan* (Cultural Manifesto) in late 1963. Members of Lekra were furious.[53] The economic situation continued to deteriorate, hostility between cultural groups worsened, and Sukarno continued to grapple with appeasing his military and the PKI.

Before WWII, there was no formal art education for adults in the Netherlands Indies. But there was a host of informal artists' cooperatives or studios (*sanggar*) that operated on a small scale in many cities and towns, including outside Java (listed by Yuliman in Chapter 3) where budding artists could work with more established ones. Sukarno was a strong proponent of education as a priority for the new nation and there were national universities in Yogyakarta, Jakarta and Bandung; Sukarno himself had studied civil engineering and architecture at the prestigious Bandung Institute of Technology (ITB).

A program of tertiary-level training for art teachers was established in Bandung in 1947 as part of the University of Indonesia, which later amalgamated with ITB.[54] In Yogyakarta, the Academy of Fine Arts (ASRI, now ISI) opened in 1950. In Jakarta, the art school IKJ (Jakarta Institute for the Arts) and later the cultural centre Taman Ismail Marzuki (as noted above) made important contributions to promoting art. Yuliman refers to the growth of art education in Chapter 3 but does not make the point that, outside of Bali, which had its own centres for teaching and learning traditional arts, Java was the focus for formal art teaching, and young artists had to travel to its centres to study. This posed particular problems for women, most of whom found it difficult to leave their families and

51 Recent studies have reconsidered the relationship between 'Cold War culture' and art history, see Phoebe Scott, Yvonne Low, Sarena Abdullah and Stephen Whiteman, 'Aligning New Histories of Southeast Asian Art', in Whiteman et al., *Ambitious Alignments*, 2.

52 Abbreviation for *Manifes Politik* (Political Manifesto). MANIPOL was Sukarno's new state philosophy based on 'USDEK', an acronym for *Undang-Undang Dasar* 1945 (the 1945 Constitution); *Sosialisme* (Indonesian Socialism); *Demokrasi* (Guided Democracy); *Ekonomi* (Guided Economy); and *Kepribadian Nasional* (Nationalism).

53 See Foulcher, *Social Commitment*, 125–26.

54 The ITB arts faculty has been through several changes of name, see further ITB, 'History', accessed 7 March 2021, www.itb.ac.id/history.

live alone in distant cities. It has been estimated that until the 1980s 'there were approximately five male students to every female student in the art schools'.[55]

'Our Country Is a Land of Spilt Blood', 1965–66[56]

During 1965, Sukarno's risky politics at home and abroad, his ambiguous support for the PKI and the parlous state of the Indonesian economy caused such tensions that many Indonesians—urban and rural—felt a crisis was looming. In the early hours of 30 September, six of Sukarno's senior generals were murdered. Claiming that the security of the nation and the president were threatened, General Suharto took control of Jakarta and led, or condoned, reprisals against members, actual or suspected, of the PKI.

Robert Cribb and Michele Ford have summarised the massacres that lasted for at least five months after the murders of the generals on 30 September 1965:

> In the course of little more than five months from late 1965 to early 1966, anti-communist Indonesians killed about half a million of their fellow citizens. Nearly all the victims were associated with Indonesia's Left, especially with the Communist Party (PKI) that had risen to unprecedented national prominence under President Sukarno's Guided Democracy. The massacres were presided over and often coordinated or carried out by anti-communist sections of the Indonesian army, but they also engaged wider elements of Indonesian society—both people who had reason to fear communist power and people who wanted to establish clear anti-communist credentials in troubled times.[57]

---

55 Quote from Wulan Dirgantoro, 'Arts: Visual Arts and Artists: Indonesia', in *Encyclopedia of Women & Islamic Cultures*, ed. Suad Joseph, accessed 7 June 2012, doi.org/10.1163/1872-5309_ewic_EWICCOM_001420.

56 Quote from Mohamad, *In Other Words*, 92. Goenawan Mohamad is no stranger to the violent deaths of close relatives. When he was a child, Dutch soldiers executed his father and his uncle.

57 See special issue of *Inside Indonesia* 99 (Jan–Mar 2010), accessed 21 March 2021, www.insideindonesia.org/edition-99-jan-mar-2010. See also recent research in Katharine McGregor, Jess Melvin, Annie Pohlman, eds, *The Indonesian Genocide of 1965: Causes, Dynamics and Legacies* (Switzerland: Palgrave Macmillan, 2018), doi.org/10.1007/978-3-319-71455-4.

Writing in 2010, Cribb and Ford point out that it has only recently been possible to begin documenting the events of 1965–66 from records kept by the New Order regime. Astri Wright, referring to the late 1980s when she was interviewing artists for her sensitive and thoughtful study *Soul, Spirit, and Mountain: Preoccupations of Contemporary Indonesian Painters*, noted: 'A great deal of the work by LEKRA artists and others was destroyed in the aftermath of 1965 and artists resist talking, even among themselves, about the period'.[58]

The New Order Is Established, 1966–73

On 11 March 1966, General Suharto was formally installed as president. He announced that his government would institute a 'New Order' and 'order' became the leitmotif of his presidency. Initially he had the support of Western powers (who were relieved to see the end of communist influence in Indonesia) and those Indonesians who had feared communism would negatively affect their land ownership, business enterprises, and religious, intellectual and creative freedoms.[59]

Such hopes were disappointed when Suharto and the military, which had become his to command in civilian as well as defence matters, controlled the 1971 elections and ensured that Suharto's new organisation, Golkar, was 'elected'. Suharto focused on the economic transformation of Indonesia described under the umbrella term of *pembangunan* (development). In return for ongoing political support, the New Order undertook to deliver economic and technological development for all Indonesians under a series of five-year development plans called 'Repelita' (*Rencana Pembangunan Lima Tahun*), which started in 1969. After the economic mismanagement of the Sukarno years, many Indonesians felt their lives would improve.

---

58 Wright, *Soul, Spirit, and Mountain*, 163, fnt 25.

59 While many artists, writers and intellectuals who were not associated with, or suspected of being associated with, 'leftist' organisations or the PKI felt huge relief that the intense cultural 'wars' were over, for others, it was the opposite. Many artists, intellectuals and writers, however slight their association with 'leftist' culture, became victims of the retribution that followed Suharto's takeover. Some were executed but most were imprisoned, detained or lived in exile outside Indonesia for many years. In 2012, Leila S. Chudori, one of Indonesia's most respected authors, published the highly acclaimed novel *Pulang*. It sympathetically describes the fictional lives of Lekra members who were forced to live as exiles in Europe after 1966 and describes the impact of the 1966 killings on the exiles and their families. An English translation by John McGlynn, entitled *Home*, was published by The Lontar Foundation, Jakarta, in 2015.

There was a major emphasis on modernising Indonesia's technology, agriculture, education and communication systems. An international oil boom boosted the national economy and private enterprise thrived with the government entering partnerships with Chinese business conglomerates. An upwardly mobile, aspirational middle class began to emerge, but many were left behind. The president and his ministers reiterated that self-denial for the common good was essential to success and that stability, constant guidance and vigilance were needed to stay on track.

The New Order included 'culture' in its five-year development plans. Keith Foulcher has analysed how it defined 'culture' to promote its national objectives:

> New Order Indonesia has lent an extraordinary level of official promotion to the visual and decorative aspects of indigenous Indonesian cultures, from the restoration of national monuments, through the reproduction of traditional architectural styles, to the teaching in 'Indonesian' contexts of regional arts such as dance, and the proliferation of traditional crafts and motifs in all aspects of daily life.[60]

Foulcher also noted that, as more and more Indonesians became involved with the New Order's agenda for shaping a 'national' culture, 'oppositionist' cultural activity entered 'into contest with the hegemony in shaping this cultural community adding to its pluralist character and contributing to its democratic potential'.[61]

Recent scholarship has pointed to the extent to which commercial artist and design group Decenta, established in Bandung in 1973 by artists Adriaan Palar, A. D. Pirous, G. Sidharta, Sunaryo, T. Sutanto and Priyanto Sunarto, was involved in formulating and representing a national culture directly at the behest of the New Order. Through large-scale commissions for building interiors and public art, the

---

60 Keith Foulcher, 'The Construction of a National Culture: Patterns of Hegemony and Resistance', in *State and Civil Society in Indonesia*, ed. Arief Budiman (Monash University: Centre of Southeast Asian Studies, 1990), 302–03.
61 Ibid., 316.

group perpetuated the idealised unified diversity of the nation, often using patterns and forms appropriated from the archipelago's indigenous cultures.[62]

There were also those who refused to enter into any partnership with the New Order's cultural projects and they fashioned their own forms of resistance and non-compliance, often at great cost to their personal freedom and, in some cases, their lives.

Resisting the New Order and Bearing Witness, 1974–80s

In January 1974, student-led demonstrations broke out in Jakarta in protest against the government's links with foreign investors and with Indonesian Chinese conglomerates. Students were gaoled and 12 publications were closed. When students were again targeted in 1978, they responded by resisting in less public ways. They founded study clubs and community-based socioeconomic projects to support farmers and other workers. 'Most conspicuous in their credo were the social democratic values centred on redistributing power from the state to civil society and from the rich to the poor.'[63] Thus began the contemporary versions of community-based, bottom-up, non-government movements that still operate in the new millennium.

The poet Rendra, who believed 'the function of the artist, the poet and the intellectual was to "guide or lead social change"', had returned from studying dramatic art in the United States in 1967 and set up his own theatre workshop in Yogyakarta.[64] Known as 'Bengkel' (Workshop) he rehearsed and performed his own dramas and poetry that became increasingly critical of corrupt leaders who neglected the welfare of ordinary people. In 1974 Bengkel was forbidden to play to audiences in Yogyakarta. When the ban was lifted for performances in 1977 and 1978,

62 These elements referenced ethnic cultures within (often contested) regions of Indonesia for government buildings and other state-commissioned works. Chabib Duta Hapsoro, '*Identitas Keindonesiaan dalam Elemen-elemen Estetik Kelompok Decenta: Representasi Praktik Depolitisasi* Orde Baru dalam Bidang Kebudayaan[i]', CHADUHA: *Tulisan-tulisan Chabib Duta Hapsoro*, 2015, accessed 26 March 2021, chaduha.wordpress.com/2015/06/29/identitas-keindonesiaan-dalam-elemen-elemen-estetik-kelompok-decenta-representasi-praktik-depolitisasi-orde-baru-dalam-bidang-kebudayaani/.

63 Bunnell, 'Community Participation', 181.

64 Hooker, 'Expression: Creativity despite Restraint', 278.

Rendra was lionised by audiences, especially by those who had initially supported the New Order but now felt disillusioned.[65] In Chapter 7, Caroline Turner refers to several artists, including Arahmaiani and Dadang Christanto, who were specifically inspired by Rendra's public reading of his poems of protest against New Order corruption and violence, student activists, and the neglect of the poorest and most vulnerable members of society who were not included in New Order mega-development policies. In Bandung, too, theatre played a key role in communicating resistance to the New Order to broader audiences, and many of the artists whose names and work appear in this book were involved in Studi Klub Teater, an influential group in Bandung in the 1980s, of which artists Tisna Sanjaya (see Chapter 4) and Arahmaiani (see Chapters 4 and 7) were key members.[66] Sanjaya describes his involvement in theatre and his burgeoning etching practice as mutually influential:

> For instance … my etchings, there are many that have titles from the theatre in the 1980s, like *The Thief's Party*. That was the title of the theatre-work by Rahman Sahbur … I was on the artistic team, making posters, making banners … at the same time, I was making etchings, and this was influenced by the scripts. And that also influenced the stage.[67]

Sanjaya's early years in the theatre formed the basis for what has become a highly formalised and disciplined practice, in which etching serves as a jumping off point, and a grounding, for works in television, painting, installation and performance art.

In 1975, a group of artists from the academies of Bandung and Yogyakarta decided to bring a breath of fresh air into the way art was being taught, especially with its emphasis on painting as the primary medium. As both Jim Supangkat (Chapter 6) and FX Harsono (Chapter 10) make clear, they wanted to create a 'New Art Movement' (Gerakan Seni Rupa Baru,

65 Barbara Hatley, 'W. S. Rendra (1935–2009)', *Inside Indonesia* 97 (July–September 2009), accessed 28 February 2021, www.insideindonesia.org/w-s-rendra-1935-2009. For more detail about Rendra's influence on art and artists, see also Barbara Hatley, 'Cultural Expression', in *Indonesia's New Order: The Dynamics of Socio-Economic Transformation*, ed. Hal Hill (St Leonards: Allen & Unwin, 1994), 226–29.

66 Established by Jakob Sumardjo and Saini KM in Bandung in 1958, Studi Klub Teater (STB) was a progressive course in modernist theatre and performance. In later years, musicians and artists, including Tisna Sanjaya, became involved. Arahman Ali, 'Komunitas Teater di Bandung', *Journal of Australia Indonesia Arts Alliance* 18 (2004).

67 Sanjaya, quoted by Elly Kent in *Artists and the People: Ideologies of Art in Indonesia* (Singapore: NUS Press, 2022), 46.

GSRB) that looked at social and political issues 'with the intention of experimenting with the search for a national Indonesian identity'.[68] Harsono remembers that the New Order's 'militaristic and repressive policies at this time' raised issues that he felt had to be addressed in his art and in his actions: 'I could no longer just interpret a situation or condition without becoming involved in that situation myself. I became increasingly involved with NGOs and activists who opposed Suharto's policies'. He acknowledges that the repression, overt and covert, practised by the regime against 'dissidents' was stressful.[69]

It was no secret that '[t]he New Order promoted gender differences'. Kathryn Robinson has written eloquently about the 'officially sponsored images of femininity' that the New Order developed to promote their ideology of the nation as a big family with women always ranked as 'subordinate to men in both state and home'.[70] While analysts inside and outside Indonesia during the period of New Order political hegemony, that is, before 1998, 'were justifiably critical of the government's efforts to domesticate and depoliticise women and to coopt them into the vast machinery of a repressive regime', in the decades that followed it was possible to see that New Order health and education policies had improved life expectancy for all citizens, that child marriages had begun to decline (though they still exist in many rural areas) and that all children were being compulsorily educated to at least the end of primary school. The impact of these policies on women and girls began to be seen in the late New Order period and thereafter, when women played increasingly public roles as activists and agents for change.[71] This was also evident in the number of women studying art at tertiary level in Jakarta, Bandung and Yogyakarta, where '40 per cent of students accepted into visual art studies' were women.[72] In Chapter 8, Alia Swastika describes in more detail the negative effects of the New Order on women artists, in particular the development of state *ibuism* (mother-ism) and the pressure on women to be both mothers and career professionals.

---

68 FX Harsono, Chapter 10 (this volume). See also Chapters 5 and 7 (this volume).

69 Ibid. See also Hatley, 'Cultural Expression', 228.

70 Kathryn Robinson, 'Women: Diversity versus Difference', in Emmerson, *Indonesia beyond Suharto*, 237.

71 For a careful and considered analysis of the complexities of the effects of New Order policies on Muslim women, as well as their responses to the increasing influence of 'Islam' (in its many manifestations), see Suzanne Brenner, 'Islam and Gender Politics in Late New Order Indonesia', in *Spirited Politics: Religion and Public Life in Contemporary Southeast Asia*, ed. Andrew C. Willford and Kenneth M. George (Ithaca New York: Southeast Asia Program Publications, 2005) 93, 97.

72 Dirgantoro, 'Arts: Visual Arts and Artists: Indonesia'.

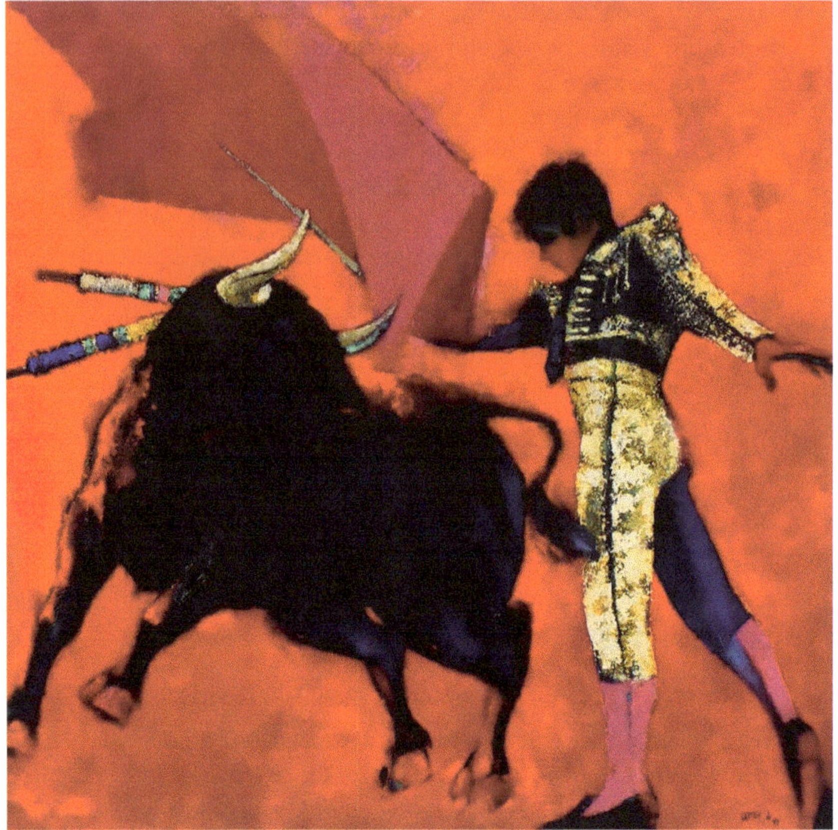

Figure 1.7: Umi Dachlan (1942–2009), West Java, *Lust for Life*, 1995.
Painting. Permission: Taufik Riantoso.

During the 1970s, Umi Dachlan (1942–2009) was one of few women who made a career in art as both an academic at ITB and as a practising artist who exhibited her work alongside male contemporaries.[73] She has been admired for the contemplative and reflective depth in many of her works as well as her technical skill.[74]

73 Ibid. For a sensitive and in-depth study of women artists in Indonesia, see Wulan Dirgantoro, *Feminisms and Contemporary Art in Indonesia: Defining Experiences* (Amsterdam: Amsterdam University Press, 2017), doi.org/10.1017/9789048526994.

74 For example: 'Blending abstract expressionist approaches with figurative symbolism, Umi's works offer a visual style that combines elegant, static minimalism and formalistic tendencies with a rhythmic play of strong, vivid colors'. See Carla Bianpoen, Farah Wardani and Wulan Dirgantoro, eds, *Indonesian Women Artists: The Curtain Opens* (Jakarta: Yayasan Senirupa Indonesia, 2007), 253.

When she was in her 60s, Dachlan painted in stronger, more vibrant colours and her work 'is marked by intense concerns about human relations and values pertaining to unequal power relations, to suppression, as well as to oppression'. In the 1980s, she witnessed a bull fight in Spain and later revealed the impact it had on her: 'I immediately recognised the similarity with conditions in our society'. She felt that the bull was like the ordinary people of Indonesia at that time, and that in the fight to the death, the odds were stacked in favour of the matador.[75] These words suggest that Umi Dachlan came to see Indonesia's ordinary people as always dominated by those in authority.

It was during this decade of the 1980s that increasing numbers of farmers were forced off their land by development projects for the upper middle class, such as housing complexes and golf courses. Huge new industrial estates attracted labourers from rural areas 'to service the booming low-wage manufacturing sector'.[76] As well, mining and deforestation caused by illegal logging by conglomerates caused environmental degradation, life-threatening mudslides and loss of livelihoods for locals displaced by multinational companies.

There was a range of responses to these disastrous conditions—'a host of new labour, environmental and women's organisations were formed, linking up with international movements and helping to transform the political agenda in Indonesia'.[77]

One of the first non-government organisations established during the New Order period, and still very active, is the respected LBH (Lembaga Bantuan Hukum Jakarta/Jakarta Legal Aid Institute). It was set up in 1969–70 by Indonesian lawyers as a pro bono organisation to provide legal aid to the have-nots and victims of human rights abuses, including political prisoners.[78] LBH was (and is) supported by the government of Jakarta; in the early years of the new millennium alone, it has helped well over 100,000 individuals in the special region of Jakarta. Other branches of LBH work elsewhere in Indonesia. In 1982 at a public conference, one of the directors of LBH Jakarta, T. Mulya Lubis, called on writers

75 Bianpoen, Wardani and Dirgantoro, *Indonesian Women Artists*, 255.

76 See David Bourchier and Vedi R. Hadiz, eds, *Indonesian Politics and Society: A Reader* (London and New York: Routledge Curzon, 2003), 161.

77 Ibid., 161.

78 See further 'Tentang Kami', LBH Jakarta, accessed 20 March 2021, bantuanhukum.or.id/tentang-kami/.

to expose 'injustice and "structural violence" which takes place against the economically and politically disadvantaged'.[79] It was artists, as well as journalists and writers, who followed Rendra and others in using their skills to draw attention to the growing state-sanctioned injustice and violence of the New Order.[80] Despite bans and even brief periods of detention, they supported victims of New Order policies and, by doing so, risked retribution for criticising those policies and the politicians and military who enacted them.

Another non-government organisation (NGO) that worked in cooperation with artists in Indonesia during the 1980s was WALHI (Wahana Lingkungan Hidup Indonesia/Indonesian Forum for the Environment). Established in 1980, WALHI works across diverse issues—for example, agrarian conflict, indigenous rights, and coastal and marine degradation and deforestation—through a platform that reaches beyond environmental issues to their impact on society, striving for 'economic, social and ecological justice for this generation and those to come'.[81] In 1985, WALHI sponsored the artistic project and exhibition *Proses '85*, which included FX Harsono, Moelyono, Bonyong Munni Ardhie, Harris Purnama, Gendut Riyanto, and which encouraged artists to undertake field work and research into social issues caused by environmental mismanagement. Harsono's documentary photographs of his work with communities affected by mercury poisoning in Jakarta Bay is echoed in the projects he has pursued in his career since, as described in Chapter 10. Moelyono too has pursued similarly 'people-oriented' (*kerakyatan)* processes in his work since the 1980s, and has continued to collaborate with WALHI and other NGOs, as described by Kent in Chapter 2.

One example of social action in support of farmers in Central Java, whose land was being forcibly acquired for a new dam at Kedung Ombo near Salatiga, stands for many others. In 1988, when students from the nearby Christian University of Salatiga learned the farmers were not only being

79 David T. Hill, 'Who's Left? Indonesian Literature in the Early 1980s', *Monash University Department of Indonesian and Malay: Working Paper* 33 (October 1984): 34–35.

80 Halim HD, a cultural organiser in Solo, Central Java, recounts how, in the early 1980s, he and other artists countered the New Order proscriptions against political activity by establishing 'working groups' (*kumandungan*), inspired by a suggestion from Rendra. They networked with similar groups elsewhere and created 'cultural pockets' as a 'channel for the efforts of the artistic community to create public space'. See Halim HD, 'Arts Networks and the Struggle for Democratisation', in *Reformasi: Crisis and Change in Indonesia*, ed. Arief Budiman, Barbara Hatley and Damien Kingsbury (Monash University: Monash Asia Institute, 1999), 289.

81 WALHI, 'Vision and Mission', accessed 26 March 2021, www.walhi.or.id/visi-dan-misi.

forced from their land but also were receiving inadequate compensation, they staged protests that attracted national (and international) support for the victims of developmentalism.

A major artistic statement of support for the farmers was Dadang Christanto's mass installation in Jakarta Bay, which was clearly visible to ordinary Indonesians who flocked to Ancol to enjoy the scenery and amusements there. The vast number of figures—naked humans who appear rigid with terror—is confronting (see Figure 1.8). Their nakedness emphasises their extreme vulnerability and suggests the overwhelming nature of the losses they have suffered without any redress to justice. Their vulnerability and the Indonesian word *manusia* (human being), used to describe them in the title of the installation, emphasise that they are humans like us, the viewers; that bonds of humanity bind us together; and that we all share 'human rights'.

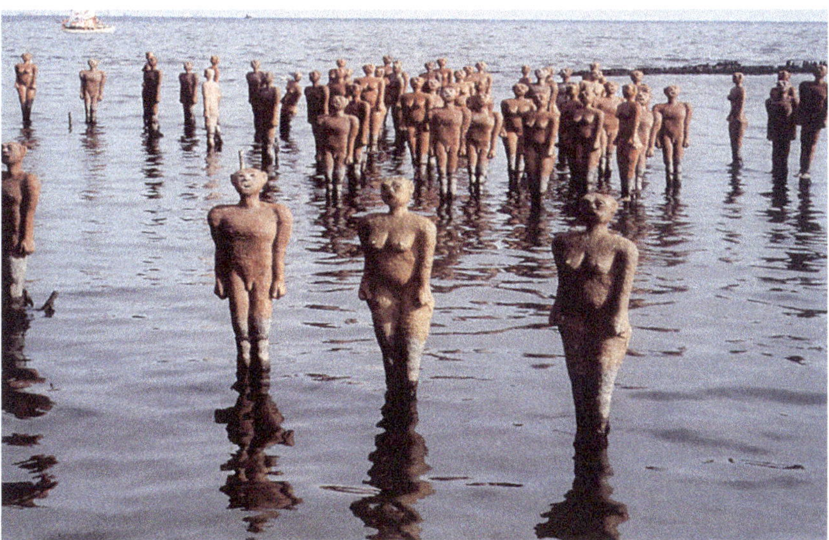

Figure 1.8: Dadang Christanto, *1001 Manusia Tanah* (*1001 Earth Humans*), 1996.

Ephemeral sculpture. One thousand life-size fibreglass figures set in the sea off Marina Beach, Ancol, North Jakarta. This work is a testimony to all humans displaced by economic development, including the farmers of Kedung Ombo (see Chapter 7). The artist was the 1,001st figure in his performance in the sea with the figures. Image courtesy the artist.

New Order development depended on access to cheap sources of labour. Wages were below poverty levels and working conditions were often unsafe, or worse. Strikes and protests were crushed by the military. The rape and murder of a young factory worker, Marsinah, by the military because she demanded better conditions for her fellows in East Java in 1993, became a public scandal.[82] Moelyono produced an installation exhibition commemorating Marsinah's life and death in Surabaya in the same year as her death, and he narrowly escaped prosecution due to representations from LBH.[83] Marsinah (and others such as Wiji Thukul, see below) became a symbol of military abuse during the later years of the New Order.

'Cultural Islam', 1980–98

In line with its depoliticisation policies, by the early 1980s, the New Order determined that the public expression of Islam would be confined to cultural expression. Political activity linked with Islam was not permitted. Respected Muslim leaders from both modernist and traditional backgrounds, such as Nurcholish Madjid and Abdurrahman Wahid, carved out a path for Islam that encouraged intellectual, educational, social and artistic activities without linking them with politics. Many, though not all, younger Muslims saw this as an opportunity to bring new vitality to Islamic thinking and to search for Islam-based solutions to socioeconomic issues such as human rights, gender equality, environmental degradation, religious tolerance and democratisation.[84] By the late 1980s and 1990s, Islamic NGOs implemented many of these ideas and spread them through training programs run by NU and Muhammadiyah groups. This continues in the new millennium and now includes training in Islam-infused courses on subjects such as entrepreneurship for women and disaster relief.

---

82 See R. William Liddle, 'Regime: The New Order', in Emmerson, *Indonesia beyond Suharto,* 47.

83 M. Taufiqurrahman, 'Moelyono: The Arts and Social Responsibility', *Jakarta Post,* 3 February 2006.

84 See further Greg Fealy, Virginia Hooker and Sally White, 'Indonesia', in *Voices of Islam in Southeast Asia: A Contemporary Sourcebook* ed. Greg Fealy and Virginia Hooker (Singapore: Institute of Southeast Asian Studies, 2006), 48. For examples of the range of views on the roles and status of Muslim women from the late New Order until 2005, see Sally White, 'Gender and the Family', in *Voices of Islam,* 273–352.

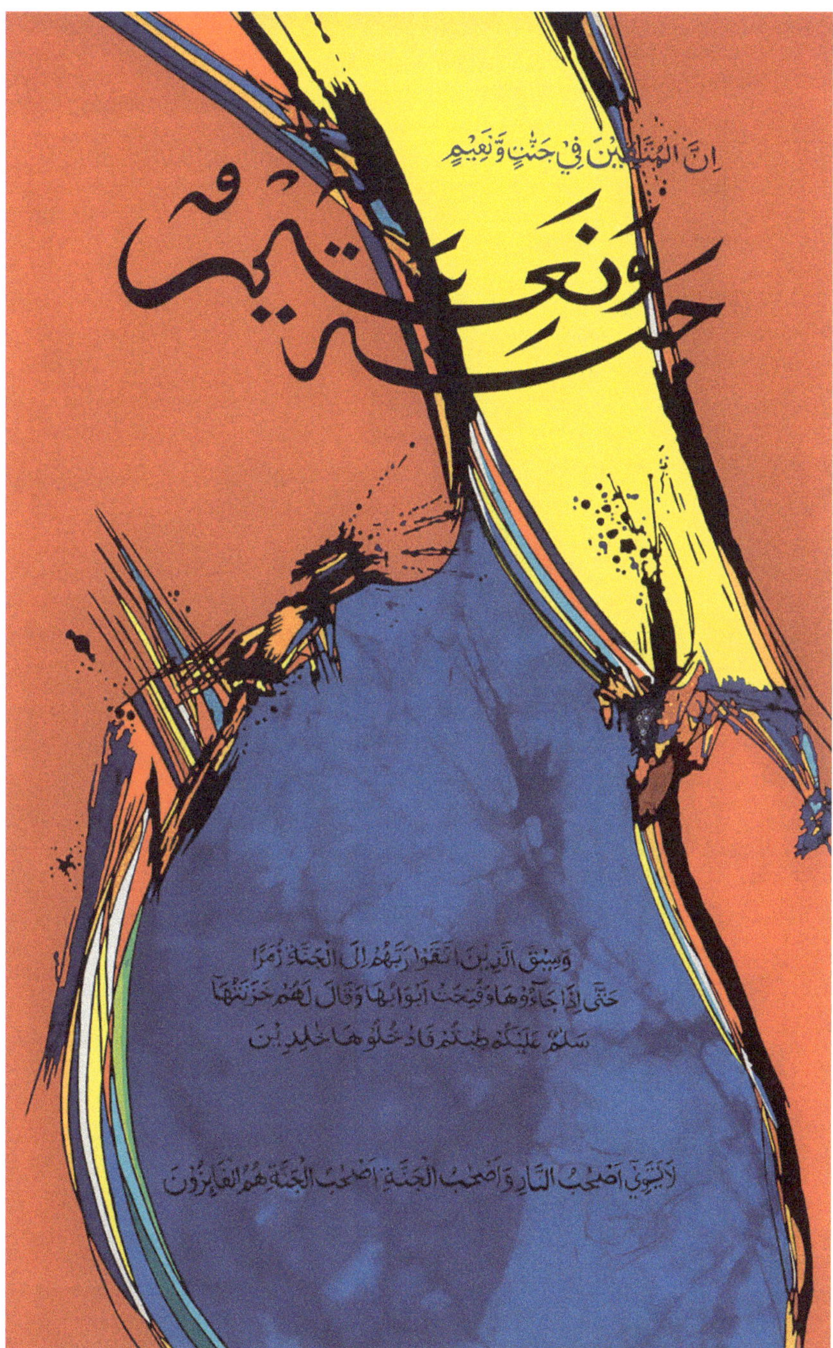

Figure 1.9: Amri Yahya (1939–2004), Indonesia, *Swargaloka – Jannaatun wa Na'iimuun* (*Garden of Delight*), 1990–95, Yogyakarta, Central Java.

Hand batik and synthetic dyes on cotton, 1840 x 1075 mm. Collection: Museum and Art Gallery of the Northern Territory. Acquired with the support of the Northern Territory Government, 1997. Image courtesy the Museum and Art Gallery of the Northern Territory. Permission: Adwi Prasetya Yogananta and family. Photographer: Mark Sherwood. [SEA 02063].[85]

The work's title uses the Classical Malay and Arabic terms for heaven/paradise to express a balance between the older and newer understandings of truth that are mirrored in the artist's choice of the traditional techniques of batik and the vibrant contemporary colours that express his design.

The emergence of increasing numbers of middle-class Muslims who shared in the economic prosperity of the New Order coincided with a worldwide revival of Islam in the 1980s. These aspirational Muslims realised they lacked a true understanding of their religion and they sought it through study groups and classes in Quran recital techniques and Arabic calligraphy. They had the money to make the pilgrimage to Mecca, to buy Islamic fashions and works of Islam-inspired art to display in their homes.

International experts in Islamic arts and cultures, such as Professor S. H. Nasr and Professor Annemarie Schimmel (both from the US) were invited to Indonesia and Malaysia to address overflowing conferences. A regular report was sent each month from Indonesia to the UK-based, upmarket publication *Arts & the Islamic World* detailing art events being held in Indonesia.[86] A special report was devoted to the blockbuster exhibition of Islamic art held in 1995 at Indonesia's national Istiqlal (Independence) Mosque, with the backing of President Suharto, which attracted 11 million viewers (see Chapter 4, this volume). President Suharto had been supportive of this major cultural project because he was seeking increased backing from Muslim organisations. Ironically, he was losing the support of sections of the military and, like Sukarno before him, Suharto was forced to play a balancing game.

85 Amri Yahya (b. 1939) graduated from ASRI Yogyakarta in 1971 and was acknowledged as one of the pioneers and innovators of modern batik art. He held many overseas exhibitions, the first in Australia in 1957 and eventually including European cities, the US, the Middle East and all parts of Asia. He lived most of his life in Yogyakarta where he died in 2004, severely affected by the loss of his art collection when fire destroyed his gallery. One of his paintings includes a reference to Australia's support for Indonesian independence, see Ron Witton, 'Amri Yahya and the Sydney University Labor Club', *Inside Indonesia*, 24 August 2014, www.insideindonesia.org/amri-yahya-and-the-sydney-university-labor-club, accessed 20 May 2022. Biographical information from the catalogue, *Wajah Seni Lukis Islami Indonesia ke-3* [Faces of the Third Indonesian Islamic Art Exhibition], 15–17 May 1996, World Trade Centre, Jakarta (no further publication details).

86 Published for the Islamic Arts Foundation, London, by New Century Publishers, from 1982, with representatives in all countries with Muslim majority populations.

As well, in 1993, a new radical Islam-based movement was established by two former leaders of the banned violent movement Darul Islam that had killed 15–40,000 Indonesians in the early to mid-1950s. The new movement, known as Jemaah Islamiyah (JI), had its own terrorist agenda. It was the leaders of JI who, in mid-2000, masterminded lethal attacks in Indonesia. Islamic terrorism by Indonesians against their fellow citizens and foreigners was to become a major threat in the new millennium.

The New Order Unravels, 1990–98

By 1990, the atmosphere of tension and disillusion felt by many Indonesians was summed up by a report of a celebration of Indonesia's forty-fifth anniversary on 16 August held at Taman Ismail Marzuki (TIM):

> the young men and women performing and attending the cultural performance at TIM that night cried out about a gloomy social reality. Their thoughts ranged over unemployment, the deteriorating environment, overcrowding of the island of Java and the future of an Indonesian population of more than 200 million, prevailing injustice, social gaps, ethnic and other social prejudices, conglomerates, corruption, lack of democracy and gloom over the lack of hope for effective participation.[87]

As well as the socioeconomic issues pervading 1990s Indonesia and the obvious corruption and nepotism rife in the regime, especially in the president's own family, violent and deadly clashes were occurring in East Timor, Aceh and Papua as the military crushed dissent. In 1991, over 90 East Timorese students were gunned down in the Santa Cruz cemetery in Dili where they had fled to shelter from the military. The massacre was caught on film, shown across the world and universally condemned.

A new generation of Indonesian students took up the cause of workers and farmers, their direct support for those suffering military or government discrimination differentiating them from student protesters of the 1970s. Instead of protesting on behalf of the 'victims' and trying to advocate for them with members of the elite, the students of the 1990s worked directly with the 'underdogs' through NGOs and direct community action.[88]

87 Hooker, 'Introduction', 1.

88 Bourchier and Hadiz, *Indonesian Politics and Society*, 162.

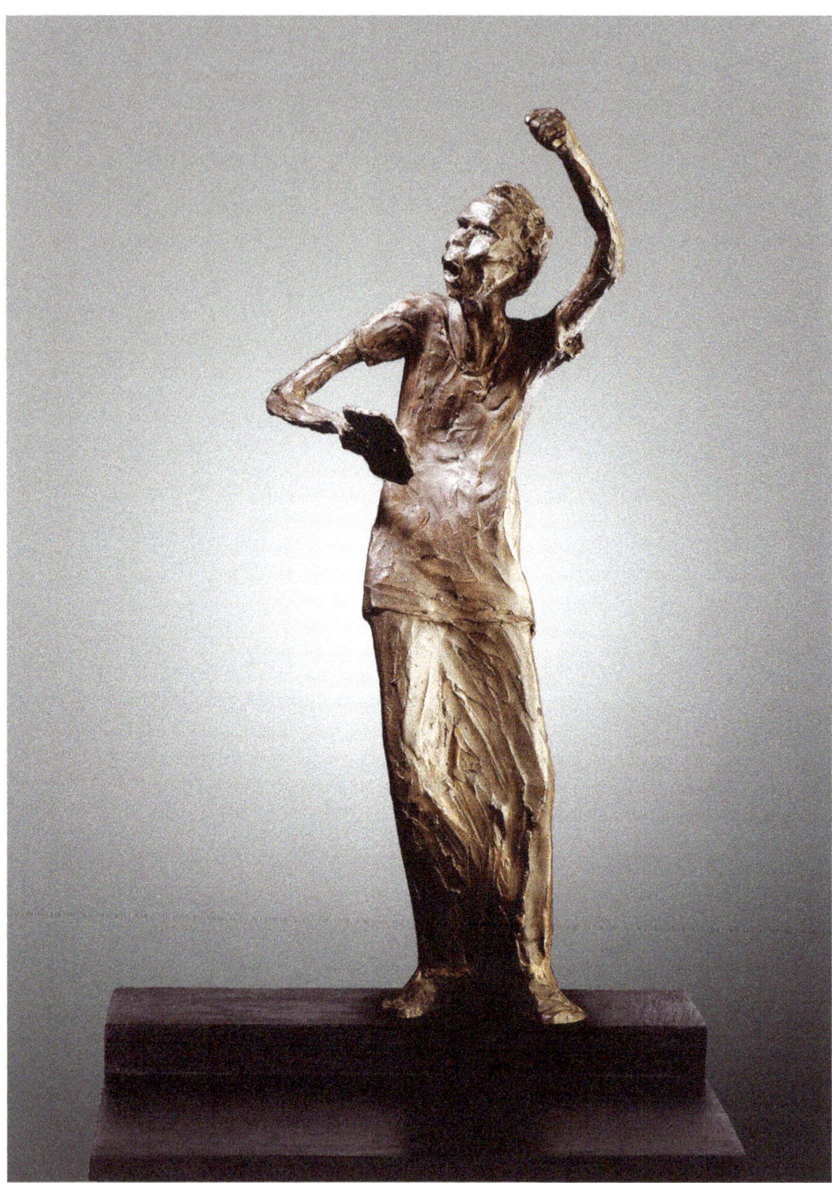

Figure 1.10: Dolorosa Sinaga, *Satu Kata Saja: Lawan!* (*One Word Only: Resist!*), 2003.

Bronze, 36 x 30 x 60 cm. Image and permission: Dolorosa Sinaga. The figure is a lifelike representation of Thukul in appearance and dress.

One example of such direct action, by a man of the people rather than a student, concerns Wiji Thukul (b. 1963), the son of a pedicab driver. He became head of the People's Art Network (JAKKER) and worked with kampong children of workers in his hometown of Solo, Central Java, to establish art collectives for them as well as supporting protesting workers and peasants. He wrote protest poems and was arrested several times. In 1996, he disappeared and, although his body has never been found, is assumed to have been killed by, or on the orders of, the military. His poems were read at protests by farmers and striking workers. This final verse of one of his poems was frequently quoted by protesters at their rallies:

> if suggestions are refused without heed
> voices silenced, criticism banned without reason
> accused of subversion and disturbing
> the peace
> then there is only one word: resist![89]

Thukul's work has regained resonance in recent years as families and advocates for the many 'disappeared' of the late New Order have found voice through human rights campaigns against legal impunity for perpetrators of violent crimes and murders.[90]

The Fall of Suharto, 1998

Indonesia was the first Asian economy to be hit by the effects of the global financial crisis (GFC) in 1997. It was also the worst affected and the economic crash is now seen as one of the prime factors contributing to the end of Suharto's presidency. As outlined above, protests against the regime had been increasing and military repression and censorship had failed to quell the dissent. Early in 1998, the Indonesian currency plummeted as a result of the GFC. This caused panic buying, the collapse of the stock exchange, closure of businesses and widespread unemployment. Educated women who had long been critical of Suharto's gender policies had been meeting together and forming organisations such as Yayasan Jurnal Perempuan (Women's Journal Association) and linking with

89 Ibid., 163, 179.

90 In 2017, a 'sparse and quietly composed film' about the poet's last days, *Istirahatlah Kata-Kata* (the film was given the English title *Solo: Solitude*), played to large audiences in Indonesia, and won awards at Film Festivals around the world. See Elly Kent, '"Istirahatlah Kata-Kata": Young Audiences Discover a Dissident Poet', Indonesia at Melbourne, accessed 26 March 2021, indonesiaatmelbourne.unimelb.edu.au/film-review-istirahatlah-kata-kata/.

international organisations such as UNIFEM. Increasingly concerned about the authoritarian actions of the regime, they needed a 'cause' to rally support for criticism of the government. When the price of milk rose 400 per cent in early 1998 as a result of the GFC, they found their cause. Calling themselves Suara Ibu Peduli (Voice of Concerned Mothers) they organised their first mass demonstration at a highly prominent Jakarta site in February 1998 and gained almost immediate sympathetic support. Titarubi (b. 1961) was one of the artists who actively supported the movement against Suharto and it was at this time, Wulan Dirgantoro notes, that themes of 'political motherhood' appear in her works.[91]

Other mass demonstrations across the archipelago were met with live bullets fired by the military, resulting in loss of life. On 12 May 1998, students protesting peacefully in Jakarta at Trisakti University were fired on by the military and four were killed. The next day mass violence broke out in Jakarta and shops and office blocks were set on fire. Hundreds of women were raped. Over 1,000 people were killed in Jakarta with more deaths in other cities. Ethnic Chinese were targeted, and tens of thousands of Indonesian Chinese left Indonesia. Many later returned.[92] On 21 May 1998, Suharto finally bowed to pressure and resigned, handing over to his vice-president, Habibie. After 32 long years of New Order rule, most Indonesians could not believe he had gone.

In the Yogyakarta LBH office in December 1998, a group of students and young artists came together as Taring Padi (Rice Tusk). With their mission to direct creative practice to actively support and involve 'the people', they 'were among the architects of the radical art actions that highlighted the Yogyakarta protest movement in 1998'.[93] The group, who created their lo-fi collective artworks in a squat in the former ASRI building, remains active and extraordinarily influential in the early 2020s (see Figure 1.11). Many young artists' political consciousness was forged in the heat of this troubled period, and political art has remained one of the dominant themes in the decades since. The events of 1998 and the effects on Indonesians of Chinese descent are discussed in Chapters 7 and 10 and

91 See further, Wulan Dirgantoro, 'Herstory in Art', *Inside Indonesia*, www.insideindonesia.org/herstory-in-art, accessed 28 February 2022.

92 This summary is based on Edward Aspinall, Herb Feith and Gerry van Klinken, 'Introduction', in *The Last Days of President Suharto*, ed. Edward Aspinall, Herb Feith and Gerry van Klinken (Monash University: Monash Asia Institute, 1999), v–viii.

93 Heidi Arbuckle, 'Of Pigs, Puppets and Protest: Radical Yogyakarta Artists Get among the People', *Inside Indonesia* 64 (2000).

have been a theme in art, literature and film in recent years. In Chapter 10, FX Harsono provides a very personal account of his artistic responses to violence against members of the Indonesian Chinese community.

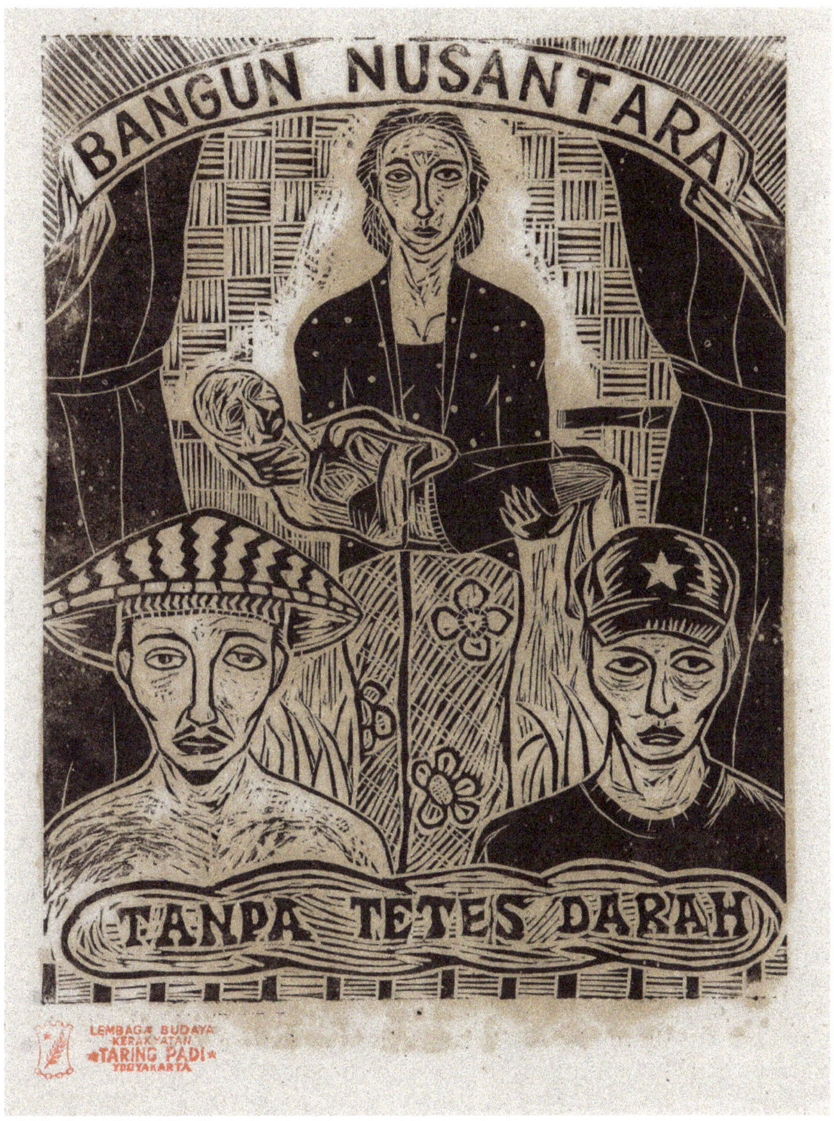

Figure 1.11: People's Cultural Institute Taring Padi, *Bangun Nusantara Tanpa Tetes Darah* (*Develop the Archipelago without Drops of Blood*), 1998, Yogyakarta, Indonesia.

Woodblock print, ink and colour on paper, 52.0 x 40.0 cm (image). Gift of Damon Moon through the Art Gallery of South Australia Foundation 2012. Art Gallery of South Australia, Adelaide © Taring Padi Collective. Permission: Taring Padi.

One assessment of the effects of the fall of the regime, made shortly after the event, suggests that, despite the human tragedies, Indonesians united to support survivors, and artists and performers were an essential part of the process of recovery:

> Though greatly shaken by economic hardship and the threat of ethnic and religiously based violence, communities are attempting to foster collaborative, inter-group activities and to provide support for the most needy. Even the horrific rapes of Chinese women during the May riots are shown to have had complex effects. While illustrating the brutal extremes of military-style violence, and processes of silencing and blaming of female victims, they have also angered and mobilised women to demand redress from the authorities, and pushed women's rights to the forefront of human rights campaigns. And gender violence becomes one of the themes taken up by cultural networks, in performances and other arts activities fostering democratic consciousness.[94]

The New Millennium, 1999–2020s

Goenawan Mohamad characterises Indonesia's history as 'a wounded history', citing the violence of the Darul Islam guerrillas in the late 1940s–60s; the PRRI-Permesta rebellion of 1958; the shooting of Muslim protesters at Tanjung Priok (Jakarta) in 1984; and the violence in East Timor, Aceh and Papua.[95] He might have added inter-ethnic and sectarian-based violence in Ambon, Halmahera and Poso in Central Sulawesi and the persecution of Indonesian Shi'a and Ahmadis.[96]

The violence did not stop immediately after Suharto resigned. The displaced military fomented ethno-religious rivalries and instigated other forms of violence in various parts of the archipelago. It took a while for the apparatus of the New Order to disband or be disbanded and for a police force to be formed and replace the application of the law by the military.

94 Arief Budiman, Barbara Hatley and Damien Kingsbury, 'Postscript', in Budiman, Hatley and Kingsbury, *Reformasi*, 386.

95 Mohamad, *In Other Words*, 228, originally published in *Tempo*, 27 February 2000.

96 See Greg Fealy and Sally White, 'Introduction', in *Expressing Islam: Religious Life and Politics in Indonesia*, ed. Greg Fealy and Sally White (Singapore: Institute of Southeast Asian Studies, 2008), 1–2, doi.org/10.1355/9789812308528, in which they also point out that there is much more to Islam in Indonesia than terrorism.

It took a while to get used to Indonesia without Suharto and his family and cronies, the re-emergence of political parties and the retreat of the military to their barracks.

Preparations for the first democratic elections in Indonesia since 1955 marked the beginning of the reform period, known as Reformasi. Without New Order restrictions on Islamic political parties, there was a flowering of Islam-based parties. They did not do as well in the national elections as their leaders had expected when allegiance to Islam did not translate into votes for Muslim political parties. However, at the sub-provincial (*kabupaten*) level, 'hard-line' or literalist Muslim groups pushed for implementation of local versions of sharia law (*Peraturan Daerah Syariah*) and in some areas these were enacted and sometimes enforced by sharia officials (referred to as 'sharia police'). The regulations focused on dress codes, especially for women, the attainment of basic levels of Quranic literacy, relationships between unmarried males and females, homosexuality and 'deviant sects' (i.e. persecution of members of Ahmadi and Shi'a groups).[97] Local protests and complaints about statues and monuments did not gain much support but, in Jakarta from 1998, a well-organised Islamic vigilante group named Front Pembela Islam (FPI, Islamic Defenders Front) embarked on targeted attacks on nightclubs, bars and brothels.[98] In 2005–06, an Anti-Pornography Bill was submitted to parliament backed by conservative Islamic political parties and supported by ultra-conservative, militant Muslim paramilitary groups such as Laskar Jihad. Blasphemy (against Islam), obscenity and pornography, as well as women's dress and comportment, were the main concerns of the proposed Bill. Representatives of moderate Islamic women's groups, as well as human rights activists, protested vigorously against the Bill and some amendments were made. But, in 2006, the FPI sued artists Agus Suwage and Davy Linggar, curator Jim Supangkat and models involved in an installation entitled *Pink Swing Park* shown in the

97 In contrast to this literalist and ultra-conservative interpretation of Islam, the Muslim mass social movement Nahdlatul Ulama organised campaigns to educate its members about the compatibility between Islam and democracy. This included respect for the place of art in Indonesian society, as long as that art did not conflict with Islamic values. See Virginia Hooker, 'Artistic Expression in Non-Arab Islamic Cultures: Views from Indonesia', *TAASA Review* 29, no. 3 (September 2020): 10–12.
98 See Robyn Bush, 'Regional Sharia Regulation in Indonesia: Anomaly or Symptom?', in Fealy and White, *Expressing Islam*, 174–91, doi.org/10.1355/9789812308528-014.

2005 Jakarta CP Biennale exhibition and forced its closure.[99] The Bill was passed into law in 2008 and remains highly controversial. FPI continued its proactive and often aggressive actions to 'protect' Islam well into the new millennium. Its charismatic, firebrand leader attracted a mass following that government claimed could threaten peace and stability, especially when authorities were calling for an end to large-scale mass gatherings as the COVID-19 pandemic ravaged Indonesia. In December 2020, FPI was officially banned for involving its members in violent activities.[100]

These highly visible, socially (and often legally) coercive manifestations of ultra-conservative Islam's influence in contemporary Indonesian society have prompted visual responses by both Muslim and non-Muslim artists, including Agus Suwage's *Tembok Toleransi* (*Wall of Tolerance*) (see Figure 1.12), which invites viewers to lean into the installation to hear the soft sounds of the call to prayer. This experience contrasts with the calls to prayer broadcast at high volume through mosque loudspeakers in many parts of Indonesia today.

Another work, an unusual, embroidered image by Eko Nugroho,[101] is a satirical depiction of a student of Islam. It was created in 2011 during the presidency of Susilo Bambang Yudhoyono, a former army officer and Indonesia's first democratically elected president, who held office between 2004 and 2014. This was a period of political stability but also of sectarianism and ongoing corruption.[102]

---

99 Pamela Allen, 'Challenging Diversity? Indonesia's Anti-Pornography Bill', *Asian Studies Review* 31 (June 2007): 101–15, especially 108, doi.org/10.1080/10357820701373275. See also Sue Ingham, 'Cultural Issues in Indonesian Biennals', *Broadsheet* 35, no. 2 (June–August 2006): 84–85. For an expert legal assessment of the case and the issues it raises for Indonesian artists who are facing prosecution, see Helen Pausacker, 'Pink or Blue Swing? Art, Pornography, Islamists and the Law in Reformasi Indonesia', in *Religion, Law and Intolerance in Indonesia*, ed. Tim Lindsey and Helen Pausacker (London and New York: Routledge, 2016), 289–316, doi.org/10.4324/9781315657356.

100 See further Afifur Rochman Sya'rani, 'The Impact of the Indonesian Government's Crackdown on Islamists', *New Mandala*, 7 January 2021, accessed 21 July 2021, www.newmandala.org/what-will-be-the-impact-of-the-indonesian-governments-crackdown-on-islamists/.

101 Born in Yogyakarta in 1977, versatile and multidisciplinary, his work was included in *Contemporary Worlds: Indonesia*, an exhibition at the National Gallery of Australia in 2019. See Introduction (this volume).

102 See further Ed Aspinall, Marcus Mietzner and Dirk Tomsa, eds, *The Yudhoyono Presidency: Indonesia's Decade of Stability and Stagnation* (Singapore: Institute of Southeast Asian Studies, 2015), doi.org/10.1355/9789814620727.

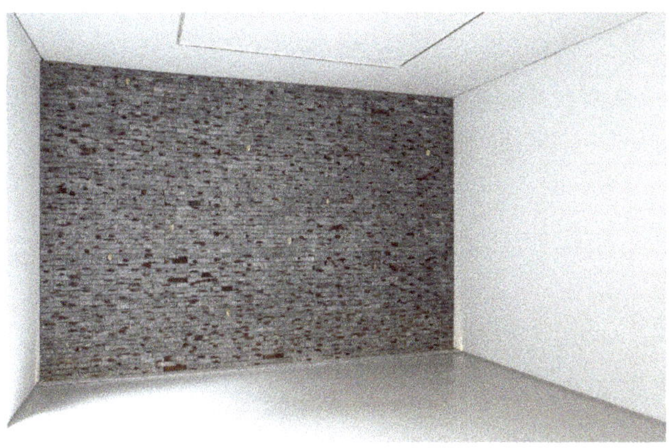

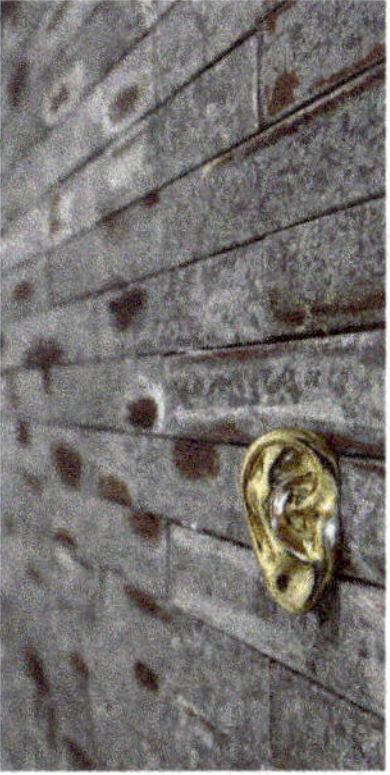

Figure 1.12: Agus Suwage (b. 1959), Central Java, *Tembok Toleransi* (*Wall of Tolerance*), 2012.

Zinc, gold-plated brass, LED lights, sounds. Shown in the exhibition *Contemporary Worlds: Indonesia*, National Gallery of Australia, 2019. Image and permission: Agus Suwage.

The interpretation of the work by James Bennett, curator of Southeast Asian Art and Material Culture at the Museum and Art Gallery of the Northern Territory, identifies the figure as a religious student who holds both a copy of a religious text and a sword (a symbol of militant Islam) and wears an armband reading '*Benci*' (Hate). The absence of the student's head 'suggests the absence of the senses associated with meaningful intelligence'. Concerning the idyllic scene that replaces the head, Bennett writes:

> A rooster perches on the roof of a dwelling, a sight that Javanese people regard as a symbol of domestic harmony and prosperity. Set against a blue sky is the sacred volcano Merapi, the dwelling place of the *jin* guardian spirits of Java, which is located near Yogyakarta where Nugroho lives. The mountain invokes the memory of the ancestral heritage of Javanese society, whose practice of Islam was renowned for its religious tolerance and inclusion.[103]

Nugroho imbued his work with symbols and allusions to Indonesia's contemporary politics, the growth of sectarianism and decline in morals, and provided an idyllic picture of an earlier time when daily life was more harmonious and simplified. But he also included flames (from the fires of hell) beneath the religious student, suggesting that unless he changes his views of hate and prejudice, he is doomed for a life of eternal damnation.

103 James Bennett, 'The Green Curtain: A Portrait of the Prophet Muhammad', *TAASA Review* 29, no. 3 (September 2020): 19.

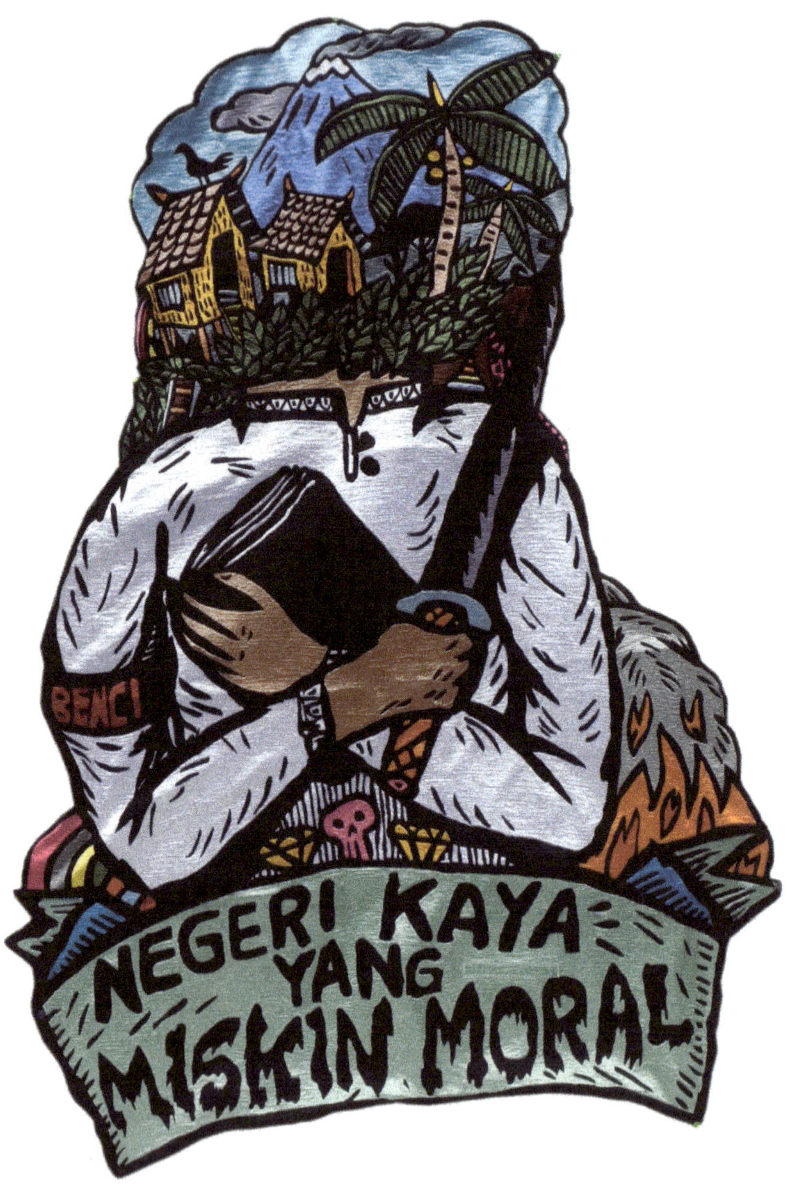

Figure 1.13: Eko Nugroho (b. 1977), Central Java, *Negeri kaya yang miskin moral* (*A Rich Country Poor in Morals*), 2011, Yogyakarta, Indonesia.

Fabric, wire, rayon thread, machine embroidery, 122.5 x 90.5 cm. Gift of the Art Gallery of South Australia Foundation 2012, Art Gallery of South Australia, Adelaide. Permission: Eko Nugroho.

Revisiting the Past

The Indonesian artists, critics and curators who pioneered the study of Indonesia's modern art began their narratives with Raden Saleh.[104] But there was little information available about him and he remained a somewhat distant figure. He came of age in the artistic sense in Europe and it was in Europe that Professor Werner Kraus located the archival materials that described Raden Saleh's successes and achievements there. In 1995, Kraus and Supangkat spoke about Raden Saleh at a public lecture, attended by Indonesian artists among others, organised by the Goethe Institute. A reappraisal began but was overtaken by the political events of the GFC and the fall of Suharto. In 2002, Galeri Semarang (in Semarang) curated a major exhibition of works by 34 Indonesian artists who acknowledged Raden Saleh as an influence on their work. Among them was Heri Dono, who has since featured his own version of Raden Saleh in scores of his paintings. In 2004, Kraus spoke in Singapore about a new, 'proto-nationalist' interpretation of Raden Saleh's painting of the Dutch arrest of Prince Diponogoro completed in 1857 (see Figure 1.4).[105] Amir Sidharta attended the talk and immediately invited Kraus to deliver it in Jakarta, which he did.[106] Thanks to the work of contemporary scholars, Raden Saleh and his works have become an inspiration to contemporary Indonesian artists and his motto, '*Ehre Gott und liebe die Menschen*' (Honour God and love mankind), is one that resonates with many of them.

---

104 There is renewed interest in the role of Raden Ajeng Kartini and her sister as supporters of women's art and crafts in her local area in the late nineteenth century. See Introduction (this volume); Enin Supriyanto, 'The Mother of Indonesian Art', in *Indonesian Women Artists*, ed. Carla Bianpoen, Farah Wardani and Wulan Dirgantoro, (Jakarta: Yayasan Senirupa Indonesia, 2007), 15–21.

105 See Werner Kraus, 'First Steps to Modernity: The Javanese Painter Raden Saleh (1811–1880)', in *Eye of the Beholder: Reception, Audience, and Practice of Modern Asian Art*, ed. John Clark, Maurizzio Peleggi and T. K. Sabapathy (University of Sydney: Wild Peony, 2006), 29–55. Kraus makes the further point that: '*The Arrest of Diponegoro* is among the first Southeast Asian paintings in the tradition of European historical painting' (p. 31). In John Clark's estimation, *The Arrest of Prince Diponegoro* is 'the first counter-colonial appropriation of academy style for a history painting'. See John Clark, 'The Worlding of the Asian Modern', in *Contemporary Asian Art and Exhibitions*, ed. Michelle Antoinette and Caroline Turner (The Australian National University: ANU Press, 2014), 67, doi.org/10.22459/CAAE.11.2014.04.

106 See also Amir Sidharta, 'Indonesian Views of Raden Saleh', accessed 22 February 2021, www.academia.edu/37630216/Indonesian_Views_of_Raden_Saleh.

In his 1970 essay 'Painting in Indonesia: Issues Past and Present', Yuliman argues that the shift to modernity in Indonesian art happened sometime in the 1930s when 'the centre of creative energy' shifted from society to the individual. This, he believes, was the beginning of a new art 'that took the form of individual expression'.[107] It was not many years after this that Chairil Anwar wrote his defiant (and self-centred) poem '*Aku*' (I)—a shift had indeed begun.

Yuliman expands on his theory of shift in the centre of creative energy to the individual in this way:

> we have developed a vision of the self as a vital centre, with potential, dignity and inviolable basic rights. The vision gives birth to the discourses and movements of renewal in social, educational, political and legal fields, which are still in process … Further, through modern intercommunication, the borders of Indonesia as an existential space are no longer the same as the geographical borders: we are witnessing the shifting of the horizons of philosophy, the realms and values of technology, horizons that are widening to encompass the world.[108]

Yuliman concludes his essay by urging Indonesians:

> to reach more deeply into the phenomena of painting—into the creative process of the artist, into the psychology of the artist, into the artistic endeavours and struggles that they traverse step by step, into all the fruits of their works and into the process of appreciation.

But, he says, 'it is precisely this that is never done by Indonesians'. If it were, says Yuliman, there would be vital and innovative discussions about art that would provide new perspectives and provide valuable support for encouraging 'an appreciation of art that is alive and intelligent'.[109]

107 Yuliman, 'Seni Lukis Di Indonesia'.
108 Ibid.
109 Ibid.

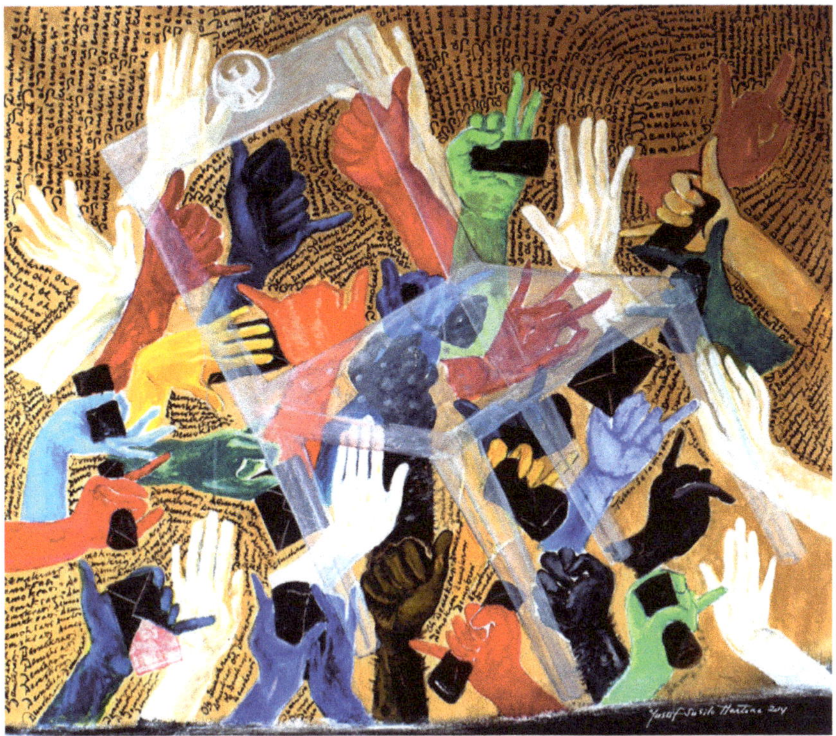

Figure 1.14: Yusuf Susilo Hartono (b. 1958), East Java, *Suara Rakyat, Suara Uang* (*Voice of the People, Voice of Money*), 2014.

Acrylic on canvas, 120 x 110 cm. Image and permission: Yusuf Susilo Hartono.

Yuliman wrote these words in 1970. He was to live another 20 years and he would have seen, as chapters in this book describe, that during that period Indonesians were reaching even 'more deeply into the phenomena of painting'. This was in part a response to his own efforts as well as the encouragement of other Indonesian art critics and artists, who exhibited their works, taught in the academies, informal studios and collectives, and explored new forms and techniques.

In June 2014, a few weeks before the presidential election hotly contested by candidates Prabowo and Jokowi, the National Gallery of Indonesia held a solo exhibition of works by respected artist and arts journalist Yusuf Susilo Hartono.[110] Entitled *Pe(s)ta Demokrasi* (Festival/map of

110 Born in East Java in 1958 into a strict religious family, his father forbad him to develop his artistic talent lest the images be considered idolatrous. Ridden with guilt, Yusuf continued to draw and paint. In 1987 he met maestro Affandi at Taman Ismail Marzuki. Affandi complimented him on his drawings and advised him not to listen to critics or others but to look inside himself and listen to his heart. Personal email to Virginia Hooker, 26 November 2013.

democracy), it took a critical look at the culture of democracy in Indonesia in a series of paintings, sketches and an installation. His works are visual readings of the fallout from Indonesia's transactional politics and they remind his viewers of the widespread corruption, vote buying and broken promises that accompany each democratic election in Indonesia. In Figure 1.14, the sea of multi-coloured hands, many throwing the hand signs that represent their political parties, clutch envelopes of rupiah notes all set against a background of beautifully patterned whorls (perhaps an allusion to the inking of a finger after a vote has been cast) that read '*Demokrasi*' (Democracy). Clearly these are the hands of people who have sold their votes. The white hands remind viewers of the high percentage of spoiled or donkey votes that are now a feature of Indonesian elections. Superimposed on the sea of hands is a chair (*kursi*) stamped with the emblem of the Republic of Indonesia, representing the parliamentary seats (*kursi*) that are at stake.

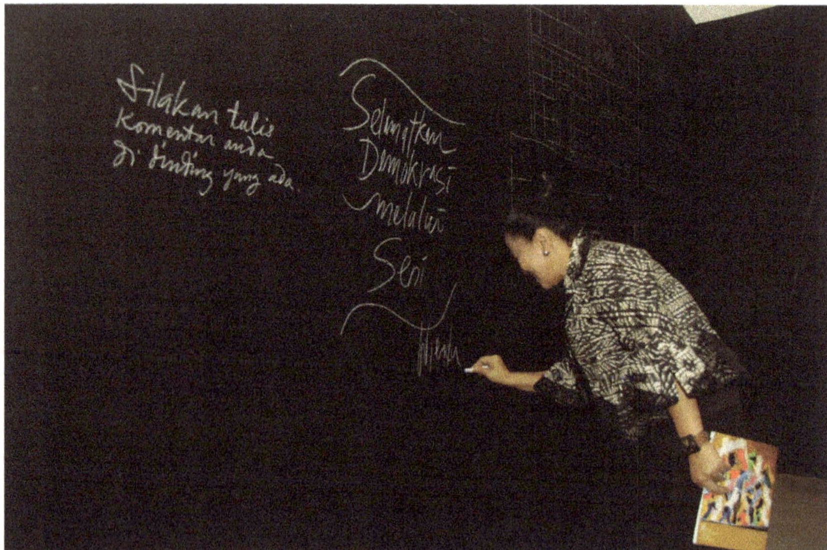

Figure 1.15: Deputy Minister of Education and Culture Professor Wiendu Nuryanti at Yusuf Susilo Hartono's exhibition, National Gallery of Indonesia, 2014.

The deputy minister wrote 'Save Democracy through Art' on the visitor's board after opening Hartono's solo exhibition *Pe(s)ta Demokrasi* (Map/festival of democracy) on the eve of the presidential elections that brought Joko Widodo to power in 2014. Photograph courtesy Yusuf Susilo Hartono.

Indonesia's artists are its intellectuals and philosophers of the visual. Deputy Minister Wiendu Nuryanti's words 'Save Democracy through Art', particularly in the context of a presidential election campaign, imply that art can play an active role in public affairs and that it should safeguard democracy. They also recognise that artists are acutely observant of the political as well as the social aspects of their society, and that they should not remain silent about abuses of power. The examples in this book illustrate how Indonesia's artists reinvent and play with 'tradition', knowing their viewers will understand the innuendos and allusions, using earthy humour and lyrical grace with all shades in between, to exquisitely express their subjects. When censorship, intimidation or even violence is used against them, they are not silenced and continue to create their art. As Minister Nuryanti's words suggest, that is why Indonesia's contemporary art matters.

2

Artistic Ideologies: Individual and Society in Indonesian Art

Elly Kent

The title of this chapter, 'Artistic Ideologies', is one I have borrowed from the eminent Indonesian art critic and historian Sanento Yuliman. Yuliman, who died in 1992, looms large over Indonesian art history, not least because his perspicuous and prescient texts firmly place Indonesian modern art in continuity with what came before, 'emerging in the midst of living art traditions'. Yuliman insisted that these living traditions emerged from the people, were widely understood and functionally crossed into many social practices. Those who demand a social function rather than esoteric individualism in modern art, Yuliman argued, are actually looking for art that can be widely understood in society.[1]

The idea that the art must be connected to society, and that it draws also on the traditions that remain in practice across Indonesia's many cultures, remains a strong influence on many contemporary artists. This has given rise to a continuous flow of discourses that engender, encourage or even mandate individual artists to engage with society in the creation of their work. This chapter explores some of these discourses, including the social realism of revolutionary modern artist S. Sudjojono (1913–1986), which he called *jiwa ketok* (the visible soul); the prescribed participatory research

1 Sanento Yuliman, 'Seni Lukis di Indonesia: Persoalan-Persoalannya, dulu dan sekarang [Painting in Indonesia: Issues, past and present], in *Dua Seni Rupa: Sepilihan Tulisan Sanento Yuliman* [Two arts: A selection of Sanento Yuliman's writing], ed. Hasan Asikin (Jakarta: Yayasan Kalam, 2001), 75, originally published in *Budaya Djawa*, December 1970.

methodology of *turba* (going down below), mandated by the Institute for People's Culture; the adoption of the concept of *gotong royong* (mutual cooperation) as a platform for collective art practice; and the adoption of conscientisation as a means of using art to empower communities. Each of these is laden with ideological overtones and historical contexts that, together, create an intellectual landscape that has been a touchstone for contemporary Indonesian art in its current forms.

The practices and concepts described here demonstrate that many contemporary artists in Indonesia are drawing on and responding to ideas that imagine a conjunction of individualist creativity and specific social responsibilities for artists, ideas that have long been embedded in Indonesian art. This situates contemporary artists in continuity with—to borrow again from Yuliman—established discourses of modern Indonesian art. Yet these discourses are not received uncritically and remain part of an ongoing dialectic with those from other disciplines, cultures and places.

To unpack these ideas around tradition, change, individuality and society in art, I begin by looking at *Kuda Binal* (*Wild Horses*). This delegated performance work by well-known peripatetic Indonesian artist Heri Dono (b. 1960), whose work also features prominently in Chapter 7, looks at the international context of the 1990s, incorporating traditional dance forms and contemporary iconography in an event that resulted in the scenes—or better yet, the experience—described below.

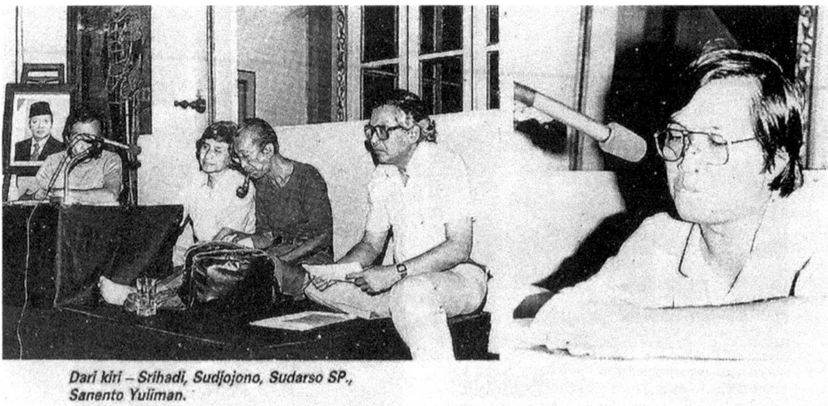

Figure 2.1: Documentation of a meeting in Surakarta in 1985, titled '*Situasi Seni Rupa Kita dan Seni Rupa Terlibat*' (*The Situation of Our Art and Art That Is Involved*).

Image courtesy Indonesian Visual Art Archive.

Wild Horses and Stonemasons: Tradition Reimagined

> The fire in the middle of the arena raged. Suddenly the sound of a drum thundered in the audience's ears, followed by the sound of a gong, and the shrill call of five trumpets. Ten riders on kuda lumping then descended into the 10 x 10 metre arena. This was the beginning of the *Kuda Binal* performance … on the western corner of the northern town square in Yogya … Idioms from traditional art and symbols of modern society were inverted in this performance. Everything reflected wildness and humour. The heads of the ten kuda lumping are not all horse-heads … some sport human heads, others resemble animals, there are even those that depict mysterious creatures. Meanwhile, the ten actors wearing old fashioned clothes are also wearing gas masks, apparatus of modern man. They dance around while spraying kerosene and setting it alight, the only form of illumination for this performance …
>
> Heri Dono's painting and mixed media merge. Just look to the animals made from cardboard carried in this performance … These forms are precisely the same as the objects that always appear in his paintings. Barong, dragons and all manner of other creatures and the costumes of the 60 actors also quickly reveal the character and colours of Heri Dono paintings. The expressions in this performance were rough and wild, so the intensity was palpable.[2]

2 Raihul Fadjri, 'Gebu Yogya 1992: Terobosan Kuda Binal' [Yogya aflame 1992: The wild horse breaks through], *Tempo* 8, no. 8 (1992), accessed 19 January 2022, archive.ivaa-online.org/khazanahs/detail/1701 (author's translation). *Kuda lumping* and *barong* are among a wide variety of rituals performed across Indonesia (and elsewhere) in which the performers identify with animals, either as 'handlers' or as the animals themselves. In *kuda lumping* a flat horse shape made of woven bamboo, rattan or leather is ridden by the dancers; *barong* resembles a Chinese lion dance, with two performers inside a costume sporting a fierce, animalistic countenance and an elaborately decorated body. Performers in these rituals often attain trance-like states, and can perform extreme feats; performances are frequently commissioned to mark significant social and community events.

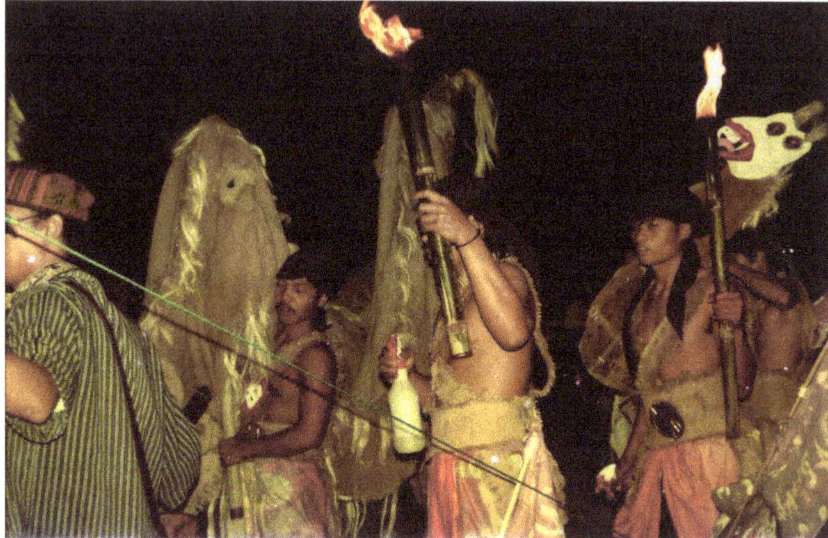

Figure 2.2: Heri Dono (b. 1960), Jakarta, *Kuda Binal*, 1992.
Delegated performance, costumes and artworks, performed in Yogyakarta's public square. Image courtesy the Indonesian Visual Art Archive. Permission: Heri Dono.

This passionate prose describes a performance often cited as a seminal work in the history of experimental performance art in Indonesia.[3] It appeared as part of the *Pameran Binal Eksperimental* (Wild experimental exhibition)—a rebellious event held to counter the formalist and formalised Yogyakarta Painting Biennale (1992)—in which the artists placed integral conceptual value on the active participation of individuals other than themselves. As the account above describes, Heri Dono inverted idioms from tradition, enlisting local grave diggers and stonemasons as dancers in a performance that parodied Central Javanese folk dance forms. In *Kuda Binal* the dancers' movements were rough simulations of the 'horse dances' to which they referred. Traditionally, the horse dances, performed with woven horse-shaped silhouettes as props, are imbued with the barely

3 See, for instance, Alexandra Kuss, 'Hak Istimewa Kelokalan Telah Berhamburan' [The privileges of locality have dissipated], in *Paradigma dan Pasar: Aspek-aspek Seni Visual Indonesia* [Paradigms and the market: Aspects of Indonesian visual art], ed. Adi Wicaksono et al. (Yogyakarta: Yayasan Seni Cemeti, 2003), 91; Jim Supangkat, 'Multiculturalism/Multimodernism', in *Contemporary Art in Asia: Traditions/Tensions*, ed. Apinan Poshyananda (New York: Asia Society Galleries, 1996); Michelle Antoinette, 'Cosmopatriots: On Distant Belongings and Close Encounters', in *Deterritorializing Aesthetics: International Art and its New Cosmopolitanisms, from an Indonesian Perspective*, ed. Edwin Jurriëns and Jeroen de Kloet (Amsterdam: Rodopi, 2007), 205–33, doi.org/10.1163/9789401205559_011.

controlled chaos of trance performance, but in Heri Dono's version they appeared more animalistic, exaggerated by the uneven ground on which they were performed and the untrained movements of the performers (see Figure 2.3). Dono says:

> They had never danced before. That was the first time. And they were bad … in terms of dance theory, they were wrong, their movements. But that was so interesting, because it became a new reference for dance … I was able to learn from the culture they usually practised, not as an academic problem, but as a new form of knowledge.[4]

Referring to European practice, Bishop argues that, before 1989, the traditions of performance art 'valorised live presence and immediacy via the artist's own body'.[5] After the end of the Cold War, this 'live presence' was attached to the 'collective body' of a social group. In Indonesia, Dono's *Kuda Binal* and other works that followed (e.g. *The Chair*, 1993[6]; *Semar Farts*, 2000) are examples of this shift away from the focus on the artist's own body. However, other artists, such as Arahmaiani and Tisna Sanjaya, continued to use their own bodies as a primary vehicle for their concepts, although both have increasingly involved others in their performances.

Kuda Binal exemplifies how artists in the 1990s adapted traditional forms to develop new, more widely accessible (or legible) visual and physical languages to communicate contemporary issues to urban audiences who were often recently arrived migrants to that space. It also provides an insight into the strategies that Indonesian artists have used to engage with society and community—the *rakyat* (the people)—through their art practice.

---

4 Heri Dono, interview with the author, 2014.

5 C. Bishop, *Artificial Hells: Participatory Art and the Politics of Spectatorship* (London: Verso, 2012), 219. In Indonesia, examples of this valorisation of the artist's body can be seen in Arahmaiani's public interventions: *Kecelakaan I* [*Accident I*], 1981; *Manusia Koran* [*Newspaper People*], 1981; Dadang Christanto's performance of the self as victim, *For Those Who Have Been Killed*, 1992–93; Iwan Wijono's *The Greenman*, 1996; and Melati Suryodarmo's feats of endurance in *Rindu* [*Longing*], 1996, and *Exergie Butter Dance*, 2000. Melati was also a student of Marina Abramović, whose work is exemplary of this tendency.

6 QAGOMA, 'APT1 performance / Heri Dono: The Chair', 25 September 2018, accessed 11 September 2022, youtu.be/mAjIsCQggOw.

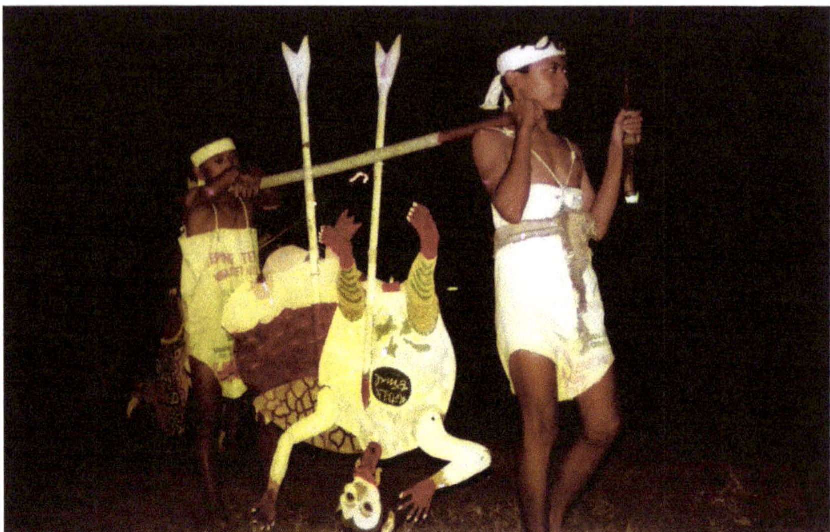

Figure 2.3: Heri Dono, *Kuda Binal*, 1992.
Stonemasons and gravediggers play the role of traditional dancers in a folk 'horse' dance. Image courtesy Indonesian Visual Art Archive. Permission: Heri Dono.

Dono's inclusion of his own paintings in *Kuda Binal* serves as an important tool in breaking down the partitioned categories of tradition and modernity, high and low art—particularly as the horse dances that inspired *Kuda Binal* are classified as 'folk' performing arts rather than the refined classical Javanese dance of the royal courts. This further demonstrates the integral role that Dono's interpretation of tradition plays in his object artworks, and in the setting of the performance itself. Modern elements like gas masks and traditional elements such as the woven horse silhouette that the performers 'rode' while they danced, were brought together to raise particular existential issues around environmental destruction and pollution (see Figure 2.3). This departitioning was also enacted through the participation of stonemasons and grave diggers in the place of dancers, which opened productive sites for the reinterpretation of traditional roles created through their failure to master the intricacies of the dance:

> The interesting thing is that psychologically, when people make mistakes in an artistic exploration (in their own field) they see it as something that shouldn't happen, because you can't make a mistake. But, if its someone from a different discipline—say I'm a painter then I make a dance, choreography—if there's a mistake I don't feel too strongly that I have failed.[7]

7 Heri Dono, interview with the author, 2014.

The primary role of participants, then, was to subvert audience assumptions and open up space for new interpretations.[8]

Heri Dono's departitioning reflects the anti-lyricism that Yuliman identified in the emerging art of the 1970s, works that moved away from the poetic and beautiful towards a more vernacular and everyday visual language. This manifested, in part, in the work of the Gerakan Seni Rupa Baru (New Art Movement)—known as GSRB—and their use of found material to produce works that Yuliman argued were 'not a slice of the imaginary world contemplated at a distance, but rather the concrete object which physically involves the viewer'.[9] In his 1979 essay 'Perspektif Baru' (A new perspective), Yuliman contends that these artists and, in particular, members of GSRB were trying to leave behind traditions that located art within a literal and metaphorical 'frame' that separated them from the sphere of lived experience.

The ideology of GSRB set the stage for artists like Dono to experiment with local and global idioms to create works equally accessible to local and international audiences. After anti-lyricism dissolved the constructions that kept Indonesian art inside literal and metaphoric frames, the next challenge for the expansion of the realm of aesthetic experience was the effort 'to reject the impression that modern art is an ivory tower and re-instate its place in the midst of the praxis of social life'.[10] The challenge was taken up by the *Pameran Binal Eksperimental.*

Bringing together disparate elements to imagine new roles and responsibilities for the artist, audience and participants, Dono drew attention to the dynamic and changing nature of tradition. He identified artists as generators of that change, creating new traditions by reordering the old. The brochure accompanying the show stated:

> Kuda Binal was born from an age-old tradition, and we recreate it here for you as contemporary art. We present it to each and every level of society. We hope it will open the door to the start of a new tradition.[11]

---

8 The accompanying flyer reminded the audience 'that this isn't tradisional [sic] horse trance dance with the traditional bamboo horse … it's *kuda binal!* So we hope that you'll watch it with an open mind', 'Heri Dono Presents: Kuda Binal' (Yogyakarta, 1992).

9 Sanento Yuliman, 'A New Perspective', in *Gerakan Seni Rupa Baru Indonesia*, ed. Jim Supangkat (Jakarta: PT Gramedia, 1979), 98.

10 From a review of the *Wild Experimental Exhibition* by ethnomusicologist Franki Raden, 'Menempatkan Seni di Masyarakat' [Locating art in society], *Kompas* (16 August 1992), accessed 19 January 2022, archive.ivaa-online.org/khazanahs/detail/1656.

11 Dono, 'Heri Dono Presents: Kuda Binal', flyer accompanying the performance, 1993, accessed 19 January 2022, archive.ivaa-online.org/khazanahs/detail/1687.

Dono explicitly expects the audience to negotiate their own meanings from the performance. As Yuliman had predicted in his 1969 essay 'Looking for Indonesia in Indonesian Painting', works such as *Kuda Binal* open a 'multitude of frameworks for Indonesian art'.[12]

The *Pameran Binal Eksperimental* also provided a platform for artists to challenge established categories of time, space and meaning in Indonesian art, creating the kind of experience that French theorist Rancière describes as an 'aesthetic regime' in which 'art and life can exchange their properties'.[13] But in *Kuda Binal,* rather than being exchanged, these properties were deliberately set on a collision path that resulted in a clash between the modern art establishment (and its separation from society) and traditional art (and its separation from contemporary life).

Living Traditions: *Gotong Royong*

In his engagement with his self-identified roots, Heri Dono's practice is a very different project to relational aesthetics, which Bourriaud identified as emerging from the philosophies of the Enlightenment, Dadaism and Marx's social interstices.[14] *Kuda Binal* invokes and inverts tradition to question the order of things, and to develop new traditions and ideas. A similar tendency can be recognised in broader art discourses in Indonesia, where cultural concepts previously tied to tradition are recast in conversation with globally resonant art theories and practices to develop new, originary art discourses.[15] One example of an originary Javanese cultural construction that has been invoked in contemporary art discourses in Indonesia is *gotong royong.*

12 Sanento Yuliman, 'Mencari Indonesia Dalam Seni Lukis Indonesia', in *Dua Seni Rupa, Sepilihan Tulisan Sanento Yuliman* [Two arts, a selection Sanento Yuliman's writing], ed. Hasan Asikin (Jakarta: Yayasan Kalam, 2001), 67.

13 Jacques Rancière, 'The Aesthetic Revolution and Its Outcomes', *New Left Review* 14 (March–April 2002): 133–51, 137.

14 N. Bourriaud, *Relational Aesthetics* (Paris: Le Presses du Réel, 2010).

15 I borrow the term 'originary' from John Clark, who cautions that we must now reconsider modern art discourses in Asia through a postcolonial lens and recognise that the resulting works are now 'originary works for the long-term and, in most cases, almost wholly endogenous genealogies of the modern'. John Clark, 'The Worlding of the Asian Modern', in *Contemporary Asian Art and Exhibitions: Connectivities and World-Making*, ed. M. Antoinette and C Turner (Canberra: ANU Press, 2014), 69–70, doi.org/10.22459/CAAE.11.2014.04.

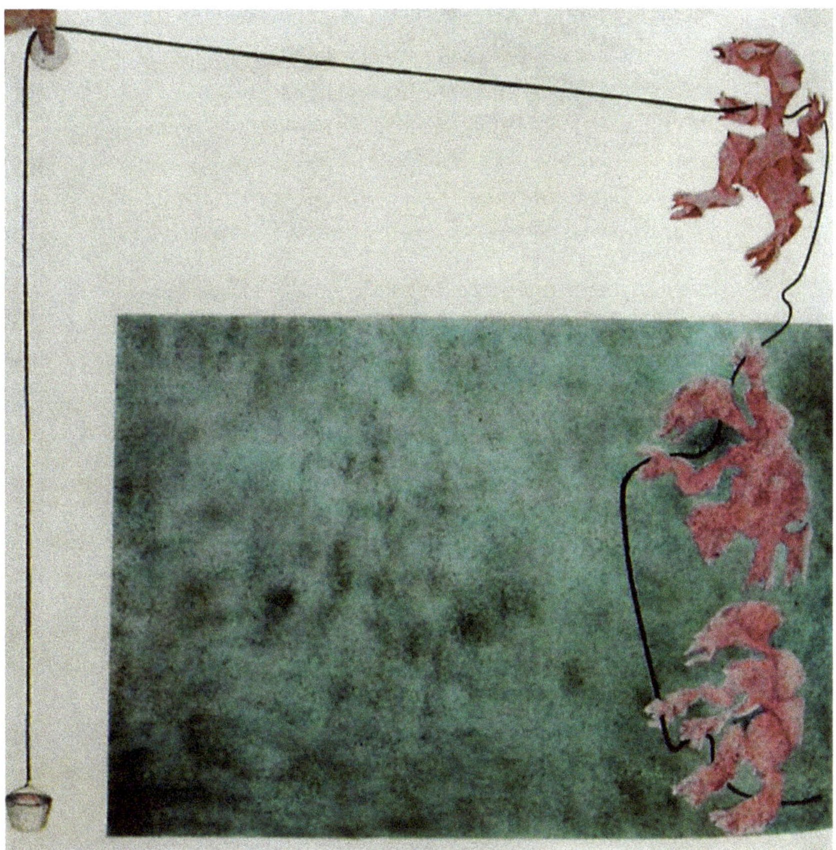

Figure 2.4: Heri Dono, *Gotong Royong (Working Together)*, 1984.
Acrylic on canvas, 97 x 97 cm. Image and permission courtesy Heri Dono.

An early painting by Heri Dono, *Gotong Royong* (1984) (see Figure 2.4), playfully illustrates this contested and appropriated social practice with a depiction of three distorted figures working in concert to lift a tiny bucket. *Gotong royong* (helping each other or mutual cooperation) is one of the fundamental principles of the modern Indonesian social system, coopted from traditional agrarian customs and promoted by the state at various points in the discourse of Indonesian nationalism and modernisation. Sukarno described the compression of the five points of the Pancasila—the five principles on which the Indonesian nation was founded—into one main principal: *gotong royong*.[16] Yet, renowned composer Suka Hardjana has questioned both the unique 'Indonesianness' of *gotong royong* and its contribution to the nation. In his keynote address to the Equator Symposium at Indonesia's prestigious Gadjah Mada University in 2014, Hardjana emphasised the universality of formalised social cooperation, arguing that the state's obsession with *gotong royong* results in a lack of emphasis on individual excellence, thus eroding national excellence.[17]

The concept has certainly been used as a tool of repression and top-down social organisation. A *gotong royong* representative council was established as part of Sukarno's political ideology of 'Guided Democracy' (1957–65), in which the role of opposition political parties was replaced by 'functional groups' such as the council. During Suharto's New Order (1966–98), a number of additional functional groups that had also included *gotong royong* in their titles were amalgamated and eventually became the basis of Suharto's Golkar political party, through which the New Order regime ruled.

Gotong royong is not only a political tool deployed as a national tradition; it is also often used to describe the system by which many Indonesians, especially those outside the middle class, access support and social welfare that might otherwise be provided by the state. In one example from 2010, following the disastrous eruption of the Mount Merapi volcano (see Map 2) near Yogyakarta that displaced 300,000 people, emergency aid and evacuations were initially organised by residents themselves, with enthusiastic support from arts organisations in the city. After residents were allowed to return to the mountain, communal effort locally described as *gotong royong* played a key role in clearing ash, sand and debris. These efforts were also supported by the coordination of local arts organisations such as Tlatah Bocah (Children's World), a network of performing artists who organise an annual children's performing arts festival.[18]

---

16 J. D. Legge, *Sukarno: A Political Biography* (London: Allen Lane, 1972). Sukarno identified the Pancasila as the five principles of nationalism, internationalism, democracy, social prosperity for all, belief in God.

17 Suka Hardjana, 'Membaca Ulang Gotong Royong Tradisi dalam Perspektif Satu' [Re-reading gotong royong traditions from the perspective of the one], keynote presentation at *Equator Symposium 2014: The One and the Many* (Gadjah Mada University, Yogyakarta: Yayasan Biennale Jogja, 2014).

18 Elly Kent, 'Semua Tempat Sekolah' [Everywhere is school], in *The Third International Graduate Student Conference on Indonesia: Indonesian Urban Cultures and Societies* (Universitas Gadjah Mada, Yogyakarta: The Graduate School, Gadjah Mada University 2011, unpublished paper).

As well as its manifestation in broader society, *gotong royong* makes important appearances in artistic discourse. In Indonesian art practice, the evocation of *gotong royong* dates back as far as the early years of the nation-state when the *sanggar* (studio collectives) still held strong influence over practice and it remains current for artists and institutions who wish to engender cooperation and social engagement.[19] In 2011, architect and arts researcher Yoshi Fajar Krisnomurti (b. 1977) contextualised the philosophy and implementation of the 2009 Biennale Jogja within a *gotong royong* framework, describing how artists and art workers cooperated, collaborated, volunteered and donated food, board, time and artworks to realise the major arts event on a limited budget.[20] In a different context, in 2014 a film documenting the working practices that were developed through the HackteriaLAB project used the principle of *gotong royong* to describe the interdisciplinary collaboration between artists and science students.[21] In 2017, Tita Salina (b. 1973) and Irwan Ahmett (b. 1978) exhibited the first iteration of an evolving diagrammatic wall drawing titled *Gotong Royong—Autobiography* during an exhibition in Poland. The drawing (Figure 2.5) illustrates a participatory conversation on *gotong royong* as artistic practice, in Indonesia and beyond, addressing many of the political, institutional, social and ideological manifestations of the concept.[22]

Gotong royong is used by the actors in these contexts to describe collaborative practices that are among other underlying influences—such as social performativity and modernism oriented to social responsibility—on participatory practices for many Indonesian artists. Yet there is, anecdotally at least, another side to *gotong royong* in the arts: the exploitation of young artists in the implementation of projects 'for the greater good' of Indonesian art in a poorly funded arts environment. In this context, emerging art workers are frequently engaged in projects led by established practitioners as participants, as contributing artists or performers, frequently without recognition or payment.[23]

19 Brita Miklouho-Maklai, *Exposing Society's Wounds, Some Aspects of Contemporary Art since 1966* (Adelaide: Flinders University of South Australia, 1991), 17.

20 Yoshi Fajar Krisnomurti, 'Gugur Gunung, Gotong Royong, and Jamming' [Falling mountains, mutual assistance and jamming], 2011, accessed 22 May 2022, www.scribd.com/doc/94386135/GUGUR-GUNUNG.

21 *Seni Gotong Royong* [Gotong royong art], documentary film (X-Code Films, 2014).

22 See Gotong Royong Participants, 'Irwan Ahmett & Tita Salina', accessed 19 January 2022, u-jazdowski.pl/en/projects/gotong-royong/uczestnicy/01-irwan-ahmett-i-nbsp-tita-salina.

23 I have had a number of informal conversations with artists on this subject, specifically in relation to the implementation of programs associated with large-scale projects such as biennales and art festivals.

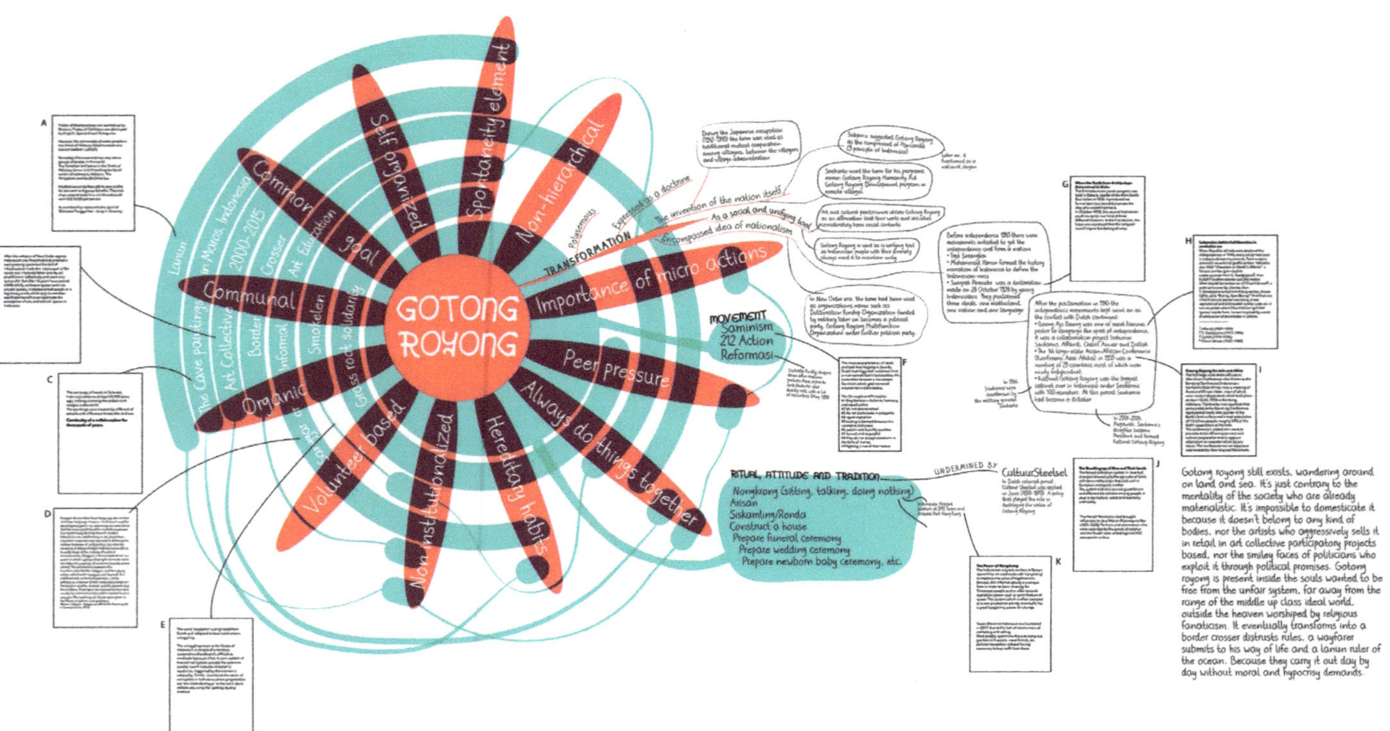

Figure 2.5: Tita Salina (b. 1973), South Sumatra, and Irwan Ahmett (b. 1975), West Java, *Gotong Royong – Autobiography*, 2014.

Evolving wall diagram, dimensions variable. Image courtesy the artists.

Anthropologist J. R. Bowen argues that, in Indonesia, 'state and local actors are both continually engaged in the construction of "tradition" in a dialogue … in which the outcome is by no means pre-determined by the state'.[24] This suggests the manner in which functions that might usually be fulfilled by the state become a field of practice for artists and institutions dealing with the failure, thus far, of the state to achieve strong welfare systems and resilient arts infrastructure.[25] This is also the controversial field that Bishop has identified as a site for neo-liberalist state cooption of participatory art practice as a substitute for strong, state-supported welfare systems.[26] Locating *gotong royong*—which focuses on the individual's responsiveness and responsibility to her society—within arts discourses that also valorise autonomous creativity raises important questions around assumptions that Indonesian (or at least Javanese) traditions are inherently and exclusively communal. These questions are fundamental to the next two, specifically art-related concepts addressed in this chapter: *jiwa ketok* and *turba*.

Living Traditions: *Jiwa Ketok*

> If an artist makes an art object, then that art object is none other than his own soul made visible. Art is the visible soul. So art is the soul.[27]

This statement by Sudjojono, published in his 1946 essay 'Art, Artists and Society', described his fundamental philosophy of *jiwa ketok*, the 'visible soul'. It has remained a point of resistance and consolidation over the decades since. In their 1987 catalogue for *Pasar Raya Dunia Fantasi* (Fantasy world supermarket), GSRB rejected the idea that the artist must retain an emotional connection to the artwork for it to be successful: 'Emotional and intuitive ways of working—let alone a state of trance, were considered taboo', a catalogue essay attributed to Jim Supangkat and Sanento Yuliman declared.[28] Yet for many present-day Indonesian artists, Sudjojono's legacy remains influential.

24 John R. Bowen, 'On the Political Construction of Tradition: *Gotong Royong* in Indonesia', *Journal of Asian Studies* 45, no. 3 (1986): 456, doi.org/10.2307/2056530.

25 In the late 2010s there were developments in the provision of arts grants by the Agency for Creative Economies, which provincially provided multi-year funding for events such as the Biennale Jogja.

26 Bishop, *Artificial Hells*, 13.

27 Sudjojono, 'Kesenian, Seniman dan Masyarakat' [Art, artists and society], in *Seni Loekis, Kesenian dan Seniman* [Painting, Art and Artists] (Yogyakarta: Penerbit Indonesia Sekarang, 1946), 69.

28 J. Supangkat, Sanento Yuliman, Arief Budiman, Emmanuel Subangun and Soejtipto Wirosardjono, *Seni Rupa Baru Proyek 1: Pasaraya Dunia Fantasi* [New art project 1: Fantasy world supermarket], ed. Taman Ismail Marzuki (Jakarta: Percetakan Gramedia, 1987), 19.

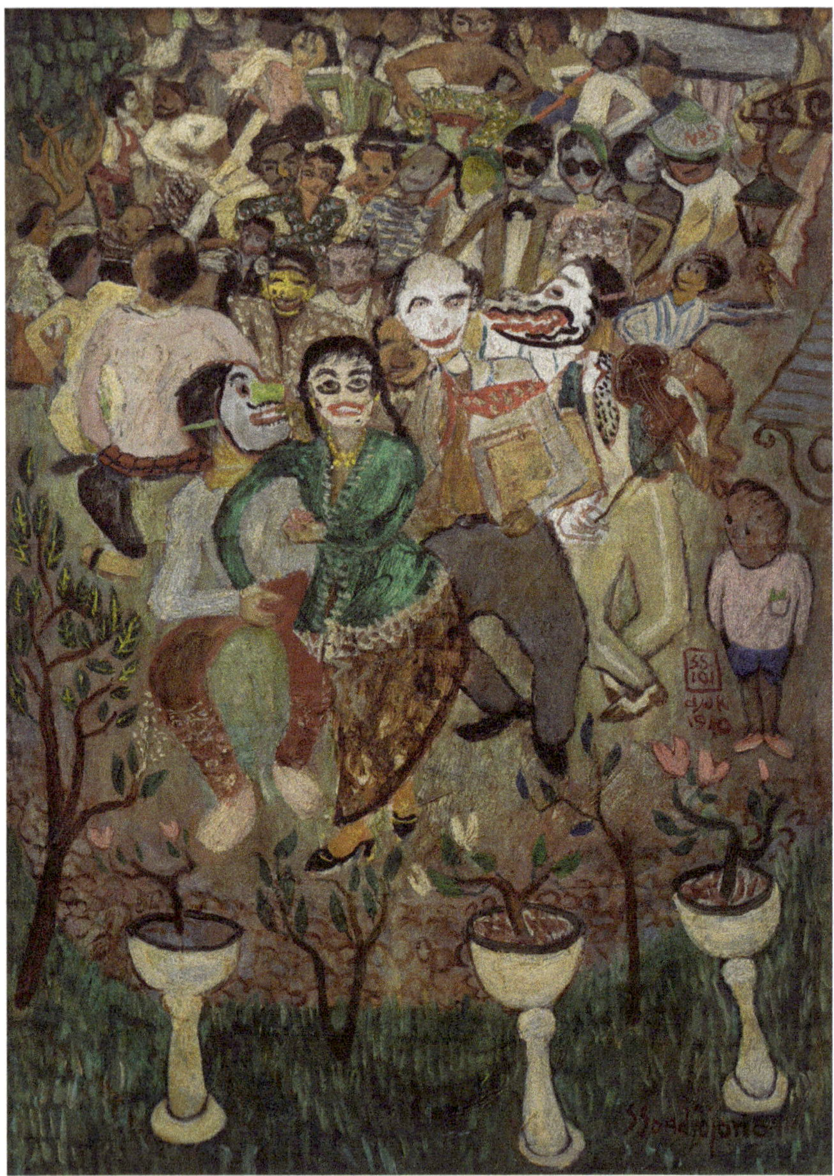

Figure 2.6: S. Sudjojono, *Tjap Go Meh*, 1940.

73 x 51 cm. Image courtesy the National Gallery of Indonesia. Permission courtesy the S. Sudjojono Center, Indonesia. *Tjap Go Meh* depicts the Chinese lantern festival of the same name, and has been subject to various interpretations and visual analyses detailed by Agus T. Dermawan.[29]

29 See Agus T. Dermawan, 'Sudjojono's Criticism in Cap Go Meh', *Jakarta Post*, 5 March 2018, www.thejakartapost.com/life/2018/03/05/sudjojonos-criticism-in-cap-go-meh.html.

Indonesian painter and theorist Stanislaus Yangni (b. 1982), for example, asserts that '(Sudjojono's) credo of the "visible soul" was the first discourse of Indonesian fine arts'.[30] She places this discourse alongside Deleuzian philosophy in her ruminations on the aesthetic in painting—contemporary and past, Indonesian and otherwise. In another example, in 2013 an exhibition called *Jiwa Ketok, Kebangsaan dan Kita* (The visible soul, nationalism and us) was held at the National Gallery of Indonesia. Contemporary artists produced diverse works demonstrating both resistance to, and nostalgia for, the kind of 'social realism' that *jiwa ketok* produced: images of the poor and the marginalised, the elderly and the ordinary reappeared but were, often as not, inverted, chalked over and recomposed with self-conscious and direct political references.

Sudjojono was well known for his fiery admonishments of slavish orientation to the West, yet he also advised young artists to study the techniques of Western painters. In 1967 Claire Holt wrote of Sudjojono:

> He believed that artists should be politically conscious and cited Picasso and Diego de Rivera as good examples. Art, he held, should be dedicated to the social and political struggle.[31]

But for Sudjojono, this commitment to the social struggle did not suggest that artists should allow themselves to be beholden to society's traditions or morals, rather that they should maintain their individuality. Yuliman argued that this focus on the individual as the centre of creative energy is one of three main tenets of Indonesian modernism. This motif recurs throughout Sudjojono's writing, including in his essay, 'Painting in Indonesia, Now and in the Future':

> Every artist: the number one thing is to be founded on the artist's own character. And an artist must be courageous in all things, and especially dare to give their ideas to the world, even though not a single member of the public regards them well.[32]

---

30 Stanislaus Yangni, *Dari Khaos ke Khaosmos: Estetika Seni Rupa* [From chaos to the chaosmos: Aesthetics of art] (Yogyakarta: Erupsi Akademia and Institut Seni Indonesia, 2012), 14.

31 Claire Holt, *Art in Indonesia: Continuities and Change* (Ithaca, NY: Cornell University Press, 1967), 216.

32 Sudjojono, 'Seni Loekis di Indonesia, Sekarang dan Jang Akan Datang', in *Seni Loekis, Kesenian Dan Seniman* (Yogyakarta: Penerbit Indonesia Sekarang 1946), 7.

This dual commitment to the sociopolitical realm through the representation of the struggles of society and to the vehement privileging of the artist as independent from society sets the 'climate' (to borrow a term from Yuliman) in which present-day Indonesian artists create both individual and participatory works.[33] For Sudjojono, the autonomy of the artist as an individual was imperative to the creation of art, which could only be beautiful if it remained truthful, created through confrontation with social realities. To this end, 'realism' is positioned as the primary goal of the artist, one inherently subjective in Sudjojono's construction. However, as Yangni argues, this does not locate 'realism' as a technique or stylistic tendency, which would lead to a dead end.[34] Rather, she contends that the 'realism of *jiwa ketok*' is associated with a consciousness of human history in the here and now. In claiming *jiwa ketok* as foundational art theory in Indonesia, Yangni reveals the ongoing interpretation of the 'visible soul' in contemporary arts practice. This continuing concern for the artists' creative autonomy remains centred on consciousness and response to reality.

Living Traditions: *Turba*

The philosophy of *turba*—going down below into society—did not negate the emphasis on the artist as the centre for creative energy.[35] In fact, Sudjojono was an influential member of Lekra and the formulation of *turba* as a philosophy of practice reflects his insistence that artists turn to realism for honest individual expression. Between 1950 and the 1960s in Indonesia, as in many places around the world, leftist ideologies were increasingly dominant in political and cultural discourse. The Indonesian Communist Party enjoyed an important seat at Sukarno's table, and socialist organisations flourished in the community. The Lembaga Kebudayaan Rakyat (Institute for People's Culture)—better known as Lekra—brought together art workers (including writers) from all disciplines to determine a functional role for the arts in Indonesia's future. Lekra's 1955 *Mukadimah* (Manifesto) declared that:

33 Yuliman, 'Seni Lukis di Indonesia', 73.

34 Yangni, *Dari Khaos ke Khaosmos*, 30.

35 *Turba* is an acronym from the phrase *turun ke bawah* or 'go down below'.

> In the field of art, Lekra urges creative initiative, and creative daring, and Lekra approves of every form, style, etc. as long as it is faithful to the truth, and as long as it strives for the utmost artistic beauty.

The *Mukadimah* also specified that 'artists, scholars and cultural workers should be on the side of the people and serve the people if they are to produce works of lasting value', thus establishing a clear ethical basis for the evaluation of artwork.[36]

At Lekra's first National Congress in 1959, *turba* was formulated as a methodology to ensure artists could meet the ethical values set out in Lekra's early manifestos. Lekra distilled its modernist, outward-looking and socialist-nationalist philosophies into the '1-5-1 Principles'. These firstly set 'politics as the commander', then defined five sub-principles pertaining to: 'combining individual creativity with the wisdom of the many', the wide distribution of high-quality art, the harmonic combination of content and form, wholesome traditions meeting revolutionary modernity and the combination of revolutionary realism with revolutionary romanticism. Lastly, 1-5-1 dictated: '1: Go Down Below, through interviews and in-depth investigation of the conditions and aspirations of the people'.[37]

It was this last aspect of the 1-5-1 Principles that came to dominate artistic methodologies. In Antariksa's account of Lekra and visual art practice, he cites former Lekra member Hersri Setiawan's (b. 1936) description of *turba* as a research method. Setiawan tells of a week he spent in the village of Saragedug, just east of Yogyakarta (see Map 2), to collect folktales: 'In the afternoon we would hoe or weed, and in the evening … while we plaited reeds we would develop discussions about folk tales with the farmers'.[38]

These folk tales became the basis for the literary works Setiawan wrote. From this we can see that, rather than benefiting those 'below' through artistic intervention, the purpose of *turba* was, at least from Setiawan's perspective, to expand the perspectives of artists and cultural workers and

36 Keith Foulcher, *Social Commitment in Literature and the Arts: 'The Indonesian Institute of People's Culture' 1950–1965* (Monash University: Centre of Southeast Asian Studies, 1986).
37 Aminuddin T. Siregar and Tempo Team, 'LEKRA: Analysis of a Discourse', *Tempo* (30 September – 6 October 2013).
38 Antariksa, *Tuan Tanah Kawin Muda* [The land owner takes a younger wife] (Yogyakarta: Yayasan Seni Cemeti, 2005), 66.

their organisations. Noting that artists are generally born into middle-class urban families, Setiawan attests that *turba's* purpose was to 'catch the heart-beat of those below' and re-voice the repertoire of art and cultural forms at this level of society. In contrast to Setiawan, for Amrus Natalsya, the head of Bumi Tarung—an artists' group that took *turba* as its primary creative process—*turba* was knowledge: social knowledge that could then be offered to an audience. However, his understanding of this knowledge was somewhat narrow and arbitrary: 'that farmers should be defended. That feudalism is bad'.

Of this contested, lauded and derided part of leftist art practice, Keith Foulcher, expert in Indonesian literature wrote:

> [*Turba*] was not only a description, but a working method. It expressed a particular concept of the relationship between cultural workers and ordinary people, and was intended to ensure that the artist was at one with the thoughts and feelings of the people, not an observer of their lives but a full participant in them.[39]

Swastika sees *turba* as the origins of participatory art practice in Indonesia, saying it 'indicates there was already a desire to be close to the subject'. She traces this desire back to activism and performance art in political demonstrations, during which artists invited fellow demonstrators to join them in performative protest.[40]

While the legacy of *turba* inspires contemporary politically aware artists, the reality in the 1950s and 1960s was somewhat less romantic. For all the good intentions to 'expand (art) out and up', according to Lekra artist Djoko Pekik, Lekra promoted only folk-art forms at the sub-district level (*kecamatan*) and 'high arts' at the regency level (*kabupaten*). Kusni Sulang wrote of objections during the 1964 conference, when artists complained that they spent too much time making banners and had little time for creative work, much less *turba.* In the same letter, Sulang claims that the models for farmers that appeared in paintings were in fact city people in farmer's clothing.[41] Musicians similarly protested that so much time was spent performing at cultural events that there was no time for composition or consideration of the context.

---

39 Foulcher, *Social Commitment in Literature and the Arts*, 110.

40 Alia Swastika, interviewed by Elly Kent, 2014. The works of artist collective *Taring Padi* (see Chapter 1) are prime examples of this tendency.

41 Antariksa, *Tuan Tanah Kawin Muda*, 79.

Foulcher has argued that Lekra's art will remain 'a site on which meanings will continue to be built', and this has proven to be the case, as those working in the arts have, in recent years, increasingly referred to the literature and theatre produced by Lekra members.[42] However, I argue that the *artworks* produced by Lekra, at least in the visual arts, have had limited impact on the discourse of Indonesian art.[43]

Lekra's philosophies, however, 'combining individual creativity with the wisdom of the many', and its conception of *turba* as a methodology that engendered artists' participation in society, have greatly influenced the aesthetic form of Indonesian art. In spite of fractured implementation and ambiguous intentions, or perhaps because of them, *turba* remains an exemplar of socially engaged art practice in Indonesia, in the minds of artists, curators and cultural workers.

Aggregrated Knowledge: Kerakyatan and Conscientisation in Indonesian Art

During the 1980s, the concept of the artist as a participant in society diverged from the concept of *turba* when artists began to actively seek ways to interpret their own experiences of ordinary life—rather than focusing on those of the 'other' as embodied in the *rakyat*. GSRB artist and writer FX Harsono (b. 1949) described this practice, and its attendant commitment to making more meaningful contributions to society through art, as 'reformative':

> Almost all reformative artists undertake some work outside their individual creative arts practice. Of course, they cannot live from their art alone, whether it is painting, sculpture or design. Initially these strategic efforts at survival were not acknowledged as a lifestyle which is at heart an artistic one, but then there emerged a new awareness among these innovative artists, that the act of earning a living and creating art form an inseparable unit.[44]

---

42 Foulcher, *Social Commitment in Literature and the Arts*, 208.

43 It should be acknowledged that many works of art and literature by members of Lekra were likely destroyed, and were certainly censored, during the purges of the New Order. Some works, particularly those of writer Pramoedya Ananta Toer, have gained international attention and wide influence, but works of art have had limited attention.

44 FX Harsono, 'Upaya Mandiri Seni Rupa Pembaruan' [Independent efforts in reformative art], in *Seni Rupa Penyadaran*, by Moelyono (Yogyakarta: Yayasan Bentang Budaya, 1997), 101–11.

Lamenting its status, Harsono identified participation in society as a defining and undervalued aspect of 'reformative art' practice. In the past, the strong relationship between social situations and creativity in Indonesia had been linked to traditional art forms like shadow puppetry.[45] However, for some Indonesian artists in the 1980s, it was instead an attempt to develop and deepen their understanding of the issues faced by Indonesian society. Harsono wrote:

> However they struggle with poverty, immersing themselves with the poor, their involvement in NGOs and their efforts to expand the concept of sociology and culture … These activities are always regarded as having no direct connection to their creation of art, and tend to be ignored by art aficionados.[46]

Revealing the tension between creative autonomy and social engagement, Harsono argued that the desire to manifest both in art practice was thwarted by modernist concepts of universalism and the pure autonomy of the arts. In later writing, Harsono used the word *kerakyatan* to describe this longstanding tendency, a term sometimes translated as 'populism' but that, in artistic discourse, refers to painting and art practices related to the fate of 'those who are repressed by the government's policies … so those that do not have the economic, social or political ability to resist'.[47] The term also appears frequently in writings about Lekra.[48]

Harsono traced the development of art concerned with the struggle of the populace through various stages of Indonesian art history.[49] He identified shifts in the understanding of who the *rakyat* are and what role the artist should take in relation to them, attributing an expansion of the concept of *kerakyatan* to the emergence of artists involved in groups like GSRB and PIPA (Kepribadian Apa/What Identity) in the 1970s.

45 J. Ewington, 'Between the Cracks: Art and Method in Southeast Asia', *Art Asia Pacific* 3, no. 4 (1996): 57–63.

46 FX Harsono, 'Upaya Mandiri Seni Rupa Pembaruan'.

47 Personal communication with Harsono, 29 July 2015.

48 Foulcher, *Social Commitment in Literature and the Arts,* 41, 111.

49 FX Harsono, 'Kerakyatan dalam Seni Lukis Indonesia Sejak PERSAGI Hingga Kini' [Orientation to the people in Indonesian painting from PERSAGI to now], in *Politik Dan Gender: Aspek-Aspek Seni Visual Indonesia,* ed. Adi Wicaksono et al. (Yogyakarta: Yayasan Seni Cemeti, 2003), 56–91 (author's translation).

The development in artists' conceptions of which sections of society were experiencing suffering, Harsono wrote, was directly related to their expanding networks:

> Drawing on their critical observations of the reality of existence and their interactions with society and groups outside the arts … they no longer identify the problems of the people as limited to the problems experienced by the *wong cilik* [little people/peasants], rather more diversely …. environmental pollution, eviction, workers, war, cultures of violence, the clash between modernity and tradition, and so on.[50]

In one of his last essays, Yuliman too discussed the sense of restlessness among largely the same artists. Yuliman quoted phrases that various artists used to refer to the shifting direction of their practice: 'publicly oriented' (FX Harsono); 'communication art' (Gendut Riyanto, 1955–2003); and 'art that is beneficial to society' (Harris Purnama, b. 1956). Yuliman stressed that their art was often the 'result of collaboration, and perhaps even with a role for the audience or the public (which thus changes their role, and that of the artist)'.[51]

This shift in attitude to art practice and to the *rakyat* resulted in an increasingly direct pedagogical function for art, which artists like Moelyono (b. 1957), Arahmaiani (b. 1961) and Tisna Sanjaya (b. 1958) then developed through their interaction with NGOs, society and non-arts groups. It can be argued that this pedagogical or didactic function develops the goals of Lekra's *turba*, a methodology that sought to expand artists' experience and knowledge so that they could accurately represent the subjects of their artwork. However, among the artists of the late twentieth century, Harsono points to academic rather than experiential catalysts, which also influenced attitudes to participation:

> Alignment (with society) begins with intellectual awareness due to educational background, not from the experience of living in the community. The younger generation, for example Moelyono, began to engage with NGOs, encountering participatory research methods.[52]

---

50 Ibid., 70.

51 Sanento Yuliman, 'Kemana Semangat Muda', in *Dua Seni Rupa: Sepilihan Tulisan Sanento Yuliman*, ed. Hasan Asikin (Jakarta: Yayasan Kalam, 2001), 151.

52 Harsono, 'Kerakyatan dalam Seni Lukis Indonesia Sejak PERSAGI Hingga Kini', 85.

The concept of conscientisation gained cadence in Indonesia with the publication of *Seni Rupa Penyadaran* (Conscientisation art) in 1997. Addressing Moelyono's art, philosophy and methodology, the book came at a time when Moelyono's work in marginalised communities was attracting considerable media and curatorial attention locally and overseas.[53] This was probably influenced by his networks with NGOs, burgeoning international interest in political art from the 'periphery' and the rapidly approaching fall of the repressive Orde Baru (New Order). The title of the book reflected Moelyono's own 'writing' of his practice, and its influence among artists in the 1980s.

In this book Moelyono preserved the specific role he sees for art as a tool in emancipation. He valorises the role of aesthetics using the classical Greek words for feeling and sensation, and links them to the 'development of dialogue that creates a critical consciousness … both through processes of working and the finished work as it is discussed with the broader community'.[54] Thus, Moelyono brings aesthetics as a sensory experience together with consciousness and the capacity for subjective criticality. In his construction, the role of art and artists as catalysts in conscientising art is explicit, although it is the *rakyat* who are positioned as subjects and drivers in this process of creating new culture:

> As creators of culture, the *rakyat* has the potential and right to visual art as a medium for dialogue … In the dialogue process, in the social reality, there is a need for concern, involvement, alignment, participation and contributions from accompanying professional or graduate art workers.[55]

---

53 See, for instance, 'Artist Moelyono Intends to Promote Social Awareness', *Jakarta Post*, 1 January 1988; 'Moelyono's Art Invites Dialog on Social Issues', *Jakarta Post*, 14 May 1997; Supangkat, 'Multiculturalism/Multimodernism'. Also note Moelyono's inclusion in *Art in Southeast Asia 1997: Glimpses into the Future*, curated by Junichi Shioda, Osamu Fukunaga and Yasuko Furuichi at the Museum of Contemporary Art, Tokyo; *Plastic (& Other) Waste*, curated by Apinan Poshyananda at Chulalongkorn University Bangkok, Thailand; Australia & Regions Artists' Exchange, *Torque*: ARX 4, The Fourth Artists' Regional Exchange, 1995, at Perth Institute of Contemporary Arts Perth, Australia; and the Third Asia Pacific Triennial of Contemporary Art, *Beyond the Future* 1999, at the Queensland Art Gallery.

54 Here Moelyono is drawing his understanding of aesthetics from Ursula Meyer, 'Conceptual Art', *Journal of Aesthetics and Art Criticism* 31, no. 1 (1972): 45. Jim Supangkat and Sanento Yuliman also draw on terms drawn from classical Greek in their writing on GSRB in the 1980s. See Sanento Yuliman and J. Supangkat, 'Seni Rupa Sehari-Hari Menentang Elitisme' [Everyday art for opposing elitism], in *Seni Rupa Baru Proyek 1: Pasaraya Dunia Fantasi* [New art project 1: Fantasy world supermarket], 14. An English translation is available at Asia Art Archive, accessed 19 January 2022, aaa.org.hk/en/collections/search/library/every-day-art-practices-against-elitism.

55 Moelyono, *Seni Rupa Penyadaran*, 44.

The specific role for artists that Moelyono identifies here was eclipsed by theories of participatory research and pedagogical aspirations in later publications, where the focus is primarily on Moelyono's work as an example of the kind of sociological praxis that Freire defined as 'reflection and action directed at the structures to be transformed'.[56]

Especially after he established working relations with NGOs, Moelyono's work has demonstrated a strong focus on applying theory and practice to enacting social change. This is evident not only in his art projects but also in his propensity for writing, rewriting and publishing accounts of his work, and the pedagogical theories he develops within this work. His earliest and most frequently (self-)cited foray into pedagogic art practice involved an unexpected opportunity to voluntarily teach drawing in a small, isolated primary school in the village of Brumbun, East Java (see Map 2). Subsequently, in 1988 Moelyono was awarded an Ashoka Fellowship, which provided a stipend, allowing him to increase his activity at Brumbun.[57] He also began to work closely with established NGOs such as WALHI (Environment Lobby) and API (Association for Sociology Researchers). API introduced Moelyono to the concept of participatory research and the pedagogical teachings of Brazilian Paulo Freire, and Moelyono quickly adopted these theories in explaining his own work:

> I came to know terms and names such as participative, participatory, methodology, dialogical, transformative, Paulo Freire, Gramsci, and others that I had never heard or imagined when I was studying at art school.[58]

In a 1989 forum, artist Siti Adiyati borrowed the term 'conscientisation' from Freire's *Pedagogy of the Oppressed* and described Moelyono's art as *Seni Rupa Penyadaran* or 'Art for Conscientisation'.[59]

56 P. Freire, *Pedagogy of the Oppressed* (New York: Continuum, 1970), 126.

57 The Ashoka Fellowships, awarded by a philanthropic organisation funded by corporate partners, provide stipends for recognised 'social entrepreneurs' to support them to continue their work.

58 Moelyono, *Seni Rupa Penyadaran*, 31.

59 Moelyono, *Pak Moel Guru Nggambar* [Mr Moel, drawing teacher] (Yogyakarta: Insist Press, 2005), 32.

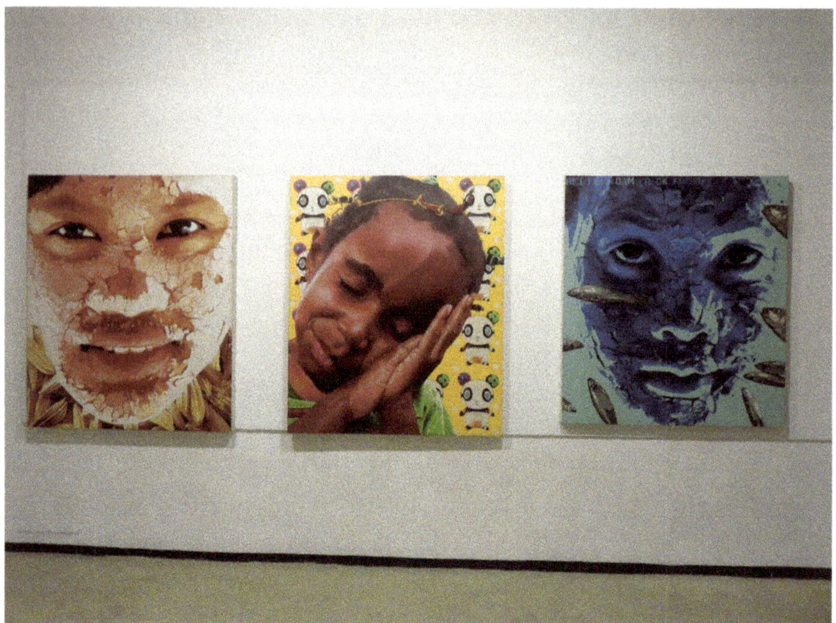

Figure 2.7: Moelyono, paintings installed in 2015 Biennale Jogja XIII – Hacking Conflict: Indonesia Meets Nigeria.

Moelyono's work continues to resonate with new generations of Indonesians. These paintings draw on the techniques he used in the *Retak Wajah* (Cracks in the face) exhibition and were among the works produced during the *Bertolak-Bersanding Parallel Events*, in which Moelyono and Joned Suryatmoko mentored participating community organisations. Photograph: Elly Kent.

In Moelyono's work there is a tension between the individual expression that contemporary art inherits from modernist discourse and the drive to play a tangible, quantifiable role in social change through deep creative engagement with others. The exhibition *Retak Wajah* (Cracks in the face), held at Cemeti Art House, clearly demonstrated this tension. The work followed up on the Waung Village project on which Moelyono's final, failed painting examination for his undergraduate degree was based 25 years earlier. Waung's swamps, previously subject to regular flooding, evaporated after the construction of the Wonorejo Dam (see Map 2). Moelyono's subsequent artworks have regularly displayed statistical data and official documents such as maps, planograms and tables alongside artefacts of rural life. However, this distinctive aesthetic decision is rarely addressed (if at all) in literature on his practice.

The exception is Nindityo Adipurnomo's impressive curatorial essay for the exhibition *Retak Wajah Anak-anak Bendungan* (Disintegrating faces of the children of the dam, 2011), which provides a nuanced account of the difficulties the maps, tables and planograms present for the artist and curator. Nindityo opines that Moelyono's use of official documentation and data contrasted with items of bucolic material culture is a strategy to bring both perpetrators and victims into the gallery space to 'record the fragility of the rural sector'. Yet, in his curatorial approach to Moelyono's work Nindityo identifies a double-edged exoticisation, describing a debate they had while preparing the exhibition:

> I felt confronted by the calculated estimations of stereotypical middle-class urbanites that Moelyono felt it was important to target with this work. Phrases like 'nouveau riche' and 'Facebook generation' came complete with specific indicators of their characteristics (fast, cheap and instant); once again I was aware of an attempt to stereotype target audiences that made me feel uncomfortable (not to say hopeless) in my efforts to build a dialogue around Moelyono's art in a gallery space.[60]

Nindityo's account of his frustration locates some of Moelyono's work, which brought 'village art artefacts' that had been submerged by the dam project into the gallery space, as an exoticisation of 'village art' for a perceived urban 'other' in need of pedagogical realignment. Yet Nindityo retains his faith in the fundamental 'anti-fetishist' qualities of Moelyono's work; his scepticism evaporates in his descriptions of the installation work that 'transforms the exhibition space into confiscated land that will … be flooded'.[61]

Conclusion

I began this chapter by reflecting on the work of Heri Dono. His *Kuda Binal* performance inverted those modernist and Javanese traditions that establish values around the expert and layperson, tradition and modernity, and individual and communal expression, and set them on a collision course with each other. In doing so, *Kuda Binal* perfectly exemplifies the

60 Nindityo Adipurnomo Moelyono and Priyambudi Sulistiyanto, *Retak Wajah Anak-anak Bendungan* [Disintegrating faces of the children of the dam], ed. House Cemeti Art (Yogyakarta: Cemeti Art House, 2011), 17.

61 Ibid., 17–19.

aesthetic regime's task of permeating the partitions between art and life, and, at the same time, shows how artists and institutions bring together local knowledge with global arts discourses to engender practices that focus on the *rakyat* as a primary subject.

While many artists of the twentieth century may have sought a definitively social role for Indonesian modernism, artists of the twenty-first century are drawing on a plethora of sources and ideas that echo, challenge and deconstruct those ideas. Contemporary Indonesian artists continue to engage with the art discourses developed across their nation's short history, adopting, as the artists of the late twentieth century did, a multitude of positions and stances around ideas of artistic responsibility and autonomous creativity. Yuliman described an artistic ideology that rigorously attended to the deconstruction of binaries: high and low, common and rarefied, everyday and extraordinary, functional and esoteric, traditional and modern. This continues through the work of contemporary Indonesian artists who have embraced Yuliman's approach. The departitioning of the commonly held distinction between the artists' individual autonomy and their responsibility to society remains a site for groundbreaking artistic explorations. But the history of their predecessors and their concerns has not been forgotten.

Acknowledgements

Heri Dono, Moelyono, Arahmaiani, Tisna Sanjaya, Nindityo Adipurnomo, FX Harsono, Tita Salina, Irwan Ahmett, Yoshi Fajar Kreshnomurti and Gunawan Julianto deserve particular thanks for their willingness to discuss their work with me and, importantly, for their writing about practice. I am also indebted to my coeditors, Associate Professor Caroline Turner and Emeritus Professor Virginia Hooker, for creating this opportunity for me to work with them, and for their patient guidance and mentorship during the course of producing this book and throughout my academic career. Parts of this essay draw on material also published in my book, *Artists and the People: Ideologies of Art in Indonesia* (NUS Press, 2022).

3

New Indonesian Painting

Sanento Yuliman
Translated by Elly Kent

Sanento Yuliman is widely recognised in Indonesia as one of the most important and influential art historians and critics in the country. Even before his doctoral studies in France in the late 1970s – early 1980s, Yuliman was building a reputation as an art critic with a deep understanding of Indonesian art history and a unique perspective on the genesis of Indonesian modernism. Much of Yuliman's writings appeared in magazines and journals such as Budaya Djaya, *and as a series of exhibition reviews published over 10 years in* Tempo. *His premature death in 1992 cut short the invaluable contribution he was making to the establishment of objective and knowledgeable art criticism in Indonesia, but a 2001 publication of selected essays, two recent books and an exhibition of his artwork and ephemera have re-established the relevance of Yuliman's writing in Indonesia.*[1] *Unfortunately, very little of Yuliman's work has been translated for readers outside Indonesia, creating a disjuncture between discourses on Indonesian art within and outside the country. The text reproduced in translation here was published as a book in 1976 and has been lauded as 'the first real art history to demonstrate formal*

1 These include *Sanento Yuliman, Dua Seni Rupa: Sepilihan Tulisan Sanento Yuliman* [Two fine arts: A selection of Sanento Yuliman's writing] (Jakarta: Yayasan Kalam, 2001); Sanento Yuliman, *Estetika Yang Merabunkan: Bunga Rampai Esai Dan Kritik Seni Rupa* [Blinding aesthetics: A collection of art criticism and essays], 1969–92 (Jakarta: Dewan Kesenian Jakarta and Gang Kabel, 2020); Sanento Yuliman, *Pasfoto Sang Iblis: Bunga Rampai Esai Kebudayaan, Karikatur, Puisi, Dan Lain-Lain* [The devils passport photo: A collection of cultural essays, caricatures, poetry and more], 1966–90 (Jakarta: Gang Kabel, 2020).

continuity across political lines'.[2] *While art historical scholarship has advanced in the intervening decades, this text represents an important window into the conceptualisation of not only Indonesian art history, but also the discourses that underpin art movements of the past and present.*

Introduction[3]

In this century two new genres of painting have developed in Indonesia. The first has flourished in Bali since the 1930s. This painting displayed several new tendencies that differentiated it from earlier Balinese painting traditions, however in general it still showed a clear connection with the art and culture of Bali. Because of this people could still refer to it as 'Balinese painting'.

The second genre was painting that developed in the big cities, especially Jakarta, Bandung and Yogyakarta, which nonetheless included some painters who were trying to use elements from regional (traditional) arts, although they could not be considered part of the developmental framework of a regional culture.

This essay brings us to the second genre.

With regards to this second category of painting, people usually position Raden Saleh, from the nineteenth century, as the pioneer. Indeed he was the first Indonesian painter to take up new techniques and styles and also—in association with this—a new aesthetic. In addition, this painter became a legendary figure for most Indonesian painters in subsequent generations. In this role, he provided strength and inspiration for them as they struggled in their lives as artists.

2 This quote comes from a summary of the thirteenth instalment of the Arts in Southeast Asia Seminar Series, which was presented by Professor Adrian Vickers on 14 September 2017. See Adrian Vickers, 'A Hundred Years of Indonesian Art', Seminar ISEAS-Yusof Ishak Institute Singapore 2017, accessed 25 January 2022, www.iseas.edu.sg/media/event-highlights/indonesian-art-in-1976-a-hundred-years-of-indonesian-art/.

3 Editors' note: the editors thank Dr Yuliman's family for permission to publish it here. Unless indicated, the spelling of personal names and the footnotes and titles of works are given as published in *Estetika Yang Merabunkan: Bunga Rampai Esai dan Kritik Seni Rupa* (2020).

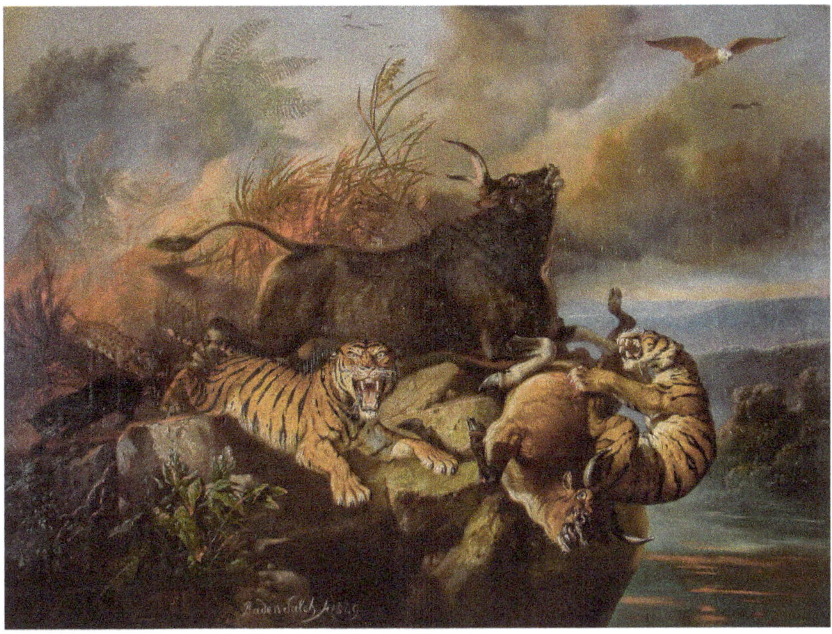

Figure 3.1: Raden Saleh, *Forest Fire*, 1849.
Oil on canvas, 300 x 396 cm. Signed 1849. Collection: the Singapore National Gallery. Public domain.

As a pioneer, Raden Saleh is in fact distanced from the first stage of the development of the new genre of Indonesian painting. There are two reasons for this. Firstly, in the absence of a cohort of fellow painters, Raden Saleh had no contemporaries in his own time, nor did he teach his painting style to a younger generation. Secondly—and this is more important—because of the difference in style.

About Raden Saleh

Raden Saleh Syarif Bustaman (1807–1880)[4] began studying painting with A. A. J Payen, a Belgian artist who was brought to the Dutch East Indies by the (colonial) government to document the Indonesian landscape. He spent a long period in Europe (1830–51), absorbing the influence of the Romantic Movement on art there. Raden Saleh's paintings

4 Editors' note: Sanento Yuliman gave a birth date of 1807 for Raden Saleh; however, the birth date of 1811 is used in a number of more recent scholarly sources and is used here in this volume except in primary sources such as this chapter and in quotations.

> are known for their dynamic style, with scenes of adventure or drama, as seen in his painting 'Between Life and Death' (1848), which depicted the struggle between a bison and a lion; 'Hunting Buffalo in Java' (1870), which showed horse riders attacking a buffalo; 'Forest Fire', which depicted various animals confused by a conflagration; 'Flood', which depicted terrified people caught in a natural disaster, and so on.[5] Raden Saleh's paintings were paintings full of spirit.

About one generation after Raden Saleh, other Indonesian artists began to appear, and in greater numbers. The new painting began to grow and develop in Indonesia.

Three Periods of Development

We can trace three phases of this development.

The first period took place in the first 40 years of this [twentieth] century. The growth of painting was based on landscapes. Of course, painters of the time painted other subjects, for instance people, however landscapes took pride of place in their art.

The second period began around 1940. In this period we can see the growth of painting that intended to express experience. Furthermore, the character and mental state of the painter, which was generally stressed and anxious—was seen as important and had to be apparent in their paintings. In painting nature, people and objects, the painter's emotions towards the object were seen as paramount.

The third period began after 1960. This period was marked by painting that was referred to as 'abstract'. In these paintings people would struggle, or completely fail to see objects familiar from reality.

Of course, this division into three time periods does not mean that painters suddenly abandoned the style of painting in one era and shifted to a different kind of painting in the following one. Even today artists paint the landscape. And young painters who emerged in the 60s or 70s were not inevitably abstract painters. This division of phases is only intended to indicate which new tendencies emerged in each period.

5 Editors' note: this may refer to a work titled: *Banjir di Jawa* or *Flood in Java*. We have been unable to find reference to a painting titled *Flood*.

First Period (1900–40)

The growth of landscape painting at the beginning of the century was supported by several factors.

Causative Factors

One of the most important factors was the presence of a number of Dutch painters, both those who were brought over by the Dutch East Indies government for official business (for instance to document the natural and urban environment and so on, in Indonesia) and those who came because they had adventurous spirits and were attracted to the environment around the Pacific Ocean. There were even Dutch painters who had been born and raised in Indonesia. These painters introduced Indonesians to the landscape painting tradition that had been developing in the Netherlands over the preceding three or four centuries.

Thus we find a number of Indonesians who were interested in becoming landscape painters, such as Abdullah Surio Subroto (1878–1941), who studied at the academy of fine art in the Netherlands, Mas Pirngadi (1865–1936), Wakidi (b. 1889) and others. The techniques and style of painting in this era were then continued by Basuki Abdullah, Sukardji, Omar Basalamah, Wahdi and others.

Another factor was the aspirations of the European (bourgeois) middle class. In Europe, landscape painting developed in tandem with the emergence of the middle class. This social class, which was essentially the class of merchants and traders, were less inclined to the paintings of Biblical stories and classical literature that the aristocrats favoured. They preferred paintings that depicted ordinary subjects, for instance landscapes. Furthermore, the views of nature took them to places where they could rest for a moment from the bustle of trading and industry in the noisy and dirty city.

Merchants, traders, Dutch civil servants and tourists brought their aspirations to Indonesia. The upper class of Indonesian society, the educated class who often socialised with the Dutch, was influenced by these aspirations.

Thus, at the beginning of the twentieth century, consumers for landscape paintings of Indonesia were formed—merchants, traders, civil servants and tourists—all wanting to have souvenirs of the Indonesian world—and also the educated classes of Indonesia. Of course it is clear that the aspirations of these consumers spread to the lower echelons of society.

Another factor that led to the development of landscape painting was, of course, the fact that most painters enjoyed painting the landscape. This pleasure—as well as the proceeds from sales and the enthusiasm of the people (who were immediately impressed by landscape paintings that seemed like 'a slice of reality')—was for painters a considerable reward for their efforts. Painters like Abdullah Surio Subroto, Mas Pirngadi and Wakidi spent much of their time getting away from busy lifestyles, escaping to quiet places like the slopes of Mt Tangkuban Perahu, or the foot of Mt Merapi, Pelabuhan Ratu beaches or the Sianok Valley, contemplating the natural landscape and painting it diligently.[6]

It seems as if in the natural environment that stretched as far as the eye could see, in its authenticity, its beauty and harmony, they found a friend who welcomed their sensitivity, and gave them comfort and enjoyment. For all of this, painters often depicted the landscape 'not' as it was in reality. On their canvases they made changes, for instance, 'shifting' a tree or scrub, and so on. It is as if by doing so they wanted to 'improve nature'. They paid great attention to the impressions generated by colour, for example, coolness or heat. This was connected with positioning of painting as something that could be 'refreshing'.

Technique

Landscape painters used techniques that were already customary and prescribed in Dutch painting, and that were taught in the fine art academies of the Netherlands. In these techniques, perspective had to be calculated precisely. The field of the painting was divided in three: the foreground, middle ground and background. One of these grounds, which would be given prominence, would be given a light source. The other grounds were muted or darkened. Colours were chosen according to the appropriate prescriptions, mixed well on the pallet in order to avoid blending on the canvas, which would make it look murky, and then applied very delicately to the canvas. In 1928, when Mas Pirngadi was teaching painting to Sudjojono, one of his students, he was disappointed to see the rough brushstrokes and dirty colours that Sudjojono had chosen. Pirngadi said:

6 Editors' note: these are picturesque sites in West and Central Java (see Map 2).

> When you depict a cloud, use white, ochre and mix in a little vermillion. Then the shadows are those colours with blue added. To show the water of a rice field, use these colours with a little more ochre and blue. Ochre is the key colour. Avoid using black and white.[7]

But Sudjojono was in fact the main opponent of the techniques, style and aesthetic of landscape painting. With this opposition he initiated the second period in the development of a new Indonesian painting.

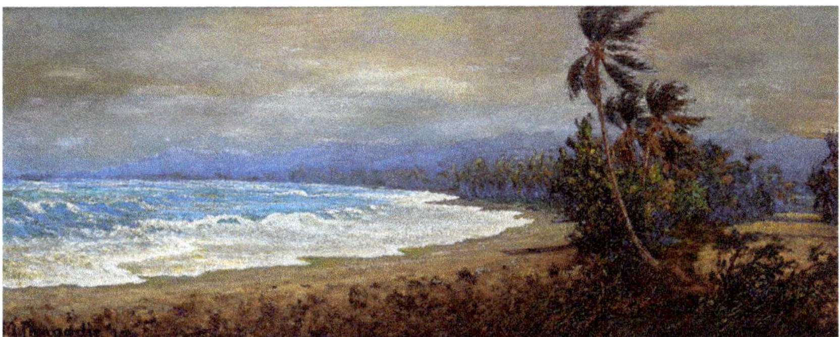

Figure 3.2: Mas Pirngadi, *Pantai Pelabuhan Ratu (Queens Port Beach)*, 1927.
Oil on canvas 30 x 75 cm. Public domain.

About Sudjojono

> Sudjojono, who was born in Kisaran, North Sumatra, around 1913, was convinced that painters should be free from rules, so that their spirit could pour out freely. Thus, painting was measured not by [the] speed with which it depicted an object, but by how intensely the passion (the connection to the subject-object) could be visualised in the lines that were brushed onto the canvas.
>
> With this view, and by positioning landscape painting in the 'Western' camp, Sudjojono and other painters found motivation for their opposition. Sudjojono himself said: 'I want to know how far behind the Europeans we are'.

7 Imam Buchori Zainuddin, 'Latar Belakang, Sejarah Pembinaan dan perkembangan Seni Lukis Indonesia Modern, 1935-1950' (thesis for the Fine Art Section of the Fine Art Department, ITB), 105–06.

These words contain a conviction that a path impassioned by the Indonesian spirit that they embodied would be a powerful resource.

In 1937, Sudjojono successfully exhibited alongside Europeans. He was praised. And about the same time he established PERSAGI [Persatuan Ahli Gambar Indonesia/Association of Indonesian Draughtsmen]. He became a key figure in this collective because of his ideas. Following this he also became an active member of POETERA [Pusat Tenaga Rakyat/Centre for the People's Power] and SIM [Seniman Indonesia Muda/Young Indonesian Artists]. His opinion that 'painting is the soul made visible' was encouraged by the atmosphere of the time, and was very influential on other painters. In 1945, Sudjojono declared 'Go to Realism'. At the time he disagreed with the painting styles that were too expressive and which produced abstraction and distortion. He saw these paintings as impossible for the people to understand. Sudjojono declared that his 'Realism' in painting was more accurate, his paintings from this period seem almost like portraits.

Sudjojono persisted with his realism until around 1958. In 1960 his paintings appear to indicate that he had returned to his earlier convictions, and feature strong brushstrokes. However the themes of his paintings had not changed much. From the beginning he revealed strong connections to the events taking place around him.

Second Phase (1940–60)

Development

S. Sudjojono and several other painters established the collective Persatuan Ahli Gambar Indonesia (Association of Indonesian Draughtsmen), shortened to PERSAGI, in 1937 in Jakarta. In its four years of activity, this collective attracted about 30 painters. PERSAGI was chaired by Agus Djaja and its members included, among others, Sudjojono, Abdul Salam, Sumitro, Sudibio, Sukirno, Suromo, Surono, Setyoso, Herbert Hutagalung, Syoeaib, Emiria Sunasa and more. With regard to the 'academic painting' (as they called it) that was developing around them, they agreed to establish their own 'academy'—by running lessons in their own homes, together. With regards to the colonialism that created an artistic atmosphere that seemed to cater only to the Dutch, and that created barriers to prevent Indonesian artists from emerging and being recognised, they agreed to break through and show the world that Indonesians too could paint and were capable of creating their own art that now carried 'the stamp of an new unified Indonesia'. Because of his skills in writing and speaking, Sudjojono became the driver and spokesperson for PERSAGI.

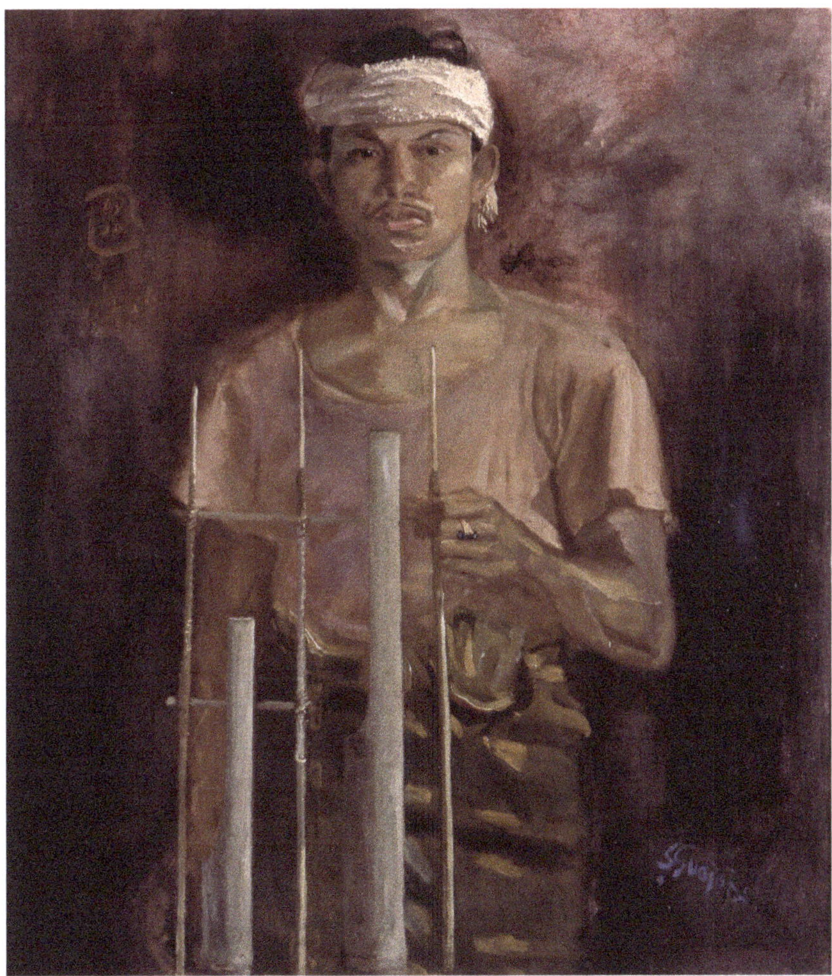

Figure 3.3: S. Sudjojono, Angklung, *Player*, 1956.

Oil on canvas, 98 x 84 cm. Collection: National Gallery Singapore. Permission courtesy S. Sudjojono Center, Indonesia.

While the PERSAGI painters were working in Jakarta, in Bandung the painters Sjafei Sumardja, Affandi and Hendra Gunawan were working. Later, Sjafei Sumardja would become known as a prominent arts educator, while the others were recognised as important painters.

With the arrival of the Japanese occupation in Indonesia (1942–45), the painters faced a new reality. The Japanese military government, in its efforts to 'foster an Eastern culture' in order to 'advance a Greater East Asian people' saw it as necessary to mobilise cultural workers and artists towards 'achieving the final victory of the war'.[8]

Hence, in 1945[9] they established the Keimin Bunka Shidoso (Cultural Centre), which provided a vehicle for artistic activities. Indonesian painters utilised this opportunity to train themselves and practise their burgeoning talents, at the same time introducing new painting styles to the broader community. Eventually the leaders of Indonesia themselves provided a place in which painters could practise, in the POETERA (Pusat Tenaga Rakyat or Centre for the People's Power).

In the cultivation of painting during this Japanese era, Sudjojono, Agus Djaja and Affandi had important roles. A number of other painters also emerged during this time, including Otto Djaja, Kartono Yudhokusomo, Henk Ngantung, Djajengasmoro, Basuki Resobowo, Baharudin, Soebanto Soeriosoebandrio, Rusli, Barli, Mochtar Apin, Dullah, Harijadi, Hendra Gunawan, Kusnadi, Kerton, Trubus and others.

The political and military upheaval that followed the Proclamation of Indonesian Independence in 1945 did not stop painting. Most painters and political leaders believed that painting had a role in the struggle. The government's shift from Jakarta to Yogyakarta in 1946 was followed by the migration of painters, and Yogyakarta became a centre for painting activity.

---

8 See the speeches of the top brass of *Keimin Bunka Shidoso* at the inauguration of the office bearers. Published in the magazine *Keboedayaan Timoer*, 1/2603.

9 Editors' note: Antariksa's research into collectivism during the Japanese occupation shows this date to be incorrect: 'Keimin Bunka Shidōsho was established in April 1943 as an auxiliary organisation of the Sendenbu, or the Propaganda Department'. See 'Cross-Cultural Counterparts: The Role of Keimin Bunka Shidosho in Indonesian Art, 1942–1945', Nusantara Archive, accessed 27 March 2021, www.heath.tw/nml-article/cross-cultural-counterparts-the-role-of-keimin-bunka-shidosho-in-indonesian-art-1942-1945/?lang=en. POETERA was in fact established prior to Keimin Bunka Shidōsho, on 9 March 1943. Ethan Mark, *Japan's Occupation of Java in the Second World War: A Transnational History* (Bloomsbury Publishing, 2018), 242, doi.org/10.5040/9781350022225.

In Yogyakarta, Affandi, Rusli, Hendra and Harijadi formed the Seni Rupa Masyarakat (People's Art) collective in 1946. A year later, in 1947, they joined with Sudjojono in Seniman Indonesia Muda (Young Indonesian Artists, or SIM), which was formed in Madiun in 1946, but moved to Surakarta in 1947 and eventually to Yogyakarta in 1948.[10] SIM comprised many painters, among them Suromo, Surono, Abdul Salam, Sudibio, Kartono Yudhokusumo, Basuki Resobowo, Oesman Effendi, Srihadi Soedarsono and Zaini.

The painters of SIM made paintings about the struggle, among them many paintings as large as 2 x 3 metres; they also made posters, held exhibitions and published the cultural magazine *Seniman* (Artist), which attracted writers like Wiratmo Soekito, Usmar Ismail, Anas Makruf and Trisno Sumardjo into SIM's orbit of activities. Trisno Sumardjo was even inspired to paint.

In 1945 Djajengasmoro and several of his friends formed the Pusat Tenaga Pelukis Indonesia (Centre for Indonesian Painters' Power, or PTPI). They made paintings for the struggle, posters and banners with the conviction that 'paint, pencil and paper will together with bullets and diplomatic words eradicate the remains of colonialism'.[11]

Due to differences of opinion, in 1947 Hendra [Gunawan] and Affandi left SIM and established Pelukis Rakyat (People's Painters). This collective also included Sudarso, Kusnadi, Sasongko, Trubus, Sumitro, Sudiardjo, Setijoso and others.

During the independence struggle there was an understanding and close connections between political leaders and painters. The Ministry of Information, the Secretariat for Youth Internal Affairs and the Headquarters for the People's Security Force all became supporters of painting by making payments, creating infrastructure and commissioning works. Painters' artworks were bought and collected by the government with the intention to establish the State Museum for the Documentation of the Democratic Struggle of the Republic of Indonesia.

10 Editors' note: for locations of these cities across Java, please see Map 2.

11 'Perdjoeangan PTPI' [PTPI's struggle], in *Revoloesi Pemoeda* [Youth revolution], 25 December 1945.

In this period the performance of painting was not only dominated by the struggle for independence and depictions of ordinary people, but also by the style of Sudjojono and Affandi.[12]

About Affandi

Affandi was born around 1910,[13] in Cirebon. He began making posters for a cinema in Bandung around 1933. In 1938 he joined PERSAGI, and after the war for independence he went around Europe to acquire the experience he felt he needed to develop his painting.

The progression of Affandi's paintings demonstrates intense passion. Although in his early paintings the objects he painted were relatively recognisable, the sense of passion was already evident. Later, the lines of his paintings became more boisterous as time passed, until his later paintings were almost abstract, and the objects that he painted were difficult to recognise.

Affandi's approach to painting can, at its boldest, be seen as a technique that trusts in the power of being overcome by emotion. An electrifying sensation, caused by his interpretation of the selected object, is then poured into the painting without much attention to the rules of painting.

Affandi's way—and those of other styles—underlies a rising conviction that the line/brushstroke is like a note from the emotion of a unique moment that may never be encountered again.

---

12 This is according to the testimony of Rivai Apin in 'Pembicaraan Lukisan' [Discussions of painting], *Mimbar Indonesia* [Indonesia forum], 28 August 1948.

13 Editors' note: the date now given in most sources for the artist's birth, including by the authoritative Affandi Museum, is 1907. However, the date of 1910 given by Yuliman is retained here since the chapter is a primary source. The birth date of 1907 is given in the caption for Affandi.

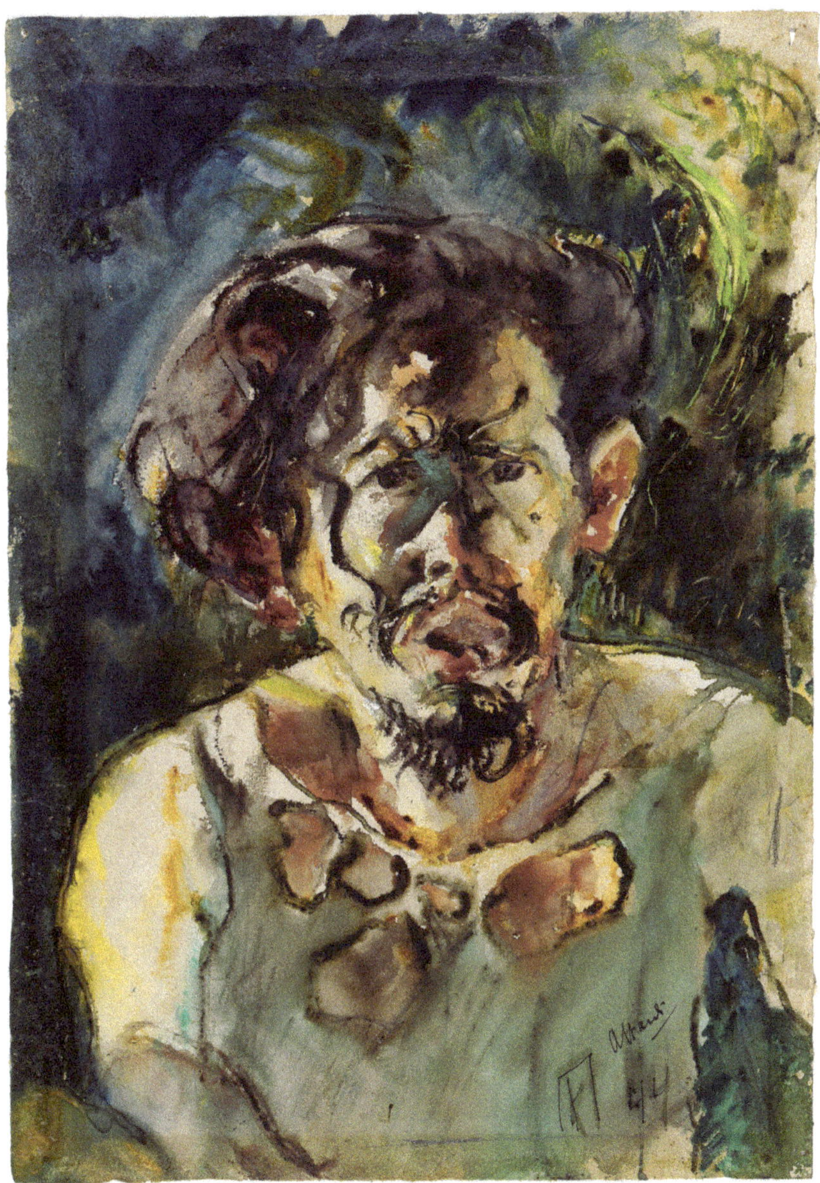

Figure 3.4: Affandi (1907–1990), Indonesia, *Self Portrait*, 1944.

Gouache, watercolour wash, paper, gum Arabic, 50.5 (H) x 32.5 (W) cm. Collection: National Gallery of Australia. Purchased 1994, 1994.1417. Image courtesy National Gallery of Australia, Canberra. Permission: Kartika Affandi and the Affandi Museum.

The involvement of painting in politics during the independence struggle was perpetuated by SIM and Pelukis Rakyat after 1950, with a strong leaning towards communist ideology. Painters who wanted to free painting from politics distanced themselves. Oesman Effendi and Zaini had already left SIM in 1949 and joined the Gabungan Pelukis Indonesia (Indonesian Painters Alliance) founded by Sutiksna and Affandi in Jakarta in 1948. In 1950 Kusnadi, Sumitro and Sasongko left Pelukis Rakyat and formed the Pelukis Indonesia (Indonesian Painters) with other members including Sholihin and Bagong Kusudiardjo.

Unlike SIM, which after 1950 became increasingly inactive, Pelukis Rakyat grew. This collective had close connections with many government figures, so Pelukis Rakyat received many commissions for paintings, sculptures and relief works for government buildings. This group also had close connections with Lembaga Kebudayaan Rakyat (Institute for People's Culture—Lekra) that was founded in 1950 by the Indonesian Communist Party, which had an increasingly strong and broad influence in Indonesia from 1950 to 1965.[14]

To counter this influence, especially after *Manifesto Politik 1959* (Political manifesto 1959, published by Lekra), other political parties also formed cultural institutions, for instance the Indonesian National Party (PNI) formed the Lembaga Kebudayaan Nasional (Institute for National Culture or LKN).

Besides Yogyakarta, before 1950 there were painters' collectives in other towns. We have already mentioned GPI in Jakarta. In Bandung there was Jiva Mukti (Spiritual Release, founded 1948; Barli, Mochtar Apin, Karnedi); in Surabaya Pelangi (Rainbow, 1947; Sularko). Then other collectives emerged. In Yogyakarta: Pelukis Indonesia Muda (Young Indonesian Painters, 1952; Widayat, G. Sidharta, Handrio); Sanggar Bambu (Bamboo Studio, 1959; Soenarto Pr, Muljadi W., Handogo S., Danarto, Arief Soedarsono); Bumi Tarung (Combat Arena, 1959; Amrus Natalsya).

14 Editors' note: at the time of Yuliman's writing, this view that the institute was an affiliate or organ of the Indonesian Communist Party was commonly held and promulgated by the New Order regime. However, the in-depth research of Keith Foulcher strongly supports the perspective 'that there is a history of LEKRA, with its own internal dynamics, quite separate from PKI [the Indonesian Communist Party] political history'. Two leaders of PKI were present at the inaugural meeting of Lekra in 1950 but the other 15 present were 'cultural workers'. See Keith Foulcher, *Social Commitment in Literature and the Arts: The Indonesian 'Institute of People's Culture' 1950–1965* (Centre of Southeast Asian Studies: Monash University, 1986), 17, 19fn37.

In Bandung: Sanggar Seniman (Artists' Studio, 1952; Kartono Yudhokusumo, But Muchtar, Srihadi, A. D. Pirous); Cipta Pancaran Rasa (Create Emotional Outpouring 1952; Angkama Setjadipradja, Abedy). In Jakarta: Lembaga Seniman Yin Hua (Chinese Artists' Yin Hua Institute, 1955; Lee Man-Fong); Matahari (Sun, 1957; Mardian, Wakidjan, Nashar, Alex Wetik); Yayasan Seni dan Design (Foundation for Art and Design, 1958; Oesman Effendi, Trisno Sumardjo, Zaini). In Surakarta: Himpunan Budaya Surakarta (Surakarta Cultural Association; Murdowo). In Surabaya: Prabangkara (1952; Karjono Js) and in a number of other cities such as Madiun, Bukittinggi and Ujungpandang.

These collectives, apart from becoming places where artists could work and exchange ideas, also became places for young artists to study. It should be noted that painting lessons were also offered by the Badan Musyawarah Kebudayaan Nasional (National Consultative Body on Culture, BMKN) in Jakarta (1956) with Oesman Effendi and Zaini as instructors.

A formal educational institute to organise education in painting was only established around 1950. With regard to general education institutions that emphasised the importance of painting and other arts in the educational process, we must mention Taman Siswa (Students' Garden), which was established by Ki Hajar Dewantara in Yogyakarta in 1922 and I.N.S., which was established by Moch. Sjafei in Kayu Tanam, Sumatra, in 1928.

However, an educational institute oriented to painting was established in Bandung in 1947: the Universitaire Leergang tot Opleiding voor Tekenleraren (Tertiary Training for Art Teachers) was headed by Dutch teachers, then later by Sjafei Sumardja from 1951, as a department in the Faculty of Technology in Indonesia University, which from 1959 became the Department of Fine Art in the Bandung Institute of Technology.

Another educational institution was formed in 1950, the Academy of Indonesian Fine Arts (ASRI) in Yogyakarta, gifted with the idealism of the pedagogist A. J. Katamsi. And this institution obtained full status as a tertiary education institute in 1968 as the Indonesia Tertiary Fine Art School Asri (STSRI or 'ASRI').

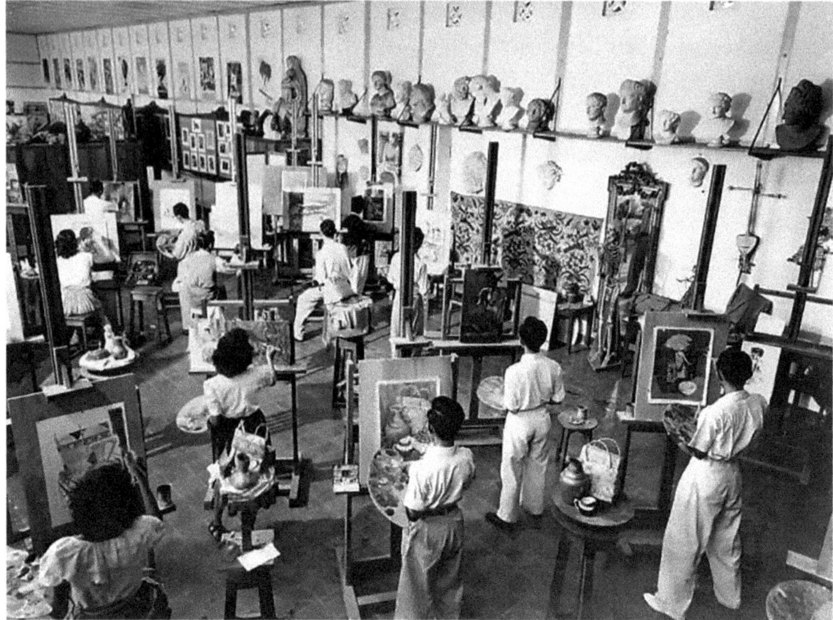

Figure 3.5: Students at the Universitaire Leergang voor Tekenleraren (University Course for Art Teachers), now the Faculty of Art and Design in the Bandung Institute of Technology, c. 1950.

Collection: Tropenmuseum, National Museum of World Cultures (CC BY-SA 3.0).

Basis of Art

There were various individual styles, various perspectives about art evident in painting during the period from 1940 to 1960. However, among this diversity we can see a general framework and within that frame there are more specific tendencies. We can say that painting in the second period was intended to express human experiences and human existence not as had been done in the previous period, which tried to depict a beautiful universe on the canvas. New painters, said Sudjojono in 1939:

> Do not only paint peaceful shelters in the rice fields and the blue mountains … but they also draw the sugar factories and the scrawny farmers, the motorcars of the rich and the trousers of the youth[15] … This is our existence, this is our reality. And painting which breathes this reality … is work that originates

15 Editors' note: alluding to Westernised young men who no longer wore the traditional dress of sarongs.

> from our everyday lives, filtered through the life of the artist, not just coming straight out of everyday life but created and hurled … compelled by an inner coercive force.[16]

Painters observe closely the world that is visible around them. Before they work, their impressions or responses to the outside world must go first automatically into their soul, then a 'psychological process happens internally'. 'Only after this process is complete will the artist paint through the agency of their hand'.[17]

Or as Trisno Sumarjo declared in 1956:

> Painters try to pay attention to everything that is there, moving and growing … the sky, the sea, the land, trees and animals … the gestures of people … those who work in the fields and in the factories or who laze about in the salons of the rich, those who are corrupt and those who struggle. They note the results; a shack or a building, traditional music or a symphony, a disco and a traditional court dance … And they process this with their creativity.

And:

> Through this practice the artist forms a special space for their spiritual lives, because this space represents their own world, it is not conquered by the physical world, which may have a role in the provision of material or 'inspiration' for the cultivation of the spirit.[18]

Indeed, in art of this second period, it seems that there are two positions when it comes to the process of painting.

First, the objective position, that is the world around the painter, the social world and the visible world. From this position, through the senses, comes an impression or a response.

Secondly, the subjective position, that it is the 'inner world' of the painter: their character, temperament, emotions, imagination and all the processes of their spirituality that cultivate and thus change—their impressions and

16 SS101 [sic], 'Kesenian Meloekis di Indonesia, sekarang dan jang akan Datang' [The art of painting in Indonesia, now and in future], *Keboedajaan dan Masyarakat* [Culture and society], no. 6 tahun 1 (October 1939).

17 S. Sudjojono, *Seni Loekis Kesenian dan Seniman* [Painting, art and artists] (Yogyakarta: Penerbit Indonesia Sekarang, 1946), 11.

18 Trisno Sumardjo, 'Kedudukan Seni Rupa Kita' [The position of our arts], *Almanak Seni 1957* (Jakarta: Badan Musyawarah Kebudayaan Nasional [Council for National Culture], 1956).

responses. Sudjojono's proposition spells out: 'painting is the visible soul'. This expression became commonplace among painters, and it was said that painting was 'self-expression', 'emotional expression'.

So in painting there appear various forms that we can recognise as objects in reality: painters depict things, but in painting the form of the object is changed by the painter's liberty to work with their own, diverse subjective powers. Furthermore, the object, or various parts of the objects can be arranged in new relationships, or even in a way that contradicts what we know of reality.

Characteristics of Style

Within this general framework there are several more specific tendencies.

First Tendency

The biggest is that painters look at their objects, then paint them directly or make sketches that are then developed into paintings. Their work is triggered by emotions that are associated with that object. They tend to distort the form of the object, its shape, proportions, colour. This happens because of the close connection between emotions and distortion. Peoples' emotions are easily moved by things that diverge from what they expect, things that are not as they should be, not normal, including form. In painting, distortion becomes a way to evoke and express emotion.

Emotions are also associated with tension and movement. In painting, strong emotions will create tension and movement in the hands of the painter, and in the impression that is recorded in forms on the canvas. Distortion itself—forms that become longer or shorter, or which are twisted—suggest the workings of powers that pull or push. Furthermore the painter tends to the dynamic arrangement of form, which is supported by lines and firm brushstrokes, as well as those that float or bend, are all features in the paintings we are discussing here. In the painters' working method, colours are mixed on the canvas and tend to be subdued; this is a feature of many paintings of the time.

Of course painters are not only moved to emotion by objects. They may be moved mostly because of the meaning of the object, its connection with their experiences and ideas, which can be associated with social life, or the life of the individual. In the period of development after 1940, many painters were interested in social experience, and many took diverse aspects of the lives of the people around them as subjects to paint. To name a few: Sudjojono, Affandi, Hendra [Gunawan], Surono, Henk Ngantung, Otto Djaja, Dullah, Harijadi, Trubus, Tarmizi, Amrus Natalsya and more—most of these were members of SIM and Pelukis Rakyat.

Emotional expressions were diverse. They could be tense and fierce, for instance from Sudjojono before 1950 and Affandi; most of the paintings from the independence struggle also exhibit these tendencies, for instance the works of Henk Ngantung and Dullah, around 1947. But there was also joy and celebration, as in the works of Hendra, or humour as in some of Hendra's work and in that of Otto Djaja.

However in this period there were not a few painters who tend to express their experiences in a more individual way, tending to expressions of personal emotions or sentiments. These artists rarely—or never—depicted social life. Examples of these artists are Basuki Resobowo, Rusli, Sholihin, Kusnadi, Oesman Effendi, Zaini, Nashar and others.

Second Tendency

Aside from emotional styles, there was also a broader tendency to more objective styles. Painters wanted to act as objective observers, and thus did not want to allow emotion to distort what they were looking at. Some painters swung between this and the aforementioned first tendency, including Sudjojono, Henk Ngantung, Harijadi, Dullah and Trubus.

In the developments of the period 1940–69, some critics were concerned to note that 'modern painting' was difficult for the broader community to understand. They advised painters to only paint 'realistic' works, in the sense of becoming objective observers and documenters.

Sudjojono himself declared in 1949 that artists should 'Go to realism', which gave rise to a polemic with Trisno Sumardjo. But among the painters of this 'realist movement' only Sudjojono and Trubus could really be said to have implemented this proclamation. However, in about 1960 Trubus revealed works that deviated from realism, and a considerable number of the works that Sudjojono exhibited in 1968 also showed a similar style.

Several communist critics, especially after President Sukarno's Political Manifesto of 1959, attacked the shift to abstraction in Indonesian painting, and promoted 'realism'. In spite of this, painters who were under the umbrella of the Lembaga Kebudayaan Rakyat (Institute of People's

Culture, an organ of the Communist Party of Indonesia)[19]—for instance the members of the Pelukis Rakyat at the time—generally continued to use various styles that were not, or were even a long way from, 'realism'.

Third Tendency

There was also a greater tendency to subjectivity. There were paintings that demonstrated qualities of fantasy. Here we use the word fantasy to refer generally to various internal [imaginative] processes such as imagination, reverie, dreams, myths and so on. Psychology shows that these processes are meaningful and connected to reality, but what emerges from these processes is organised according to a logic than differs from that of reality as we know it in our conscious state. Fantasy can create images that are pleasant, and others that are frightening and terrifying. But all of this emerges from internal tensions that may be sub- or even unconscious, and that seek resolution through irrational processes.

These fantastical paintings reveal to us the logic of fantasy, not the logic of reality. Sudjojono's *Sayang Kita Bukan Anjing* (*It's a Pity We're Not Dogs*, 1943) depicting two dogs with human heads, is a fantasy. So too is Harijadi's *Biografi II di Malioboro*[20] (*Biography II on Malioboro*, 1947), which shows people in a scene assembled not according to the laws of space in reality, but with people flying around. In paintings like these, we can still recognise objects, but different objects—or with various parts of them arranged in relationships that diverge from those we're familiar with in reality. These arrangements follow the logic of fantasy.

Painters who exhibit this tendency to styles that embrace fantasy include Agus Djaja, Sudibio, Sukirno, Handrio (before 1958) and Sudiardjo.

Fourth Tendency

The fourth tendency is towards decorative styles. In these paintings we recognise objects (trees, leaves) but their forms are stylised, turned into patterns. Characteristics of this style include lines or the impression of lines (because every shape must be clearly delineated), repetitive rhythms (because of repetition or the alignment of patterned elements) and neat and controlled compositions. In this tendency Kartono Yudhokusumo painted a perspective view of the guerrilla arena in Wonosari (1947),

19 Editors' note: see fnt 14 for clarification of this erroneous claim.

20 Editors' note: the main street in Yogyakarta.

a view of Dieng (1949) and even Bandung. In many of his paintings after 1950, Hendra seemed to move towards stylisation and a preference for the decorative traditions of Indonesia. Then came Batara Lubis—a painter who was deeply interested in decorative forms and who admired Kartono Yudhokusumo. He painted various scenes of the lives of the people in this style. We could say that this tendency to the decorative style spread from Hendra and Batara Lubis to other painters in Yogyakarta, like Widayat, Alibasyah and Bagong Kusudiardjo.

With these developments, the decorative style took another path. Painters did not stylise a particular object as a model in front of them (as did Kartono and Batara Lubis), but instead arranged various visual elements (line, colour, etc) to become shapes that only reminded people of objects in a general way, for instance a person, but not a portrait of a specific person. This is evident in paintings by Abas Alibasyah, Widayat and Suparto. We could say that these developments represent a shift from depiction (which refers to a specific individual object) to metaphor (which refers to a generalised concept). Thus the objective camp, which we mentioned at the outset, that is the external and visible world, the world of impressions or visual responses that are gleaned from the world around the painter, moved further away. Here the tendency to abstraction is even greater.

Towards Abstract Painting, 1955–60

In mentioning a broader tendency to abstraction, in fact we have broached the fifth tendency of the second period. However, this tendency points to a more important issue, which is the characteristics of the shift to the third period.

This tendency emerged particularly among a number of painters in Bandung, Jakarta and Yogyakarta. In Bandung there was Ahmad Sadali, Mochtar Apin, Srihadi, Popo Iskandar, But Muchtar and Jusuf Affendy. In Jakarta there was Oesman Effendi. In Yogyakarta there was G. Sidharta, Fadjar Sidik, Handrio and Abas Alibasyah.

In Bandung, this began with Sadali in 1953. Painters remodelled the form of objects into flat motifs, which was achieved by intersecting straight and curved lines. The whole painting was created with lines dividing up the surface of the canvas, as well as colours that evenly filled the geometrical fields created by the intersection of lines. Thus what was immediately apparent in the painting, or what dominated one's vision, was an arrangement of colourful lines and geometric fields, with the form of the object 'submerged' under this network.

Around the same time in Jakarta, Oesman Effendi divided the form of objects with lines and geometric fields too, so that, to borrow the words of a critic who was disappointed with Oesman Effendi's exhibition in 1957, it seemed that 'we are merely seized by a constructivist arrangement of lines, colours and fields'.[21]

In Yogyakarta, academic education at ASRI and exhibitions of works by Bandung painters in 1955 and 1958 prompted several painters to pursue abstraction more enthusiastically. This tendency was strengthened by G. Sidharta's return from his studies in the Netherlands in 1958. Sidharta arranged various shapes, fields, colours, lines and textures. These arrangements very much remind the viewer of the objects that we recognise in reality, but their shapes have been dissected, deconstructed and flattened.

Approaching 1960, Handrio quickly grasped the concept that painting, through the arrangement of its elements, could be a kind of 'visual music'. He tried working with this concept around 1963–64. He abstracted and reshaped musical instruments into geometric arrangements. For Fadjar Sidik, 1957–58 was a critical period. Through his observations of the developments in society around him, he became suspicious of styles that merely followed the general tendencies outlined above.

In 1960 he made a number of sketches, vignettes and paintings by arranging flat motifs together with quite clear basic geometric shapes, and which seemed to move in the space like living creatures. Often a motif will bring up a memory of various kinds of living beings including humans, animals and plants. Approaching 1960, the decorative style in Yogyakarta progressed with larger abstract works like those from the oeuvre of Widayat (from 1955) and Abas Alibasyah, as mentioned above.

So, while in earlier tendencies painters depicted objects, however distorted, stylised or manifested through fantasy, in this fifth tendency painters created forms freely. The reference to objects could be said to be merely a 'hold' on the idea in the midst of an abstract arrangement of shapes, or

21 Basuki Resobowo, 'Tugas Seni Membuka Mata dan Hati' [The task of art is to open eyes and hearts], *Siasat* 1 (Mei 1957).

just a pebble cast to begin painting. Painters created visual arrangements expressive of emotions (lyricism), and to satisfy their feelings about form (aesthetics).

This fifth tendency took painting outside of the framework of the general tendencies in the second period mentioned earlier. It revealed a new direction and thus prepared the way for subsequent developments.

This new development was the emergence of abstract painting in Indonesia. But this development must not induce us to ignore an important aspect of the history of painting in Indonesia, that of continuity.

Continuity is not just evident in the stages that distance the visible outside world, but also primarily in a kind of 'artistic ideology'. What this means is a shared complexity of thought, attitude and emotion, which becomes the shared basis for different individual practices, and which endorses diverse kinds of practice.

There are two important elements in this artistic ideology, first, respect for the painter as an individual who is free to create their own form and style. Of course, there is a force that opposes this, but this respect remains strong and widespread among painters. The second element is the belief, which, due to the communication among painters in the *sanggar* (atelier), at meetings and in educational institutions, has become a kind of teaching, that the elements of form and their arrangement, regardless of the object they depict, can give rise to, realise, or express valuable artistic emotions, sensations or experiences.

Sudjojono already believed—in the PERSAGI era, and also in subsequent years—that painting was the 'visible soul': that that character would appear in the quality of the brushwork, colours and shapes that appear in the formal elements and their arrangement and also that, therefore, painters could create major works even if they depicted small or insignificant objects.[22]

22 See a collection of S. Sudjojono's essays in *Seni Loekis, Kesenian dan Seniman* [Painting, art and artists] (Yogyakarta: Penerbit Indonesia Sekarang, 1946).

Later, around 1949, Basuki Resobowo proposed a similar perspective even more emphatically. He said: in order to see painting one needs visual powers, so that one can respond emotionally to the shapes, lines and colours 'without needing to think too much about what the object is intended to be'.[23]

Nashar said it more succinctly: 'With regards to Artistry, it's not a matter of what is being painted, but how'.[24]

This artistic ideology is what became the resistance to the growth of 'realism' and, conversely, the basis for the endorsement of the various kinds of distortion that appeared in painting after PERSAGI. It also became the basis for a larger tendency to abstraction from 1955 to 1960 and in many of the paintings since then. Finally, this ideology became fertile ground for the emergence of abstract painting.

Third Period, after 1960

Of course, all the styles we have discussed previously can be found after 1960. But what marked this third period was the growth of abstract painting.

Overtures to Abstract Painting

The term 'abstract' has several meanings. Here we use it to refer to a type of painting that does not depict forms that we know as objects or things that we can see in our surrounding reality: people, animals, plants, landscapes and so on. Paintings in this style don't depict objects (hence they are called 'non-objective abstracts') or paint figures (hence they are also called 'nonfigurative abstracts').

Of course this doesn't mean that abstract painting does not have any connection at all to the forms we recognise. Both painters and viewers of paintings live in a world of forms. The shape of humans, animals, trees, rice fields and mountains are a part of that world of form, and it is this that is usually painted. But there are also other shapes/forms. The earth can

23 Basuki Resobowo, 'Pahatan Kaju dan Sket-sket dari Soeromo dan S. Soendoro' [Wooden sculptures and sketches by Soeromo and S. Soendoro], *Indonesia*, June 1949.

24 *Pameran Lukisan-lukisan: Nashar, Oesman Effendi, Trisno Sumardjo, Zaini, 12–31 Maret 1963* [Painting exhibition: Nashar, Oesman Effendi, Trisno Sumardjo, Zaini, 12–31 March 1963], exhibition introduction.

be seen from an aircraft, objects can be observed very closely (the surface of the land, or a stone for example) or we can look at objects through a microscope (micro-organisms, cells networks arranged like crystals, and so on), revealing to us a wealth of diverse visual forms.

There are also man-made forms: the shapes created by architects, mechanics, civil engineers etc. And finally there are forms that we find in mathematics, those made with rulers, compasses and so on. Our reception of this diverse world of forms, both physiological and psychological—occurs against the background of our experiences of form—an important factor in how we experience abstract paintings. The best preparation for 'understanding' or 'enjoying' abstract painting is the wealth and depth of our experience in this diverse world of visual forms.

Period of Growth in Abstract Painting

We have already mentioned a number of painters who showed a greater tendency to abstraction approaching the 1960s. All of them leaned towards abstract painting in the period after 1960; some for a moment, and others who continued their exploration of the style.

SRIHADI, in 1960, left behind the style that had occupied him up to that point, which he felt was 'too cold'. He left behind the discipline of geometry and depictions of objects and made two kinds of experiment. In the first experiment the canvas carried an explosion of bright colours. In another experiment he stuck pieces of paper on the canvas and then mixed these with spontaneous sweeps of colour. From this experiment, Srihadi produced an abstract painting. Thus, abstract painting emerged in the development of new Indonesian painting. But for Srihadi it was fleeting. He painted this way only from 1960 to 1962.

About Srihadi

> Srihadi became familiar with the work of 'painting' during the war in 1947, as a volunteer he sketched important events. He was born in Solo, in 1931, and here he gathered with Sudjojono, Affandi and others who were in SIM at the time. Indirectly he gained an education in painting from these painters.[25]

25 Editors' note: Srihadi died in 2022.

> In 1953 he studied in Bandung (now the Department of Art in the Bandung Institute of Technology). Here he learned to paint through the arrangement of lines, colours and space in a painting. In Srihadi's paintings from this time there are a number of large lines that are arranged rhythmically, neatly. The object became unimportant, and in its place emerged harmoniously arranged colours.
>
> Three or four years of painting later, Srihadi felt painting was dead and only depicted the sweet and beautiful. He felt trapped. The dynamism he felt in the past, in his paintings, made Srihadi want to animate his paintings. So from 1959 he began to reduce the lines in his works. Then in 1960–61, he painted free and dynamic scribbles with transparent colours. And here, through developing the 'concept' of painting, Srihadi produced 'abstract' painting.
>
> Srihadi didn't stick to his encounter with abstraction for long, after 1962, through dots of colour in his paintings, he found forms that resembled figures: so Srihadi returned to painting objects, including the horizon. In 1971 he even added the element of story to his paintings.

A. SADALI, in 1963, left behind geometric painting. His canvases depicted wide, bright colours and referenced no objects at all. In subsequent developments, Sadali's canvases depicted sombre colours like ochre, deep blue and black. Texture began to play an important role. These textures appeared as if they were result of much effort and many natural processes; stretching and wrinkling, cracking and breaking, peeling and tearing, erosion and weathering, processes of aging and destruction.

In Sadali's painting from this period there are no strong, wide brushstrokes that record the energy and emotion of the painter, and that activate our attention. All of the cracking and texture, the many scribbles and trembling, short scratches make every surface of Sadali's paintings rich, challenging us to examine it calmly and closely, to be still and to contemplate. Obsolescence and strain, age and excess are indeed matters that should make us reflect. More so if Sadali places lustrous trickles of gold and gold leaf on his canvases or shapes that we can read as symbols:

a verse of holy text in Arabic script, a black cube that reminds us of the Kaabah, mountain shapes (*kekayon* = the tree of life) or movement from bottom to top (vertical).

Sadali's attention to texture as an element of great importance in his paintings was achieved by using thick paint and sometimes attaching pieces of cloth to his canvas. These increasingly prominent textures brought his work into a state of relief. From around 1970, Sadali attached thick padding to his canvases.

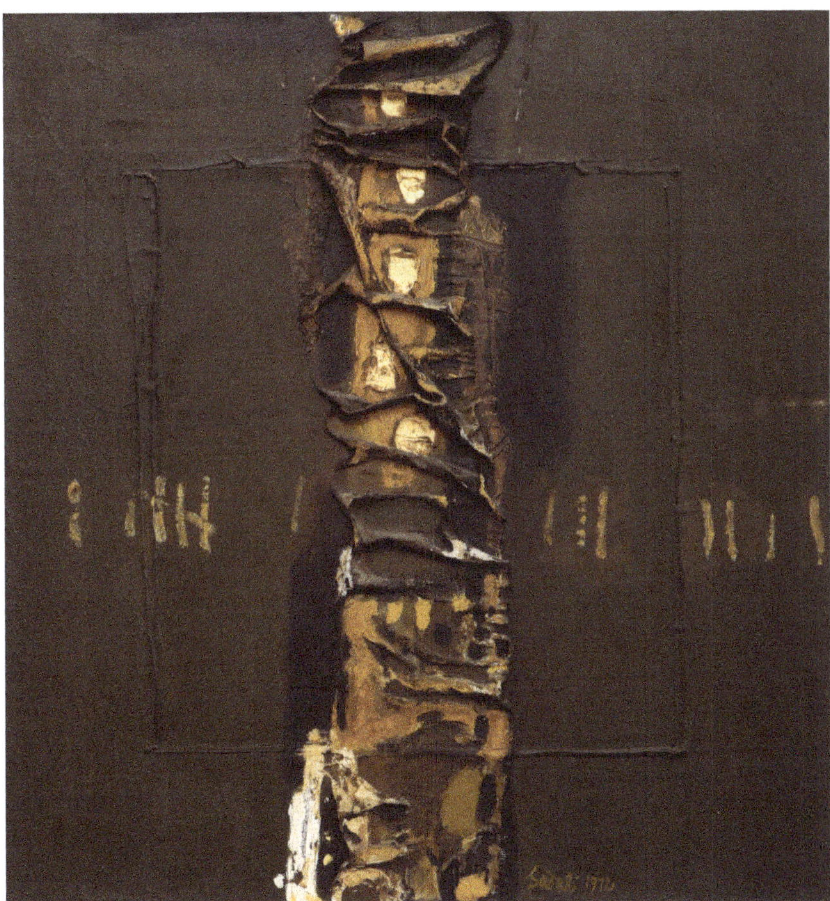

Figure 3.6: Ahmad Sadali, *Untitled 28*, 1974.

Oil on canvas, 65 x 65 cm. Image with permission of the artist's family. Photograph by Adi Rahmatullah.

FADJAR SIDIK, in 1963, produced abstract paintings in the form of geometric arrangements. However his more important abstract paintings were made after 1968.

As mentioned above, in 1960 Fadjar Sidik made a number of small sketches and vignettes, in the form of motifs composed from circles, triangles and so on, with these parts forming the shape of animals, humans and plants. After 1968 he discarded all these fantastical creatures. He then composed simple shapes based on circles, half circles and crescents, triangles, trapeziums, parallelograms and so on. Tens of shapes like this were lined up and scattered across the picture plane with bright, even hues of blue, red and yellow.

Fadjar created quite stunning degrees of irregularity because he always included variations in each basic shape and in their positions. In this way he avoided exactitude and precision, eschewing geometric rigour and mathematical systems. His paintings have elements of the feeling of nature (shapes in the form of moons, rocks, degrees of irregularity), and the living world (the shapes and rhythms of leaves). With these associations, Fadjar Sidik was able to achieve lyricism.

HANDRIO, in 1963–64 made abstractions and distortions of musical instruments. In 1965 he left the instruments behind and his paintings became arrangements of flat shapes and geometric forms. In subsequent developments he created illusions of space with these geometric forms. The results, like those apparent in his work from 1968, were a kind of construction that resembled architecture. Complex and dynamic geometric spaces intertwined seamlessly and endlessly to give emotional and symbolic overtones to Handrio's paintings. And indeed, Handrio gave the title *Labirin* (*Labyrinth*) to his works (1968).

OESMAN EFFENDI, who around 1960 painted abstractions that were a long way from natural forms, began abstract painting in 1968. Contrast, harmony and variations in curved lines, brightly coloured spots pressed into the canvas. All of this forms an open composition with elements that move freely and rhythmically. Oesman Effendi's paintings are like musical compositions. Titles like *Alam Perahu* (*The World of Boats*), *Pemandangan* (*View*) and so on, show how the painter saw his own paintings, or indicate the experience that his art drew on. Paintings like this have become lyrical experiences, about nature, or life, without painting nature or objects from life itself.

Many painters expressed their experiences of nature without painting objects from nature itself. They depend on the expressive power of visual elements and their arrangement. Even so, often, through division of the picture plane to form a horizon, through colours that are impure and rich with nuance, through the marks of texture, through the irregularity and variation of shapes and their arrangements, these paintings depicted forms that appeared to have their prototypes in nature. The painters didn't paint nature, but the paintings had associations with, and the feeling of nature.

In this category we find the paintings of But Muchtar, Mochtar Apin, A. D. Pirous and Jusuf Affendy in the period 1968–69.

A. D. PIROUS took Arabic calligraphy as his main subject for painting from 1970. Here we find paintings that take another art form as their source of expression: the art of writing in Arabic on manuscripts and tombstones, as is frequently found in Aceh, where Pirous was born. Sometimes Pirous takes a holy verse and tries to distil its meaning through all the elements of his painting. Sometimes he may only take the movement and rhythm of that calligraphy.

We don't intend to speak about abstract painters one by one. The main purpose of the discussion above is to provide a picture of some of the styles that have emerged in Indonesia since 1960.

We have indicated that the third period, that is the period from around 1960, was the time in which abstract painting in Indonesia developed. From the way that we delineate these periods, it is clear that the intention is not to declare that there was only abstract painting during this third period. However, at the very least, we can say abstract painting was the strongest realisation or manifestation [of painting], and in developments after 1960 it appears to have been particularly prominent.

The emergence of abstract painting redirected painters' attention from a focus on aspects of experience that were tied to the presence of objects or things: views, people in the market, trees, boats and so on, towards a focus on more abstract experiences.

The experience that was 'transmitted' through Sadali's paintings, for instance, was not an event from the social realm, or an experience of a fragment of the landscape, or an emotional expression that he was moved to by such things. What was conveyed was the experience that was evoked by looking at the process of destruction and decay and in nature and life; not the destruction and decay of this or that object, but the process of destruction itself. When Oesman Effendi painted *Alam Perahu* or *Pemandangan*, his attention was not drawn to an experience that was bound to or glued to the form of a boat or a view. He was interested in the aspects of the experience that are more essential, more musical. Thus, as we have seen, many painters express their experience of nature without painting objects in nature itself.

The stimulus that shifted attention to more abstract experiences was also what lay behind the strength of the increased tendency to abstraction after 1960.

Popo Iskandar immediately comes to mind. This painter continued to take lyrical and existential experiences of nature as his starting point and he also maintained a relationship with particular objects from nature: the beach, a glimpsed landscape, flowers, cats, bamboo. However after 1970 he expressed his lyrical experiences with as few expressive tools as possible (as little colour and line as possible, etc). Thus the bamboo becomes white curved lines on a white field.

Several other painters worked on paintings that began as improvisations without thought of a particular subject. Then, if a form emerged, they developed that form as much or as little as was needed to take our thoughts to an object with which we're familiar, even though that is never as clear as the objects in paintings prior to 1960. Among those painters were A. D. Pirous, Jusuf Affendy and Rustam Arief, in the period 1960–70, as well as Amri Yahya, D. A. Peransi and others.

There were also painters, in this third period, who created 'abstract fantasies'. A 'world' inhabited by animated objects and figures was created on the canvas, although their identities were obscure. A fantasy far from the world as we know it. This can be seen in the paintings of O. H. Supono.

This new freedom of which we speak, also meant freedom to line up, or gather on the same platform, images of objects that originate in different realities. For instance, images from the world of things and images from the world of symbols and signs. This appeared, for instance, in some of Srihadi's painting, and some of the works of young painters like Siti Adiyati, and more so in works by Suatmadji, who collected images that not only came from different realities, but also different styles.

Freed from ties to objects, painters explored different arts and different experiences. Painters could even develop their sensitivity to diverse ranges of experiences, building new perspectives and looking at various 'realms of experience' simultaneously. Thus it is as if we are asked to quickly jump from one world to another from one different style in one experience, all in one painting.

We could say that this period nurtured numerous kinds of new sensibilities with more multifaceted characteristics, and explorations of more complex experiences. The push in this direction explains why the changing styles of painters after PERSAGI were more dynamic than those of older painters. Compared to the changing styles of Sadali, Srihadi and Fadjar Sidik, the stylistic developments of Sudjojono, Affandi and Hendra [Gunawan?] feel static.

From the explanation above, it seems sufficiently clear that we have witnessed an experiment in experience, and this also means an experiment in form. Various forms have been explored, tested. Compared to painters in preceding periods, painters during this third phase evidently found intrigue and pleasure in visual elements and their various possibilities. For many young painters, the problem of form seems to have a primary role. In the paintings of Aming Prayitno, for instance, there are times when he only experiments with texture. Experimenting in this third period meant experimenting with materials and techniques.

Painting no longer alone means brushing paint over a canvas; a painter might attach pieces of paper, fabric, glass, metal and so on. Painters sew, weld, puncture the canvas and so on. Painters can act as assemblers and attach all kinds of objects and material with very advanced technology, as we see in works by Saptohudoyo. A number of other painters have experimented with the [wax-resist] technique of batik, including Abas Alibasyah, Amri Yahya, Bagong Kusudiardjo, Mudjita, Mustika and others.

A 'spirit of experimentation' is perhaps the correct expression with which to refer to this important impulse in painting after 1960. Mochtar Apin was a painter who clearly demonstrated this. He delved into several styles simultaneously over a short period of time. Perhaps this is a sign of restlessness in explorations of experience. For Mochtar Apin, creating a work is not based on a known starting point, but a process that develops slowly and haltingly, with the intention of giving form to something in the subconscious. And all of this activity is experimental.[26]

General Critiques of the Third Period

Abstract painting in this third period, although featuring many variations, is united by one characteristic: lyricism. It is all an expression of the painter's emotions and sensations in experiencing the world. A painting is an expressive field, a place where it is as if painters 'project' their emotions and the beating of their feelings, recording the life of their soul. The painting is thus seen as a realm of imagination that has its own purpose, an imaginary or *irreal* world.

The world that appears in the picture plane is not connected to and is not even a conduit from the real-concrete world in which we who view the painting exist. It occupies a virtual world. As if to strengthen this imaginary plane the painting is contained with a frame, 'isolating' itself on the wall. In this way it presents forms that are not pictures of objects we know from our surroundings, but a world of imagination, that inside the realm of the picture frame is seen as an incarnation of the painter's emotions and inner being in experiencing nature and the real world. A painting is an imaginative world, a lyrical world. Inside it, emotions are filtered and made manifest.

However, in this third period, we should note other phenomena among a number of young artists that go against this lyricism. These appeared around 1970. This anti-lyricism appears in two types.

In the first type, associations with nature and life, as well as emotions, are pushed aside. Of course there are feelings here, that is to say forms, or, in this case, a feeling of mathematical order, and rationality in form. Paintings become the arrangement of two or three simple geometric shapes that are repeated and arranged according to mathematical principles. These appear in paintings by B. Munni Ardhi, Harsono and Nanik Mirna in 1970–73. In other matters, painting is research, analysis, measuring and calculating, in the service of finding and revealing optical indicators within systematic structures, as in the paintings of Anyool Subroto and Sugeng Santosa.

26 See the catalogue *Pameran Grup 18; 18–27 Agustus 1971, Jakarta* (Jakarta: Group 18 Exhibition, 1971).

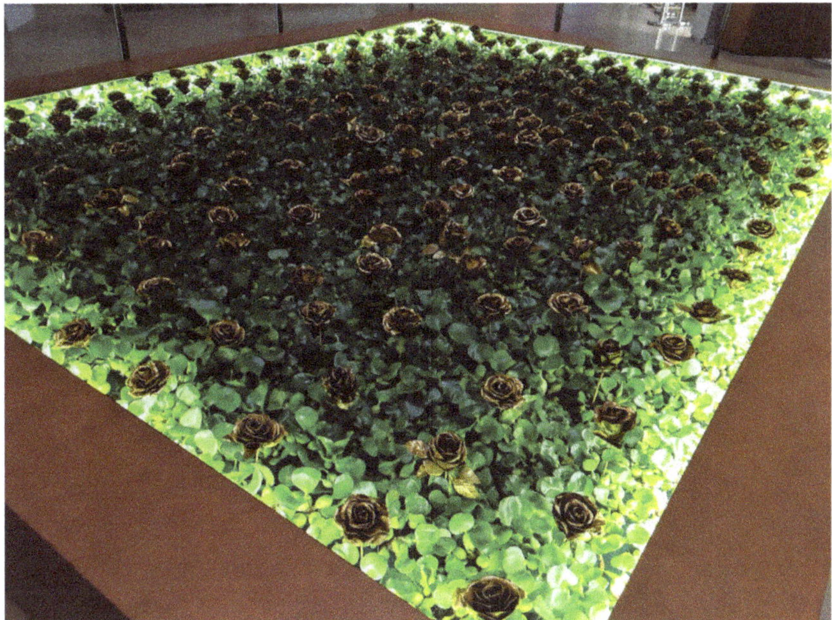

Figure 3.7: Siti Adiyati, *Eceng Gondok Berbunga Emas* (*Water Hyacinth with Golden Roses*), 1979, remade in 2017.

Pond, water hyacinths and plastic flowers, dimensions variable. Collection: the artist. © Siti Adiyati, image with the artist's permission.[27]

In 1973 Danarto exhibited a number of large blank canvases in geometric shapes, without frames. In this experiment painting became the viewer's own environment, forming a spatial place that exists and moves. Painting is no longer a fragment of an imagined world isolated on the wall, contained with a frame and contemplated from a distance. Painting becomes a concrete structural environment of its own, in which the viewer can observe and move. As Danarto said, he intended his work to be 'simultaneously architecture, painting and sculpture'. Danarto can be seen as bridging pure form (dissociated from nature and life, without emotion) and anti-lyricism of the second type.

In this second type, anti-lyricism appears in tendencies to the actual and the concrete. If lyricism filters and transforms experiences and emotions into the imaginary world, then in this tendency it is as if the artist is avoiding that filtering and transformation. It is not a picture of objects

27 Editors' note: see Chapter 8 for a more extended discussion of the artist's works and the context of this installation work.

that we look at, but the objects themselves on display. It is not a feeling of disgust that is filtered and satisfies the imagination, but rather a real and immediate sensation of disgust that is presented directly, without distancing it, which makes people turn away in disgust.

The experience is intended to achieve the most concrete and actual form possible. Art works are not a slice of the imaginary world to be contemplated at a distance, but a concrete object that physically involves the viewer. This was apparent in the *Pameran Seni Lukis 74* (Painting exhibition 74; B. Munni Ardhi, Harsono, Nanik Mirna) and *Pameran Seni Rupa 75* (Fine art exhibition 75; Jim Supangkat, Hardi, Harsono, B. Munni Ardhi, Siti Adiyati and others). If we must call their works 'paintings' it should be noted that their work is not 'painting' in the usual sense.

Background to New Indonesian Painting

Works of art are born from the soul of the artist, through processing media, that is working with materials, tools and particular techniques. It is unquestionable that the work of art often depicts things particular and unique to the individual. But the soul of the artist, from which the work of art is born, grows and takes its form, is a matrix in which all the forces of history are at work. Here is where the connection that brings together the issues of the artist with those who are not artists. And it also results in the impression of a connection between one concept from a tendency and a concept from another tendency.

New Indonesian Art, which has grown in Indonesia, just like art in general, cannot wholly be understood without locating it in the context of the larger framework of Indonesian society and culture. In other words, without locating it within the whole force of history.

Several historical powers are at work in the development of New Indonesian Painting.

First, cultural heritage. Basically, cultural heritage is part of the formation of a person's character, which is the basis of their relationship with the reality around them, and in this lies the spiritual connection between human intuition, human emotions and an unformulated reality. This connection, in Indonesia [now] and even more so in the past is not an empirical, rational, straightforward and objective one. Indonesian society, despite changes that have taken place this century (especially in larger cities, where painting has developed), still appears to retain elements of the old culture.

To mention several of these characteristics, there is evident pleasure in the awesome, a tendency to depict something weird and supernatural, and to approach it via the mysterious. In visual art one of the clearest roles for cultural heritage is in the painting that we call 'decorative style'. This has long occurred although with different bases.

Another is the power of history, which comes through social events and phenomena that take place around the artist, social life in upheaval, the struggle for the nation, the destruction of the integrity of traditional communal society, a national consciousness that motivates change, upheaval and reform and the aspirations of society; all of this creates a spiritual climate that is tense and anxious. This is reflected in the second style of painting. The growth of national consciousness that triggered the Youth Pledge of 1928 was also a social phenomenon that strongly influenced the advent of New Indonesian Painting. It manifested an enthusiasm for the creation of new art that differed from the traditional art that existed in regional cultures, and also a passion for showing the world that Indonesia as a nation could create its own painting.

The influence of the West was a reality that also had historical force. The colonial period, for instance, created contact between Indonesian painting at the point of its formation, and Western painting. Then, advances in global communication and the mixing of world civilisations resulted in visual art becoming a specific issue. Hence we see in the development of New Indonesian Painting an eagerness to seek new possibilities in the world of art through the history of the development of Western, European, Modern, Indonesian Art, systematically arranged in that order.

However not all of what is in Western painting was influential in Indonesia. The painters of the second period, for instance, were familiar with the various painting styles of the West, but they didn't make use of all of them. The most popular Western painter was Vincent van Gogh, the pioneer of expressionism who lived in the nineteenth century. Another example was the analytical, rational and geometric style of painting that had grown in the West since the beginning of the twentieth century but was not adopted by even one Indonesian painter until the years approaching 1960 when the influence of this style began to appear. Only after 1970 do we begin to see the influence of the West. The process of social change in Indonesia and the spiritual climate that accompanied it, explains this kind of 'selectivity'.

New painting that grew in Indonesia was, in every way 'Indonesian Painting'. Which is to say it was formed through the powers of Indonesian history. Of course this was yet to attain a stable existence, because it rested on supports that remained weak. It was confined to big cities and there even further confined to small sections of the educated and wealthy.

However, in spite of this, painting institutions, while not strong, proliferated. The number of educational institutions for artists grew, most important among them STSRI 'Asri' in Yogyakarta, the Department of Visual Art in ITB [Bandung Institute of Technology], and the Academy of Art, in the Jakarta Arts Education Institute. There were galleries for exhibitions in the major cities, among the most important being the Jakarta Arts Hall, the Exhibition Space at the Ismail Marzuki Centre and the Cultural Hall in Jakarta. Some collectors with interesting collections emerged in several cities.

Issues about art and painting made an appearance. Already a number of [new] approaches are being developed through more organised research into history and ideas. This can certainly fill the space that was previously occupied with the problems of Western painting. And it can also provide a rationale for Indonesian Painting, which is often greeted with suspicion.

So, there are many signs that, slowly but surely, Indonesian painting continues to grow.

4

'God Is Beautiful and Loves Beauty': Aesthetics and Ethics in Islam-Inspired Art

Virginia Hooker

Most Indonesian Muslims are familiar with the Prophet Muhammad's saying, 'God is Beautiful and loves beauty', and the balancing statement, 'God is Good and loves goodness'.[1] In Islam, 'Beauty' and 'Goodness' are two of the '99 Names' that Muslims use to describe the attributes and qualities of God, qualities that are also the 'the guiding principles for Islamic ethics, piety, and good moral conduct'.[2] The Prophet Muhammad urged Muslims to strive to acquire the characteristics of God as much as it is possible for humans to do, because the very effort will guide them to lead pious lives.

The two sayings have particular significance for Indonesian artists whose work is inspired by Islam. Quranic descriptions of God creating a universe of wonder and beauty to be a source of pleasure and enjoyment for all humans inspire them to express that beauty in their art.[3] They believe that art inspired by the Quran bears witness to God's majesty and power

1 Recorded in Imam Muslim's (d. 875 CE) collection of *hadīth*, the sayings and actions of the Prophet Muhammad and his companions.

2 Quran *Al-Hashr* 59: 23. See further Samer Akkach, 'Beautiful Names of God', in *The Encyclopaedia of Islam Three*, ed. Kate Fleet, Gudrun Krämer, Denis Matringe, John Nawas and Everett Rowson (Leiden Boston: Brill, 2015), 54–57. All translations from the Quran are taken from M. A. S. Abdel Haleem, *The Qur'an* (Oxford: Oxford University Press, 2004).

3 For example, Quran *Qaf* 50: 6–10.

and to create such art is an act of worship. It follows, they believe, that when individuals are affected and moved by the beauty of Islam-inspired art to reflect on the power of God the Creator, they will want to follow His injunctions, apply them in their daily lives and thus live ethically and with goodness.[4]

This chapter begins with an analysis of the works of three well-known Indonesian male artists to examine how they have combined aesthetics with Quranic values—that is, ethics—to create works that respond to events in Indonesian politics and society. It concludes by examining the contribution of a female artist who also questions the values and ethics of those with power, but in innovative ways that underline 'the right of women to define for themselves their voice and their own language'.[5] It is a chapter about contexts and choices. Each of the male artists has acknowledged the influence of Indonesian history and social change on their work and has written or spoken about how their choices in life and art are shaped by Islam. Ahmad Sadali (1924–1987), A. D. Pirous (b. 1932) and Tisna Sanjaya (b. 1958) encourage their audiences to reflect on and engage with their work through the thoughts and emotions they experience when viewing it. The affect of the aesthetic of their works, they hope, will remind or prompt viewers to remember God the Creator of all beauty and to remember the Quranic values of goodness and ethical behaviour.

Sadali's works demand the most effort from his audience, but he assists them with visual 'clues' that are integral parts of his arresting paintings. In his paintings, Pirous often uses Quranic verses in Arabic calligraphy to express the themes of his work and he refers to 'visual ethics' as part of his style. Sanjaya literally spells out his themes in keywords inscribed onto his works and in dialogues with members of his audience. In his performance installations, he includes prayers, rituals and images that symbolise the

4 For more detail, see Toshihiko Izutsu, *Ethico-Religious Concepts in the Qur'ān* (Quebec: McGill-Queen's Press, 2002), 18, 252–53. In the post-Independence context, recorded discussion about the nature of Islamic art and literature in the new nation goes back to at least 1951. For example, one Muslim writer stated that: 'Islam desires an art which can unite and merge the beautiful, the good, and the true'. See E. U. Kratz, 'Islamic Attitudes toward Modern Indonesian Literature', in *Cultural Contact and Textual Interpretation,* ed. C. D. Grijns and S. O. Robson (Dordrecht: Foris Publications Holland, 1986), 69. For the surge of Islamic cultural consciousness that emerged in the 1950s, see Jennifer Lindsay and Maya Liem, eds, *Heirs to World Culture: Being Indonesian 1950–1965* (Leiden: KITLV Press, 2012), 75–117 and 283–314, doi.org/10.26530/OAPEN_403204.

5 Astri Wright, 'Red and White Refigured: Indonesian Activist Art in Progress', *ART AsiaPacific* 26 (2000): 63–64.

metaphysical. These themes, and active audience participation in his works during his live performances, serve to engage viewers directly with the ethical issues that concern him and, he believes, will also concern them.

Each of these artists has an established reputation in Indonesia and is recognised internationally. Sadali and Sanjaya are from Sunda (West Java) and Pirous was born and grew up in Aceh (northern Sumatra) but moved to West Java in 1955 where he still lives (see Map 3). They were (and in Sanjaya's case still are) senior staff members of the Faculty of Fine Arts and Design at the Bandung Institute of Technology (ITB), Indonesia's oldest tertiary education institution. They each came to prominence at different times, yet they are linked by four factors: Islam as their source of inspiration, thinking and values; belief in the transformational power of art; the conviction that this transformational power is activated by the affect of beauty (aesthetics); and, lastly, their concerns about the negative effects of unethical behaviour and violence on their fellow Indonesians, Muslim and non-Muslim, and on the environment God created for all humans.

Sadali and Pirous went to school during the last years of Dutch colonialism and the Japanese occupation of Indonesia between 1942 and 1945. They saw Sukarno proclaim the birth of Indonesia as an independent nation-state in 1945, and experienced the bitter and bloody armed struggle against the Dutch to achieve full independence in 1950. Sadali, Pirous and Sanjaya have each, at different times, witnessed bitter civil violence and seen the effects of mass murders, or prolonged imprisonment, on hundreds of thousands of individuals and families. They have witnessed the division of local communities riven by prejudice, corruption, ideologies (communism and Islamic extremism) and inequality. On the plus side, they have each enjoyed international travel and periods of study in America, Europe, other parts of Asia and Australia. Their works have been shown and recognised in Muslim and non-Muslim societies outside Indonesia. They have experienced the honour of being recognised within Indonesia as among its leading cultural ambassadors and nationally acclaimed artists, despite the criticisms of aspects of Indonesia's society and political leadership that are expressed in some of their artworks.[6]

6 Examples of how these criticisms are expressed are given below.

They are linked also by their embrace of 'the new', particularly in exploring new ways of understanding their religion (as described later in the chapter), and new ways of expressing that understanding in their artistic practice. The Quran, the record of divine revelations to the Prophet Muhammad, provides the spiritual framework for all Muslims. Three of its messages are touchstones for most believers: first, the unity and uniqueness of God (*tawhid*); second, the belief that this physical, earthly life is ephemeral but after death will be followed by an eternal spiritual existence; third, the obligations of humans to God and to each other as expressed in the verses:

> Hold fast to God's rope all together; do not split into factions …
> Be a community that calls for what is good, urges what is right, and forbids what is wrong: those who do this are the successful ones.[7]

Muslims interpret these verses as a description of the vertical ties (of spiritual belief and obligation) that link human beings to God and the horizontal ties between humans living together as social beings seeking peace and harmony. These vertical and horizontal relationships of trust and obligation are expressed symbolically in many artworks inspired by Islam.

The female artist is Arahmaiani Feisal (b. 1961). Her contribution to Indonesian contemporary art is widely acknowledged (see Chapter 7 by Caroline Turner). Like the male artists in this chapter, Arahmaiani has also embraced 'the new' and she communicates her art in diverse ways. In contrast to them, she travels regularly and widely to engage with members of various communities in different parts of the world as creators of and participants in collaborative projects. The projects often include performances by Arahmaiani and members of the community as integral parts of their process and these may be recorded on video and viewed by anyone with access to them.[8] Many of her artistic references to Islam draw attention to its abuse by individuals and groups who have hijacked it for their own purposes of power and control or who interpret it extremely literally. Arahmaiani is a contemporary of Tisna Sanjaya and, like him, is from Bandung. There are other similarities that will be discussed in the final sections of the chapter.

7 Quran *Āl 'Imrān* 3: 103 and 104.

8 An excellent account of this aspect of Arahmaiani's oeuvre is by Anissa Rahadiningtyas, 'Arahmaiani: Nomadic Reparation Projects, Environmentalism, and Global Islam', *Post* (Museum of Modern Art, MoMA), 11 August 2021, accessed 14 August 2021, post.moma.org/arahmaiani-nomadic-reparation-projects-environmentalism-and-global-islam/.

Artistic Ideologies

Sanento Yuliman (1941–1992) was formulating his ideas about modernity and art in Indonesia at about the same time as Sadali and Pirous were experimenting with new styles in their works. Although Yuliman does not specifically mention art inspired by Islam, he was very familiar with the artistic styles of both men who were his seniors in the faculty where each was employed. Ahmad Sadali was dean of the Faculty of Fine Arts at ITB in 1976 when Yuliman published his long essay 'Seni Lukis Baru Indonesia' (New Indonesian painting; see Chapter 3).

Elly Kent alerts us to the importance of Yuliman's identification of an emerging ideology in Indonesian art.[9] Yuliman describes it as 'a complexity of thought, attitude and emotion which becomes a shared basis for different individual practices and which extends across time periods'. Its two basic elements, according to Yuliman, are: first, 'respect for the painter as an individual who is free to create their own form and style'; second, 'that the elements of form and their arrangement, regardless of the object they depict, can give rise to, realise, or express valuable artistic emotions, sensations or experiences'.[10] It is important to note that in Indonesian, as in English, the words for artist, painter, weaver, potter and so on indicate no gender discrimination.

Yuliman, as Kent shows, was also interested in the ways style influences how viewers experience art. For example, he argues that, in the style he terms 'lyricism':

> A painting is an expressive field, a place where painters 'project' themselves and the beating of their feelings, recording the existence of their soul. The painting is thus seen as a realm of the imagination which has its own purpose, an imaginary or *irreal* world.[11]

By contrast, in a different style that Yuliman calls a form of 'anti-lyricism', artists choose *not* to filter or transform the objects in their art but to show the objects themselves:

9 Elly Kent, 'Untranslated Histories: Sanento Yuliman and Indonesian Art History', unpublished paper presented to the Indonesia Council Open Conference, The Australian National University, Canberra, 20 November 2019, 5.

10 Quotations from Chapter 3 (this volume).

11 Ibid. (original emphasis).

> The experience is intended to achieve the most concrete and actual form possible. Art works are not a slice of the imaginary world to be contemplated at a distance, but a concrete object that physically involves the viewer.[12]

The inclusiveness of Yuliman's 'new artistic ideology' can encompass the aesthetic ideology of artists who see beauty and goodness as the ethical foundation that supports their artistic practice. However, Yuliman's distinction between styles of art that are experienced through the filter of the imagination, and art experienced directly and physically, is challenged by the works of artists described in this chapter. Had Yuliman lived longer he might well have revised this dichotomy as he indicates in the following quotation from his writings. In his determination to go beyond the approach to 'modern' Indonesian art in the 1960s, Yuliman wrote: 'we must make astute empirical observations of artworks and artistic practice rather than turning to *a priori* desires and ideas', and thus 'give birth to new perspectives, new knowledge, and new questions'.[13]

The works of Sadali, Pirous and Sanjaya range in style from 'abstract lyricism' (Yuliman's term for Sadali's paintings) to performance installations in the case of Sanjaya (which Yuliman would categorise as 'anti-lyricism' in style). Yet, despite their contrasting styles, the Islam-inspired art of Sadali, Pirous and Sanjaya relies on the 'affective impact' of its aesthetic qualities to stimulate viewers' sense of ethical values—values based on the Quran and centred around 'goodness'. Their appeal is made through the aesthetics of their art so that empathy, imagination, memory, emotion and the responsibility to behave in an ethical way are the paramount links between art and its transformative impact through reflection and sensibility.

Ahmad Sadali: 'Because of God and for Humanity'

Ahmad Sadali was born in 1924 in the very beautiful mountainous province of Sunda (West Java). His family owned businesses and land, and his father, a devout Muslim, was founder of the local Muhammadiyah

12 Ibid.

13 See Kent, 'Untranslated Histories', 2–3, based on Yuliman's *Seni Lukis di Indonesia: Persoalan-Persoalannya, dulu dan sekarang* [Painting in Indonesia: Issues, past and present], *Budaya Djawa*, December 1970, 75–76.

branch. Founded in Indonesia in 1912 and the oldest of Indonesia's Muslim mass social organisations, Muhammadiyah members were inspired by the modernist thinking of the Egyptian religious scholar Muhammad Abduh (1849–1905).[14] Muhammadiyah schools provided a Western secular and a religious education. Sadali thus had a sound grounding in modernist attitudes to Islam, interpreting the Quran and Hadith in ways compatible with living in the contemporary world.

Sadali was 21 when Sukarno declared Indonesia's independence and he started studying medicine. In 1948 he left that degree to enrol in the first intake of students in the Art Department (as it was then) at ITB.[15] Indonesians regarded ITB during the 1950s as the centre of modernist aesthetics in Indonesia, valuing its appreciation of innovation, originality, rationalism and creativity in line with a culture of modernism oriented towards progress and universalism. The Dutch artist Ries Mulder (a follower of the cubist Jacques Villon) was highly regarded by his students (who included A. D. Pirous as well as Sadali) as a lecturer in painting. Considered an exceptional teacher, he taught using slides and large pictures of famous works. He encouraged his students to read widely and invited them to borrow books from his own extensive library, holding an open house for discussions with his students or other members of staff, and sharing classical music with them.[16]

After graduation in 1953, Sadali was appointed a permanent lecturer. He represented Indonesia in international art events in Europe, Asia, the UK and the US. Awarded a Rockefeller Foundation scholarship, he studied in the US between 1956 and 1957. Sadali was chair of the ITB Department of Fine Arts between 1962 and 1968 and professor of Visual Art and Design from 1972 until his death in 1987. He was also one of the founders of Salman Mosque, the first mosque built on an Indonesian university campus, where he also gave lectures on Islam to ITB students.

14 See also Chapter 1 (this volume).

15 Astri Wright, *Soul, Spirit, and Mountain: Preoccupations of Contemporary Painters* (Kuala Lumpur: Oxford University Press, 1994), 18–21, for her comparison of the art academies in Bandung and Yogyakarta. She also provides an insightful overview of Sadali's thinking on his art, based on secondary sources because he died before she could interview him (pp. 70–71).

16 Details about Ries Mulder and modernism at ITB based on information in Yustiono, 'Interpretasi Karya Ahmad Sadali dalam Konteks Modernitas dan Spiritualitas Islam dengan Pendekatan Hermeneutik' [A hermeneutic approach to interpreting the works of Ahmad Sadali in the context of modernity and Islamic spirituality] (PhD diss., Bandung Institute of Technology, 2005), 84–88. It should be noted that, years later, Pirous told Kenneth M. George that 'Mulder was too hard on me' and that he felt humiliated by some of his comments. See Kenneth M. George, *Picturing Islam: Art and Ethics in a Muslim Lifeworld* (UK/US: Wiley-Blackwell, 2010), 32, doi.org/10.1002/9781444318265.

In 1968, when he was 44 and serving as dean of his faculty, Sadali seems to have made a deliberate decision about the relationship between his religion and his art. He publicly stated that his art would be 'because of God and for humanity'.[17] From 1968 onwards, his artistic style, which had previously been cubist or semi-abstract, became fully abstract; he is often referred to as 'the father of Indonesian abstract art'.[18]

With hindsight, and drawing on Sadali's public talks and writings, it becomes clear that he made a deliberate choice to respond to the massacres, repression and fear that characterised the post-1965 period of Indonesian history through his art. Only relatively recently have some Indonesians who lived through the violence of 1965–66 been willing to speak publicly or be interviewed about the effect of the violence and the climate of fear on those who survived.[19] Art historian Wulan Dirgantoro has researched the effects of trauma on a range of artists who were teaching or studying in Sadali's faculty during the mid to late 1960s for their impressions of that period. Some remembered rumours of pits or holes being dug by communists as burial sites for the 'capitalists' they planned to kill, and some of the art staff heard their names were on communist death lists because they had studied in America. After Suharto seized power in 1965–66, people remember that some staff and students disappeared and were never seen again, their colleagues assuming it was because they had communist affiliations. Wulan Dirgantoro argues that all who survived that period are 'victims of the extreme violence and ongoing state terror campaigns'.[20] It was in this atmosphere of fear, suspicion and post-violence trauma, followed by an increasing emphasis on the training of scientists and technologists, that Sadali painted, led the Faculty of Fine Arts at ITB and taught his students. At the same time, he was formulating the philosophy that became his moral, ethical and aesthetic guide for the rest of his life.

---

17 Sadali said this at a press conference held in 1968 as part of an exhibition of his works, see Yustiono, 'Interpretasi Karya Ahmad Sadali', 226.

18 See Wulan Dirgantoro, 'Aesthetics of Silence: Exploring Trauma and Indonesian Paintings after 1965', in *Ambitious Alignments: New Histories of Southeast Asian Art, 1945–1990*, ed. Stephen H. Whiteman, Sarena Abdullah, Yvonne Low and Phoebe Scott (Sydney: Power Publications and National Gallery Singapore, 2018), 220, fnt 24, quoting Mamannoor's opinion that there are probably several origins for abstraction in modern Indonesian art.

19 Moving examples of stories by survivors are presented in Putu Oka Sukanta, ed., *Breaking the Silence: Survivors Speak About 1965–66 Violence in Indonesia*, trans. Jennifer Lindsay (Clayton, Victoria: Monash University Publishing, 2014).

20 Dirgantoro, 'Aesthetics of Silence', 203, 206.

Building Communities with Insight

As the nation's oldest and most experienced university for education and research into science, engineering and technology, ITB was expected to lead the way in introducing new technologies that would transform Indonesia's economy and raise living standards to reach the targets set out in Suharto's five-year development plans. Sadali differed from his ITB colleagues, many of whom felt that there was no place for religion and spirituality in the modern, secular world. Sadali strongly believed that reason, feeling and faith were part of a whole, not dialectically opposed. He also knew that the exact sciences, for which ITB was famous, did not include courses on the humanities and religion and thus could not nurture the spiritual and ethical aspects of students' lives.

Sadali has described how his days began with dawn prayers followed by reading the Quran and reflecting on what he had read before beginning to paint. He said his art expressed what he experienced and what he saw with the eyes of his heart after prayer and reflection, or after gazing on the beauty of the universe. He referred to this practice of inner reflection as '*zikr*'—being mindful of God through meditation.[21] Sometime after 1968, Sadali conceived a spiritual response to materialism, developmentalism and fear, and he would talk, lecture and write about that response until his death in 1987.

Sadali's response was based on two verses in the Quran. He interpreted them as God's guidance to those who wished to gain understanding and insight about this world and the next, and the purpose of their existence. Taken from the Quran, chapter *Āl 'Imrān* 190–91, they read:

> There truly are signs [*ayāt*] in the creation of the heavens and earth, and in the alternation of night and day, for those with understanding/insight [*uli-l-albāb*], [191] who remember [*yazkurūna*] God standing, sitting, and lying down, who reflect [*yatafakkarūna*] on the creation of the heavens and earth: 'Our Lord! You have not created all this without purpose—You are far above that!—so protect us from the torment of the Fire'.

For Sadali, the key concepts in the verses are God's creation of 'signs' or 'clues' in the universe (such as the alternation of night and day) that are intelligible by individuals who use their powers of reflection, meditation

21 Ahmad Sadali, 'Fikir dan Dzikir', in *Kumpulan Materi LMD dan SII, Kaderisasi YPM Salman ITB* (Bandung: Salman Mosque, 1987), 135–38.

and sensibility (*zikr*) as well as their powers of reason and logic (*fikr*) to understand this world and the next. Only by using these twin powers (of reason and logic, and inner reflection and emotions) would individuals be able to fully develop their potential and attain the status of *ulī-l-albāb* (people with knowledge and insight). Then they would understand God's signs—both revealed and concealed—and understand that God alone has the power to grant eternal life.

The Eyes of the Heart: Beauty and Zikr

Sadali was concerned that all people strive to balance their reason and reflection and gain spiritual insight, but he also referred to the special ability of artists to perceive reality because of their heightened sensibility and inner awareness. He expanded on this in several talks he delivered to conferences in Malaysia and Pakistan, as well as in Indonesia, during the 1980s. The equilibrium between *fikr* and *zikr* remained the foundation for his thinking, but with his 'art' audiences he also talked about aesthetics. To do so, he linked the concepts of beauty (*keindahan*), inner reflection and sensibility (*zikr*), and art (*seni*).

Sadali drew on one of the works of the great twelfth-century Muslim scholar al-Ghazali to illustrate the two ways of 'seeing'. In his *Kimiyā' Sa'āda*, al-Ghazali explained that children and animals perceive external beauty with their 'outer' or physical eyes. Inner beauty, the deeper, concealed, eternal nature of God, can only be understood by adults through the 'eyes of their soul and the light of vision'. For Sadali, the key to developing the 'eyes of the soul' was the practice of '*zikr*':

> The more developed the practice of *zikr*, the greater the capacity of the inner eyes and the outer eyes to see form aesthetically—in the broadest sense—that is [form] created by God including humans themselves and [form] created by humans as art. [And the practice of *zikr* enables it] to be expressed as art' [as summarised by Yuliman].[22]

The function of art, according to Sadali, was to serve as a reminder (*tazkira*), something that prompted reflection and connected viewers with God. Beauty touches the sensibilities and only through them can

---

22 Sanento Yuliman, 'Dimensi yang Tersisihkan' [The neglected dimension], in *Dua Seni Rupa: Sepilihan Tulisan Sanento Yuliman*, ed. Asikin Hasan (Jakarta: Yayasan Kalam, 2001), 105–06. Originally published in *Perspektif*, January–February 1988, that is, about five months after Sadali's death.

beauty be captured, experienced and appreciated. When beauty brings pleasure, he believed, it makes humans aware of God's transcendence and omnipotence so that they give thanks.

In 1986, just a year before his death, Sadali was asked to write a catalogue note for his paintings being shown in a major exhibition in Jakarta. He responded with a poem entitled, 'Like Life Itself'. In it he describes the process of integrating his lived experiences with his inner reflections and expressing that process through his art. He seems to allude to the massacres of 1965–66 and their aftermath when he refers to the judgement awaiting all in the Hereafter and the responsibility each individual bears for his or her own actions.

Like Life Itself

Like life itself
to be attempted as well and as purely as possible
though the result comes only later, in the Hereafter

Like a circle
of which only a tiny part can be enclosed with words
like all works without words
the complete content is found only in the painting itself
the amount that can be grasped depends on the capacities of the
observer who approaches it

Every happening works for me
new experiences
each painting
a different world
different from those done previously
sensations, intuition, mysterious inspiration
process and the completion of process
each unique, self-contained
yet all tell a story
about what is present on the canvas
what takes shape in the process.
How could it be otherwise?

The result is only then apparent
After the process finally ends
Like life itself.[23]

23 Ahmad Sadali, 1986, quoted in Yustiono, 'Interpretasi Karya Ahmad Sadali', 77, my translation.

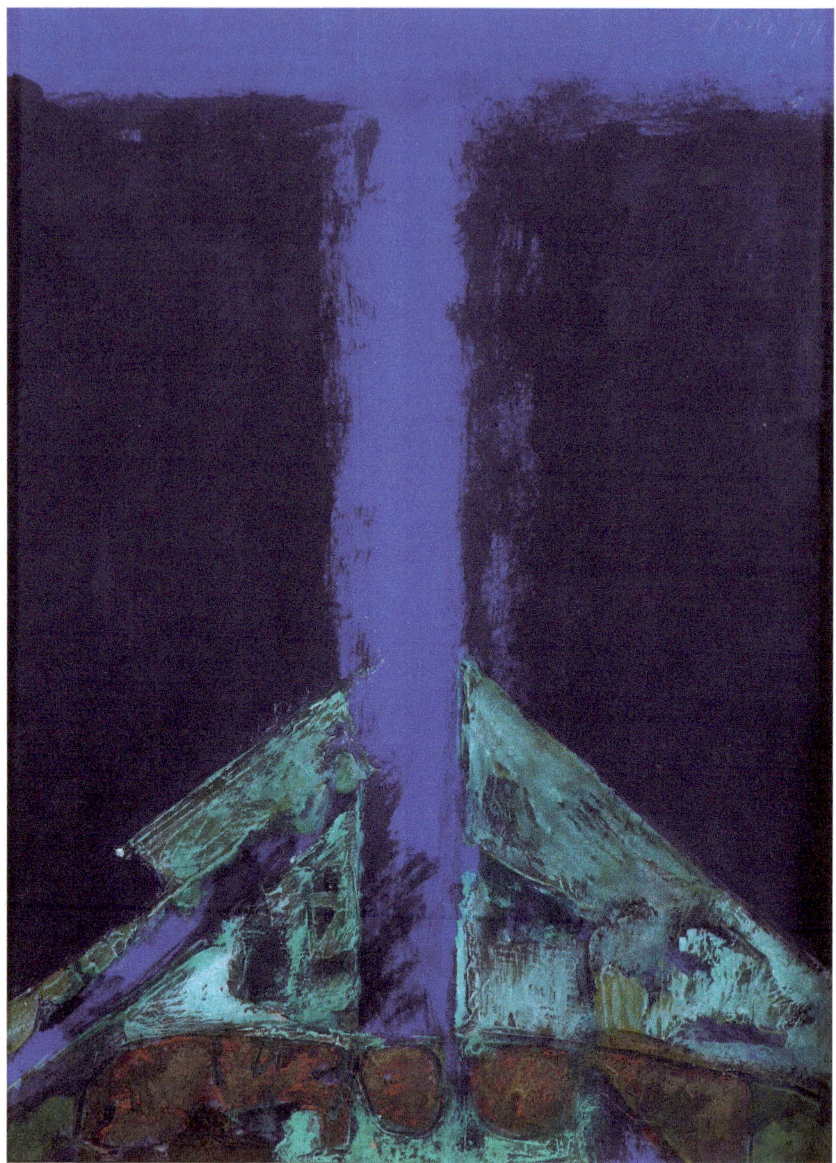

Figure 4.1: Ahmad Sadali, *Gunungan dengan Garis Vertikal Biru* (*Mountain Shape with Blue Vertical Line*), 1974.

Acrylic on paper, 26 x 36 cm. Photograph courtesy Edwin Rahardjo. Permission: Ravi Ahmad Salim.

In his poem Sadali describes life as a process, an ongoing cycle of interaction between knowledge and experience gained in the material world, and the sensations and feelings those experiences evoke, leading to a sense of the metaphysical world. That interaction ends only when life ends, and it is that interaction that is the wellspring for his art.

The painting in Figure 4.1, completed in 1974, six years after Sadali declared publicly that his work would be inspired by Islam, is an example of his style, including his Rothko-like preference for minimalist titles.

The confident tone and bold colours in this work capture the viewer's attention. The centrally placed vertical line of cobalt blue shoots up to the top of the painting, like the rope linking humans with God. Texturing breaks up the smooth surface, while earth tones—Sadali's way of indicating the ephemeral—are mixed with, or perhaps layered beneath, the triangle of turquoise. The band of irregular shapes along the lower edge of the work provide the mountain's foundation and are given life with flecks and spots of red on their ochre surfaces. Every viewer will notice different things in this complex painting, but each will probably feel (with the eyes of their heart) the power inherent in the work.

Sadali's philosophy was not only a path to individual salvation. By emphasising personal responsibility for an individual's actions, Sadali was offering all humans, Muslims and non-Muslims, a guide to ethical behaviour based on reflective responses to the aesthetics of his art.

A. D. Pirous: 'Aesthetic Pleasure and Ethical Pleasure Together'[24]

In 1970, while on a Rockefeller scholarship to study high-viscosity etching techniques in Rochester, New York, the 38-year-old Pirous visited as many art galleries and exhibitions as he could. For the first time, he could view the originals of modern artworks he had only seen as reproductions. He could find no examples of modern Indonesian art but, in the Metropolitan Museum of Art and some private galleries, he came across works of 'Islamic art'—'sometimes plates, sometimes ceramic fragments, sometimes manuscripts, miniature paintings, or calligraphic writings'. He was struck by memories of his childhood in Aceh, where

24 George, *Picturing Islam*, 61.

he was surrounded by similar things and thought: 'This is a part of my own body, a part of my own blood. Why didn't I see it before? How come I did not see it before?' He realised that his art education in Bandung had included only European thought and materials and that his own culture had not been included. He had to go to New York to recognise his Islamic heritage. He seized it with the words: '*This*, *this* is my property, *this* is my treasure'.[25]

Pirous would later use the word 'enlightenment' to refer to his 'discovery' of Islamic art and its significance for him. Born in Aceh in 1932, Pirous's parents were both devout Muslims. Although his mother was knowledgeable about the Quran and Arabic calligraphy and was interested in Sufism,[26] he did not have a formal Islamic religious education. He left Aceh in 1950 to complete his secondary studies in cosmopolitan Medan (see Map 1). There he decided to train to become an artist and, in 1955, he left for Bandung to study at ITB's Faculty of Fine Arts, in the same department as the older Sadali. Anthropologist Kenneth M. George, who has made a lifetime study of Pirous and his art, draws on descriptions by Sanento Yuliman of Pirous's work between 1959 and 1965 in these words: 'The work tended toward "lyric expression"—thematic or symbolic representations of nature, landscapes, everyday people, and everyday objects'.[27]

In 1964, Pirous was appointed a permanent staff member; he held his first solo exhibition in Jakarta in 1968. The following year he was in New York and about to experience his 'enlightenment'.[28]

In 1970, after returning to Bandung from the US, Pirous began working on Islam-themed works, starting with abstract representations of Quranic calligraphy that were illegible and puzzled viewers. This made him think more carefully about his new style. The Quran recorded the sacred words of God, could not be altered in the slightest way and had to be treated

25 Ibid., 42–44 (original emphasis).

26 Sufism or mysticism (known in Islam as *tasawuf*) is one of the classical 'sciences' of Islam, together with the study of the Quran and the saying of the Prophet Muhammad, Islamic law and the history of Islam. It is considered the inner balance to Islamic law (sharia) and practices such as special prayers and inner reflection (*zikr*, as described by Sadali) are believed to facilitate a mystical awareness of God's presence. See further Julia Day Howell, 'Introduction: Sufism and Neo-Sufism in Indonesia Today', *Review of Indonesian and Malaysian Affairs* 46, no. 2 (2012): 1–24.

27 George, *Picturing Islam*, 33.

28 Ibid., 52–53 and Chapter 1 for biographical details of Pirous.

with the utmost reverence. After reflecting on this, Pirous felt it would be a service to others if he could combine his artistic creativity with the ethical values of the Quran. He described his realisation in this way:

> Me what is my life all about? What is a good person? A good person is someone who is useful to others. If I give them something they want, I will be useful. And so I decided to be useful. This is the concept of *khairuqum an-fa'aqum linnas*—a person useful to others … So I sacrificed myself, putting a limit on my free expression, but I came back to values that I could explore more frequently and more meaningfully in the Quran. I planted in the paintings concepts and philosophical values that would make them more enjoyable. *Aesthetic pleasure and ethical pleasure together.*[29]

This, and other examples of Pirous's reasoning, reveal how he uses self-questioning to examine his own motives and motivations for his decision to practise Quran-based art. Unlike Sadali, he does not quote the authority or works of Islamic scholars or religious authorities. He uses his own power of reflection, analysis and self-knowledge to reach his conclusions. This is evident too in his explanation of how he 'uses' the Quran:

> The Holy Qur'an itself may not be changed, but to understand it, you must be free to interpret it. Each and every person may interpret it and glorify its essence, its message. So I take a verse and I try to animate it with my personal vision, with my personal understanding. Now why did I take that verse at that moment? And what is it that I want to say in such a personally meaningful way? If it all comes together and is read by someone else, that's what you call expressiveness, that's what you call spirituality. The meaningfulness might come from something I read, something I saw, something I dreamt about, or something I heard in a story and gets into the back of my head. And if it stirs me as an artist, I will want to put it onto my canvas. When I express it in *visual language*, that's when I use my aesthetic knowledge: composition, color, texture, line, rhythm, everything. I use all of that to make my dream real, so that it can be felt. So that I can tell a story. At last, the painting, its meaning, the Qur'anic verse, all of it becomes clear.[30]

29 Ibid., 61, English translation by George (original emphasis).

30 Ibid., 85 (emphasis added).

Pirous and 'Visual Language'

In the late 1980s, Pirous and several other prominent Indonesians persuaded President Suharto to support a large-scale exhibition of Islam-inspired art to be held in 1991 at Indonesia's national mosque in Jakarta, Mesjid Istiqlal (Independence Mosque). In his preface to the catalogue for the exhibition, Pirous noted that the exhibition was the first to use the national mosque as the venue for an exhibition of 'modern Indonesian art inspired by Islam', and that he hoped it would help the public to understand the nature of modern Islam-inspired art.[31] Held during the holy fasting month of Ramadan in 1991, the exhibition attracted 6.5 million visitors. A second Islamic art exhibition held at the Independence Mosque to mark the fiftieth anniversary of Indonesia's independence during Ramadan in 1995 was even more popular, attracting over 11 million viewers.

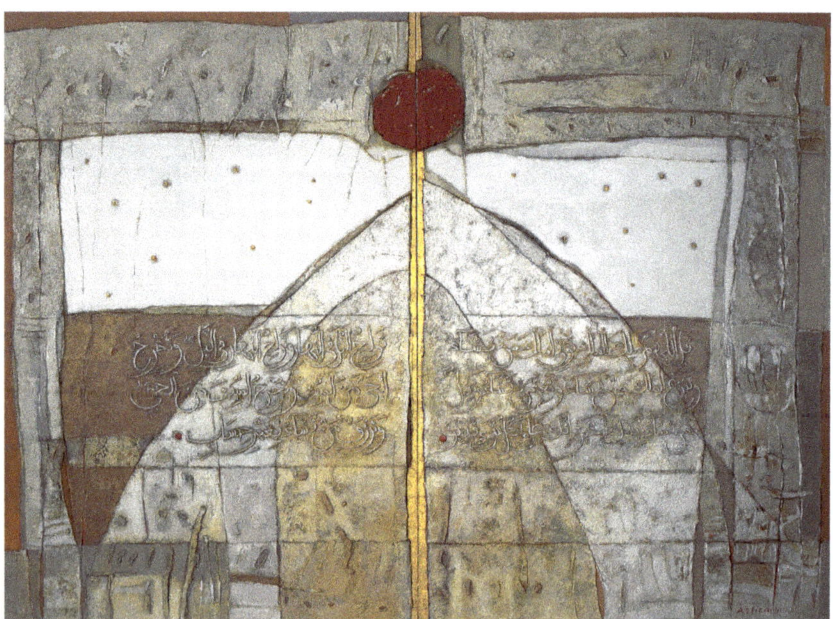

Figure 4.2: A. D. Pirous, *Amanat kepada Sang Pemimpin: Tentang Mahligai Kefanaan, Tentang Awal Akhir Kehayatan* (*An Admonition to the Leader: Concerning the Transient Palace and the Beginning and End of Life*), 1995.

Marble paste, gold leaf, acrylic on canvas, 175 x 260 cm.[32] Photograph courtesy Kenneth M. George. Permission: A. D. Pirous.

31 Setiawan Sabana et al., eds, *Katalog Seni Rupa Modern* (Bandung: Badan Pelaksana Festival Istiqlal, 1991), 1.

32 Description taken from George, *Picturing Islam*, colour plate 18 following p. 46.

Pirous was closely involved with both exhibitions. In the second, he entered a large, eye-catching work, with impressive use of gold leaf (see Figure 4.2).[33] Pirous described the context and stimulus for his painting in response to a comment I had emailed him. I had suggested that, although there are many expert commentaries and interpretations of the Quran, individual Muslims remain free to form their own understandings. This is his reply:

> Indeed it is correct that the Quran is interpreted not translated by the experts. So there is a limited freedom for the exegetes, which later becomes the guide for Muslims. Certainly in the process of *ijtihad* [independent legal reasoning] the users from then on will give it a more contextual quality. This is what happened when I took Chapter Ali Imran, verses 26 and 27 to enrich the painting *An Admonition to the Leader*.
>
> At that time there was a pressing situation that made me anxious and wanting to caution all parties to think again. Around 1995 the New Order government was very violent, many leaders in power went totally too far. It was as if power was something eternal and unending even though everything is transitory and every moment has an end as the Chapter *Āl 'Imrān* verses 26 and 27 state. In the world of art certainly there is a freedom which is rather personal to express a message. It is as if there will be two identities which can become one, the identity through the language of visual expression (style) and the identity of conveying the message (content). Even if the content of the message is the same it will be expressed differently by a range of artists.[34]

The English translation of verses 26 and 27 from Quran *Āl 'Imrān* that Pirous includes in his painting reads as follows:

> You give control to whoever You will and remove it from whoever You will; You elevate whoever You will and humble whoever You will. All that is good lies in Your hand: You have power over everything. You merge night into day and day into night; You bring the living out of the dead and the dead out of the living; You provide limitlessly for whoever You will.

33 George, *Picturing Islam*, 104.

34 A. D. Pirous, personal email to Virginia Hooker, sent from Indonesia 13 June 2013, my translation.

Pirous's motivation for choosing this Quranic verse was the sociopolitical situation in Indonesia in 1995. The early 1990s saw unprecedented levels of corruption, collusion, and nepotism in President Suharto's regime, including the behaviour of Suharto's own children. This period also saw the Dili massacre by Indonesian troops in East Timor (1991), followed by increasing brutality. Open displays of abuse of power at the highest levels of the regime prompted Pirous to remind President Suharto of the divine source and transitory nature of all power. Although President Suharto opened the exhibition and senior members of his New Order government attended, no public comment was made about the verses Pirous had chosen to inscribe onto his painting. Three years later, Suharto was forced to step down as president.[35]

Tisna Sanjaya: 'An Art Full of Spiritual Values'[36]

The fall of Suharto in 1998, the irresistible push for change and a new millennium full of hope ushered in Indonesia's Reformasi (Reform) era. There were more opportunities for open, public debate, the mushrooming of activist groups organised by members of civil society and a deepened sense of being part of global movements facilitated by internet platforms that Indonesians used with skill and enthusiasm. The new millennium also brought well-organised forms of extremist (sometimes termed 'radical') Islam, terrorism, ongoing incidents of sectarian violence, large-scale natural disasters and environmental degradation. Against this background, Tisna Sanjaya developed his mature forms of artistic practice.

35 Pirous continues to paint. Between December 2020 and March 2021, Pirous and his family organised a virtual exhibition of his paintings entitled *Pameran Seni Rupa 88 tahun A. D. Pirous: 'Tetap Bergulir Mengalir', Tur Virtual Serambi Pirous* [Art exhibition for the 88 birthday of A. D. Pirous, 'keep rolling flowing', a virtual tour of gallery Serambi Pirous] featuring 26 new works. The works included both his 'classic' Islam-themed calligraphic art as well as studies of flowers and plants, thus bringing together his early and mature styles.

36 Jaklyn Babington and Carol Cains, eds, *Contemporary Worlds: Indonesia* (Canberra: National Gallery of Australia, 2019), 101. The original Indonesian attributed to Tisna Sanjaya reads, '*seni yang mengandung nilai-nilai spiritual*'. My translation.

Born in Bandung, West Java, in 1958, Tisna Sanjaya describes himself as 'an artist, a teacher and a bearer of culture'.[37] Sanjaya remembers growing up surrounded by traditional Sundanese art and culture[38] and in an atmosphere of pluralist and inclusive Islam that he refers to as 'Islam *pluralis*' (pluralist Islam). His appreciation of traditional Sundanese culture and Islam as a religion that embraces diversity of expression have remained lifelong influences on his art. His father founded and constructed the Nur al-Huda Mosque in Bandung and there gave lessons in Islam to his own and local children.[39]

As a child, Sanjaya won prizes for drawing and he initially trained as an art teacher at the Bandung Teacher's College between 1978 and 1979. But, like Sadali and Pirous, he wanted to be an artist so between 1980 and 1986 he studied drawing and etching in the Graphic Art Department of ITB's Faculty of Fine Art and Design. Sadali and Pirous were senior staff members while he was a student, but he was in a different department and had little contact with them. After graduating from ITB, Sanjaya was awarded scholarships to study etching in Germany at undergraduate and masters levels. During this period he gave several solo exhibitions in Germany, Paris, Japan and Singapore. His exhibition in Paris in 1998, entitled *Art and Football for Peace*, expressed his passion for art, peace and football. He continued to exhibit in Indonesia throughout his period of study in Germany and to hold residencies in Europe, Southeast Asia and Australia.

---

37 The Indonesian reads, '*perupa, pengajar dan budayawan*'. This quote is taken from the curriculum vitae Sanjaya sent me via WhatsApp on 16 February 2020. I thank him for providing answers to my WhatsApp questions as well as visual materials of his work. Unless otherwise indicated, information about Dr Sanjaya's work and art comes from his WhatsApp communications to me.

38 West Java, known as 'Sunda', proudly maintains a language and culture that is totally distinct from that of Central and East Java. Famous for a delicate vegetable and fish-based cuisine, distinctive dance and musical styles featuring bamboo instruments the angklung and suling flute and proudly Muslim, there are still pockets of ancestor worship, animism and belief in a mythical beast known as *reak*, which Sanjaya sometimes includes in his art. See further Ellen Kent, 'Entanglement: Individual and Participatory Art Practice in Indonesia' (PhD diss., The Australian National University, 2016), 243–45, doi.org/10.25911/5d5146060c32c. As well as the flat shadow puppets (*wayang kulit*), the Sundanese have their own distinctive rod puppets, *wayang golek*. Kent describes how Sanjaya has appropriated and developed a popular Sundanese folk character (who is used to teach children 'correct behaviour') called Si Kabayan, with himself playing an eccentric version of the character in a regular TV show. See Kent, 'Entanglement', 230ff.

39 For a thoughtful and astute assessment of Sanjaya's life and work, see Kent, 'Entanglement', 229–63. Elly Kent generously shared her information with me and facilitated my contact with Tisna Sanjaya.

In 1999, when he had returned to Indonesia, Sanjaya was invited to participate in the Third Asia Pacific Triennial of Contemporary Art at the Queensland Art Gallery. Every year since then, his work has been included in major exhibitions of Indonesian art in Venice, North Asia, Southeast Asia, the United States and Australia, particularly at AsiaTOPA in Melbourne.[40] Like Sadali and Pirous, Sanjaya's art has been recognised with national and international awards. He is currently a lecturer in the graphic arts program in the Faculty of Fine Arts at ITB.

Sanjaya has noted that a distinguishing characteristic of his generation of Indonesian artists, those studying and graduating in the 1980s, is their confidence to experiment with developing their own approaches, style and 'language'. For Sanjaya, this included incorporating performance into his etching, painting and installation works. He had formal theatre experience when he worked as a set designer and actor in productions of the Bandung Theatre Study Club (STB). Together with other art students who also performed with STB, Sanjaya is one of the earliest Bandung-based performance artists.[41]

Art Purifying Dialogue (*Seni Penjernih Dialog*)

In 2019, Sanjaya completed an installation commissioned by the National Gallery of Australia (NGA) for its exhibition, *Contemporary Worlds: Indonesia* (see Figure 4.3). Its considerable scale, three-dimensional form, complex elements and almost overwhelming detail would seem to be a complete contrast to the style of beauty and colour that characterise the works of Sadali and Pirous. Yet, Sanjaya's choice of title for his installation, *Seni Penjernih Dialog*—meaning that art can purify dialogue—and the three words, '*Etik, Pedagogik, Estetik*' (Ethics, Pedagogy, Aesthetics), written on each of the three steps leading onto the platform of his installation, align his work with the ideals of Sadali and Pirous.

40 For more detail on Sanjaya's exhibitions in Australia, see Edwin Jurriëns, 'Art Is Capital: Between Cultural Memory and the Creative Industry', *Art & the Public Sphere* 7, no. 1 (2018): 43–62, doi.org/10.1386/aps.7.1.43_1.

41 Ibid., 46. Jurriëns lists Arahmaiani, Isa Perkasa and Marintan Sirait as fellow performance artists shaped by STB.

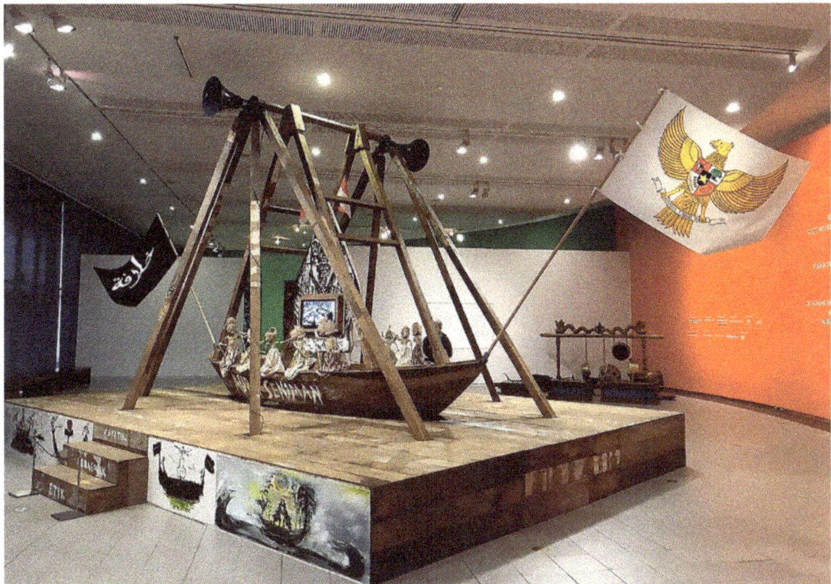

Figure 4.3: Tisna Sanjaya, *Seni Penjernih Dialog* (*Art as Purifying Dialogue*), Contemporary Worlds: Indonesia, NGA, 2019.

Installation; spoken word performance; single-channel video. Photograph and permission courtesy Tisna Sanjaya.

Sanjaya has referred to his installation as a work with special meaning and purpose. In the book accompanying the *Contemporary Worlds: Indonesia* exhibition, he explained that his aim was to:

> Discover a new way, an alternative way, to bring peace, inspiring and never previously done. And also to try to find a balanced voice for humanity, a special local civility, and an art full of spiritual values.[42]

The following sections analyse the installation and its component elements of art (the installation) and performance (purification and dialogue). The performance component was only possible when Sanjaya was physically present and he was in Canberra for about one week in June 2019 after the exhibition opened.[43]

---

42 My English translation of the original Indonesian, which reads '*menemukan cara baru, cara alternatif untuk mengupayakan perdamaian, cara yang inspiratif dan belum pernah dilakukan. Juga berusaha untuk menemukan suara kemanusiaan yang imbang, kesantunan lokal yang khas, dan seni yang mengandung nilai-nilai spiritual*', as in Babington and Cains, *Contemporary Worlds*, 101.

43 Art historian Susan Ingham has identified the following general characteristics of Indonesian performance art: it is ephemeral, and the relationship between performer and audience varies according to context, place and the dominant culture of the audience. It is challenging to assess because each performance is unique. See further Indonesian Contemporary Art, 'Going Global: Indonesian Visual Art in the 1990s', accessed 20 February 2020, www.reformasiart.com/, especially 'Global Artists'.

The Installation

Sanjaya's installation dominates its space and demands attention. It is a life-sized, curved wooden boat, resting on a raised wooden platform that Sanjaya designed to be used for 'installation art & for performance art to convey an artistic statement for peace'.[44] The boat is supported by a superstructure of sturdy wooden beams to resemble a traditional Sundanese 'swing boat' (*kora-kora*). 'Swing boats' are usually sited in public playgrounds or fairgrounds to provide fun rides. Sanjaya's NGA version has a twin that is sited permanently on the bank of a river in Bandung. Sanjaya performed also on the Bandung swing boat and recorded a dialogue he had with a group of invited Bandung officials and residents. The artist linked the boats through a video recording of this Bandung dialogue played on a screen incorporated into the mast and 'sail' of the NGA boat. Thus, the Bandung-recorded dialogue, embedded in Sanjaya's artwork, links Indonesia with Australia.

Three steps link the platform to the floor of the gallery. A word is written on each step: in descending order, '*ESTETIK*', '*PEDAGOGIK*', '*ETIK*'. On one side of the boat is written '*AURA SENIMAN*' and on the other side '*AURA IDEOLOGI*'. At one end of the boat is a flag bearing the symbol of Pancasila (the national ideology of Indonesia, see Chapter 1); at the other end is a black flag on which is written in white Arabic script '*Khilafa*' (Islamic governance or caliphate). The ideologies represented by the flags are in competition and tension in contemporary Indonesia, and Sanjaya signals this by placing them at opposite ends of the boat.

The point of stability and balance for a 'swing boat', as it moves from one side to the other, is the centre. Sanjaya has chosen a range of symbols to indicate the significance of this balance point, emphasising that it is neither 'Pancasila' nor '*Khilafa*' but a point midway between them. A large 'sail' in the form of a '*gunungan*' (a mountain shape, used in traditional Indonesian puppet dramas to indicate beginnings, endings

44 My translation. See Sanjaya's notes in Indonesian accompanying the sketch design of his installation that he provided to the curators of *Contemporary Worlds: Indonesia*. The Indonesian reads: '*Idenya dari kora-kora ini tempat permainan warga, menjadi meja untuk seni instalasi & performance art untuk menyampaikan statemen seni untuk perdamaian*'. See Babington and Cains, *Contemporary Worlds*, 100.

and transformations)[45] is inscribed with a fantastical monster figure holding aloft, in each hand, a Pancasila icon and a weird mask-like head, all surrounded by a background of pseudo-Arabic script. Inserted into the *gunungan* is a small TV screen that shows a video loop of people in dialogue. Encircling the foot of the 'mast' are the figures of *wayang golek*, Sundanese doll-like rod puppets. Each of these symbols, like the loudspeaker at the top of the mast, reflect and amplify Sanjaya's themes of pluralist Islam and traditional Sundanese culture in dialogue with Pancasila ideology and extremist Islam. The traditional Sundanese puppets, symbolising centuries of local culture and beliefs, seem to support and encourage a peaceful dialogue between extremist Islam and Pancasila.

One further aspect of the installation art is noteworthy. Sanjaya has painted a series of cameo sketches on panels around the edge of the platform on which the boat rests. They can be read as microcosmic and more detailed representations of the macro-themes represented by the boat and its 'cargo'. It is not possible to do the cameo sketches justice here, except to say that many of them include figures executed in the '*reak*' style of sketching that Sanjaya uses to capture the form and atmosphere of the trance-like rituals associated with a mythical Sundanese ghost creature.[46]

One of the cameos, not in the *reak* style, is sited immediately next to the steps leading onto the platform and bears two pairs of imprints of Sanjaya's hands (see Figure 4.4), The lowest pair serve as a base out of which 'grows' a stem that bears a red flower. At the base of the stem is written '*ikhlas*' (sincere, pure) and halfway up the stem is a perfect circle—with no beginning and no end—that represents the eternal nature of God. Within the flower, the words '*seni*' (art), 'peace' and 'dialog' are inscribed. Sweeping out of the base formed by the lowest pair of hands are black candelabra-like lines that end with imprints of the palm and fingers of Sanjaya's hands. The left hand has Pancasila written above it and the word '*setuju*' (agree), while the right hand has '*chilafa*' (*khilafa*) written above, and several words of basic Islamic belief such as '*tauhid*' (the unity

45 For further details about the gunungan and its significance, see James Bennett, 'The Shadow Puppet: A South-East Asian Islamic Aesthetic', in *The Image Debate: Figural Representation in Islam and Across the World*, ed. Christiane Gruber (London: Gingko 2019), 181, 182, doi.org/10.2307/j.ctv1wmz3m6.13.

46 Kent, 'Entanglement', 233–37, 243–44, provides a detailed description and analysis of *reak* performances and Sanjaya's visual representations of them.

of God) and '*iman*' (faith). One reading of the cameo is that, at a point midway between Pancasila and *Khilafa*, the artist (Sanjaya's hands) can create beauty that holds opportunities for dialogue and peace.

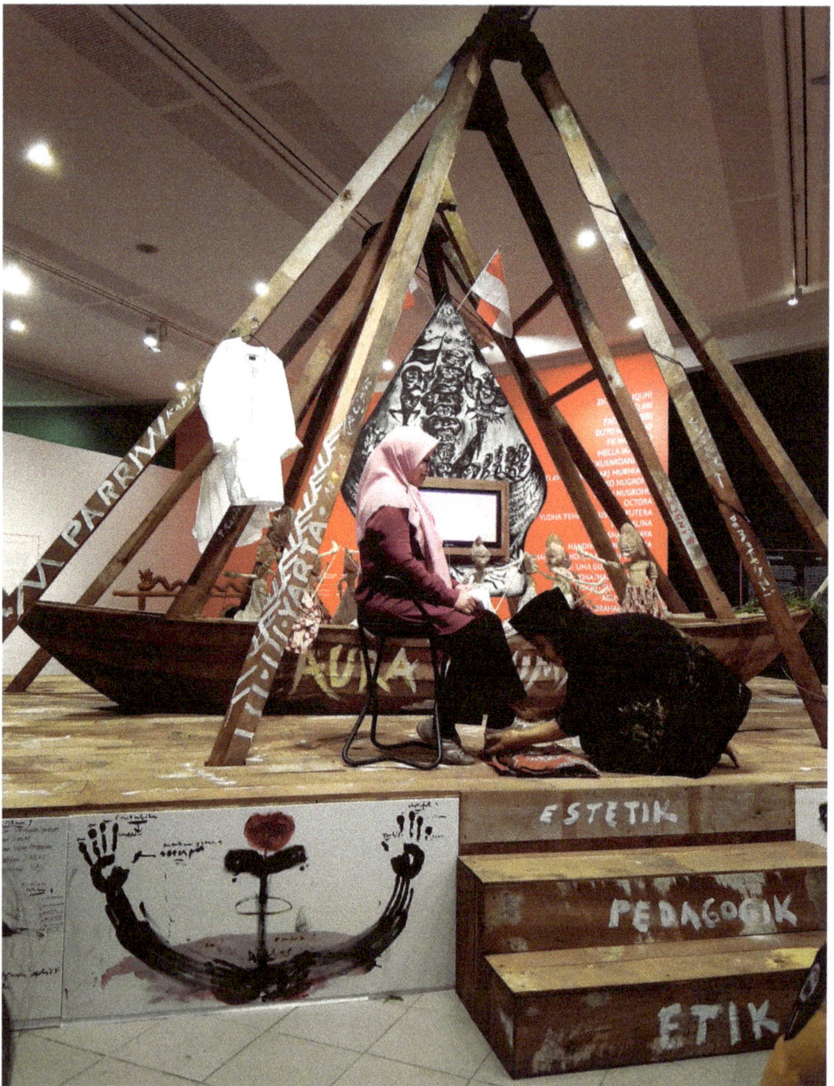

Figure 4.4: The artist bathing the feet of Dr Haula Noor, whom he had invited to participate in the performance on the day following the exhibition's opening.

A scholar of Indonesian Islam, Dr Noor spoke to the audience about the Quran and peace. Note also cameo sketch of artist's hands and flower as described above. Photograph courtesy Cut Nurkemala Muliani.

This reading can be extended to explain '*AURA SENIMAN*' and '*AURA IDEOLOGI*', the twin statements on each side of the swing boat. Sanjaya dedicates his art (*aura seniman*) to represent two ideologies (*aura ideologi*) in the hope that supporters of each can engage in a dialogue that respects diversity and difference and results in a new ethic of civility.

Performance Art as Purifier: Jeprut

Viewers familiar with Sanjaya's performance art, in particular his 'Art is a Prayer' performance at AsiaTOPA in Melbourne in 2017, would note similarities with his performance two years later on and around the platform of his swing boat installation in Canberra.[47] Accompanied by gamelan music, Sanjaya began each performance by quietly chanting prayers in Arabic and ritually cleansing himself, his performance space and his installation with water.[48] Inviting a female spectator onto the performance platform, with her permission he removes her shoes and gently washes, dries and kisses her feet. In Canberra, Sanjaya then enveloped himself in a covering and, speaking quietly to himself, crawled and shuffled around the performance platform, before inviting viewers to ask questions or engage in dialogue. In this way, Sanjaya enacted the title of his work, 'Art Purifying Dialogue', by using water to purify himself and his art and then to engage in dialogue with his audience.

Sanjaya's performances in Melbourne and Canberra were presented in a style he and several other artists pioneered in Bandung in the mid-1980s. It was later called '*jeprut*', a Sundanese word for the sound made when something tight cracks or snaps, releasing a burst of energy. Indonesia studies specialist, Edwin Jurriëns, suggests that *jeprut* is performed by artists 'who feel an imbalance between themselves and their surroundings, and who wish to obtain and share a full bodily and spiritual understanding of the problem that is disturbing them'.[49] Sanjaya's choice of a swing boat at rest as the subject of his installation as well as his emphasis on its point of equipoise, midway between the Pancasila emblem and the *khilafa* flag representing extremist Islam, highlights his concern with balance in its many contexts. Choosing *jeprut* as the mode for his performance enables

47 The Melbourne performance is described in Jurriëns, 'Art Is Capital', 50–52.

48 The prayers Sanjaya recited are 'Sholawat Nariyah', as taught to him by his father, prayers Muslims offer to God when they seek successful and safe outcomes. I am grateful to Dr Muchammadun, State Islamic University of Mataram, Lombok, for explaining the significance of these prayers.

49 Jurriëns, 'Art Is Capital', 44.

Sanjaya to experience and to express the imbalance he perceives and feels between Pancasila as an inclusive national ideology and extremist Islam with its intolerance of diversity and pluralism.

Agents of Change: 'Be a Community That Calls for What Is Right'[50]

This chapter began with the suggestion of the late Sanento Yuliman that, rather than placing Indonesian works of art in pre-existing frameworks, 'new perspectives, new knowledge, and new questions' will emerge only as a result of 'astute empirical observations of artworks and artistic practice'.[51] The artistic ideologies of the three Islam-inspired artists outlined above acknowledge the Quran as the source of their understanding of aesthetics and ethics. Each artist chooses styles or modes of artistic expression that can be seen both by physical eyes and by 'inner eyes', which see, as al-Ghazali noted in the twelfth century, with the 'eyes of the soul and the light of vision'. The dichotomy between 'abstract' and 'concrete' styles of art and the ways they are perceived becomes irrelevant if the 'inner eyes', which use the imagination and sensibility, are always engaged when viewing art.

Each artist has developed their individual spiritual practices of reflection or meditation (*zikr*) to connect with the metaphysical or 'inner' aspect of Islam that is experienced through emotion, sensibility and intuition. As Sadali and Pirous explain, reading the Quran often stimulates the inner reflections that inspire their art. Sadali's 'artistic ideology' is also inspired by the Quran's descriptions of the qualities of 'insightful humans', that is, individuals who strive to balance *fikr* and *zikr* (reason and sensibility).

There seem to be similarities between Sadali's descriptions of *zikr* and the emotional and intuitive state of *jeprut* performers enter when seeking balance and solutions to problems that disturb them. It might not be taking the comparison between the mindful, metaphysical states of *zikr* and *jeprut* too far to remember that Sadali often referred to his works as '*tazkira*' (from the Arabic root '*zikr*')—'reminders' or, in contemporary language, 'wake-up calls' to viewers to engage with the works using their

50 Quran *Āl 'Imrān* 3: 104, a Quranic quotation that most Indonesian Muslims know and would automatically complete with the words, 'and forbids what is wrong'.

51 Yuliman, *Seni Lukis di Indonesia*, 77, as discussed by Kent, 'Untranslated Histories', 3.

inner eyes, and to respond to the feelings and emotions they experience. In a similar way, Sanjaya's *jeprut* performances in *Seni Penjernih Dialog* might be wake-up calls to his audience to attend to the themes of his installation and to take action to redress the imbalance he perceives in Indonesian society by connecting with God and with each other in peace and in dialogue. Elly Kent makes a similar point about Sanjaya's performances in other contexts. Acknowledging the difficulty of assessing the impact of Sanjaya's efforts, through art and performance, to influence change for the greater good at a local or national level, she describes her personal responses as follows:

> My own experience of the affective power of Tisna's performative participation and the resonance of his work in triggering emotion and feeling, demonstrated the aesthetic success of his work on an individual, experiential level.[52]

Arahmaiani Feisal: 'A New Awareness of Humanity and a New Social Consciousness'

It is here we return to Arahmaiani Feisal, who, like Sanjaya, was an early member of the *jeprut* group in Bandung and an active member of the Bandung Theatre Club. She is also a talented dancer, singer and poet and developed her own style of performance. It is practised and creative and has its own aesthetic qualities that encompass her voice in speech and music, poetry as well as prose, combined with grace of bodily movement. In very obvious contrast to Sanjaya, her body is female, her voice is female and she offers her viewers a new form of activist art. As noted by Caroline Turner in Chapter 7, Arahmaiani's courage in addressing 'taboo' subjects and her creativity seemed without bounds and in the 1990s her name became well known within and outside Indonesia.[53]

In the context of this chapter, with its focus on Islam, ethics and aesthetics, it is revealing to refer to Turner's description of Arahmaiani's *Manifesto of a Sceptic*, a performance piece she presented at various times in the 2000s. During the performance, Arahmaiani described the role of art as 'a liberating force' that 'should encourage a new awareness of humanity

52 Kent, 'Entanglement', 263.

53 For examples of her courage in speaking out, and for further details of her education and theatre training, see Turner, Chapter 7 (this volume).

and a new social consciousness' and a force that could affect values—we might even understand this as ethics—that are alternative, changed, or even values that are turned upside down.[54] As Anissa Rahadiningtyas observes, from 2006, 'performance and installation became Arahmaiani's mediums of political and environmental activism, through which she progressively articulates the importance of collaboration as a strategy of reparation'. She notes also that, from that time, Arahmaiani's works 'seek to show the experience and reality of Muslims and women actively contributing to shaping the image of global Islam'. She quotes Arahmaiani as explaining how her participatory and collaborative art projects actively engage those who work on them, join in with them or see them 'in building a foundation for a more open, democratic, equal, and tolerant society'.[55]

The videos Arahmaiani makes of these projects preserve this form of art in ways that a painting might, in the sense that aspects of the project are selected for filming and the visual choices of the person filming (and/or the choices of Arahmaiani herself) determine the content and form of the video. Editing, like erasure and changes to a painting, can further shape the final form of the film. But video has an advantage not available to painting. It transports an event out of a specific place so that it is not restricted to one site of exhibition or viewing. Video takes Arahmaiani's art out of museums and galleries to screens anywhere and, similarly, brings her art project from Tibet, or Bali or Europe into any gallery or museum. Audiences do not have to come to her. Walls and international borders do not restrict the viewing of her work. She is indeed 'shaping the image of global Islam' and, perhaps, building foundations for political, social and economic change.[56]

Were Sanento Yuliman still alive to witness the installation works of Sanjaya and Arahmaiani he might describe them as 'anti-lyrical'. But their performances extend the installations with physical, musical, verbal presentations that add a level of aesthetic individualism to the installation that Yuliman might have found stretched his 'anti-lyricism' category. Whatever their form, the new millennium artistic enterprises of Sanjaya and Arahmaiani continue the broad and inclusive view that Quran-based ethics and values are essential pre-requisites for individual

54 Turner, Chapter 7 (this volume).

55 Rahadiningtyas, 'Arahmaiani: Nomadic Reparation Projects, Environmentalism, and Global Islam'.

56 Some of Arahmaiani's performances are professionally documented and edited. A few are posted on YouTube or Vimeo. Email communication from Anissa Rahadiningtyas, 5 October 2021.

and social welfare in all senses. Their art creates the space and inspiration for reflection and reparation and, as Sadali emphasised, the opportunity to build communities with insight.

With their deep commitment to balance in all spheres of human life, it is important to recognise that the artistic ideology of Islam-based aesthetics and ethics as developed by Islam-inspired artists is inclusive and addresses all human beings and all God's creation. The art created by these artists is accessible to all who have sight and keeps Revelation relevant to contemporary times and particular issues. Art that grows out of these convictions takes Islam beyond the realm of the jurists and specialist religious scholars and makes it accessible to 'ordinary' people, Muslims and non-Muslims, across time and borders.

Acknowledgements

Emeritus Professor A. D. Pirous, Dr Tisna Sanjaya MA, Dr Didin Sirojuddin AR and Dr Anissa Rahadiningtyas have been more than generous in their responses to my questions. Dr Yustiono (ITB, Bandung) very kindly entrusted me with a copy of his unpublished dissertation based on the thinking and works of his mentor, Professor Ahmad Sadali, and gave me permission to quote from it. Dr Haula Noor from State Islamic University Syarif Hidayatullah, Jakarta, and The Australian National University, engaged in dialogue with Sanjaya during one of his Canberra performances and shared with me her knowledge of Sundanese traditions. Edwin Rahardjo from Edwin's Gallery and Professor Kenneth M. George provided photos of the works of Sadali and Pirous, respectively, and Sam MacKenzie provided a detailed image of Sanjaya's cameo painting for me. My thanks to you all. My patient and wonderful colleagues Dr Caroline Turner and Dr Elly Kent have offered expert comments and suggestions, for which I am deeply grateful.

5

The Contemporary in Southeast Asian Art: The 1970s

T. K. Sabapathy

I

This chapter was originally presented as a keynote paper at the conference convened by and at The Australian National University (ANU) in association with *Contemporary Worlds: Indonesia*, an exhibition at the National Gallery of Australia in 2019 and the first, I understand, in recent years at that institution for curating Asia as manifesting contemporary art worlds.

I am reminded of another occasion scaled expansively, of the fervour attending it as presaging a dawning of a new age in Brisbane, 1993, when and where the Asia Pacific and its contemporary were artistically incarnated, triennially, on the premises of the Queensland Art Gallery, transforming it significantly.

Even as we are in Canberra, I pause at Brisbane 1993. At that inaugural Asia Pacific Triennial (APT), the Asia Pacific was curated as consisting of three sub-regions, namely: Southeast Asia, East Asia and the South Pacific. 'South-east Asia' bore a hyphenated presence—south as separated from east—and in turn was made up of six nations: Indonesia, Malaysia, the Philippines, Singapore, Thailand and Vietnam. I focus on Indonesia, as it is the subject in the exposition and conference.

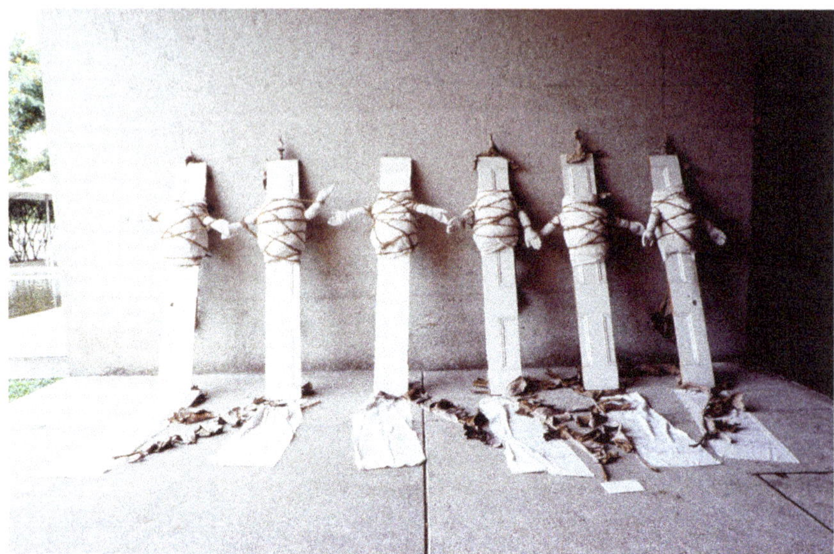

Figure 5.1: FX Harsono, *Just the Rights*, 1993.
Installation comprising wood, cloth, foam rubber, rope, organic materials. First Asia Pacific Triennial, Brisbane. Collection: the artist. Photographer: Richard Stringer. Image courtesy QAGOMA and the artist.

Nine artists were nominated, each showing a body of works. FX Harsono was one of them and he is the reason I pause at Brisbane 1993. Among his works displayed then is titled *Just the Rights* (1993; see Figure 5.1). The other artists were Dadang Christanto, Heri Dono, Nyoman Erawan, Sudjana Kerton, A. D. Pirous, Ivan Sagito, Srihadi Soedarsono and Dede Eri Supria (Figure 5.2).

Harsono had been featured in the Artists' Regional Exchange (ARX) in Perth, 1992, a year before appearing at the APT, where a production titled *Power and Oppression* (1992) was installed. This work is illustrated in the catalogue issued for the inaugural Asia Pacific exhibition. While its display at Perth in ARX is acknowledged in the caption, there is no comment on this matter or on the work and its inclusion in the text, written by Jim Supangkat, introducing Harsono (Figure 5.3).

What might we make of it? We could read it as illustrating a kind or type or category of work produced by this artist, thereby signalling to viewers in Brisbane and in Australia a precedent for or kinship with what is shown in the APT. We could read it also as registering Harsono's artistic footprints in Australia so that he is seen appearing in Brisbane not as a complete unknown in and to the artistic milieu in Australia. Let us pursue this thought a little further.

SOUTH-EAST ASIA

INDONESIA

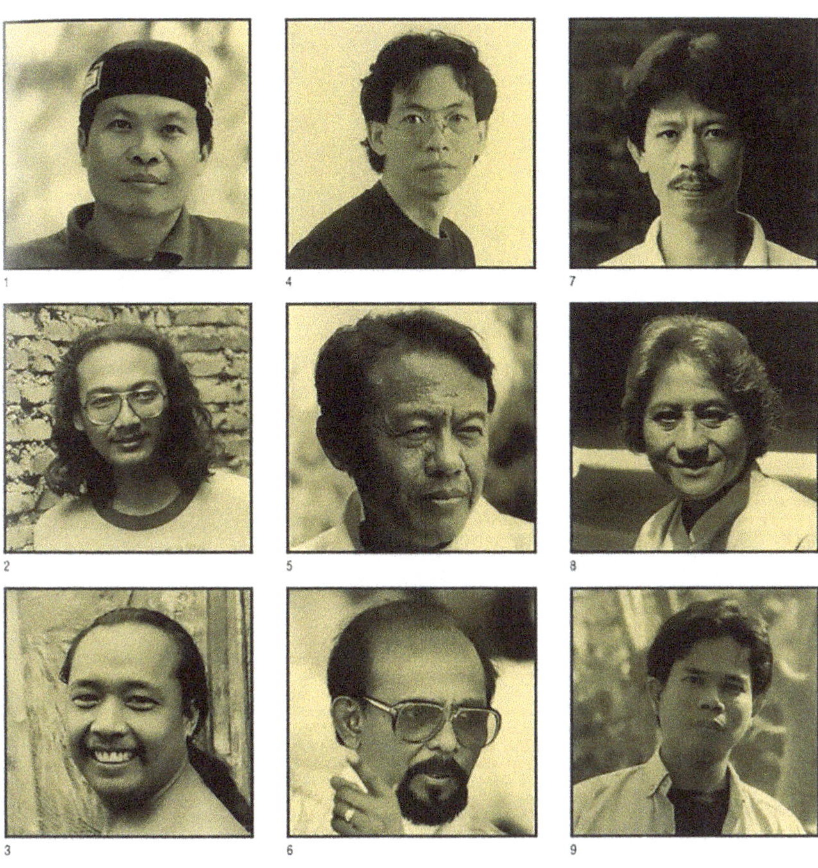

1 DADANG CHRISTANTO
2 HERI DONO
3 NYOMAN ERAWAN
4 FX HARSONO
5 SUDJANA KERTON
6 A.D. PIROUS
7 IVAN SAGITO
8 SRIHADI SOEDARSONO
9 DEDE ERI SUPRIA

Figure 5.2: Photographs of Indonesian artists reproduced in the catalogue of the First Asia Pacific Triennial, Queensland Art Gallery, 1993.

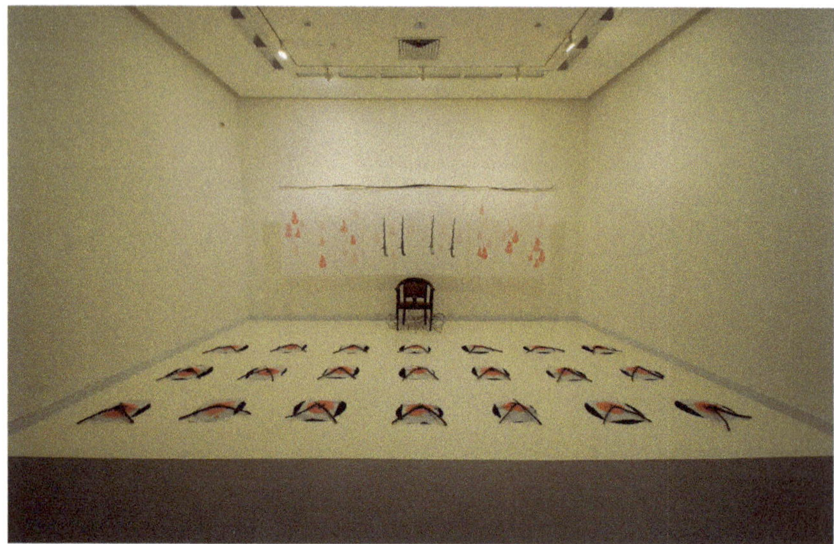

Figure 5.3: FX Harsono, *Power and Oppression*, 1992.
Shown in Artists' Regional Exchange (ARX) exhibition, Perth, Australia, 1992. Image courtesy the artist.

I draw attention to Harsono to underline the importance of examining crossovers by artists as they migrate and by artworks as they circulate from site to site within bordered precincts, and across them, in order to discern deeply the provenance of individual practices and productions. The term provenance may sit uneasily, inattentively when applied to examining contemporary art worlds; yet conceptually and methodologically it is apt.

I direct attention to Harsono to underline the usefulness of forging networks for linking artworks that are curated over time and space, networks that draw attention to relatedness or separateness of artworks, thereby dispelling the apparent strangeness, inexplicableness of their appearance, and instead propose inflected pathways for apprehending them. How these are distilled when exhibiting creative productions as experientially compelling in their particulars are among heartbeats propelling curatorial decisions and orientations. Anticipations are for encountering a work resonantly—yes! Anticipations are also for encountering a work as yielding varied interpretive desires and interests.

I draw attention to Harsono to underline propensities for trans-locating a practice and artworks, hinting at the cumulative impact of such itinerancy on curating and seeing art. Of course he is not exceptional in any of these respects as trans-located-ness is acclaimed as a defining attribute in being contemporary in the art world. There are other interests and destinies.

In one instance Harsono is hoisted onto exalted registers, cast as embodying exemplariness when assessing recent art in Indonesia and Southeast Asia. Agung Hujatnikajennong offers such a measure and reckoning. It appears in an essay he writes for a publication issued for an exhibition dealing with conceptual approaches and strategies employed by contemporary artists in Southeast Asia; its title is *Concept Context Contestation. Art and the Collective in Southeast Asia* (CCC) shown at the Bangkok Art and Culture Centre from December 2013 to March 2014.

We read his appraisal:

> FX Harsono's work *What Would You Do If These Crackers Were Real Pistols?* (1977) has been specially remade for this exhibition [see Figure 5.4]. This work becomes an important sample especially in relation to the social and political context in Southeast Asian countries that still seem to stand out as co-existing factors that created differences and similarities of interest in regional art practice. In CCC, FX Harsono occupies a unique position as one of a few living artists who connects successive art developments since the 1970s. He has experienced the ups and downs of Indonesian political transitions in the country. The development of his art has consistently demonstrated a genealogical link between conceptual strategies and the issue of contesting power in Indonesia.
>
> It is useful to re-read FX Harsono's trajectory and use Indonesia as a case study for how endogenous and exogenous factors have shaped current conceptual practices in Southeast Asia.[1]

1 Agung Hujatnikajennong, 'Trajectories/Contingencies. Indonesian Contemporary Art and the Regional Context', in *Concept Context Contestation: Art and the Collective in Southeast Asia*, ed. Iola Lenzi (Bangkok: Bangkok Art and Culture Foundation, 2014), 20. *What Would You Do If These Crackers Were Real Pistols* was remade again for *Awakenings: Art in Society in Asia 1960s–1990s*, shown in Japan and South Korea and then at the National Gallery of Singapore from 14 June to 15 September 2019. S. Sudjojono is the supreme patriarch of Indonesian art. In recent writings, claims for exemplariness are advanced for individuals esteemed for political/social activism as artists in the 1980s. For instance, Aminudin Siregar propels Semsar Siahaan into singular prominence when he says:

> There may not be another artist who better represents the development of Indonesian art in resisting the despotism of the Soeharto, The New Order regime whether through artworks or sociopolitical activities than Semsar Siahaan (1952–2005). He is a representative of the rebel generation of the 1980s, his name shines since studying as a student at the Institut Teknologi Bandung campus.

Aminudin T. H. Siregar, 'He Who Comes as an Invalid and Wounded', in *Semsar Siahaan: Art, Liberation*, ed. T. K. Sabapathy (Singapore: Gajah Gallery, 2017). Histories of Indonesian art are, as with accounts of art elsewhere, cast emphatically along patrilineal trajectories.

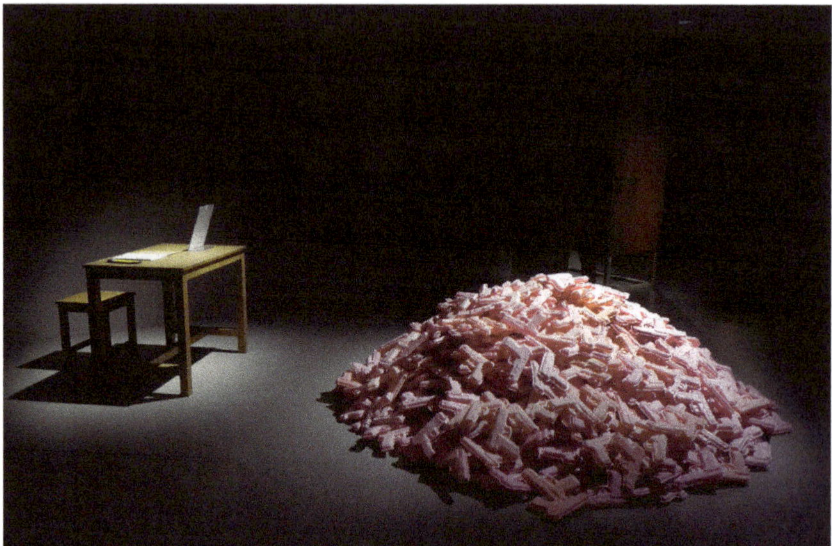

Figure 5.4: FX Harsono, *What Would You Do If These Crackers Were Real Pistols?* 1977–2018.

Crackers, wooden table, chair, book, pen and instructions, dimensions variable. Collection: the artist. Image courtesy the artist.

In his estimation, aspects of contemporary art in Indonesia and Southeast Asia are historically telescoped into conforming to the life and creative practice of an individual. We may recoil from valorising of one artist as manifesting the wellspring source of the new historically, although Hujatnikajennong inserts his claim thoughtfully. Hence, it would be a gross misinterpretation to leave this citation unaddressed, conveying impressions of Harsono hijacking what Agung Hujatnikajennong has to say in this essay.

Titled 'Trajectories/Contingencies: Indonesian Contemporary Art and the Regional Context', Hujatnikajennong proposes perspectives for assessing exhibitions of Southeast Asian contemporary art featuring works, gestures, testimonies exemplifying conceptual interests or traits, spanning the 1970s and the 1990s, in exhibitions in locations in the region. It is not a survey; it is a discussion of complexities entailed when examining the region and its art as historically formative—via exhibitions. Harsono is raised to unrivalled prominence in this account, as is Indonesia.

In the year Agung Hujatnikajennong publishes his essay (i.e. 2014), there appears *Contemporary Asian Art and Exhibitions: Connectivities and World-Making*, published by ANU Press. Edited by Michelle Antoinette and Caroline Turner, it is made up of writings on the modern and the contemporary by several authors, and research facilitated by The Australian National University. A year earlier, in October 2013, the Asia Art Archive in Hong Kong convened a symposium on 'Sites of Construction: Exhibitions and the Making of Recent Art History in Asia'. As the title indicates, the symposium's interest is twofold: firstly to examine claims that exhibitions are formative sites for developing, representing histories of especially modern art; secondly, and arising from this, how might exhibitions be studied historically. *Yishu. Journal of Contemporary Chinese Art* devoted its entire March/April 2014 issue to it, publishing papers that were presented and transcripts of panel discussions at the end of the symposium. Exhibitions are increasingly examined; they are hot topics for research, publications and conferences.

The essay I have earlier discussed by Agung Hujatnikajennong is the third in a trilogy he writes on the contemporary, publishing in the English language. Each is written for an occasion held at a specific location; all are affiliated with exhibitions. The suite of texts constitutes potentially significant readings on the contemporary in art, chiefly in Indonesia although Hujatnikajennong's analysis may be read as having wider pertinence. I say potentially as it needs to be examined and discussed. For the present I offer these observations; brief as they are, it would be undeserving to merely pass by them.

The first essay, titled 'The Contemporary Turns: On the Indonesian Art World and the Aftermath of the 80s', is for a publication issued for an exhibition, both named *Beyond the Dutch: Indonesia, the Netherlands and the Visual Arts, from 1900 until Now* with the exhibition at the Centraal Museum, Utrecht, from October 2009 to January 2010.[2]

The art world in Indonesia in this instance is initially defined by patronage determined by acquisitions of artworks via commercial agencies and transactions driven at the onset by domestic demands dominated by powerful, collector conglomerates amassing extensive private collections,

2 Agung Hujatnikajennong, 'The Contemporary Turns: On the Indonesian Art World and the Aftermath of the 80s', in *Beyond the Dutch: Indonesia, the Netherlands and the Visual Arts, from 1900 until Now*, ed. Meta Knol, Remco Raben and Kitty Zijlmans (Amsterdam: KIT Publishers; Utrecht: Centraal Museum, 2009), 139–45.

and subsequently by global/corporate capitalism. Yet the contemporary is not cast completely in their shadows. Hujatnikajennong sharply points to sites, spaces, agencies, such as artists' initiatives, regional expositions, biennials—even as these are entangled with state/national imperatives—as also providing alternative representations and mediations and as constituting patronage. And then, as John Clark dramatically and pointedly identifies, there appears in these arenas 'a new kind of actor' who brings into art worlds a 'notion of the contemporary as a new kind of art practice'. A practice no longer assessed and assessable by prevailing interpretive codes but by 'a new aesthetic fuelled by directing access to subjects of daily life'.[3]

The new actor is the curator; not any or all but, John Clark underlines, particular curators 'who at critical times performed and built careers' that are 'intertwined with the rise of new contemporary spaces, often in cultures which lacked formal and permanent museums of modern and contemporary art'.[4] This appears in a foreword written for Patrick Flores's *Past Peripheral: Curation in Southeast Asia*, an important comparative study of curators, especially in Indonesia in the 1970s and Thailand in the 1980s. *Past Peripheral* was published by the National University of Singapore Museum in 2008, a year before Hujatnikajennong's essay appears.

And Hujatnikajennong cites Flores's analysis in his account, whose tenor separately and collegially substantiates John Clark's observations as I have reported them. The actor who emerges prominently, dominantly in Indonesia, is Jim Supangkat, whose curating of especially the ninth Jakarta Biennale in 1993, precipitated seismically wideranging debates, disputes and partisanship, altering discourses on the modern and the contemporary in Indonesia. Hujatnikajennong scrutinises these entangled trajectories methodically while underlining difficulties when weighing them historically and regionally.

The second essay, titled 'The Contemporary Turns: Indonesian Contemporary Art of the 1980s', is for an exhibition-cum-publication called *Negotiating Home, History and Nation: Two Decades of Contemporary Art in Southeast Asia 1991–2011*, by and at the Singapore Art Museum, the exposition running from March until June 2011.[5] Similarities between

3 John Clark, 'Foreword', in *Past Peripheral: Curation in Southeast Asia*, by Patrick D. Flores (Singapore: NUS Museum, National University of Singapore, 2008), 2.

4 Ibid.

5 Agung Hujatnikajennong, 'The Contemporary Turns: Indonesian Contemporary Art of the 1980s', in *Negotiating Home, History and Nation: Two Decades of Contemporary Art in Southeast Asia 1991–2001*, ed. Iola Lenzi (Singapore: Singapore Art Museum, 2011), 85–90.

the Utrecht and Singapore texts are acknowledged and publicised as the latter being a reworked, revised version of the former. Its republication underlines the editor's view of its importance and continuing pertinence.

I return to the third essay in Agung Hujatnikajennong's trilogy, written for *Concept Context Contestation* in Bangkok in 2014; in it Harsono is installed as exemplary when writing histories of recent Indonesian and Southeast Asian art, art identified, represented and examined as contemporary. The time span Hujatnikajennong allocates is the 1970s, a decade defined by the Black December incident/statement and by the inaugural exposition by the Gerakan Seni Rupa Baru Indonesia (GSRB, the Indonesian New Art Movement) in 1975.

As Hujatnikajennong tells it, one morphs into the other almost naturally. Again Harsono is named, along with Siti Adiyati, B. Munni Ardhi,[6] Ries Purwana and more, as spearheading a transformation of a protest gesture (with immense cost to the lives of those who delivered it) into a gathering of artists with disparate interests and dispositions, assembling from different locations (all in Java of course), to form a loose, fluctuating collective with ambitions for altering the foundations, impact, significance of the practice, production and showing of art. The GSRB ignited intense discussion; it was disparaged and commended.

More than any other group, it is now identified as marking the advent of the contemporary. So much so it is now customary to say Indonesian contemporary begins with the Gerakan Seni Rupa Baru Indonesia in 1975. For that matter, the GSRB has been written on from its onset and continues to be written on—by those from within its formation and those who behold its representations from other constituencies. Foremost among writers from within are Jim Supangkat and Sanento Yuliman. Siti Adiyati is never mentioned; yet she writes lucidly, advocating aims and destinations of the new in the new movement in clear terminology and by employing vivid analogies.

This is not an occasion to recount any of these in detail. The GSRB was not a topic in the NGA exhibition or in the conference at ANU, although it was not completely absent from either of these. In the NGA exposition, the contemporary was represented from 1998 onwards, the year marking the overthrow, the ouster, the departure of Suharto from the presidency and the end of the New Order regime. A year preceded

6 Editors' note: an alternative spelling is Bonyong Munny Ardhie.

by sustained civil action mounted by disparate bodies stemming from calls for eradicating inequality, poverty and injustice; actions mounted at immense consequences for individual lives; action that is collectively referred to as Reformasi.

Nineteen ninety-eight: a year signalling endings—momentously; and a year promising beginnings—fervently.

Beginnings and endings precipitating, according to NGA curator Carol Cains:

> the sudden, unfamiliar opportunity for innumerable individual voices, beliefs and opinions to be broadcast created a declaratory cacophony accompanied by tactical manoeuvres as numerous social and political groups jockeyed for prominence.[7]

The pace and tumult vividly captured in Cains's prose continue to be lived until today, yielding at times different destinies and at times persisting in unchanged conditions. And for Cains they materialise in Jompet Kuswidananto's *Staging Collectivism* (2013), installed in the exhibition (Figure 5.5).

I am not sufficiently familiar with the NGA exhibition (not having viewed it prior to writing this paper) to deal with it here.

I aim to step back and sideways and talk of the contemporary historically by examining a handful of representations in locations in the region other than Indonesia. The focus is chiefly on the 1970s, comparable to some of Agung Hujatnikajennong's preoccupations—with tracking wellsprings for showing, seeing and writing the new, the different in art practices. In large measure, readings of Hujatnikajennong's trilogy of texts are aimed at gaining entries to what I wish to say here. In this sense too, writings by Chaitanya Sambrani, Elly Kent and Carol Cains for the NGA publication have accompanied thoughts and preparations for this occasion. Each of the texts is deeply inflected by historicalness, distinctively, and I am glad for such companionship.[8]

---

7 Carol Cains, 'Contemporary Worlds: Indonesian Art at the NGA', draft text.

8 Chaitanya Sambrani, 'Archipelagic Cosmopolitanism: A Prehistory of Contemporary Art in Indonesia', in *Contemporary Worlds: Indonesia*, Jaklyn Babington and Carol Cains (Canberra: National Gallery of Australia, 2019), 15–20; Elly Kent, 'Looking for Indonesia in Contemporary Art', in *Contemporary Worlds: Indonesia*, Jaklyn Babington and Carol Cains (Canberra: National Gallery of Australia, 2019), 23–26. I thank Carol Cains, Chaitanya Sambrani and Elly Kent for forwarding their texts to me pre-publication.

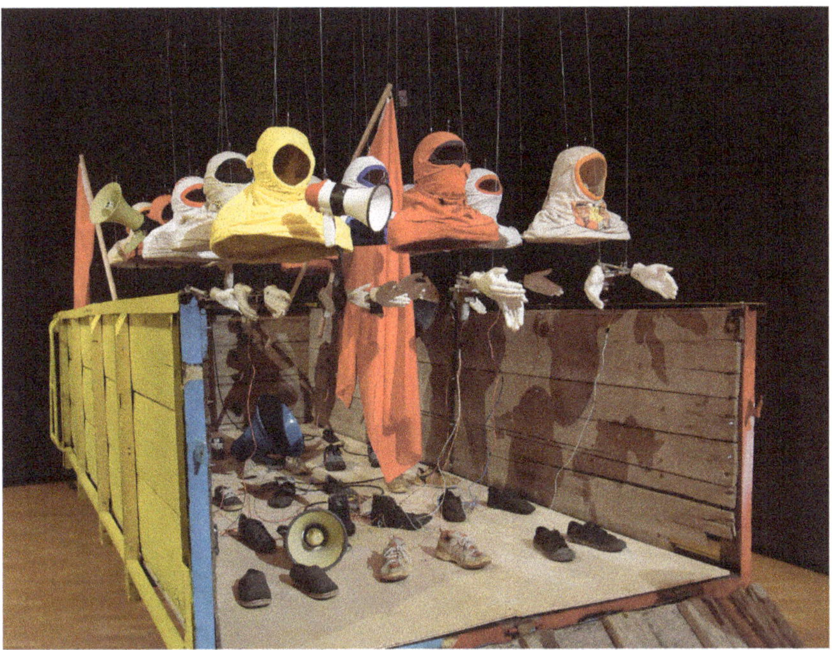

Figure 5.5: Jompet Kuswidananto (b. 1976), Central Java, *Staging Collectivism*, 2013.

Installation as installed at National Gallery of Australia, Canberra, 2019. Image by Timothy Tobing/DFAT on Flickr (CC BY 2.0).[9]

When nominating the decade of the 1970s, the purpose is not to fix, consolidate chronologies for contemporary art's beginnings, but to indicate a time frame for detecting a parting of ways, scrutinising shifts whereby prevailing values, modes of practice and interpretation are interrogated; elbowed to make room for actions, positions that are different; room for registering claims that practices of art are overtly related to conditions of daily life or that conditions of daily life are vital resources for art practices and for materialising them as works of art. Resources fuelling such engagements are also derived from encounters with representations in locations in Europe, Japan, the USA and Southeast Asia.

9 Accessed 20 January 2022, flickr.com/photos/kedubesaustralia/48428169937/.

II

Between 1972 and 1974, Cheo Chai-Hiang set down his thoughts on art and its predicaments in three texts, written for audiences in Singapore. In 1971 he departed for England, enrolling as an undergraduate in the art department of Brighton Polytechnic and subsequently in a graduate program at the Royal College of Art, completing studio-based studies in visual art in 1978. The foundations for his creative practice were consolidated during these years, as were orientations for his thinking on art.

Prior to his departure for art studies, he was briefly a student at the then Nanyang University studying literature; subsequently he joined a teachers' training college where he gained rudimentary knowledge of painting and drawing. Pursuing these with self-study, he produced pictures, exhibiting them with the Modern Art Society, established in 1964, of which he was a member, a society that vigorously articulated the modern as the avant-garde in Singapore and in Southeast Asia, and as having a worldly compass—a worldliness embodied, represented largely by the Western, newly resurgent post–World War II capitalist hemisphere.

The writings I discuss were produced while he was studying in England. Two were written in Chinese and one in the English language. Even as he was away, he was not absent. Cheo maintained a close brief on the goings-on in Singapore art, intervening, provoking with creative gestures, artworks and writings. The writings were directed at and for Singapore artists and their publics. While they are site specific, they may be read as pertinent for thinking of the region.

The first, in 1972, in the Chinese language, was for a monthly magazine reporting on a wide range of topics; its title 'New Art, New Concepts' (the new is tirelessly registered and claimed along many fronts in Southeast Asia, a new that is of the 70s). In this essay he outlined strategies for striking out in directions that are new, cultivating and thinking new ways for producing art—art that speaks differently, art seen apart from prevailing works whose import tended to fold inwards. The following are listed as desirable goals. Concepts, ideas are mentioned as paramount; he says so at the beginning of his text and again towards the end. I quote: 'the changes in art do not only occur in subject matter, content, materials and techniques; the crucial changes occur in considerations of ideas and concepts'.[10] Formalism is rejected or swept aside as a presiding artistic principle. An artwork may now be made from simple, ordinary, non-artistic materials; it need not satisfy conventional aesthetic values and need not even be visually satisfying, but strike viewers as experientially connected with the world.

The second, in 1973, is written for the Modern Art Society's eighth annual exhibition. It was mailed to the residence of its president, which was also the postal address of the society. Cheo's text was not a review of the exhibition in that year. It was a no-holds barred appraisal of prevailing trends in Singapore, judging them sterile. He restates goals outlined a year earlier, directing them forcefully towards criticising the commoditisation, precocity of art. Practices of art are restricted; he urges discarding limits and adopting open, porous attitudes towards the world. He introduces the artist as contemporary, socially connected even convivial and says: 'contemporary artists do not mind others participating in the making of their work. In a way, the whole activity becomes less exclusive and more gregarious'.[11]

The third text, in 1974, was written in the English language as a foreword for the Modern Art Society's exhibition that year. In it the contemporary is named clearly, forcefully, prominently. Its mandate as a creative practice is set out, as are outcomes. All of these are laid out, nugget-like, in five brief paragraphs. Paragraphs 1 and 2 read as follows:

> 1. Contemporary art has in fact reached a point when artists are prepared to adopt anything as a medium to work with. What is important is not the execution of an art work but the idea. The speculation about the nature of things is sometimes more interesting than the rendering of actual appearances.
> 2. An artist should be able to deal with any kind of material and transform it into something that affects the spectator physically, intellectually or emotionally.[12]

10 Cheo Chai-Hiang, 'New Art, New Concepts', *Cheo Chai-Hiang. Thoughts and Processes (Rethinking the Singapore River)*, ed. T. K. Sabapathy and Cecily Briggs (Singapore: Nanyang Academy of Fine Arts & Singapore Art Museum, 2000), 115–17. Originally published in *Singapore Monthly Magazine*, 1972, in Chinese. English translation by Lai Chee-Kien.

11 Cheo Chai-Hiang, 'Written for the Occasion of 8th Modern Art Exhibition', in Sabapathy and Briggs, *Cheo Chai-Hiang*, 119. Originally published in *Sin Chew Jit Poh*, January 1973, 4. English translation by Cheo Chai-Hiang.

12 Cheo Chai-Hiang, 'Foreword', *Singapore Modern Art Exhibition Catalogue* (Singapore: Modern Art Society, 1974). Republished in Sabapathy and Briggs, eds, *Cheo Chai-Hiang*, 121.

Cheo Chai-Hiang's thoughts in these texts were beamed from the vantage of regarding Singapore from the outside, from seeing its artists and art along perspectives he was cultivating while studying in England. Yet, his is not solely an external, expatriated view, fuelled by newly inflected ideals absorbed unthinkingly by a freshly arrived, starry-eyed student, enthralled by the metropolitan milieus in England and in Europe. The tone in his writings is informed, rigorous and subtle; its tenor is weighted towards affecting change in a particular site. He explains terms, elaborating them with references to historically marked instances and adopts a dialogic stance.

Cheo remarks that the visual field is crowded and competitive; painting—and this is significant for Singapore and for Southeast Asia—can no longer claim a commanding presence for visual representation. Other media, formats, technologies—all of which are vigorously promoted and directed by the Singapore government then for economic, industrial development—are capable of producing images far more compelling and seductive. Those who practise painting will have to seriously reckon with these advances, redefine the foundations for its continuance (we encounter analogous assertions in the Black December Statement in 1974). He urges artists to discard the straitjacket stifling them, and instead cultivate critical openness, connectedness in creative practice and for the reception of artworks, artworks that are no longer embalmed by inwardly turned aesthetic doctrines but that resonate with living experience. To do so, practitioners and viewers are asked to unyoke themselves from restrictive, rigid orthodoxies some kinds of modern practices had congealed into.

The tone and tenor fly in the face of reigning political ideologies. These were unflinchingly aimed at mobilising peoples of a newly constituted modern state (i.e. Singapore) into yielding their lives as material resources for economic development, uniformly and conformingly. To think, act and live otherwise is to do so unproductively outside the prescribed political arena. Cheo Chai-Hiang was well aware of this, writing his thoughts subtly yet pointedly. Ho Ho Ying, the society's president to whom the second text was mailed, considered it as significant to the extent it required a broad readership. He submitted it to a Chinese language newspaper where it was published. These are not defiant acts; they are publicised in the mass media, in spaces set apart from the glare of headlines and editorials, and available readily.

While Cheo Chai-Hiang's analysis and exhortations lean towards unravelling the new as the contemporary, he does so by addressing artists and art agencies rooted in the modern, in Singapore, from which he emerged. What he says would not otherwise make sense. As it would not otherwise too when regarding the Black December disruption/statement and, for that matter, the emergence, the advocacies of the GSRB. Their pertinence for propelling the new, the different, is measurable when weighted with or against the modern as reigning aesthetic regimes in the 1970s, regimes that may well be troubled from within.

Patrick Flores illuminates this situation when he says:

> an argument can be made about the seventies as a flash point in the history of modernity in Southeast Asia. In mapping out the coordinates of certain shifts in this history, it is important to locate that point at which the modern would be challenged and made to yield to a condition of post-ness. The latter may be described as post-modern or contemporary; in whatever way it is conceived, the legacy of an always-already precarious modernity is threatened.[13]

Flores repositions the modern vis-à-vis the contemporary, beaming headlights onto its predicaments in the seventies. All is no longer completely well in the world that is the modern! As an argument it is useful for substantiating the historicalness of the contemporary as I am describing it.

Cheo Chai-Hiang's writing was read attentively, at least in and by the Modern Art Society, although not passively. There were written responses, countering his positional claims and reasserting the society's artistic goals. Matters came to a head in 1972.

In that year Cheo mailed a submission for display from Brighton, England. It consisted of instructions to the Modern Art Society's exhibitors in Singapore to draw a square, 5 feet in dimension, partially on a wall and partially on the floor adjoining it. The drawn square, without an image, was to bear the title *Singapore River*, referring to landscape paintings featuring this river, a perennial feature in pictures produced in the 1950s

13 Patrick D. Flores, 'The Demands of Abstraction: Exhibiting the Non-Objective in Manila in 1953', conference paper presented at 'From a History of Exhibitions towards a Future of Exhibition Making', Auckland Art Gallery, Auckland, 2013, 1, unpublished.

and 1960s. It was not considered for inclusion as there was no work as such, no work that was tangible, no work created by an artist for curatorial assessment.

Ho Ho Ying wrote a lengthy account for its exclusion. It was a letter written in the Chinese language and mailed to Cheo in Brighton, England. He acknowledged the seriousness of Cheo's thinking, but it had insufficiently to do with art. He recognises the importance of innovation, of not being restricted by aesthetic dogma. Even so, he safeguards foundational principles as they are inalienable. Here is a paragraph encapsulating some of these ideals; reading it is to hear the modern writing back!

> Art, besides being new, also has to possess intentionality and particularity in order to strike the viewer's heart. Imagine an artist installing nothing other than a bare cube in a big public square, and declaring, 'This is real art'. The viewer can also place a dead tree in the middle of a park and say this is art too. This is definitely confusing art with non-art. I personally believe in the importance of the created form in art, but I can't accept those found objects that are neither well thought out nor carefully fabricated.[14]

The divide between two worlds cannot be more starkly etched. Cheo Chai-Hiang was not surprised by any of this. Towards the end of the second text written in 1973 for the Modern Art Society's annual show, a year after receiving this letter, he points out that issues he raises are not removed from or alien to the modern in art. 'Modern art', he recalls, 'is the constant struggle to go beyond its defined boundaries' and 'whoever tries to pre-set a rigid boundary will sentence it to oblivion'. And this has, for him, come to pass. As it had at the Major Indonesian Painting Exhibition convened by the Jakarta Council in December 1974, instigating its disruption by a handful of student-artists, an intervention now known as the Black December event. There too the matter had to do with boundaries constraining modernist practices and of painting.

The contemporary and the modern are entangled, complicatedly and troublesomely.

---

14 Ho Ho Ying, 'Art, Besides Being New, Has to Possess an Intrinsic Quality in Order to Strike a Sympathetic Chord in the Hearts of the Viewers', in *Liu Kang and Ho Ho Ying. Re-Connecting. Selected Writings on Singapore Art and Art Criticism*, ed. T. K. Sabapathy and Cheo Chai-Hiang, trans. Cheo Chai-Hiang (Singapore: Institute of Contemporary Art Singapore, LASALLE-SIA College of the Arts, Singapore, 2005), 24. Originally published in Ho Ho Ying, *Critical Essays on Art* (Singapore: Singapore Art Museum, 1999).

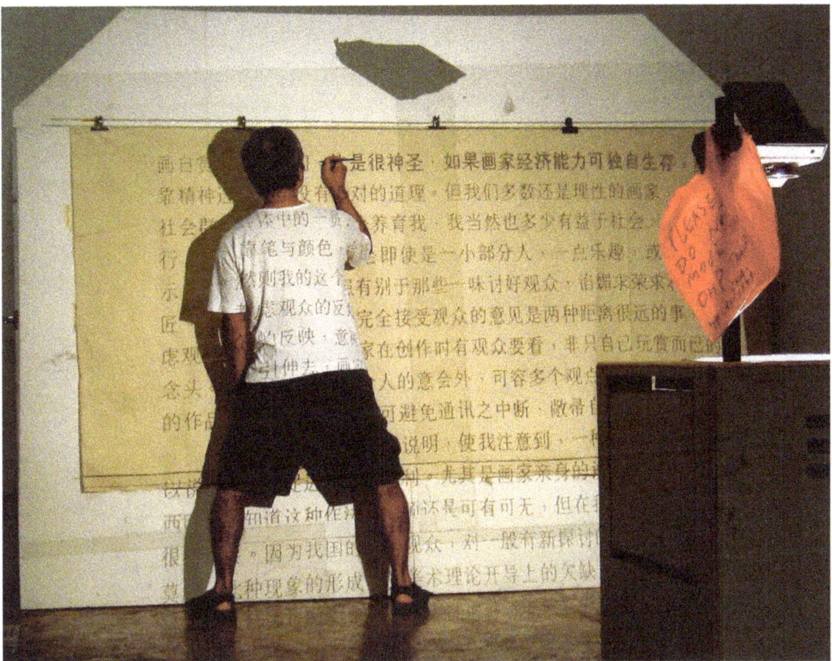

Figure 5.6: Cheo Chai-Hiang, *Artist at Work on Dear Cai Xiong (A Letter from Ho Ho Ying)*, 1972/2005.

Pencil on unprimed canvas. Dimensions various. Image courtesy the artist.[15]

The struggle for freeing oneself from the grip of inwardly turned, exclusive aesthetic doctrines by experimentally breaking constraints, by exploratory widening the scope for creative practice so as to be in the world openly and critically are, for Cheo Chai-Hiang, writing in the early 1970s, 'precursors' to 'what has been happening in the contemporary world'.

In all these regards and bearing in mind my brief description of political demands made of the newly formed, modern Singapore, Cheo's closing remarks in this 1973 text are unerring and for us prescient:

> These are questions for artists of the seventies to think deep and hard about. It is a testing time for artists. It also poses big challenges for mankind. We need to be more open when we look at the world. We also need to be more courageous and have faith in ourselves when engaging in new experiments.[16]

15 See T. K. Sabapathy, 'Intersecting Histories: On the Contemporary in Southeast Asian Art', Leap 26, 11 June 2014, accessed 20 January 2022, www.leapleapleap.com/2014/06/intersecting-histories-on-the-contemporary-in-southeast-asian-art/.

16 Cheo Chai-Hiang, 'Written for the Occasion of the 8th Modern Art Exhibition', 120.

It is circumspect and it is assertive.

Before leaving Cheo Chai-Hiang I draw attention to his conversion of that letter from Ho Ho Ying into a monumental representation; on four large canvases, he transcribes the letter, magnifying a private communication albeit consisting of important matters into assuming a public spectacle (see Figure 5.6). The circumstances prompting this work have to do with a spate of rejections that Cheo met when submitting works as public commissions.

III

In August 1974 Redza Piyadasa and Sulaiman Esa brought a year-long collaborative research-based creative project to fruition and publicised it in the writers' corner, a room for readings and book launches, in the Dewan Bahasa dan Pustaka (a government agency for promoting Malay as the national language and literature written in it) in Kuala Lumpur. It was called *Towards A Mystical Reality: a documentation of a jointly initiated experience by redza piyadasa and suleiman esa*[17] (hereafter TMR). A publication bearing the same title was issued as a salient component of this documentation.[18] The two have insisted that the publication is the real thing in this project. Mention of artist, art, exhibition, are avoided in naming it, underlining the radicalness they sought to deliver up front. Although in the text proper, art, artists are fervently discussed.[19]

17 Editors' note: the lower case for the second part of the title, including the names of Piyadasa and Esa, and spelling of 'sulieman' are as they appear on the front cover of the catalogue.

18 Editors' note: *Towards A Mystical Reality: a documentation of an experience by redza piyadasa and suleiman esa*, Kuala Lumpur, undated. A range of images and extracts from the text of *Towards A Mystical Reality* can be found on a number of internet websites including Sulaiman Esa's own website and the M+ Archive Hong Kong. Esa was selected as an artist for the First Asia Pacific Triennial in Australia in 1993 and his work *Garden of Mystery 1* (1992) was purchased by the Queensland Art Gallery | Gallery of Modern Art. Piyadasa was an adviser and co-curator for the Malaysian artists for the First Asia Pacific Triennial.

19 *Towards A Mystical Reality: a documentation of jointly initiated experiences by redza piyadasa and suleiman esa*, Kuala Lumpur, undated. All citations are from this publication. Literature on this exposition and publication is quite extensive, although a bibliography of writings has not been compiled. The following are useful: Siti Zainon Ismail, 'Satu Esei untuk Piyadasa' [An essay for Piyadasa], *Dewan Sastera* (May 1975): 48; R. Piyadasa, 'Satu lagi jawapan untuk Siti Zainon' [Another reply for Siti Zainon], *Dewan Sastera* (June 1975); Salleh Ben Joned, 'Kencing dan Kesenian' [Peeing and art], *Dewan Sastera* (July 1975), republished in English by the author as 'The Art of Pissing', in Salleh Ben Joned, *As I Please* (London: Skoob Books Publishing, 1994), 19–29; T. K. Sabapathy, *Piyadasa*, (Kuala Lumpur: Archipelago Publishers, 1978), 31–38; T. K. Sabapathy, *Piyadasa. An Overview, 1962–2000* (Kuala Lumpur: Balai Seni Lukis Negara, 2001), 37–59; Simon Soon, 'An Empty Canvas on Which Many Shadows Have Already Fallen', *Reactions—New Critical Strategies. Narratives in Malaysian Art*, Vol. 2, ed. Nur Hanim Khairuddin and Beverly Yong with T. K. Sabapathy (Kuala Lumpur: Rogue Art, 2013), 55–69.

As a display it consisted of things cast away as refuse or matter-of-factly used; things retrieved by the two of them from diverse locations, including their respective homes. The very stuff Ho Ho Ying refuses to admit into his art world.

Although ordinary and discarded, each of these was shown as artefacts are in art exhibitions—raised on plinths, suspended on walls and from the ceiling. A label bearing details on provenance and purpose for showing accompanied every item. The information does not mimic the tenor of data furnished for artworks and reading texts when seeing them. References to aesthetic intentions or formal properties are excluded. In their stead one reads anecdotal notations as to when, where from, a thing had been retrieved and how it might be of incidental interest in the display. Each of these comes over casually, obviously and unremarkably.

TMR has been discussed in a number of publications. As with GSRB it has been written on from its onset, commendably and disparagingly, never fading from attention. As with GSRB too, it is singled out as the most significant flashpoint illuminating the departure from the modern as the reigning aesthetic orthodoxy and as 'opening the floodgates of the contemporary'[20] in Malaysian art practices.

I summarise TMR's aims and move to deal with its prehistory. They are as follows:

1. sow seeds for creating, spurring a new art in Malaysia and Asia
2. free artists from the dominance of the West by cultivating foundations affiliated with Asian philosophical traditions, seen as congenial for creative practices in the present
3. bypass formal principles as defining for the making and appraising artworks and, in their stead
4. present stimuli, provocations that may entail visual, concrete objects for apprehending reality directly and from one's lived, cultivated experiences.

---

20 'Interviews with Prominent Art Personalities by Nur Hanim Khairuddin: Simon Soon', in *Raja'ah: Art, Idea and Creativity of Sulaiman Esa from 1950s–2011*, ed. Nur Hanim Khairuddin (Kuala Lumpur: Balai Seni Visual National/National Visual Arts Gallery), 141. Simon Soon's observation is as follows: 'TMR did open up the floodgates to the contemporary but it was by no means the ONLY exhibition that did that and certainly not the first'. He is also cited as remarking: 'I think that TMR is an important flashpoint from the modern into the contemporary in its radical reevaluation of the aesthetic paradigm' (p. 141).

The familiarity of such an inventory is not surprising. We encounter it when examining textual representations of certain kinds of art in the 1970s in locations in Southeast Asia. They are articulated variously, with differing resonance arising from specific social-political conditions and expressed distinctly in particular languages. When reading Cheo Chai-Hiang's texts I highlighted ambitions, aims that are at times symptomatic and at times declaratory of the contemporary in art. These traits may be aligned comparably when interpreting the TMR as I have reported it and earlier in this account with reference to Black December and GSRB.

I track back from 1974, back from *Towards A Mystical Reality* and round off this paper. I introduced it as marking a fruition of creative collaboration between Sulaiman Esa and Piyadasa. It did not come about just for that project but predates it by quite a while. The two were students in London, had shared accommodation there, fuelling each other's thinking on art and fortifying their mission to shake Malaysian artists into recognising new realities. They were colleagues as teaching faculty in the school of art and design, MARA Institute of Technology (in Malaysia), and were a formidable force in art education.

In 1970 they held an exhibition, titling it *Experiment '70* with three other artists, all allied by interests in minimalist strategies, in two- and three-dimensional productions, developing cool, detached, serialised methods for designing, fabricating works as art. Their aims were positioned as antithetical to the dominant strains in painting in Malaysia in which expressivity/expressiveness were upheld as aesthetically and existentially paramount.

Artists in *Experiment '70* direct attention to the primacy of materials, to thought-and-processes in practice and production. These were cast, however, in modernist parlance, envisaging art that is created as edging towards a kind of terminus for modernist possibilities. For instance, Piyadasa claims: 'my work is conceptual in nature', it 'exists as visual documents' even as he concedes that his works are sculptures.[21] As notions, they simultaneously are anchored in modernity while aspiring to be freed from it.

Sulaiman Esa and Piyadasa persisted with strategies unveiled in 1970 and two years later in a joint exposition they called *Dokumentasi 72*, presented framed planes and pigmented surfaces barely, residually, recognisable as

21 *Experiment '70*, Kuala Lumpur, 1970, unpaginated.

pictures. They had depleted the parameters of painting and sculpture as these had been advanced as defining the modern in visual art in Malaysia, in their practices. This is not to imply that painting and sculpture as such are finished. Indeed these are reconfigured, enlivened in part at least by young artists on seeing *Experiment '70* and *Dokumentasi 72* and in part by impetus gleaned from imagery, technologies of representation in the domain of mass media as well as sharp perceptions of political and social violence.

To say they had emptied painting and sculpture in their practices is to signify that pathways leading to *Towards A Mystical Reality* are developed systematically. And that TMR, esteemed as it is, as inaugurating the contemporary in Malaysian art did not erupt suddenly, inexplicably. It emerges gradually, spanning four years; it emerges from collaborative orientations of two artists' practices and thinking, directed at interrogating the terrain of the modern while traversing it, and then exiting it by prospecting criteria, methods for making a different kind of art. As remarked earlier, the contemporary and intimations of the contemporary are complicatedly entwined with the modern. One is, historically, unthinkable without the other, at least in the 1970s.[22]

Towards A Mystical Reality was initiated five years after outbreaks of racial violence in Malaysia, in May 1969. Collectively and colloquially referred to as 'May 13', it ended an alignment of power set along separate ethnic identities designated chiefly as Malay, Chinese, Indian, stitched into forming an accommodating coalition. In the reconstructed post-May 13 Malaysia, such an alignment persisted although separateness is heightened. Access to power, resources and nationhood are zealously guarded and contested within separate grids. Being Malay and Muslim are constituted as paramount.

22 For writings on art in the 1970s in locations in Southeast Asia see the following: Patrick D. Flores, 'Missing Link, Burned Bridges: The Art of the 70s', *Pananaw2: Philippine Journal of Visual Arts* (Manila: National Commission for Culture and the Arts, 1998), 52–63; Ahmad Mashadi, 'Southeast Asian Art during the 1970s', in *Telah Terbit (Out Now), Southeast Asian Art Practices during the 1960s to 1980s* (Singapore: Singapore Art Museum, 2007), 14–24; Ahmad Mashadi, 'Framing the 1970s', *Third Text* 25, no. 4 (July 2011), ed. Patrick D. Flores and Joan Kee, 409–17, doi.org/10.1080/09528822.2011.587686; Safrizal Shahir, 'Dynamism Sophistication: Malaysian Modern Art in the 1970s', in Khairuddin and Yong, *Reaction – New Critical Strategies*, 70–80; 'Interviews with Prominent Art Personalities by Nur Hanim Khairuddin', in Khairuddin, *Raja'ah: Art, Idea and Creativity of Sulaiman Esa from 1950s – 2011*, 134–65; Ringo Bunoan, *The 70s. Objects, Photographs & Documents* (Manila: Ateneo Art Gallery, 2018).

In the midst of these manoeuvres a cultural congress was convened in 1971 to determine new directions. This is a complicated issue, largely unexamined. I touch on it as it is germane to the lives of Piyadasa and Sulaiman Esa, to their relationships/collegiality and their respective art practices.

In the congress, proposals for a national art were forwarded; such an art was envisaged favourably as springing from Malay/indigenous traditions. Proposals such as these were debated and contested. Towards the end of the 1970s and throughout the 1980s discussion of such traditions and creative practices were transformed by precepts from Islam, precepts spurred by religious/ethnic imperatives spurred by Malay-Muslim Malaysia and the proclamation of an Islamic republic in Iran in 1979, which had global ramifications. In 1982 the Malaysian government introduced an Islamisation program, seeking to inculcate Islamic values in various facets of the life of Malay-Muslim communities. This affected every artist. It affected Sulaiman Esa and Piyadasa profoundly.

The two had participated in the congress of 1971. The latter read a paper on the modern in Malaysian art in which he unambiguously underlined its history as shaped by multicultural, worldly wellsprings and not by any one cultural resource or ideology; a worldview he maintained throughout his life—in his creative practice, his teaching and writing. Sulaiman Esa, on the other hand, immersed himself in the study of Islam, its history, art and culture; he also embarked upon field studies of weaving and woodcarving among rural Malay communities. The two went their separate ways.[23]

23 Zainol Sharif hints at the difficult, complicated circumstances in which these two forged their respective creative trajectories after TMR. He remarks that Sulaiman Esa's 'Islamic works came in the wake of the global reassertion of Islam. It also seemed like a profound manifestation of his personal struggles as an artist and social being'. By way of a riveting metaphor, Zainol Sharif connects and distinguishes the two:

> If Sulaiman has been awakened by the thunder of Islamic revolution, his mystical fellow-traveler through reality, Redza Piyadasa, too has not been deaf to the amplified decibels from the minarets. His mixed-media collages incorporating silk-screened images of photographs [collectively named as *The Malaysian Series*] emerged amidst the government's Islamisation programme. And if Piyadasa was not deaf to the call from the minarets, he also was not blind to the obvious connections between ethnicity and Islam in the country. His images of recent ancestors of present-day Malaysians are aesthetic reactions echoing the latent and manifest fears of Malaysians, Muslims and non-Muslims alike, of political and social marginalization.

Zainol Sharif, 'Towards an Alter-Native Vision: The Idea of Malaysian Art since 1980', in *Vision and Idea. ReLooking Modern Malaysian Art*, ed. T. K. Sabapathy (Kuala Lumpur: National Art Gallery, 1994), 81–82. For a discussion of Sulaiman Esa's dilemma, thoughts and practice immediately after TMR, see T. K. Sabapathy, 'The Secret and the Sacred: Pictures by Sulaiman Esa', *Translating Southeast Asia, Moving Worlds, a Journal of Transcultural Writings* 15, no. 1 (2015): 77–81.

TMR marked the culmination of their artistic collaboration; it also marked the end of their collegiality and relationship.

TMR was initiated and received in such a milieu. It steered a course away from an inward national turn and instead turned to cultivating prospects so that Asia could be encompassed artistically in the present, and to simultaneously claim it mattered in the world. It was possible to do so fearlessly and briefly, in the early 1970s.

IV

I have described circumstances in which kinds of art produced in the early 1970s as well as thoughts written on such art are distinguishable as the contemporary. Individuals, instances named are seen as departing, differentiating from the modern, as it is represented in art domains in the region. This is not to indicate the modern is displaced, replaced; it is to direct attention to other values, separate destinations forwarded, claimed as significant; so much so the modern as such is affected by them. I have leaned towards reading texts in which the contemporary is on one hand symptomatically discerned and on the other heard declaratorily.

Two nominations are examined closely: writings by Cheo Chai-Hiang, and texts and works by Sulaiman Esa and Piyadasa. There are others I wished to have discussed, especially Roberto Chabet and Raymundo Albano and their curating of new art within and outside of the Cultural Center of the Philippines in Manila, in the early 1970s.

Cheo Chai-Hiang and Piyadasa/Sulaiman Esa are contemporaneous. However there is no evidence of contact between them, that they were acquainted with one another's thoughts, actions, productions. Hence, we surmise that initiatives for advancing a sense of the contemporary spring from the make-up of individuals or collectives, and their worldviews; from historical factors particular to specific locations and to living in them, and not from a single, identifiable wellspring or from interconnected resources within the region of Southeast Asia.

Be that as it may, when reading these texts I have maintained sight of one in relation to another, interweaving them, bringing to bear implications arising from what is written in one instance or occasion on another, when the two are not known historically to be related, aligning their readings so that they yield comparability pertaining to the contemporary in art in the early 1970s, in and across locations. These are for me beginnings in seeking to connect sites and temporalities within the region of Southeast Asia, and to subsequently develop methods for examining them.

6

A Brief History of Indonesian Modern Art[1]

Jim Supangkat

Regarded as Indonesia's foremost curatorial voice of the late twentieth century, Jim Supangkat was born in Makassar, Sulawesi (see Map 1), and later studied aesthetics and philosophy at university in Bandung (Institute Teknologi Bandung). He was a founder of the Gerakan Seni Rupa Baru (Indonesian New Art Movement) in 1975 and was a highly influential artist before concentrating on curating because of what he saw as the lack of curators in Indonesia at that time. Supangkat has played a key role in both Indonesian contemporary exhibitions and in taking Indonesian art to international audiences. This essay, originally published in English in 1993, is reproduced here as a significant primary document.[2] *The essay was written for an international audience at a time when Indonesian art was connecting with global contemporary art to introduce those audiences to the history of Indonesian art.*

1 Editors' note: text in the captions to illustrations in this essay has been provided by the institutions and the editors, not the author.

2 Jim Supangkat, 'A Brief History of Indonesian Art', in *Tradition and Change: Contemporary Art of Asia and the Pacific*, ed. Caroline Turner (Brisbane: University of Queensland Press, 1993), 47–57.

Since modern art is believed to be a universal phenomenon, modern art in developing countries has been expected to develop in the same way as it has in Paris or New York. But the fact is, it has not. Lack of communication, lack of information, the influence of local conditions, the distortion of perception all mean that modern art in developing countries has taken different directions.

It is understandable then that modern art in developing countries became a confusing phenomenon for critics and art theorists in the international art circle and has never been taken seriously. The unanswered question is: how far could modern art principles be interpreted so as to have different implications and meaning in another context? Modern art, which is based on Western art, particularly the tradition of high art established in the sixteenth century, has a frame of reference which resists interpretation. Modern art is in some sense ambiguous. It strongly believes in searching for new international values but, on the other hand, is also still connected to the tradition of Western art. The implication is that modern art has only one possibility to achieve: that is an achievement based on a Western frame of reference. The logical outcome is a monolinear development as seen mostly in Europe and America.

In many developing countries, including Indonesia, modern art grew out of Western art as it was adapted, sometimes over a very long period of time, during the colonial period. This is an important point to understand. Conditions changed after independence and in developing countries modern art frequently became anti-Western. This led to an emphasis on theoretical cultural debate, a confrontation between Eastern and Western values, and a focus on a search for national or Eastern identity. The fact that modern art in developing countries could deny its Western roots was a difficult phenomenon for most critics in the international circle to accept, especially as internationalism has worked against a reliance on national identity.

The national identity issue was no doubt the main reason for the distance that emerged between modern art in developing countries and the international circle. The introduction of the concept of pluralism in the 1970s and 1980s offered the possibility of an accommodation and greater understanding, since pluralism denies internationalism's absolutism and accepts national boundaries as a basis for a differentiated achievement. Thus modern art in developing countries could be seen to have both an international and a national context.

While pluralism is still not widely accepted in the international critical circle, and although information on the concept is still limited in developing countries, theoretically the evolution of modern art in developing countries can only be understood through this principle.

The Western Influence on Indonesian Modern Art

Western culture, including Western art, entered Indonesia in colonial times. Indonesia was a Dutch colony for 350 years, but the Western way of life influenced only a limited number of people—the upper level of society, mostly feudal families or plantation owners. They adopted Western culture through education and close contact with Western society, especially the Dutch colonial government whose policies created a feudal atmosphere by using this upper level of society to control the lower classes. In contrast, most of the common people still lived in a traditional way, and virtually without education. Western art, in colonial times, thus became known only within a select group and there were few Indonesian artists.

Despite this, the art activities of the upper level of society at the beginning of the nineteenth century were the basis of Indonesian modern art. Indonesian modern art grew out of Western culture. It was not a continuation and development of traditional arts, which have a different frame of reference. If Indonesian expression showed in the works, it was a result of the artist's cultural background, not the result of traditional art principles.

Since there were so few Indonesian artists in colonial times it is difficult to point to a particular Indonesian art. But the work of Dutch artists who lived in Indonesia, some of them born in Indonesia, showed differences when compared with Dutch artists working in the Netherlands. One could draw the conclusion, although purely hypothetical, that art development in colonial times already had specific local characteristics. These Dutch artists should also, therefore, be acknowledged as pioneers of Indonesian modern art.

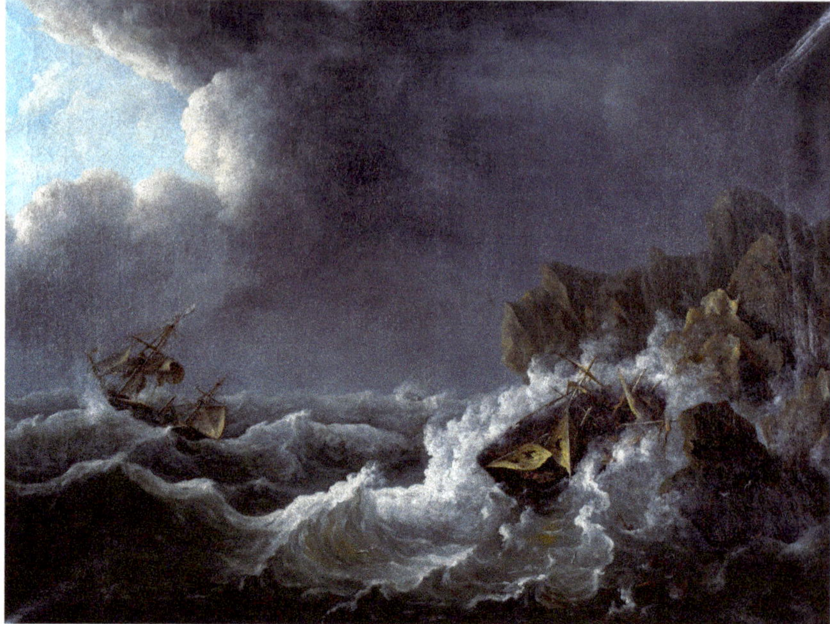

Figure 6.1: Raden Saleh, *Shipwreck in Storm*, 1840.
Oil on canvas, 74 x 98 cm. Collection: Galeri Nasional Indonesia. Image courtesy Galeri Nasional Indonesia.[3]

One Indonesian artist who, despite the obstacles, became well known at home and abroad in the nineteenth century, was a Javanese prince named Raden Saleh (1807–1880).[4] He and some early Dutch artists marked the beginning of modern art in Indonesia if we accept the theory that modern art began with neoclassicism and romanticism. Paintings and drawings made by Dutch artists before Raden Saleh were not meant as works of art, since they merely purported to function as a documentation of Indonesian rural life, landscapes, wildlife, and architecture.

Raden Saleh and a Dutch artist named Jan Daniels Beynon were the best-known Indonesian artists of their time. Like their counterparts in Europe, they were professionals who usually undertook portraiture commissions

3 Editors' note: in his important book, *Indonesian Modern Art and Beyond*, Supangkat described Raden Saleh's painting *The Arrest of Prince Diponegoro* (see discussion Chapter 1 and Figure 1.4) as setting forth 'the spirit of freedom' and as taking a stance sympathetic to the prince in his 'struggle' against the Dutch. See Jim Supangkat, *Indonesian Modern Art and Beyond* (Jakarta: The Indonesian Fine Arts Foundation, 1997), 24. See also Figure 3.1 for a further example of Raden Saleh's painting.

4 Editors' note: the date of 1811 for Raden Saleh's birth is now the generally accepted date but 1807 is retained here because this is a primary source.

of important people. Both were influenced by the romantic movement. Saleh and Beynon regularly visited Europe and spent some time in Paris. In their paintings, the principles of European romanticism could be clearly seen (such as in studies of violence among wild animals, attacks on humans and the latter's terrified expressions).

It is difficult to draw definitive conclusions about Raden Saleh since there are few sources and publications on him and not many of his works survive. But in Indonesian art history, Raden Saleh is credited with being the pioneer of Indonesian modern art. Most of his best works are now the property of the Indonesian presidential palace. Among his other important works are *The Fight* (a scene of a lion attacking a horse rider) and *The Bull Hunters* (hunters in traditional costumes fighting a group of wounded bulls). A reproduction of his masterpiece *A Matter of Life and Death* (two lions attacking a bull) is now in the collection of the Rijksmuseum in Amsterdam—the original painting disappeared in Paris in 1931.

The Spring of Indonesian Modern Art

Indonesian modern art really came into existence between 1930 and 1940. At that time there were two groups of artists who differed from each other in style and principles. The birth of Indonesian modern art was signalled by the confrontation of these two groups. One group, under the influence of two senior painters, Abdullah Soeriosoebroto (1878–1941) and Mas Pirngadi[5] (1865–1936), continued to make representational paintings, in the tradition that had developed since the days of Saleh. Their paintings followed the orderly principles and techniques referred to as academic. Nearly all the group had studied in the Netherlands. Like earlier Indonesian painters, these artists were members of the upper level of colonial society. Their works were realistic-ideal depictions of beautiful landscapes, and sometimes also flattering individual portraits.

The other group was led by a rebel painter named Sudjojono (1914–1986)[6] who had once been one of Abdullah Soeriosoebroto's followers. Sudjojono could not accept Abdullah's strict academic painting methods.

5 Editors' note: see Figure 3.2.

6 Editors' note: the date now most often used for Sudjojono's birth is 1913 but 1914 is retained here as this is a primary source.

His rebellion was also related to the fact that Sudjojono was a member of a political group that fought for Indonesian independence. Abdullah, in Sudjojono's opinion, was a collaborator who worked too closely with Dutch colonial society.

At the same time, a group of art lovers in the colonial society of the 1930s organised exhibitions of original European modern paintings, such as works by Vincent van Gogh, Braque, Cezanne, Gauguin, Max Ernst and Modigliani.

No doubt Sudjojono was influenced by those works, technically and spiritually. He identified himself as a modernist and judged Abdullah's academic paintings as tending towards classicism. These paintings, he stated, were merely expressing a notion of an ideal and peaceful life—'The Beautiful Indies'. He accused the artists of being members of colonial society and not Indonesian. For decades Sudjojono's overly nationalistic point of view influenced Indonesian critics and art historians, who denied Abdullah Soeriosoebroto's role in the development of Indonesian modern art.

The group of artists organised by Sudjojono were mostly uneducated painters such as poster painters, comic strip artists, advertisement designers and others who had never been acknowledged as artists. Because of their involvement with the nationalist movement, they identified themselves as 'Indonesian' artists. Apart from Sudjojono, two of the best-known and most influential of these artists were Affandi (1907–1990) and Hendra Gunawan (1918–1983).

The works of all three painters were expressionistic in style, and highly emotional in content. Their themes and subjects, which could be called a kind of social realism, were drawn from the struggle for independence, poverty, injustice, war and the life of people at the grass roots level. Their social realism in an expressionistic style, painted in heavy brushstrokes, fitted the conditions of that time, dominated by the spirit of the struggle for independence.[7]

7 Editors' note: for a fine example of Hendra Gunawan's work, see the National Gallery Singapore, accessed 4 October 2021, collections.nationalgallery.sg/#/search?Search=hendra%20gunawan&SearchType=b, especially his painting *War and Peace*, related to the independence war.

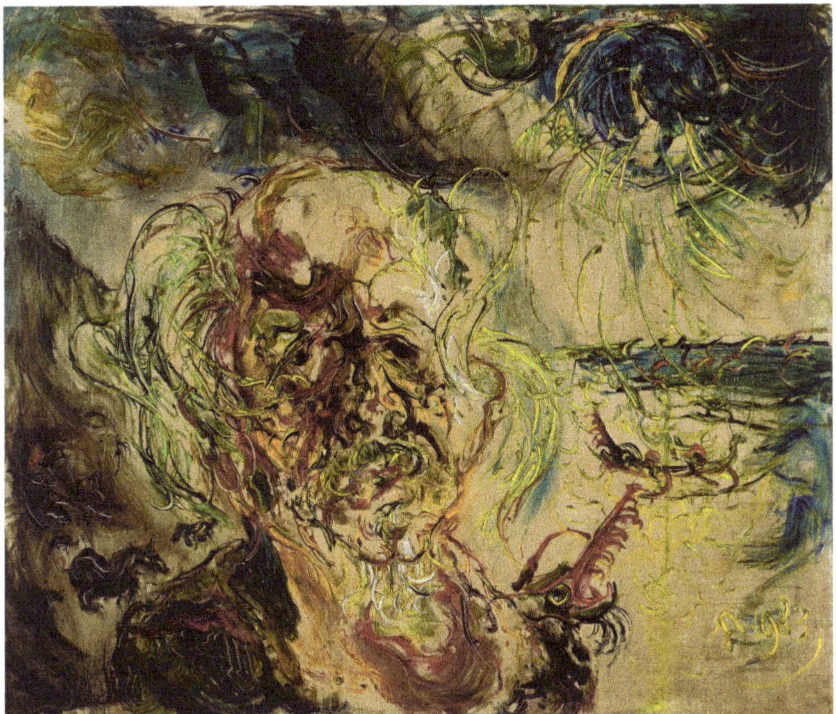

Figure 6.2: Affandi (1907–1990), Indonesia, *Self Portrait in Kusamba Beach*, 1983.

Oil on canvas, 130 x 149.5 cm. Collection: Queensland Art Gallery | Gallery of Modern Art. Purchased 1994 with funds from the International Exhibitions Program. Celebrating the Queensland Art Gallery's Centenary, 1895–1995. Image courtesy QAGOMA and permission Kartika Affandi and the Affandi Museum.

Sudjojono, Affandi, and Hendra Gunawan became the most influential artists in Indonesia after independence and the expressionistic style they introduced influenced Indonesian modern art for a long time (1940–70).

Even today some major artists still work in this expressionistic style. There are artists who still believe in social realism, painting the poor, and who even sometimes still work with revolutionary themes. Among these are Sudjana Kerton and Djoko Pekik. Poverty is still a reality for many in Indonesia. Both Kerton and Pekik often paint the everyday life of the common people and the struggles of the poor.

Others who still practice an expressionistic style have developed it in a very individual way. Srihadi Soedarsono, for example, the most acclaimed painter in present-day Indonesia, has developed a very original individual style of expression.

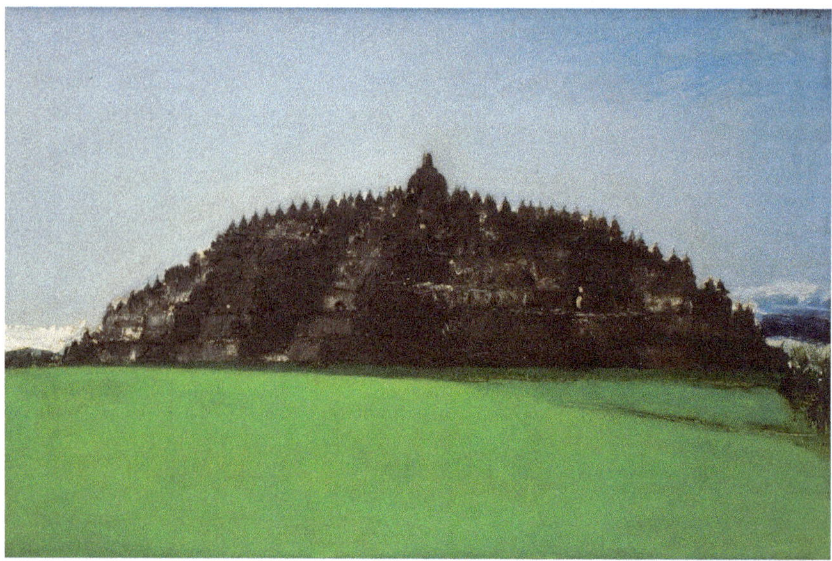

Figure 6.3: Srihadi Soedarsono [Sudarsono] (1931–2022), Solo, Indonesia, *Borobudur II*, 1982.

Oil on canvas, 95 x 140 cm. Collection: Galeri Nasional Indonesia. Image courtesy Galeri Nasional Indonesia and the artist. Permission: the artist.

Srihadi was influenced first by the social realism of the 1940s, then by action painting which he studied in the United States in the 1960s. In this period he produced abstract expressionist paintings, although this phase of his art was brief. Srihadi never totally became a nonfigurative painter. There has always been subject matter in his paintings, although it is not always clearly seen.

His landscapes, townscapes and seascapes utilise very expressive brushstrokes across the canvas which divide the space into two sections by a horizon line. Then, with some highly emotional strokes, he paints objects not far from the horizon and leaves the rest of the canvas nearly empty, covered only with a thin bright colour.

In his latest paintings Srihadi, who lives in Bandung in Java, has been working in his studio on Bali Island. Much of his recent work is filled with the atmosphere of Bali—landscapes, everyday life, dancers, traditional feasts, and so on. He has a special interest in painting the movement of Balinese dancers. With expressive lines and brushstrokes he evokes the dynamic movement of the dancers and the rhythm and sensuality of the dance.

Srihadi believes that the traditional atmosphere in Bali, where many people still live in a traditional way, has a creative spirit which stimulates and inspires him. Srihadi has consciously tried to adapt traditional arts to express his emotions and ideas. This is a common tendency in Indonesian modern art.

Another artist who has tried to combine modernism and traditionalism in the search for national identity is Gregorius Sidharta Soegiyo. This Dutch-educated artist attempted to apply traditional decorative patterns to the concepts of synthetic cubism in the 1960s. In the 1980s, inspired by mythological themes, he worked on contemporary sculptures using handicraft techniques. His experience in the domain of modern art and his knowledge of traditional arts (he grew up within a traditional Javanese family) has enabled Sidharta to understand the characteristic elements of both forms of art. His sculptures, paintings and prints represent a new expression—a modern art with Indonesian images.

Srihadi and Sidharta are both professors at Bandung Institute of Technology. This art academy is known as the centre of modernism in Indonesia. The teachers here work with modern art styles by adapting abstract expressionism, minimalism, neoplasticism, geometricism, etc., in some ways only adjusting attitude with changes in the international constellation (but this is modernisation, isn't it?). Not many of them, then, have ever achieved a completely individual expression in their styles.

Works by professors of the academy have a reputation for being difficult to understand. Because very few people could appreciate their work, the modernistic styles practised here, though based on a correct Western aesthetic, have only minimum recognition. Their influence in Indonesian modern art development then was also limited.

These realities are important in understanding modern art's evolution in developing countries. Because of a lack of information, exploration of new styles, expression and values are not understood by most of the people. This limitation has forced the development of modern art to take a specific course.

Indonesian modern art's development has been dominated by the art of painting and in paintings the decorative style is predominant. Nearly 80 per cent of Indonesian artists are painters, and nearly half of them work in the decorative style. This style is characteristic of another art academy, the Indonesian Institute of the Arts in Yogyakarta. Major artists who could be said to be founders of this style are Widayat, Handrio and Soenarto Pr, who in the 1960s founded a very influential artists' workshop, Sanggar Bambu (Bamboo Workshop).

At first glance, decorative painting could be criticised as only expressing superficial beauty, or a craft aesthetic. This is not the case. The decorative style in Indonesia has been explored in various ways and produced many individual styles.

It can be argued that this decorative style in modern times is a sign of an Indonesian traditional arts influence. Traditional arts in Indonesia are not based on one form of aesthetic. It is nearly impossible to generalise about Indonesian traditional arts, since there are more than 300 ethnic groups and each tribe has its own tradition and, of course, specific art expression.

But behind the diversity there is a similarity in decorative expression. This is not just a surface beauty. The decorative expression usually has a symbolic meaning. Ornaments, for example, had communication purposes, such as revealing the hierarchy in society, or were used for status or because of a belief in their magical power.

There are some traditional arts in Indonesia which developed into a sophisticated art, such as Javanese court art. Though it still has a decorative tendency, Javanese art has a descriptive and written aesthetic related to Javanese philosophy. Some of the aesthetic principles were similar to high art concepts.

Another indicator that supports the argument that the decorative arts achievement is not-just-surface-beauty is the development in Bali Island. Though this island is part of Indonesia, it is difficult to include Bali's art in Indonesian modern art development. Based on its strong tradition, Balinese art has a clearer empirical development when compared to the rest of Indonesia. In its development, Bali's art has adapted many foreign influences, in the past those of individual Dutch artists and today modern and contemporary art ideas. Yet despite these influences, Balinese identity can still clearly be seen. In Bali, as elsewhere in Indonesia, many traditional arts still exist and develop. There is no doubt that these traditional arts are part of the reality of life for Indonesian modern artists. Whether they like it or not, it is difficult to avoid the influence of traditional arts.

The decorative style has a strong tendency to be just high craftmanship and could easily be degraded to a meaningless expression. Many Indonesian decorative paintings faced this reality. After decades without development, there was a move towards the degradation of decorative paintings in the 1980s together with a move towards highly commercialised styles. Along with this, private galleries flowered in the same years. There was a sudden and fast-growing art market in the 1980s, described by Indonesian art historian Dr Sanento Yuliman as a 'boom of decorative paintings'.

Following the rise in prices at American auction houses, prices of paintings in Indonesia rose to unbelievable levels. But the art business, of course, was not based on a real knowledge of investment. High prices launched speculatively by art dealers, not based on a market mechanism, were understandably very unstable.

As a result of the sudden interest, exhibitions and art activities grew rapidly in big cities. Art, especially the art of painting, was widely recognised to a degree never seen before in Indonesian history. But this surge of activity cannot be said to have brought real progress in art. The appreciation of art in general is still poor. There has been almost no achievement in nonpainting art expression since nearly all of the galleries tend to exhibit commercial decorative paintings. This phenomenon of art sociology shows once again how modern art could be adapted with a very biased perception in developing countries. But the conclusion is not that modern art does not exist. Though modern art began as a universal phenomenon, and existed in all nations as a modern way of expression, this does not mean that it should have a universal standardised development.

Indonesian Contemporary Art

The word 'contemporary' was first used in Indonesia in 1973 at an exhibition of sculpture in Jakarta organised by Gregorius Sidharta Soegiyo. Soegiyo used the word 'contemporary' to explain the exhibition because, in his opinion, some of the sculptures exhibited could no longer be categorised as modern.

Most of them used constructed and welded techniques. By contrast, before this exhibition, the art of sculpture in Indonesia, which had made very little progress, employed almost solely wooden and marble sculpting and bronze casting techniques. The conception behind the works was a strong belief in the artist's touch and formal measurement.

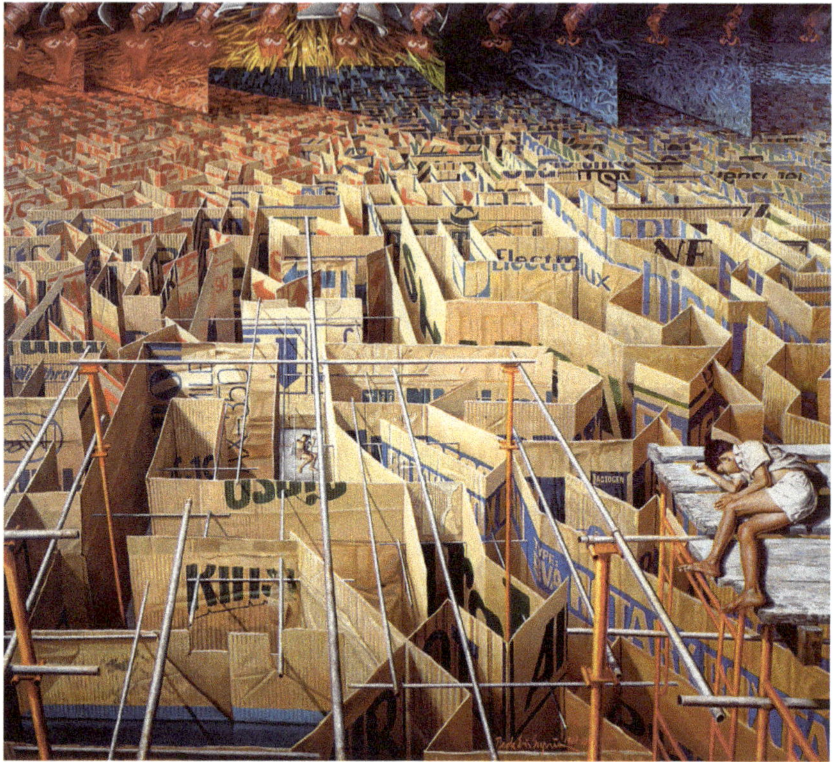

Figure 6.4: Dede Eri Supria (b. 1956), *Labyrinth* (from 'Labyrinth' series), 1987–88.

Oil on canvas, 207.3 x 227.5 cm. Collection: Queensland Art Gallery | Gallery of Modern Art. The Kenneth and Yasuko Myer Collection of Contemporary Asian Art. Purchased 1993 with funds from The Myer Foundation and Michael Sidney Myer through the Queensland Art Gallery Foundation. Image courtesy QAGOMA. Permission: the artist.

But the use of the term 'contemporary' was not followed by further discussion or debate within an art circle dominated by modern-oriented principles. The word 'contemporary' faded away. So it is difficult to draw a clear line between modern and contemporary art in Indonesia.

Contemporary principles re-emerged in 1975. In this year a group of young artists organised a movement, later known as the Indonesian New Art Movement. In the very beginning the movement was a rebellion within the two main art academies, the Bandung Institute of Technology and the Indonesian Institute of the Arts in Yogyakarta. The rebellion was merely academic, a debate on modernist principles and new points of views related to contemporary art. The young artists who took part were against the international style, universalism and the dominance of the art of painting in Indonesian modern art.

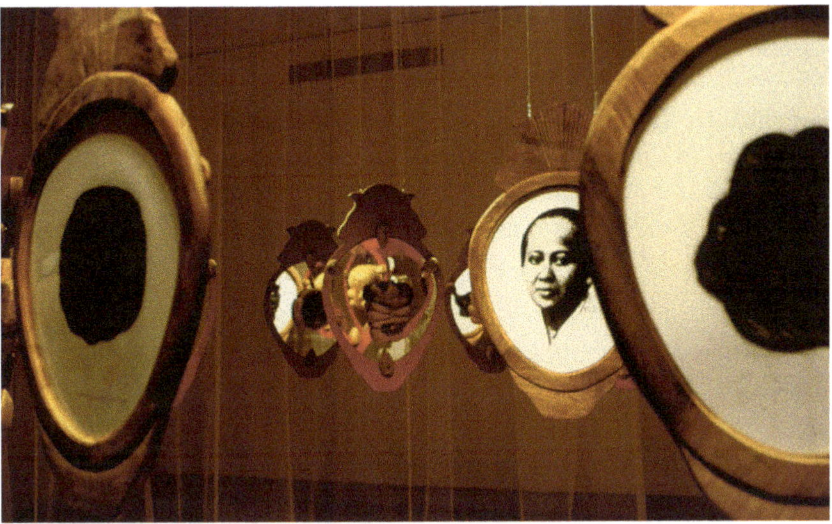

Figure 6.5: Nindityo Adipurnomo (b. 1961), Indonesia, *Introversion (April the Twenty-First)*, 1995–96.

Carved wooden objects, photographs, mirrors, cast resin, found objects, gauze curtain, paper, glass, hair, nylon and fibreglass, 390 x 616 cm (diam.) (installed), 21 parts: 75 x 45 x 15 cm (each, approx.), curtain: 390 x 2520 cm. Collection: Queensland Art Gallery | Gallery of Modern Art. Purchased 1996 (1996.206a-v.). Queensland Art Gallery Foundation. Image courtesy QAGOMA. Permission: the artist. The work refers to Kartini (Raden Ajeng Kartini) (1879–1904), the nineteenth-century Javanese female aristocrat who wrote and published a 'Handschrift' (Manuscript) on artisans especially women artisans and who is honoured for her work and advocacy for women's education every year on her birthday: 21 April, Kartini Day.

The movement promoted social criticism, political art and new art forms (installation, ready-mades, found objects, collaborative work). The movement also introduced a new definition of art and the concept of the principle of pluralism. From 1975, the movement arranged several exhibitions in Jakarta and Bandung, to strong reactions from critics, artists and scholars. Exhibitions organised by the movement were never accepted as a serious art phenomenon, mostly because the idioms used were not understood. In 20 years the movement has had a very limited influence. The boom in decorative paintings in the 1980s was a clear example. The dominance of the art of painting in Indonesia was stronger than it had been 10 years before.

The movement showed renewed influence at the beginning of the 1990s. A new development in Indonesian contemporary art has emerged, along with contemporary art developments internationally. Many artists have begun to realise the importance of becoming international. In a sense the debate on national and international contexts of modern or contemporary art has ended.

In the last few years, this can clearly be seen in the development of installations as an idiom. Dadang Christanto, Nyoman Erawan, Heri Dono (Figure 6.6) and Harsono are among the artists who usually exhibit installations. In the art of painting there have been several tendencies: photorealism, surrealistic images, social criticism, symbolism and works expressing women's dilemmas. Some artists already established within these styles are Ivan Sagito and Agus Kamal (surrealists), Dede Eri Supria (Figure 6.4), Sudarisman (social criticism), and Lucia Hartini (expressing women's dilemmas).

Meanwhile, interest in modern and contemporary art in developing countries has grown in the international circle. Slowly but surely, the pluralism principle has gained in influence. Japan and Australia should be mentioned in particular as countries that facilitate the growth of developing countries' contemporary art, especially in the Asia Pacific region, which should be seen as a growing centre of world contemporary art. For Indonesian contemporary art this presents, without doubt, a new horizon for growth.

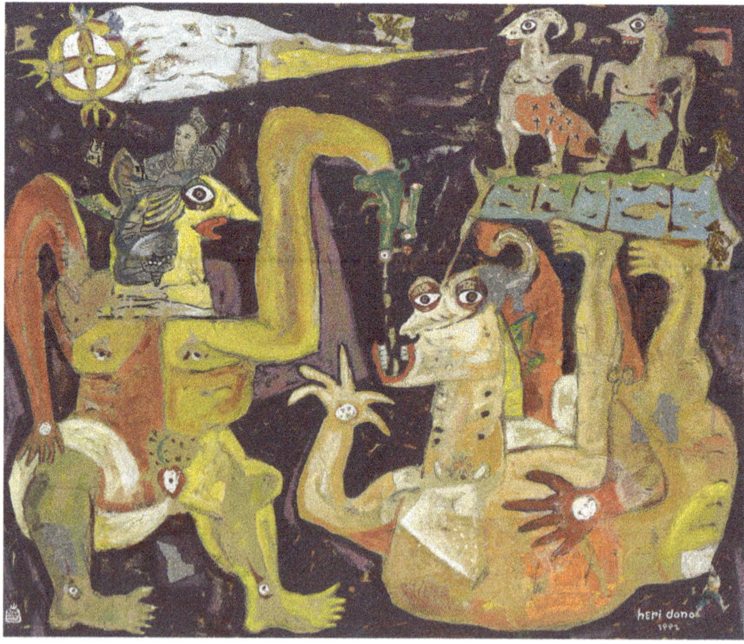

Figure 6.6: Heri Dono (b. 1960), Indonesia, *Makan Pelor* (*Eating Bullets*), 1992.

Synthetic polymer paint and collage on cardboard, 66 x 77 cm. Collection: Queensland Art Gallery | Gallery of Modern Art. Purchased 1995. Queensland Art Gallery Foundation. Image courtesy QAGOMA. Permission: the artist.

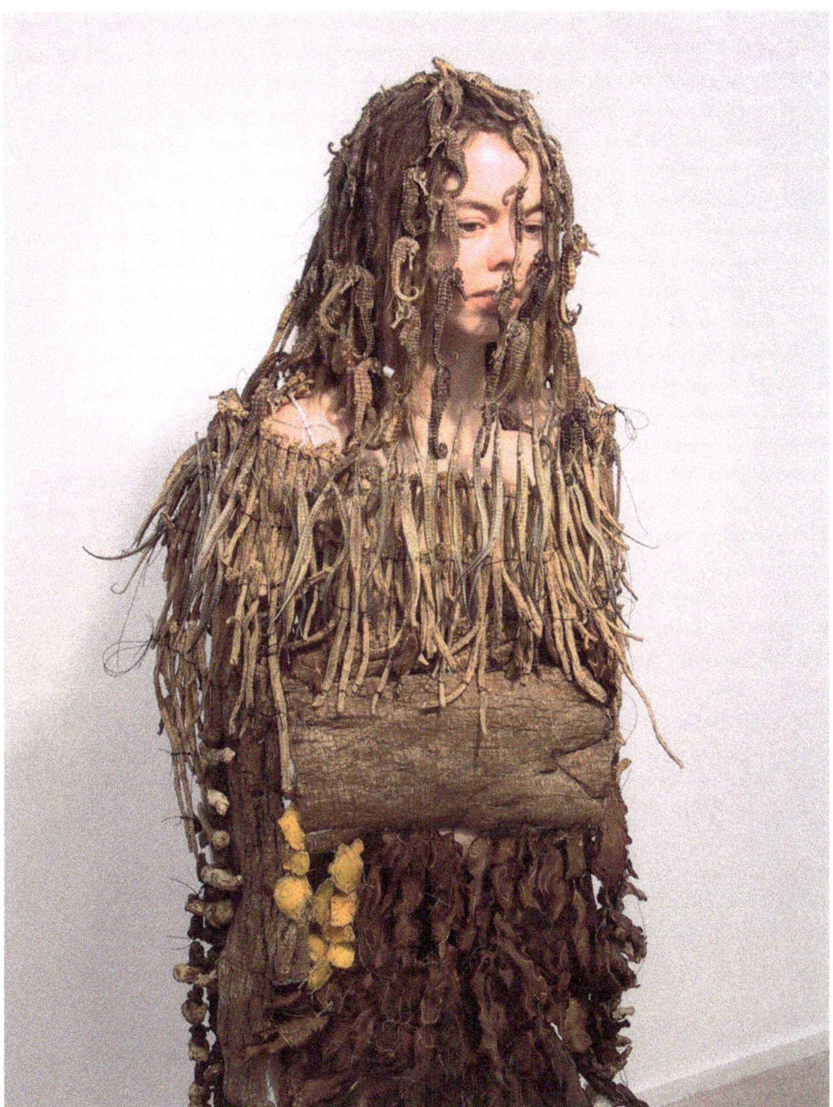

Figure 6.7: Mella Jaarsma, *The Healer*, 2003.

Costume made of Chinese and Indonesian traditional medicines, medical drinks and DVDs. Image and permission courtesy the artist. Costume worn by Elly Kent in exhibition in association with The Australian National University Art and Human Rights project; component curated by Christine Clark at Canberra Contemporary Art Space, 2003. *The Healer* is part of three costumes, the others being *The Feeder* and *The Hunter*, the latter made from military uniforms. It is also connected to a series of costume works such as Jaarsma's work for the Third Asia Pacific Triennial in 1999, *Hi Inlander*, and other works on the subject of cross-cultural encounters, cultural identities and, later on, refugees. It consists of plants and ingredients for Chinese and Indonesian traditional medicine (including seahorses), some of which hang into a wok and are cooked to create the Indonesian medicinal drink *jamu*. Jaarsma has stated: 'A military mission is not only about sending troops to war but also about food and medicine'. The work was produced during the beginning of the Iraq war. At the same time, the Indonesian military entered the province of Aceh to end the independence movement. 'It represents humankind's inevitable connection with killing, healing and feeding.'[8]

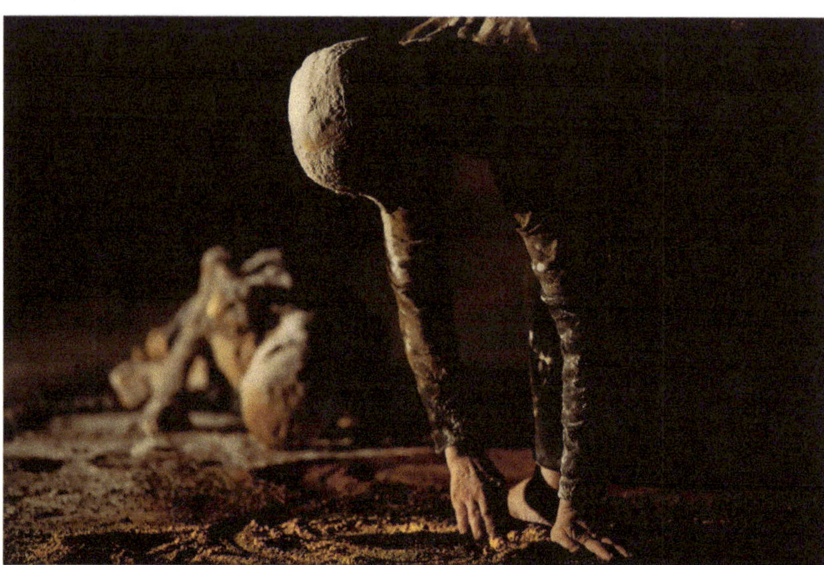

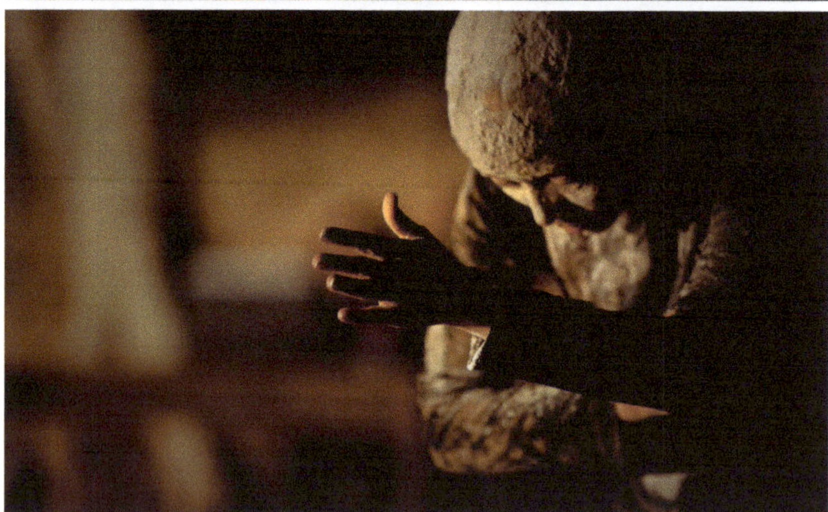

Figure 6.8: Marintan Sirait, *Long Distance Call from Home*, 2012.

8 Mella Jaarsma, quoted in '*The Warrior, the Healer, the Feeder*', accessed 14 December 2021, mellajaarsma.com/installation/the-warrior-the-healer-the-feeder/. On *Hi Inlander*, see QAGOMA Collection, accessed 27 January 2022, collection.qagoma.qld.gov.au/objects/13281.

Documentation of performance at 'Undisclosed Territory', Surakarta, 2012. Photograph by Arief Budianto. Image courtesy the artist and Arief Budianto. Supangkat illustrated an earlier performance by the artist from 1995 in his important book *Indonesian Modern Art and Beyond*. Marintan Sirait has been involved as a performance artist and with social projects since the late 1980s when she was a student in the group Sumber Waras experimenting with movement and sound. She is a transdisciplinary artist who has participated in a number of international biennales and, as Christine Clark notes, has been an instrumental figure in enabling cross artform dialogue and experimentation through various initiatives.[9]

9 Clark notes that with husband Andar Manik, she has created Dalemwangi Art Space, an artist-musician family compound. Sirait has recently established Kalyana Learning Centre (2020) and is also the founder of Jendela Ide Indonesia Foundation (1995–ongoing), a culture centre for youth, and Rumpun Indonesia Foundation, a women's media centre for social change. Sirait articulates that Dalemwangi Art Space (2018–ongoing) 'is a space similar to a laboratory where we try and let art grow … we seek … collaborations across art forms and develop shared experience and new awareness across collaborators, participants and audiences'. Interview with Christine Clark, 15 November 2019, Bandung; Christine Clark's communication with the editors, 29 October 2021. See also essay by Enin Suprianto, 'Marintan Sirait', *Catalogue of the Second Asia-Pacific Triennial* (Brisbane: Queensland Art Gallery, 1996), 101.

7

Redefining the Contemporary in a Global Context: Indonesian Art in the 1990s

Caroline Turner

Introduction

The 1990s was a tumultuous period of immense social, economic and political transformations in Indonesian history and also in art. The New Order of President Suharto came to an end in 1998 ushering in the period of Reformasi. At a global level, the decade also witnessed shifts in power balances with ongoing economic and political impacts and an unparalleled expansion of the international art world as well as the emergence of new discourses redefining contemporary art.

FX Harsono, Heri Dono, Dadang Christanto and Arahmaiani Feisal, all influential innovators in Indonesian contemporary art, were also among the Indonesian artists most exhibited internationally in the 1990s. I discuss their art in this chapter in both local Indonesian and international contexts and in relation to a critical question in art theory more generally—that is, whether 'art can provide new models for cultural, social and political understanding' in the artists' own local communities and, in a globalising world, contribute to understanding cultural identities and new ways of perceiving the world.[1]

In Chapter 2, Elly Kent analysed the artistic ideologies that underpinned Indonesian art in the post-independence era.[2] By the 1990s, artistic developments were greatly affected not only by the mutability of Indonesian society and art but also by geopolitical transformations in the world. As historian Glen Barclay has noted, the global geopolitical 'tectonic plates' shifted in the second part of the twentieth century with first Japan then China and India becoming leading players globally and other nations, including Indonesia, rising economically and politically.[3]

These geopolitical and economic changes were to lead to a reconceptualisation of global frameworks for art and challenged the accepted theory of an art centre dominated by Europe and North America.[4] The decade of the 1990s is now widely accepted as a watershed for global art history, theory and practice and the time when art theorists began to stress the need for new languages for contemporary art from outside a Western-dominated art world. As art historian Hans Belting wrote in 2009:

> Contemporary art, a term long used to designate the most recent art, assumed an entirely new meaning when art production, following the turn of world politics and world trade in 1989, expanded across the globe. The results of this unprecedented expansion challenged the continuity of any Eurocentric view of art.[5]

---

1 Caroline Turner and Jen Webb, *Art and Human Rights: Contemporary Asian Contexts* (Manchester: Manchester University Press, 2016), 111, take up this question in terms of human rights. Some material in this chapter is drawn from research conducted under Australian Research Council funded grants on art in Asia.

2 See also Elly Kent, 'Entanglement: Individual and Participatory Art Practice in Indonesia' (PhD diss., The Australian National University, 2016). Sanento Yuliman and Jim Supangkat both examine the significance of these ideologies, see Chapters 3 and 6 (this volume).

3 Glen St John Barclay, 'Geopolitical Changes in Asia and the Pacific', in *Art and Social Change: Contemporary Art in Asia and the Pacific*, ed. Caroline Turner (Canberra: Pandanus Books, 2005), 14–29.

4 While historical art from Asia had long been accepted into Western museums, modern and contemporary art had, for the most part, been framed as 'derivative' of Western art. In the 1990s, this was refuted by scholars—for example, at John Clark's seminal conference at The Australian National University in 1991, 'Modernism and Post-Modernism in Asian Art', and at the conferences for the Asia Pacific Triennial in 1993, 1996 and 1999.

5 Hans Belting, 'Contemporary Art as Global Art: A Critical Estimate', in *The Global Art World: Audiences, Markets and Museums*, ed. Hans Belting and Andrea Buddensieg (Ostfildern: Hatje Cantz, 2009), 39.

The early chapters in this volume provide examples of how well informed Indonesian artists were about world developments and new artistic connections. Many travelled or studied abroad, especially after 1945.[6] It was not until the late 1980s and early 1990s, however, that Indonesian contemporary artists began to be regularly invited to major contemporary international exhibitions based in Western countries. Jim Supangkat, the most influential Indonesian curatorial voice for contemporary art in the last decade of the century, wrote in 2005 that there was growing interest in art of the 'Third World' (his term) in the 1990s, but before that 'Indonesian art had been ignored by international art circles for decades'. He added that:

> If one reviews the record of international contact before 1990, only once in the 50 years from 1940 to 1990 did Indonesia participate in a major international event. It was when Affandi—the most widely recognized painter in Indonesia—presented his paintings in the Second São Paulo Biennale in 1953. In contrast between 1990 and 2000, Indonesian contemporary art was shown in more than 100 international and regional art events, including prestigious international art events.

As a result, the Indonesian art world 'made room' for contemporary art.[7]

6 The earliest Indonesian to study and make an artistic reputation in Europe was the nineteenth-century Javanese aristocrat Raden Saleh (see Introduction and Chapter 1, this volume) who, as Supangkat says (Chapter 6, this volume), is 'credited with being the pioneer of Indonesian modern art'. Clark refers to Saleh's painting *The Arrest of Prince Diponegoro* (1857; see Chapter 1, this volume) as 'the first counter-colonial appropriation of academy style for a history painting'. John Clark, 'The Worlding of the Asian Modern', in *Contemporary Asian Art and Exhibitions: Connectivities and World-Making*, ed. Michelle Antoinette and Caroline Turner (Canberra: ANU Press, 2014), 67, doi.org/10.22459/CAAE.11.2014.04. Both Sukarno and Suharto pursued international cultural relations. On Indonesia's post-independence cultural connections, see Jennifer Lindsay and Maya H. T. Liem, *Heirs to World Culture: Being Indonesian, 1950–1965* (Leiden: Brill, 2012), doi.org/10.26530/OAPEN_403204; Brigitta Isabella, 'The Politics of Friendship: Modern Art in Indonesia's Cultural Diplomacy, 1950–65', in *Ambitious Alignments: New Histories of Southeast Asian Art, 1945–1990*, ed. Stephen H. Whiteman, Sarena Abdullah, Yvonne Low and Phoebe Scott (Singapore: Power Publications and National Gallery Singapore, 2018), 83–105.

7 Jim Supangkat, 'Art and Politics in Indonesia', in Turner, *Art and Social Change*, 218–28, 220. Supangkat stated that it was not mainstream art in Indonesia, 'which espouses the art of beautiful painting', that attracted international attention. Yet audiences internationally were interested in this art. For example, audiences at the Asia Pacific Triennial (APT) exhibitions in Australia have been extremely enthusiastic about art related to spirituality and religion, such as the abstract and Islam-inspired paintings of A. D. Pirous (see Chapter 4, this volume). The Eurocentric viewpoint that Belting referred to is well expressed by Supangkat when he revealed that, at the Festival of Indonesia in the United States in 1990, major US art museums were not interested in taking the modern and contemporary art component that included some of Indonesia's foremost artists and even suggested the exhibition 'be shown in anthropological museums instead'. Jim Supangkat, 'Indonesia: Multiculturalism/Multimodernism', in *Contemporary Art in Asia: Traditions/Tensions*, ed. Apinan

Major exposure of Indonesian art in the United States and Europe began around 1990 with the Festival of Indonesia in the US followed by an exhibition organised in the Netherlands by the Amsterdam-based Gate Foundation in 1993.[8] Indonesian contemporary artists had earlier been invited to participate in the groundbreaking Fukuoka Asian Art exhibitions in Japan.[9] In the 1990s, the Asia Pacific Triennial (APT) exhibitions in Brisbane, Australia, beginning in 1993, and the Asia Society (US) exhibition *Traditions/Tensions* in New York in 1996 were important in including Indonesian artists. In the 1990s, Indonesian artists, as Supangkat noted, were selected for prestigious contemporary international exhibitions and for the growing number of biennales of contemporary art, a significant number of which were established outside Europe and North America.[10] Many were in Asia, where a new regional art discourse was in formation. As well, biennales and museums began to appoint curators from the former 'periphery'.[11]

Poshyananda (New York: Asia Society Galleries, 1996), 70–81, 77. Affandi's work had also been shown by invitation at the 1954 Venice Biennale but the next Indonesian to be invited into the main Biennale exhibition was Heri Dono in 2003. Indonesia had its own pavilion from 2003 and that year included Christanto and Arahmaiani among the artists. See Bharti Lalwani, 'Indonesia at the Venice Biennale: In Conversation with Carla Bianpoen and Rifky Effendy', Culture 360, 6 May 2013, accessed 28 November 2020, culture360.asef.org/magazine/indonesia-venice-biennale-conversation-carla-bianpoen-and-rifky-effendy/. Despite the hesitancy of US museums, the US exhibition was important. The catalogue was published as Joseph Fischer, *Modern Indonesian Art: Three Generations of Tradition and Change 1945–1990* (Jakarta: KIAS Festival of Indonesia: 1990), an invaluable handbook for researchers, as was Astri Wright's groundbreaking book, *Soul, Spirit, and Mountain: Preoccupations of Contemporary Indonesian Painters* (Kuala Lumpur: Oxford University Press, 1994), which was based on her 1991 PhD thesis. Wright also wrote a key chapter for the Fischer book. Claire Holt, *Art in Indonesia: Continuities and Change* (Ithaca, NY: Cornell University Press, 1967), remains a key reference. See also Cornell University Library, 'The Claire Holt Papers', accessed 20 January 2022, rmc.library.cornell.edu/holt/.

8 *Indonesian Modern Art: Indonesian Painting since 1945* (Amsterdam: Gate Foundation, 1993).

9 The Fukuoka Art Museum initiated exhibitions of contemporary Asian art from the late 1970s. Networks were developed by the Japan Foundation through its Asia Center in Tokyo for exhibitions and conferences in the 1990s. ASEAN has provided opportunities for exchange. The Singapore Art Museum has, since 1996, been a centre for Southeast Asian contemporary art, complemented by the National Gallery, Singapore, from 2015. See Caroline Turner, introduction to *Contemporary Asian Art and Exhibitions*, ed. Antoinette and Turner.

10 Anthony Gardner and Charles Green, *Biennials, Triennials, and Documenta: The Exhibitions that Created Contemporary Art* (Hoboken, New Jersey: Wiley-Blackwell, 2016), 3. Gardner and Green state that biennales 'have come, since the 1990s to define contemporary art' and many visitors 'encounter contemporary art solely within their frames'.

11 For example, Thai Apinan Poshyananda curating *Traditions/Tensions* in 1996, Nigerian-born Okwui Enwezor curating *Documenta* (Germany) in 2002 and Indonesian group *ruangrupa* appointed as curators for the 2022 *Documenta*. The first three APTs also used a model of collaboration with curators and writers from each country. Until the 1990s, artists from elsewhere than Europe and North America (the so-called 'centre' of modern and contemporary art) were referred to as being from the 'periphery'.

Supangkat and others note the significance of international engagement for Indonesian contemporary art. Participation in international events could offer artists resources, alternative platforms and the freedom for experimentation not readily available in Indonesia. However, questions have at times been raised about the framing of the art and whether local contexts and history would be understood by international audiences.[12] It is important, I believe, to recognise that many Indonesians had already participated in the emerging new regional art discourses.

Academic and curator Agung Hujatnikajennong writes of the significance of art protests of the 1970s that led to new directions for Indonesian art in the 1980s and the emergence of regional exhibitions, symposia and publications in the Asia Pacific in the 1990s that helped shape a 'paradigm shift' in that decade. Indonesian artists over the ensuing two decades, he writes, became more 'aware of their identity as a result of complex encounters with their historical and colonial past'. He suggests that, as well as looking back, the artists connected to 'the global art forum' and developed their practices 'in parallel with their growing understanding of their involvement in the global communication system with its decisive technological and information changes'.[13]

Art historian Terry Smith has described contemporary art as 'becoming—perhaps for the first time in history—truly an art of the world' meaning it comes from the whole world.[14] Smith has defined three distinctive currents in contemporary art theory and practice. The second of these currents, and one I would suggest is particularly relevant to Indonesia:

12 Other concerns were artists becoming coopted into a Western-dominated art system and market. See Arham Rahman, 'Post-1989 Indonesia: Investigating the Position of Our Art in the Era of Globalised Art', accessed 2 November 2020, www.academia.edu/21592067/Post_1989_Indonesia_Investigating_the_Position_of_Our_Art_in_the_Era_of_Globalised_Art.

13 Agung Hujatnikajennong, 'The Contemporary Turns: Indonesian Contemporary Art in the 1980s', in *Negotiating Home, History and Nation: Two Decades of Contemporary Art in Southeast Asia 1991–2011,* ed. Iola Lenzi (Singapore: Singapore Art Museum, 2011), 85–90, 89, 85. See also Sabapathy, Chapter 5 (this volume).

14 Terry Smith, 'Currents of World-Making in Contemporary Art', *World Art* 1, no. 2 (2011): 171–88, doi.org/10.1080/21500894.2011.602712.

> has arisen from movements toward political and economic independence that occurred in former colonies and on the edges of Europe, and is thus shaped above all by clashing ideologies and experiences. The result is that artists prioritise both local and global issues as the urgent content of their work.[15]

Indonesian artists such as Harsono, Dono, Christanto and Arahmaiani fit Smith's designation well, in particular his statement that they prioritised 'both local and global issues as the urgent content of their work'.[16] As Kent writes in relation to Dono, they experimented 'with local and global idioms, to create works equally accessible to local and international audiences'.[17] It was an Indonesian expression and may also be viewed as part of the decentring process in global contemporary art that gathered momentum in the 1990s.[18] This process, I suggest, did not just involve artists from 'the periphery' being invited into contemporary art circuits during that decade, but their active involvement in a reconceptualisation of contemporary art practice and discourse.[19]

---

15 Terry Smith, 'Worlds Pictured in Contemporary Art: Planes and Connectivities', *Humanities Research* XIX, no. 2 (2013): 11–25, accessed 27 March 2022, press-files.anu.edu.au/downloads/press/p245111/html/ch01.xhtml?referer=&page=5. As I noted in the APT1 catalogue in 1993:

> What is apparent is that the artists within this region are confident in their local and regional specificity as well as in incorporating ideas which cross national boundaries—an art which engages with international art practice but is not dependent on international ideas imposed from the 'centre'.

Caroline Turner in *First Asia-Pacific Triennial Catalogue* (Brisbane: Queensland Art Gallery, 1993), 8.

16 My analysis of these artists' work is based on discussions with them since the early 1990s.

17 Kent, Chapter 2 (this volume).

18 An early forum was the Rockefeller–Asia Society conference in Bellagio, Italy, in 1997 (at which I represented Australia). There was strong criticism from Latin American, African and Asian delegates of the lack of artists from those regions in major global exhibitions. The first world Biennial Conference in Gwangju, Korea, in 2012 demonstrated the extent of the change over the next 15 years. The concept of decentring art is discussed, for example, by Partha Mitter in his 'Interventions: Decentering Modernism: Art History and Avant-Garde Art from the Periphery', *The Art Bulletin* 90, no. 4 (2008): 531–48, doi.org/10.1080/00043079.2008.10786408. Recent research has challenged the belief that innovations in contemporary artistic practice in the twentieth century were always reliant on the transfer of ideas from EuroAmerica to those on the 'periphery'. Important publications on this include Reiko Tomii, *Radicalism in the Wilderness: International Contemporaneity and 1960s Art in Japan* (Cambridge MA: The MIT Press, 2016). Indonesian artists frequently utilised approaches drawn from local Indonesian modes of art as described in Chapter 2. Their approach to installation and performance, for example, was often significantly different from Western art practice, drawing on time-honoured modes from dance, theatre, ceremonies and storytelling. For a discussion of the complexity of these issues in Southeast Asian art historiography, see Nora A. Taylor, 'The Southeast Asian Art Historian as Ethnographer?', *Third Text* 25, 4 (2011): 475–88, doi.org/10.1080/09528822.2011.587948.

19 This is not to suggest that international involvement and recognition was a necessary validation for artists.

There are four interrelated themes that I want to explore in the art of the individuals I discuss below in relation to the question posed at the beginning of this chapter regarding art's role in providing models for the future:

1. These artists envisaged their role as one connected to everyday life, a perspective they shared with many if not most Indonesian artists. This also related to Sanento Yuliman's belief that art should not be separated from lived experience.[20] As interpreted by FX Harsono, this role came with a particular responsibility to society.[21] They did not, therefore, confine art to theoretical and aesthetic realms, a perspective adopted by some Western art historians, as noted by art historian Donald Preziosi. Writing in 1989, he described such a perspective as seeing:

   > art as a second reality alongside the world in which we live day to day, rather than as one of the powerful social instruments for the creation and maintenance of the world in which we live.[22]

   One of the essential contributions of artists beyond EuroAmerica to global art discourses, I have argued, was their commitment to the concept of art with a direct and necessary responsibility to society.[23]
2. They shared an interest in the organisation of social and political structures as part of this belief in a responsibility to society. Their art was addressed especially to the marginalised and ordinary people often left behind in an era of globalisation and rapid economic change, both in Indonesia and elsewhere.[24] This could include an art witnessing to injustice and political oppression. A key component is empathy, identified by Harsono in relation to his own work in Indonesia, an attribute that is also a prerequisite of effective cross-cultural dialogue in international contexts.
3. Questions of identity, inclusion and ethical relationships between human beings, especially in diverse and even divided societies, all critical subjects of the twentieth and twenty-first centuries, were central

20 Kent, Chapter 2 (this volume).

21 See Harsono, Chapter 10 (this volume).

22 Donald Preziosi, *Rethinking Art History: Meditations on a Coy Science* (New Haven and London: Yale University Press, 1989), 49.

23 Caroline Turner, 'Indonesia: Art, Freedom, Human Rights and Engagement with the West', in Turner, *Art and Social Change*, 196–217.

24 Kent, Chapter 2 (this volume), shows the historical evolution in Indonesia. See also Virginia Matheson Hooker, 'Expression: Creativity despite Constraint', in *Indonesia beyond Soeharto: Polity, Economy, Society in Transition*, ed. Donald K. Emmerson (New York: M.E. Sharpe, 1999), 262–94, for a detailed discussion of the context of art under Suharto, including censorship and the cultural policies of the New Order.

to their art. The concept of identity, while it incorporated individual identity such as ethnicity, religion or gender, was in Indonesian art also attached to cultural and collective community identity.

4. In all these respects, their art concentrated on means of perceiving and even reinventing the world in new ways. This frame of reference is frequently referred to as 'world-making'[25] and in the late twentieth century had wide implications by connecting to broader global discourses related to human values, human rights and the future of humanity.

FX Harsono: Art and Social Responsibility

FX Harsono is without question one of the Indonesian artists most committed to expressing these themes in his art. As he told Hendro Wiyanto:

> I've never viewed myself only as my own self or as a lone individual. It is the awareness that I am part of the community that always encourages me to create works that have as their point of departure social issues, the things that are external to me.[26]

For him, the role of an artist does not just consist in making art but comes with a 'responsibility to society', requiring the need for empathy in human and artistic relations for 'without empathy, the community is just a voiceless object'.[27]

As the catalogue to the exhibition of Harsono's art at the Singapore Art Museum in 2010 states: 'Any discussion of the history of contemporary art in Indonesia would be incomplete without an examination of FX Harsono's art and practice'.[28] Harsono has been a crucial theorist as well as an experimental artist in Indonesia and is also recognised as a major voice in the emergence of contemporary Asian art. Since the 1970s when,

25 A term coined by Nelson Goodman in *Ways of Worldmaking* (Indianapolis: Hackett Publishing, 1978), doi.org/10.5040/9781350928558.

26 Hendro Wiyanto, *What We Have Here Perceived as Truth, We Shall Some Day Encounter as Beauty: A Solo Show by FX Harsono* (Jakarta: Indonesia Galeri Canna, 2013), 95.

27 See Harsono, Chapter 10 (this volume).

28 *FX Harsono: Testimonies* (Singapore Art Museum, 2010), accessed 14 August 2020, www.trfineart.com/wp-content/uploads/2016/08/SAM-Harsono-Retrospective-Brochure.pdf. See Kent, Chapter 2 (this volume); T. K. Sabapathy, Chapter 5 (this volume). Harsono was included in the exhibition, *Awakenings: Art in Society in Asia, 1960s–1990s* (Japan, Taiwan and Singapore, 2018–2020), examining artists as catalysts for change. For his many international exhibitions, see 'FX Harsonso', Tyler Rollins Fine Art, accessed 21 June 2020, www.trfineart.com/artist/fx-harsono/#artist-works.

as a young art student, he challenged existing hierarchies for art, he has engaged in a dedicated exploration of questions of social and political justice, both through his art and in his work with NGOs working for societal transformation.[29] This was undertaken in the context of significant limitations on freedom of expression under the New Order.[30] Agung Hujatnikajennong states: 'The development of his art has consistently demonstrated a genealogical link between conceptual strategies and the issue of contesting power in Indonesia'.[31]

Harsono was born in 1949 in Blitar, East Java, and has Chinese as well as Javanese ancestry. He was brought up as a Catholic. His father was a professional photographer whose photographs later provided inspiration for his son's artworks examining killings of Chinese Indonesians in the late 1940s.[32] When the New Order came to power in 1965–66, Harsono and other Indonesians of Chinese descent were forced to give up their culture, religion and family names.[33]

Harsono played a critical part in the development of contemporary art discourse in Indonesia. He was co-founder in 1975 of the Gerakan Seni Rupa Baru (New Art Movement, GSRB). Although it ended in 1988, the GSRB was foundational to the period discussed here. There was, however, a price to pay for challenging the social order. As Sabapathy states in Chapter 5 in relation to GSRB artists, theirs was 'a protest gesture with immense cost to the lives of those who delivered it'.[34] The artists associated with GSRB utilised installation and performance and developed collaborative art

29 Harsono (this volume) states: 'I took up social and political issues with the intention of experimenting with the search for a national Indonesian identity'. See Turner and Webb, *Art and Human Rights*, for more on Harsono's ideas of his own identity, including his 'hybrid' identity. See also John Clark, 'Negotiating Change in Recent Southeast Asian Art', *Southeast of Now: Directions in Contemporary and Modern Art in Asia* 2, no. 1 (March 2018): 43–92, doi.org/10.1353/sen.2018.0002, for a discussion of Harsono's art in a wider context of artists negotiating both personal and collective identities; John Clark, *The Asian Modern* (Singapore: National Gallery Singapore, 2021), 333–45.

30 A depoliticised art, culture and Islam was favoured by the regime and censorship of the media and the arts was effected to control dissent. Harsono (this volume) says this was less for the visual arts. Nonetheless, artists and writers faced censorship and arrest, and, as the case of poet Wiji Thukul in 1996 shows, even death (see Chapter 1). A number of artists had spent time in gaol after Suharto came to power in 1965—including the brilliant painter Hendra Gunawan, who was imprisoned for more than a decade.

31 Quoted by Sabapathy, Chapter 5 (this volume). See also Kent's analysis of Harsono, Chapter 2 (this volume).

32 Harsono' artwork, *Preserving Life, Terminating Life #2* (2009), using his father's photographs, is illustrated in Chapter 10 (this volume). Harsono is the child pictured with his parents.

33 Rights restored under Abdurrahman Wahid during his presidency 1999–2001.

34 Sabapathy, Chapter 5 (this volume). Harsono, for example, was expelled from university for his actions in supporting the Black December Statement in 1974.

practices to critique policies of the New Order that had resulted in ruthless, exploitative, economic development; the destruction of traditional ways of life; corruption; and environmental disasters such as the crippling Minamata disease among children caused by industrial contamination. Harsono's monumental installation of 50 panels, *The Social Change*, on a beach near Yogyakarta in 1983 exemplifies research underpinning art on these subjects. It was a commentary on the social costs of unregulated capitalism. A later installation work, *Voices from the Bottom of the Dam* (1994), referenced the murders of three farmers by the Indonesian military for demonstrating against a project to flood their rice fields to construct a dam, and included poignant materials such as clothing worn by the farmers.[35]

By the 1990s, Harsono was producing powerful art works with a clear social message that were shown in Indonesia and abroad in major contemporary exhibitions. The translocation of these works into international contexts broadened their meaning to include wider discussions of human rights, democracy and political repression. The installation *Power and Oppression* (1992) was shown at the Artists' Regional Exchange (ARX) exhibition in Perth, Australia, an important artist-initiated event focused on Southeast Asian artists.[36] It comprised mounds of earth covered with apparently bloodstained cloths and broken branches, facing a chair ringed with barbed wire. The allusion to oppressive, even brutal, authority was unmistakeable. In *Just the Rights*, exhibited at APT1 in Brisbane, Australia, in 1993, Harsono attached what looked like bound human bodies to wooden boards and included a copy of the Universal Declaration of Human Rights. This was followed in 1994 by images of hands, one tied by ropes, spelling out the word 'democracy/*demokrasi*' in international sign language, a work shown in Japan, Australia and the US.[37] The symbolism of this work was clear to audiences in those countries, but, as Harsono tells us, the spies who came to his exhibition in Indonesia apparently could not decipher the meaning.[38]

35 Other socially directed artists created art about political violence, for example, Semsar Siahaan's and Moelyono's powerful works about the rape and murder by the military of a woman trade unionist, Marsinah, in May 1993. See Grace Samboh, 'Consequential Privileges of the Social Artists: Meandering through the Practices of Siti Adiyati Subangun, Semsar Siahaan and Moelyono', *Southeast of Now* 4, no. 2 (October 2020): 205–35, doi.org/10.1353/sen.2020.0010.

36 Images of *Power and Oppression* and *Just the Rights* reproduced in Chapter 5 (this volume), and *Voice without a Voice/Sign* [*Demokrasi*] in Chapter 10 (this volume). On ARX and the APT, see Christine Clark and Caroline Turner, 'Cross-Cultural Exchanges and Interconnections from the 1980s and 1990s: ARX and the APT', *Australian and New Zealand Journal of Art* 16, no. 2 (2016): 167–84, doi.org/10.1080/14434318.2016.1240649.

37 Fukuoka Art Museum, Queensland Art Gallery and *Traditions/Tensions* exhibition.

38 Harsono (this volume).

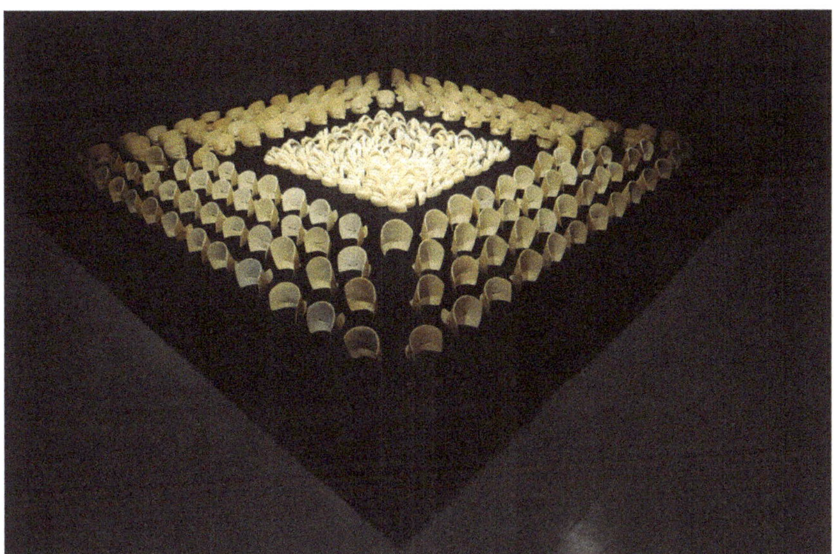

Figure 7.1: FX Harsono, *The Voices Controlled by the Powers*, 1994.
Installation with wooden masks and cloth. Dimensions variable. Image courtesy the artist.

The Voices Controlled by the Powers (1994) consisted of traditional *wayang* masks sawed off at the mouth, symbolising the denial of free speech by the New Order and the banning of the journal *Tempo* in that year (Figure 7.1). It was shown in Indonesia and later in the US in *Traditions/Tensions*. Harsono's contributions to global art discourses on human rights and democracy through these exhibitions and others after Reformasi has been extensive and recognised. In 2015, for example, he was awarded the inaugural Joseph Balestier Award for the Freedom of Art.

Indonesia was hit hard by the Asian financial crisis of 1997 and suffered a severe economic collapse and political instability.[39] Harsono created his now famous performance, appropriately named *Destruction* (*Destruksi*), for the *Slot in the Box* exhibition organised by Cemeti Gallery in Yogyakarta (1997) to address concerns regarding the fairness of elections.[40] He wore a Western suit but with it the make-up of the demon

39 The rupiah experienced a dramatic fall in value, food prices rose, GDP declined and millions became unemployed (see Chapter 1, this volume).

40 At the National Gallery of Australia in 2014, Harsono stated that, although there had been a law in 1997 banning such activity in public spaces, many people defied this to attend. Cemeti, founded in 1988 by artists Nindityo Adipurnomo and Mella Jaarsma, was a major site for contemporary art.

king Ravana from the Ramayana. He set fire to, and used a chainsaw to destroy, three *wayang* masks on chairs—the masks representing the only three political parties that Suharto permitted to contest elections and the chairs being a symbol of authority or power (Figure 7.2; see also Figure 1.14).

The financial crisis was followed in May 1998 by organised attacks on Chinese Indonesians who were traditional targets in troubled times. Hundreds of people, mainly Chinese, were killed, shops were looted and at least 200 Chinese women were raped. This violence in the words of historian Jemma Purdey 'was not normal or everyday. Unlike most anti-Chinese violence in Indonesia, it took place on a national scale, carried out by military agents with extreme brutality and purpose'.[41] The May 1998 riots proved a turning point for those seeking change in Indonesia. Indonesian women especially were shocked and appalled by the rapes of Chinese-Indonesian women.[42] Harsono made several artworks about the violence and rapes including *Burned Victims* (1998), a work of searing emotional intensity.[43] He also worked with NGOs to help victims.

In recent decades, Harsono has continued to be an advocate for social advancement through artworks that include his series on the history of Chinese Indonesians, undertaken so that younger generations in Indonesia will know this dark history, and in the hope, he has said, that it will never be repeated.

---

41 Purdey writes: it 'brought terror to the entire nation. Its victims were mainly women, urban poor and Chinese Indonesians, but the audacity and impunity assumed by its perpetrators shocked all of Indonesia'. Jemma Purdey, *Anti-Chinese Violence in Indonesia, 1996–1999* (Singapore: Asian Studies Association of Australia in association with Singapore University Press, 2006), 140, 143, doi.org/10.1163/9789004486560.

42 While the numbers are not verifiable, a fact-finding mission established by the Indonesian government reported over 1,000 dead. Coordinated rapes, evidence suggests, were used by the New Order in situations of unrest such as Aceh. Melani Budianta noted at an ANU conference in 2004 that Indonesian women banded together after the rapes. See also Kathryn Robinson, 'Indonesian Women from *Orde Baru* to Reformasi', in *Women in Asia: Tradition, Modernity and Globalisation*, ed. Louise Edwards and Mina Roces (Sydney: Allen and Unwin, 2000).

43 Other artists responded to the rapes, including Christanto and Arahmaiani.

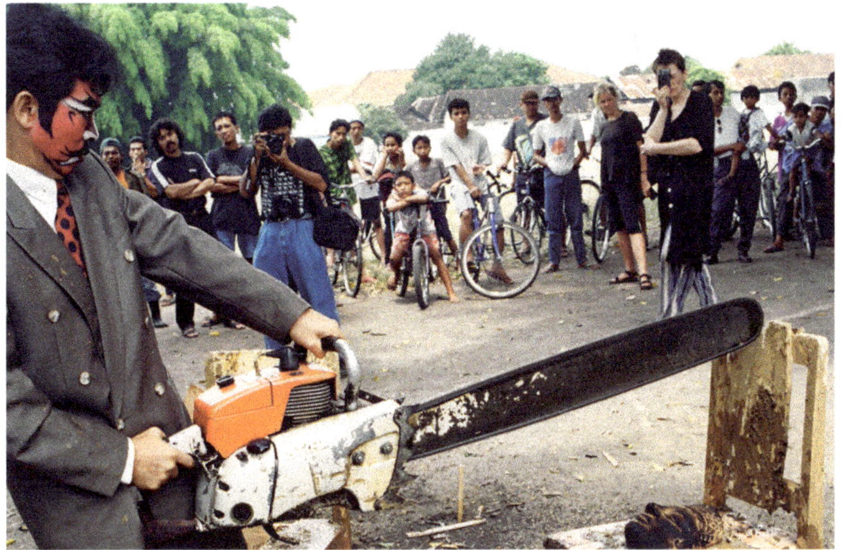

Figure 7.2: FX Harsono, *Destruction* (*Destruksi*), 1997.
Performance with wooden chairs, masks and chainsaw. Image courtesy the artist.

Heri Dono: Experimenting in Creating New Art from Old Traditions

In the 1990s, Heri Dono was almost certainly the most internationally exhibited Indonesian artist. His website notes that he has participated in 31 international biennales and many other exhibitions.[44] Dono stresses the critical importance of communication in his art, communication that is highly effective in local and international contexts. He has collaborated in his work with musicians and dancers and, as Kent describes in her evocative description of *Kuda Binal*, with grave diggers, stone masons and amateurs.[45] Dono is a multidisciplinary artist known internationally as a painter and for his highly original and engaging installations and dynamic performances, usually involving a number of performers and inspired by, and updating themes of, traditional *wayang* shadow puppetry and the Hindu epics, the *Mahabharata* and *Ramayana*, stories that transcend time and seek a balance between good and evil.

44 'Heri Dono', accessed 24 October 2020, heridono.com/heri-dono/.
45 Kent, Chapter 2 (this volume).

Dono's art is distinctive in combining a lively humour with penetrating social comment in his communication with audiences in Indonesia and beyond. His imagery includes *wayang*, contemporary popular culture, comics, cartoons and television. Supangkat highlights the 'expressive, wild and humorous' images in Dono's paintings and cites such artworks as the installation *Watching the Marginal People* as reflecting the tendency of Indonesian artists from the 1980s to look again to the grassroots life of ordinary people.[46] This interest in the everyday lives of people is a distinctive feature in his work. Embedded in his worldview also are concepts related to Javanese cosmology, spirituality and morality, although he is interested in Indonesian cultural traditions beyond Java.[47]

Like Harsono, power is a major preoccupation in his art, as are the negative aspects of power such as political falsehoods and the manipulation of ideas. These are subjects immensely relevant to the contemporary world. Although, as artist and academic Pat Hoffie writes, Dono adopted the role of a 'joker', he nonetheless presents a very serious conception of the role of art.[48] He told art historian Astri Wright: 'An artist is someone who wants to service art—but more important to me is, how can art serve humanity'.[49] In Dono's art there is, however, as Kent suggests, room for multiple interpretations and he clearly resists one interpretation of their meaning.[50]

Dono was born in 1960 and had a middle-class upbringing as the son of a father who had joined the army under Sukarno. His mother was a teacher whose family were associated with the Yogyakarta Sultanate. From an early age he pursued an independent path and dropped out of the Indonesian Institute of the Arts in Yogyakarta three months before graduation.[51] Instead, he chose to study with the *wayang* master Sigit Sukasman.

---

46 Jim Supangkat, 'Heri Dono', *The First Asia-Pacific Triennial of Contemporary Art* (Brisbane: Queensland Art Gallery, 1993), 13.

47 As shown in his work, *Wayang Legenda*, 1988.

48 Pat Hoffie, unpublished interview with Heri Dono, 1998. I am grateful to Professor Hoffie for access to this interview.

49 Wright, *Soul, Spirit, and Mountain*, 236. Wright was one of the first art historians to discuss his work. Dono also suggested to Wright that his art was concerned with 'tragedy'.

50 Kent, Chapter 2 (this volume). Hoffie, unpublished interview, cites catalogues in which Dono discusses 'the spiritual value of art work' and 'the role of the artist as communicator', and in which he described art as 'the thousand dimensions of truth' and as 'harbouring meaning that is open to a multiplicity of interpretations'.

51 ISI or the Institut Seni Indonesia Yogyakarta.

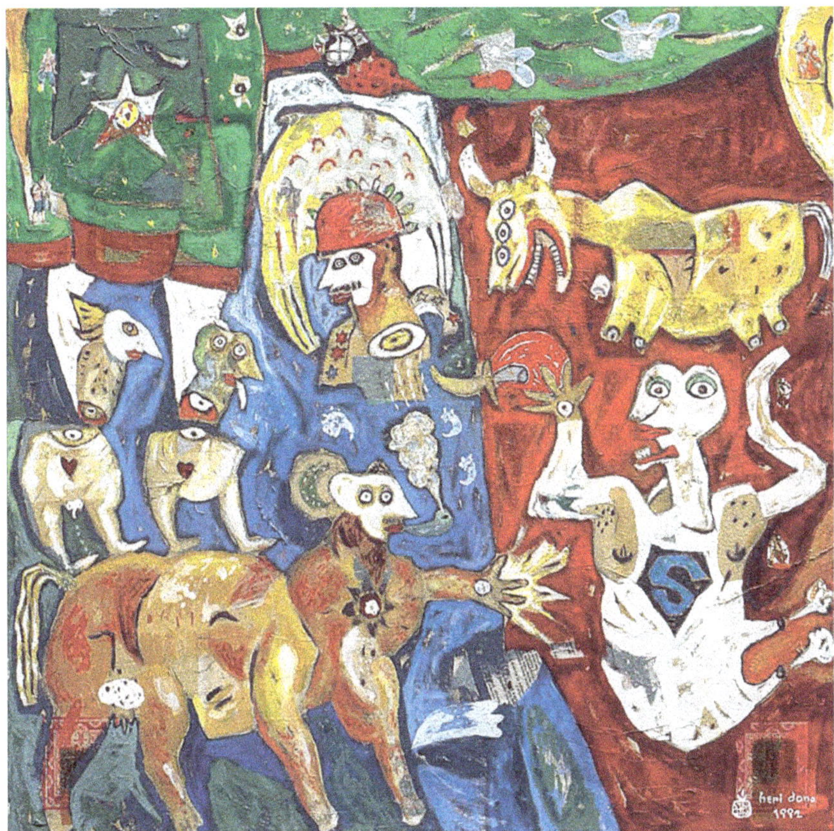

Figure 7.3: Heri Dono (b. 1960), Indonesia, *Campaign of the Three Parties*, 1992.

Synthetic polymer paint and collage on canvas, 98 x 98.5 cm. Collection: Queensland Art Gallery | Gallery of Modern Art. Acc. 1993.394. The Kenneth and Yasuko Myer Collection of Contemporary Asian Art. Purchased 1993 with funds from The Myer Foundation and Michael Sidney Myer through the Queensland Art Gallery Foundation. Image courtesy QAGOMA. Permission: the artist. The information from the QAGOMA website states: 'This work by Dono is based on the artist's impressions of contemporary Indonesian politics in which the red figures represent the Partai Demokrasi Indonesia (PDI), yellow figures represent the Golangan Karya group (Golkar), and green signifies the Partai Persatuan Pembangunan (PPP). The white 'superman' figure represents power'.[52]

52 See QAGOMA collection, accessed 11 March 2022, collection.qagoma.qld.gov.au/objects/14332.

Dono has suggested, or certainly did so before the fall of the New Order, that his works were not about politics or even social problems, but he has conceded that his art mirrors politics and society.[53] And we might add that humour and satire such as Dono employs is often a form of resistance. Apinan Poshyananda has said it is hard to accept his denial of political themes in his art.[54] I would suggest that, if Dono has countered the idea of being described as a 'political artist', his art does open opportunities for questions to be explored and critical debate about social and political issues, such as in *Campaign of the Three Parties*, which is about elections under the New Order (Figure 7.3). His subjects have ranged from famine in Africa to sociopolitical satire. His work *Gamelan of Rumour*, for example, shown at APT1 in 1993, was an experimental sound piece put together with low-tech pieces found in local markets to create a mechanically operated musical instrument.[55] Poshyananda argues that works such as *Gamelan of Rumour* (1992), *Watching the Marginal People* (1992) and *Fermentation of the Mind* (1993) 'each comment in varying degrees on the tendency of Indonesian authorities to use propaganda and censorship to implement national policies and to control the minds of the masses'.[56]

In Dono's performance *The Chair*—a meditation on the theme of power—actors play the part of puppets who challenge the absolute control of the puppeteer. His installation work *Ceremony of the Soul* (1995), a complex combination of themes related to Javanese spirituality and contemporary Indonesian society has, as a central element, stone figures whose torsos were carved by cemetery workers in a place where spirits are said to gather. As Poshyananda points out, however, the robotic figures suggest both obedience and the military (Figure 7.4).[57]

53 'I am not involved in political or social problems … but my paintings, maybe they mirror politics or society. The main thing is that the social structure must be turned around 180 degrees', quoted in Hoffie, unpublished interview. See *Mythical Monsters in Contemporary Society: An Exhibition by Heri Dono* (Singapore: Gajah Gallery, 1999), 2. His website states that he comments on 'sociopolitical' issues, see 'Heri Dono', accessed 24 October 2020, heridono.com/heri-dono/.

54 Apinan Poshyananda, 'Playing with Shadows', *Contemporary Aesthetics,* special volume, issue 3 (2011): unpaginated, accessed 20 September 2020, hdl.handle.net/2027/spo.7523862.spec.307. Paintings such as *Campaign of the Three Parties* (1992) show the three parties, PDI, GOLKAR and PPP, approved by the New Order. *The Secret Boxes* purchased by the Singapore Art Museum was later revealed to be about the killing by Indonesian troops of demonstrators in East Timor. Since Reformasi, Dono has reinforced the larger historical contexts of his art, for example, with works related to Suharto's death and also to Donald Trump's presidency in the US.

55 Dono experiments with sound and puts together works with helpers who normally repair goods like refrigerators or radios. Hoffie notes Dono's interest in collecting from local markets (such as the World War I gas masks used in *Kuda Binal*). Hoffie, unpublished interview.

56 Apinan Poshyananda, 'Roaring Tigers, Desperate Dragons in Transition', in Poshyananda, *Contemporary Art in Asia,* 31–32.

57 Poshyananda, 'Roaring Tigers, Desperate Dragons in Transition', 32.

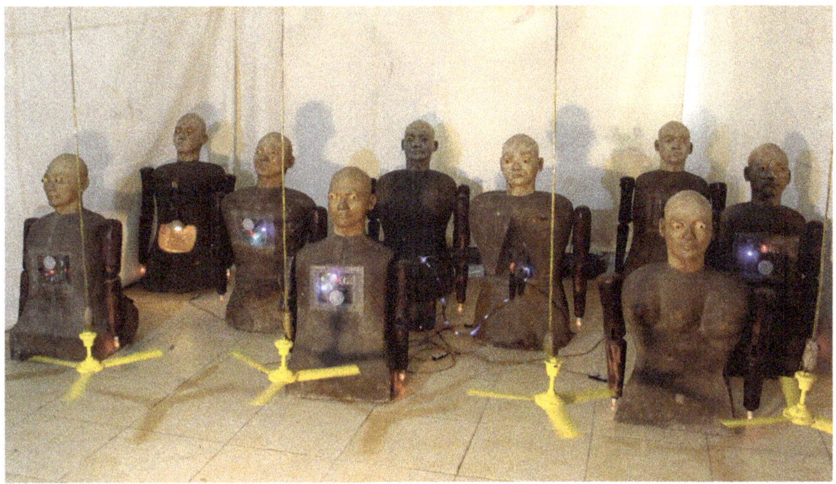

Figure 7.4: Heri Dono, *Ceremony of the Soul*, 1995.

Stone, fibreglass, plastic, radio and tape player, lamps, fans, wood. Nine figures: 70 x 60 x 50 cm each. Collection: the artist. Shown in exhibitions *Traditions/Tensions* Asia Society, New York, 1996, and Fourth Asia Pacific Triennial of Contemporary Art, Queensland Art Gallery, Brisbane, 2002. © Heri Dono. Image courtesy the artist.

Possibly his most politically charged work was his installation for the Museum of Modern Art, Oxford, in 1996, when the Indonesian Embassy in London demanded that the catalogue be withdrawn from sale.[58] The installation displayed frightening images of soldiers, some with artificial legs, camouflage and a complex layering of issues that included military power and the ecological destruction of the environment. In the catalogue of that exhibition the following quotation was attributed to Dono:

> To destroy the feelings of fear, to be able to talk freely, to develop individual opinion. This is dangerous to the government, but I am optimistic. Information and human freedom cannot ultimately be stopped.[59]

---

58 David Elliott, 'Dono's Paradox: The Arrow or the Kris?', *Art and Trousers: Traditions and Modernity in Contemporary Asian Art* (Hong Kong: Artasiapacific, 2021), 248–53. I am grateful to Professor Elliott for correspondence on this exhibition and access to the essay pre publication. Professor Elliott outlines concerns from the Embassy at the time about what they stated were 'misrepresentations' of the political situation in Indonesia under then president Suharto and also explains the issues facing the artist and museum (p. 253).

59 David Elliott and Gilane Tawadros, eds, *Heri Dono* (London and Oxford: Institute of International Visual Arts and Museum of Modern Art Oxford, 1996), 41. *Blooming in Arms* was the name of the installation.

Dadang Christanto: Witnessing to Injustice

Another Indonesian artist who has devised ways of addressing both local and global concerns and establishing direct connections with diverse audiences is Dadang Christanto. Christanto's art is undoubtedly haunted by the events of 1965–66 in which his father was one of the victims, but it is also informed by a deep sympathy and empathy with all human suffering. Through painting, installation and performance, he has created art that witnesses to injustice and speaks eloquently to audiences.[60]

Christanto was born in 1957 in Tegal, a village in Central Java (see Map 2). In 1965 when he was eight years old, his father, a Chinese-Indonesian shopkeeper, was taken away by local militias as a suspected communist supporter and never seen again. It is supposed he was one of hundreds of thousands of victims who were imprisoned or killed, whose bodies have never been found and whose families and descendants suffered discrimination until the end of the New Order.[61]

But Christanto's project is not confined to Indonesia—he is, and has always been, concerned with violence across the world and in any time or place. He has confronted these realities particularly through his *Count* project, begun in 1999, that aimed to count all the victims of violence in the twentieth century. Choosing the broader focus of injustices in the world can perhaps help to put terrible events of the past behind us. As Jacques Derrida wrote of the twentieth century: 'No degree of progress allows one to ignore that never before in absolute figures have so many men, women, and children been subjugated, starved or exterminated on earth'.[62]

Christanto grew up in his small village where his mother ran a batik shop. He remembers that he and his siblings were asleep when his father was taken away and has described how for months after his father's arrest his

60 For a list of his many exhibitions see Jan Manton Gallery, 'Dadang Christanto', accessed 9 June 2020, www.janmantonart.com/dadang-christanto.

61 Turner and Webb, *Art and Human Rights*, 49–57. Christanto is not certain his father was a member of the Communist Party, which was legal under Sukarno and one of the largest in the world. He may have allowed them to use his premises. Ariel Heryanto states that Indonesians of Chinese descent were not the specific targets in the killings although many were killed. Ariel Heryanto, *State Terrorism and Political Identity in Indonesia: Fatally Belonging* (London: Routledge, 2006), 9, doi.org/10.4324/9780203099827.

62 Jacques Derrida, *Spectres for Marx* (London: Routledge, 1994), 85.

mother took food to the local prison hoping he was there.[63] Perhaps one of the most traumatic aspects of their situation, shared with many other victims, was that the events could never be spoken of during the New Order and also perhaps the knowledge that some of their neighbours could have been involved in the killings.[64]

Christanto was admitted to the Indonesia Institute of Art in Yogyakarta as a student of painting, despite screening processes that could deny entrance to the families of those accused of being associated with the Indonesian Communist Party or having left wing sympathies. After graduation he connected with the Bengkel Theatre founded by iconic poet and playwright W. S. Rendra[65] and also with a Catholic education foundation for social justice, working with the Swiss Jesuit, human rights activist and follower of liberation theology, Fr Ruedi Hoffman.

Since then he has been involved in making art that, while relating to Indonesia, reaches out to audiences in many countries with a universal message related to human suffering and human rights with the aim of illuminating a sense of shared humanity. In 1987, Christanto took part in a revival of the GSRB in the exhibition *Fantasy World Supermarket*, exhibiting a work about a *becak* driver who committed suicide when he lost his livelihood. Another early work was *Golf* (1991), purchased by the Fukuoka Asian Art Museum. The subject was the appropriation of agricultural land for golf courses for the pleasure of the wealthy. It depicted a man hitting a golf ball that turns into a *wayang* demon. Another highly emotionally charged work was *Bureaucracy* (1991) in which a row of heads arranged like a stand of puppets each licks the back of the head in front. The foremost head wears a soldier's helmet. In 1993, Christanto's installation, *For Those: Who Are Poor, Who Are Suffer(Ing), Who Are Oppressed, Who Are Voiceless, Who Are Powerless, Who Are Burdened, Who Are Victims of Violence, Who Are Victims of a Dupe, Who Are Victims of Injustice* was selected for APT1 in Brisbane, Australia. Under the repressive Indonesian censorship laws at that time, it was not

63 Interviews with the artist, 2015.

64 All records were suppressed until 1998. For a discussion of how 1965–66 affected Indonesian society beyond direct victims, see Wulan Dirgantoro, Chapter 9 (this volume); Dirgantoro, 'Aesthetics of Silence: Exploring Trauma and Indonesian Paintings after 1965', in Whiteman et al., *Ambitious Alignments*, 199–224.

65 On Rendra, see Barbara Hatley, 'W. S. Rendra 1935–2009', *Inside Indonesia*, 16 August 2009, accessed 2 October 2020, www.insideindonesia.org/w-s-rendra-1935-2009; Hooker, 'Expression: Creativity despite Constraint', 277–80.

possible for the artist to even suggest that the work was about Indonesia. Like many of his works, it was made of natural materials and the artist had laboured for more than a year to create it, his hands bleeding, he has said, 'like my heart'.[66] The 36 hanging pieces sculpted from bamboo gave the appearance of a forest, an allusive metaphor that the artist used to suggest that trees are silent witnesses to violence. The central sculptural element was in the shape of a human body on thin wooden stakes, representing the arrows that held up the body of Bhishma in the *Mahabharata.* In his mesmerising and emotional performance, which left many viewers in tears, the artist's body was covered with clay—possibly a reference to buried victims. In many of his performances Christanto's movements relate to time-honoured ways of honouring the dead, including acts of bowing, washing, strewing flowers or burning (Figure 7.5).

The artwork, the artist stated in his artist talk, was a memorial to suffering 'in every time and place'. But it was also, he revealed nearly a decade later, a response to both the 1965–66 killings and the Dili cemetery massacre in 1991 when the Indonesian military fired on unarmed demonstrators in East Timor, which Indonesia had invaded and occupied in 1975. A student friend of Christanto's was one of those killed.[67] The audience responded to the work as a space of mourning. By the end of the exhibition, there were numerous flowers and notes left by visitors in front of the artwork. Most were not about Indonesia but, as the artist had suggested, commemorated suffering in world contexts with personal stories of grief and loss. Many mentioned the then current war and atrocities in the former Yugoslavia. Many others referred to a young Aboriginal dancer, Daniel Yok, who had died in Brisbane after an encounter with the police a few blocks from the gallery shortly before the exhibition opened. The audience thus made the artwork also a memorial to his death.[68]

---

66 Discussion with the artist in 1992 when I selected the work for the exhibition. This interest in traditional materials can also be seen in the Philippines in the art of Santiago Bose and Roberto Villanueva.

67 Interviews with the artist, 2002–20.

68 Some messages related to black deaths in custody in Australia, the subject of a Royal Commission in 1991.

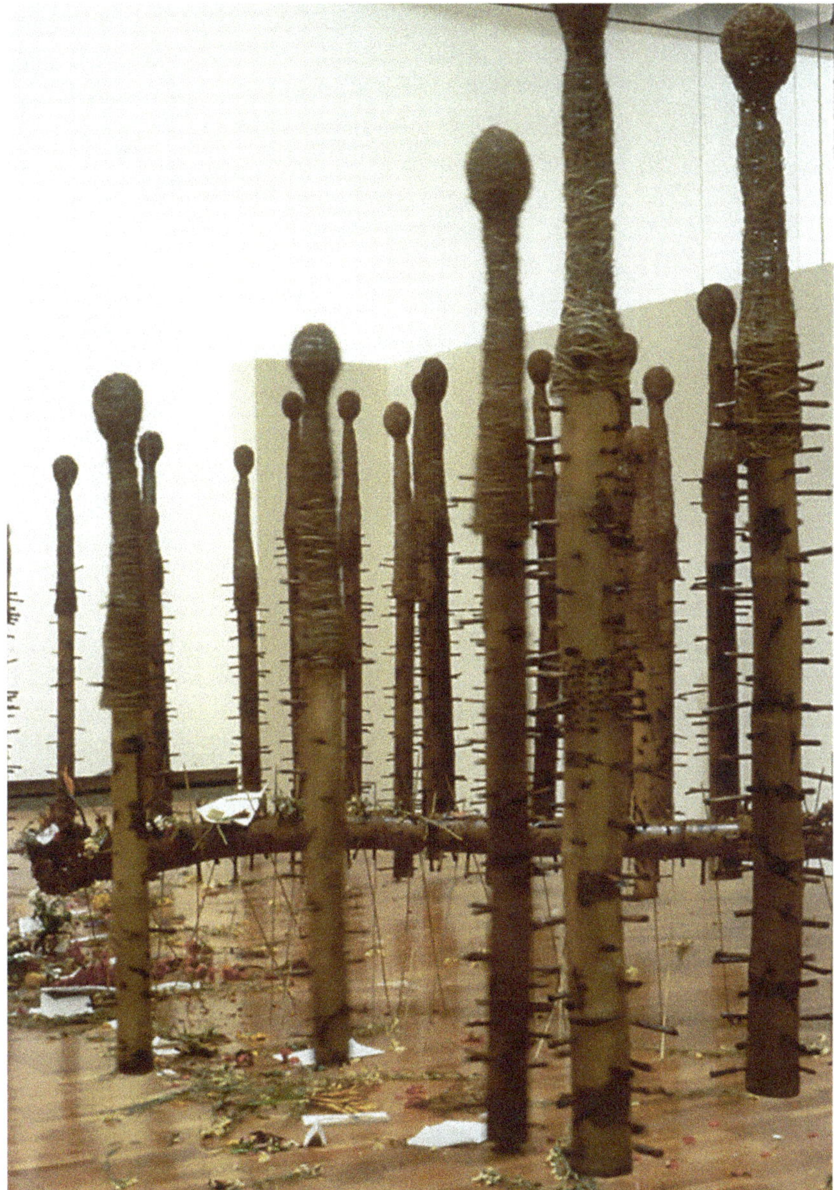

Figure 7.5: Dadang Christanto (b. 1957), Indonesia, *For Those Who Have Been Killed*, 1992–93.

Thirty-six bamboo cane pieces of varying lengths and artist's performance. *For Those: Who Are Poor, Who Are Suffer(Ing), Who Are Oppressed, Who Are Voiceless, Who Are Powerless, Who Are Burdened, Who Are Victims of Violence, Who Are Victims of a Dupe, Who Are Victims of Injustice* (1993). Collection: Queensland Art Gallery | Gallery of Modern Art. The Kenneth and Yasuko Myer Collection of Contemporary Asian Art. Purchased in 1993 with funds from The Myer Foundation and Michael Sidney Myer through the Queensland Art Gallery Foundation. Image courtesy QAGOMA.

Some viewers seeing his installation of a pyramid of ceramic skulls at the *Traditions/Tensions* exhibition in New York in 1996 identified it with the Cambodian genocide of 1975–79. One visitor to Christanto's exhibition in Japan, *They Give Evidence,* left a message that appeared to apologise for Japan's occupation of Java in the Pacific War; others in Hiroshima related the figures to the victims of the atomic bomb dropped on that city in 1945. Australian viewers of his work *Heads from the North,* in which bronze heads (portraits of his parents) float in a pool of water, have associated the work, not with Indonesia, but with refugees drowning while trying to reach Australia or Europe.

Christanto's monumental 1996 installation *1001 Earth Humans/1001 Manusia Tanah,* comprised 1,000 life-size figures placed in the sea at Ancol, outside Jakarta (with the artist the 1,001st). It was an unspoken testimony to the dispossession of villagers in the construction of the Kedung Ombo Dam in the mid-1980s (see Chapter 1 regarding this issue and for the image) and all the ordinary people condemned as collateral damage of economic development. Another major work, shown in Japan and Australia, was *They Give Evidence/Mereka Memberi Kesaksian*, an assemblage of larger-than-life naked sculptures, male and female, their extended forearms bearing bundles of clothes, as if witnessing on behalf of victims. He created *Fire in May/Api di Bulan Mei* (1998) at APT3 in 1999. He and his family were now living in Australia. He declared it was 'a tribute … to the people, mainly Chinese, who died when mobs torched businesses and homes in the Indonesian riots'. But it was also a tribute to all who had died by violence and he referred specifically to the events in East Timor and to his *Count* project.[69]

His art after the fall of the New Order has continued to be directed to the victims of 1965–66, as Dirgantoro discusses in Chapter 9 in this volume, and to victims throughout the world, including victims of war, terrorism and disasters such as the devastating tsunami of 2004 and the overwhelming flows of mud in East Java in 2006, a tragedy most probably caused by unregulated drilling for gas.[70] He has also reflected on themes such as the loss of traditional knowledge, collective memory and history in Indonesian culture such as in the painting *Pahang* (Figure 7.6).[71]

69 Forty-seven papier mâché figures were set alight. A struggle for independence from Indonesia was in process in East Timor at the time.

70 Interview with the artist. His art since Reformasi has also referenced those gaoled and detained under the New Order, such as Indonesian writer Pramoedya Ananta Toer. See Chapter 1 (this volume).

71 Sasha Grishin, 'Review of "Lost"', *Canberra Times,* 20 February 2018.

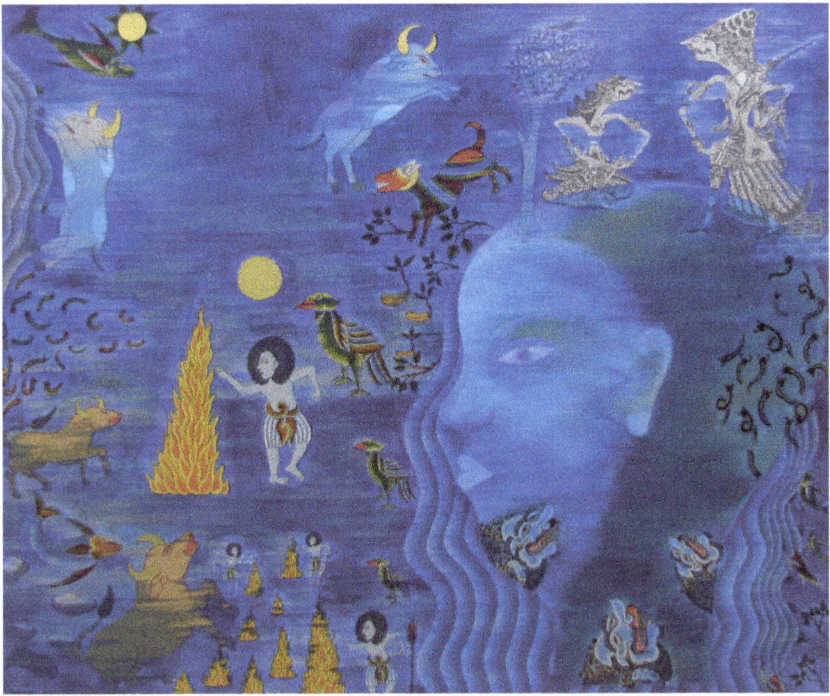

Figure 7.6: Dadang Christanto, *Pahang*, 2015.
Painting. Acrylic and gold paper on canvas, 114 x 135 cm. Image courtesy Nancy Sever Gallery Canberra and the artist.

Arahmaiani: Between the Material and the Spiritual

Arahmaiani is unquestionably the best-known artist internationally among Indonesian women artists who emerged in the 1990s.[72] Dirgantoro suggests that, in the 1990s, she was often the only woman representing Indonesia abroad.[73] Arahmaiani is also considered a pioneer of contemporary performance art. She was born in 1961 and comes from an intellectual Muslim family. Her father was a noted Islamic scholar and

72 She prefers to be known only as Arahmaiani.

73 Wulan Dirgantoro, *Feminisms and Contemporary Art in Indonesia: Defining Experiences* (Amsterdam: Amsterdam University Press, 2017), 176, doi.org/10.1017/9789048526994. For Arahmaiani's exhibitions, see Arahmaiani, 'About the Artist', accessed 14 March 2021, www.trfineart.com/artist/arahmaiani/.

her mother introduced her to Javanese Hindu-Buddhist cultural legacies.[74] An intellectual and a poet, she has, when asked about influences on her art, named, among others, Indonesian poet, dramatist and activist W. S. Rendra and German artist Joseph Beuys, both of whom combined art with activism.[75]

Arahmaiani's art addresses broad issues of humanity and crosses borders between philosophy, literature, poetry and social and ecological activism, linking the spiritual and material in sophisticated dialogue. She has explored in her art not only her Muslim faith but also Java's Hindu-Buddhist heritage and more ancient forms of Javanese spirituality, including animism.

In her groundbreaking study of Indonesian feminisms, Dirgantoro discusses her art under the two main themes of religion and gender, but notes that Arahmaiani herself does not like the application of the Western term 'feminist' to her art.[76] Dirgantoro tells us that when Arahmaiani was growing up she was inspired by spending time in the extensive library of renowned Indonesian female poet, philosopher and advocate for women Toeti Heraty.[77] Kent stresses her work with communities as a key feature of her art.[78] Dirgantoro (Chapter 9, this volume) applies the term 'cosmopolitan' to her art.

Arahmaiani has commented in interviews that she has learned much from the different circumstances of her life and the many cross-cultural situations she has experienced. When I first met her in 1996 she described

74 Pat Binder and Gerhard Haupt, 'Arahmaiani' [notes after an interview], May 2003, accessed 8 November 2020, universes.art/en/nafas/articles/2003/arahmaiani. See discussion of her art and Islam by Virginia Hooker, Chapter 4 (this volume). Anissa Rahadiningtyas also discussed Arahmaiani's art in terms of Islam during The Australian National University Indonesia Institute Webinar in 2021. See Epilogue (this volume).

75 Her work, *I Love You* (*After Joseph Beuys Social Sculpture*) (2009), alludes to Beuys whose concept of art and healing may have also been influential. See also Edwin Jurriëns, 'Gendering the Environmental Artivism: *Ekofeminisme* and *Unjuk Rasa* of Arahmaiani's Art', *Southeast of Now* 4, no. 2 (October 2020): 3–38, 16, doi.org/10.1353/sen.2020.0006, who notes that in the 1980s she 'continued her informal education in theatre and performance art' with Teater Bengkel founded by Rendra. Arahmaiani graduated from the Bandung Institute of Technology in 1983, studied at the Paddington Art School, Sydney, in the 1980s, and at the Akademie voor Beeldende Kunst en Vormgeving, Enschede, the Netherlands, in the early 1990s.

76 Dirgantoro, *Feminisms and Contemporary Art in Indonesia*, 187. Dirgantoro discusses the link between feminism and performance and the way GSRB artists used the body as a site for resistance (171).

77 Dirgantoro, *Feminisms and Contemporary Art in Indonesia*, 178.

78 Kent, 'Entanglement', Chapter 4.

her lifestyle as that of a 'nomad'. She has alluded to the fact that she was arrested while a student in 1983 for participation in street performances that, at the time, were deemed political activism. Extremely important to her art are environmental[79] and art projects involving cross-cultural communication with communities relating to diversity and inclusion. She believes passionately that art has a role in society and in humanity's responses to crises, and suggests that the future direction for art should be a space in which cultural and spiritual values can serve the development of society.[80]

Arahmaiani has spoken out on many issues. Among these has been her criticism of dogmatic religious views and she has fearlessly denounced both militarism and patriarchy. For example, in 1999 she spoke in the Philippines about her role as a Muslim woman artist in Indonesia:

> I realize it [is] a difficult way that I have chosen. The repressive government is operating on the basis of militarism in combination with Javanese Muslim feudalism and [a] patriarchal system, which I believe, breed a culture of violence—physically and psychologically. The system never gave enough room for women to express themselves freely apart from being a good mother, a good wife, a good daughter or sister, though she might also be a career woman at the same time.[81]

In her *Manifesto of a Sceptic*, a performance from the 2000s, Arahmaiani set out her idea of the role of art. Some key points from the statement she made during the various performances include:

> Art belongs to everyone and cannot be dictated to by interest of the market, politics or religion.
>
> It is a liberating force and should encourage a new awareness of humanity and a new social consciousness.

79 See Jurriëns, 'Gendering the Environmental Artivism', which deals in depth with this aspect of her art.

80 Arahmaiani, 'Art of the Earth and of Graves', July 2007, accessed 27 March 2022, universes.art/en/nafas/articles/2007/art-of-the-earth-and-of-graves. She has worked with communities in Indonesia and elsewhere on projects related to alternative ways of living, traditional medicine and to regain the spiritual in everyday living. See also 'Politics of the Unseen: Visual Practice, Spirituality and Resistance in Contemporary Indonesia', Webinar, University of Melbourne, 2020. See Kent, Epilogue (this volume), on Indonesian artists' responses to current crises.

81 Flaudette May V. Datuin, 'Passing through Fire: Pain and Transformation in the Art of Arahmaiani', *Art AsiaPacific*, no. 26 (2000): 66–71. Her work *Burning Body-Burning Country (II)* (1999) was shown in Manila.

She also stressed that art should be a 'meeting point between material and spiritual, masculine and feminine', a 'vessel combining sacred and profane in one space' and a 'tool to examine and access reality'. Most interestingly, she considers art to be 'a combination of courage, rebellion, rational and moral intelligence and conscience' and a force offering 'alternative values, changing values and even turning values upside down'.[82]

She has never been afraid to confront difficult issues. The *Jakarta Post* in 2017 described the controversy that had occurred when her painting *Lingga-Yoni* (1993) was shown in Jakarta in 1994 and the reaction of conservative Muslims, noting that the painting:

> aroused their ire because it featured the Hindu image of male and female genitalia, Malay-Arabic letters saying: 'Nature is a book' and a copy of an inscription from the first Hindu kingdom in Java.[83]

The painting has an interesting history. It was shown in *Traditions/Tensions* in New York in 1996, sold to a friend in Thailand, and finally purchased by the privately owned Museum of Modern and Contemporary Art in Nusantara (MACAN) in Jakarta in 2017. A second version was shown in New York and purchased by the Herbert F. Johnson Museum of Art at Cornell University.

There were also protests about her installation *Etalase* in the same Jakarta exhibition in 1994, because the holy Quran, a statue of Buddha, a pack of condoms, a Coca Cola bottle, a mirror, a box of sand, a fan, a musical instrument and a photo were assembled together in a display case.[84] It was withdrawn from display in Jakarta because of threats to the artist due to her choice of items for display and her use of the holy Quran. *Etalase* was shown again in *Traditions/Tensions* in 1996 and later in the exhibition *Global Feminisms* at the Brooklyn Museum of Art curated by Maura Reilly and Linda Nochlin in 2007. The museum's description reads:

82 See, for example, *Manifesto of a Sceptic* (2009). There were several versions of this performance with some variations on the wording to be seen on YouTube.

83 A. Kurniawan Ulung, 'Arahmaiani Stays True to Herself', *Jakarta Post*, 7 September 2017, accessed 5 November 2020, www.thejakartapost.com/life/2017/09/07/arahmaiani-stays-true-to-herself.html. Arahmaiani stated that the work expressed the principles of female and male found in many religions.

84 Ibid.

'Her installation, *Etalase*, brings together disparate symbols of Islam, Western culture, and sexuality',[85] but this underestimates, I suggest, the rich complexity of the symbols in the work.

I will concentrate here on her work *Nation for Sale* (Figure 7.8) and associated performance *Handle without Care* at APT2 in 1996 (Figure 7.7) as encompassing the themes set out earlier in this chapter. Both artworks were highly effective in communicating her belief that a selfish way of living and a profit-driven exploitative capitalist system needs to be changed.

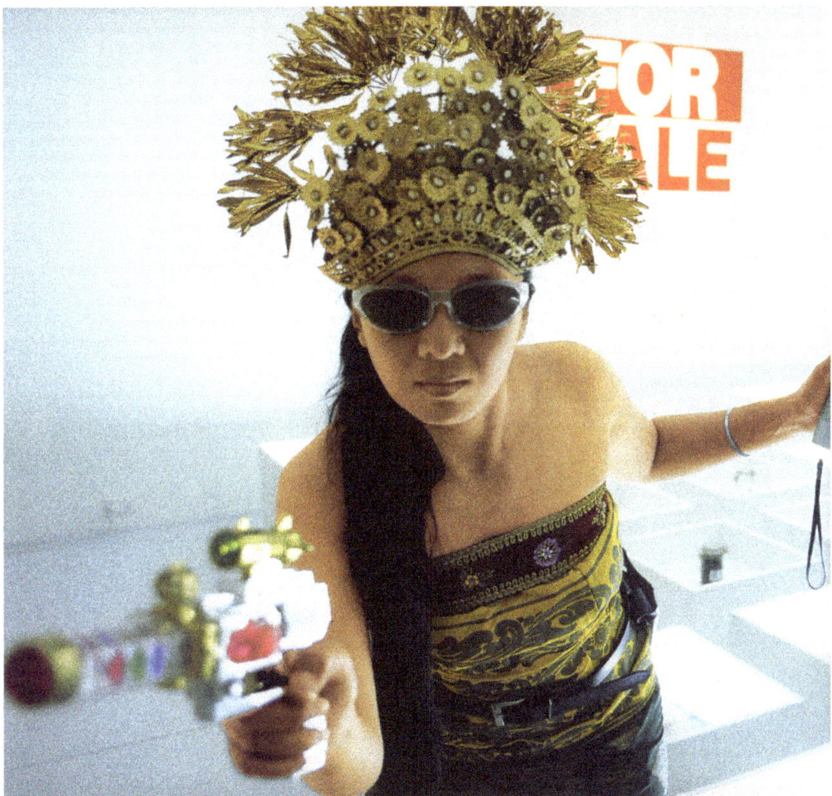

Figure 7.7: Arahmaiani (b. 1961), Indonesia, *Handle without Care*, 1996.

Performance by the artist with audio and video component for the Second Asia Pacific Triennial of Contemporary Art, Queensland Art Gallery, Brisbane, 27 and 28 September 1996. Video available online QAGOMA. Image courtesy the artist.

85 Brooklyn Museum, 'Arahmaiani', accessed 12 November 2020, www.brooklynmuseum.org/eascfa/about/feminist_art_base/arahmaiani.

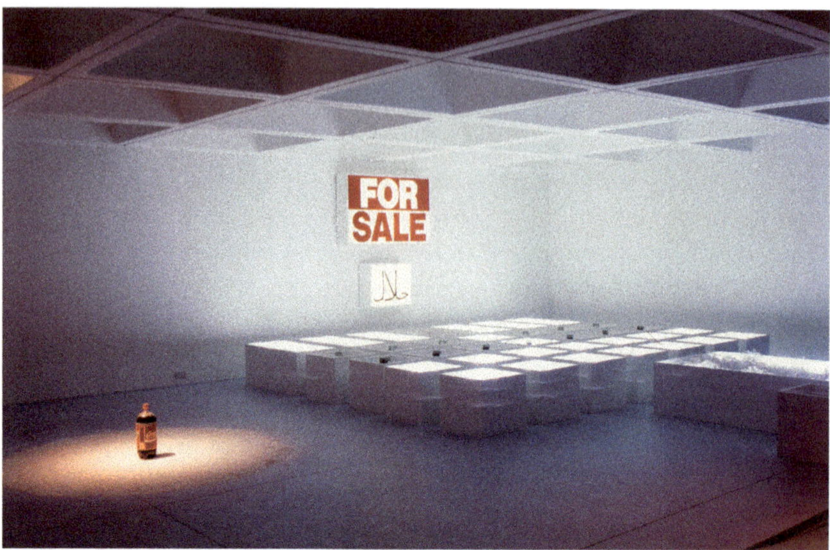

Figure 7.8: Arahmaiani, *Nation for Sale*, 1996.

Installation comprising photographs, plastic toys, soil, water, pills, mirrors, plastic bags, timber, paper, neon, Coco-Cola bottle, photographs by Marian Drew and Manit Sriwanichpoom. The Second Asia Pacific Triennial of Contemporary Art, Queensland Art Gallery, Brisbane, 1996. Photograph: Richard Stringer. Image courtesy: QAGOMA. Permission: the artist. For Nindityo Adipurnomo's work in the same exhibition see Chapter 6.

Nation for Sale was about Western cultural imperialism as well as economic and gender exploitation. It featured, among other items, a Coca-Cola bottle, condoms, as well as plastic American toy soldiers wielding machine guns. M. D. Marianto states that it referenced ordinary people in Indonesia being seduced through popular culture while their sources of livelihood and culture were destroyed by neo-colonialism. He called *Nation for Sale* a metaphor for Indonesia at the time where people had been displaced from their lands for factories, women had become commodities and 'the holders of the social and economic reins' profit so that the nation is, in effect, sold.[86] In her accompanying defining performance, *Handle without Care*, Arahmaiani wore a Balinese dancer's costume and Western sunglasses and moved gracefully through the installation carrying, among other objects, a toy machine gun. It was impossible, having witnessed the performance in 1996, for Australians not to associate the Balinese costume with Australian and other Western tourists' exploitation of the

86 M. Dwi Marianto, 'Arahmaiani', *The Second Asia-Pacific Triennial*, exhibition catalogue (Brisbane: Queensland Art Gallery, 1996), 81.

tourist island of Bali.[87] Arahmaiani's focus was on the vulnerabilities of contemporary women in Indonesia in a globalised world. It is interesting to compare this work with Nindityo Adipurnomo's equally elegant installation in the same exhibition, *Introversion (April the Twenty-First)* (1995–96), that commented on hierarchies in Javanese society through the symbolism of the *konde*, the formal hair arrangement worn by upper-class Javanese women, combined with images of Kartini, the nineteenth-century Indonesian female aristocrat who advocated education for women (see Figure 6.5).[88]

The challenges for Indonesia in a globalising world that Arahmaiani explored in this early work have, in recent years, taken on a much broader global compass and complexity. Her community work in Indonesia after events such as a devastating earthquake in Yogyakarta in 2006 have translated into international settings and new dimensions of the 'cosmopolitan'. Arahmaiani has taken her art most recently to the Tibetan plateau, a region widely known as the 'third pole' because of the significance of its water supplies to feed critical Asian river systems (Figure 7.9). The five-year project involves Buddhist monks and the Tibetan community planting trees and clearing rubbish and the community returning to growing their own food rather than importing it. It relates to numerous issues affecting the environment, including climate change. This might be termed not only environmental activism but also 'world-making' in the face of potential global catastrophe. It is dependent on both intensive cross-cultural negotiations and world-making on a transnational and transcultural scale. Arahmaiani's work in these projects mirrors art historian Marsha Meskimmon's suggestion of the 'cosmopolitan imagination' as 'future-oriented and generative' and of the affective capacity of contemporary art in allowing empathetic intersubjective connections between people across cultural and linguistic borders, 'transforming our relationship with/in the world'.[89]

---

87 Arahmaiani was not the only Indonesian artist to comment on multinational exploitation. Dede Edi Supria's painting *Labyrinth* (1987–88) shows a labyrinth of boxes with the names of multinational companies and the bodies of two Indonesian boys lying dead or injured (see Figure 6.4, this volume).
88 On Kartini, see Kathryn Robinson, 'Kartini and "Kartini"', *New Mandala*, 21 April 2018, accessed 4 November 2020, www.newmandala.org/kartini-and-kartini/.
89 Marsha Meskimmon, *Contemporary Art and the Cosmopolitan Imagination* (London: Routledge, 2010), 8, doi.org/10.4324/9780203846834. See also Meskimmon, *Transnational Feminisms, Transversal Politics and Art Entanglements and Intersections* (Abingdon: Routledge, 2020), 52, doi.org/10.4324/9780429507830. Meskimmon does not specifically write about Arahmaiani in these texts but does very effectively discuss ecofeminism in the context of cross-cultural engagement.

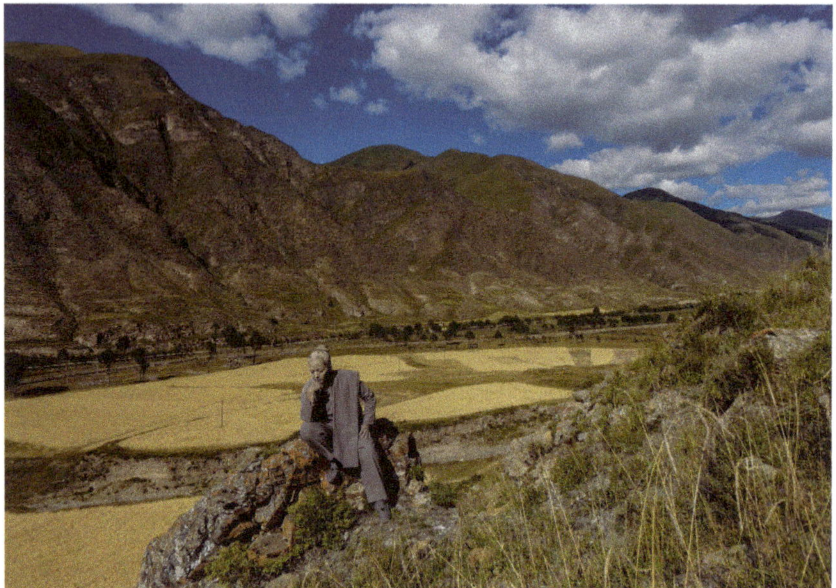

Figure 7. 9: Arahmaiani, *Shadow of the Past, Tibet*, 2018.

Still from video of performance. Image courtesy the artist. This performance can be seen as a meditation on the spiritual traditions of humanity referring particularly to historical links between Buddhism in Java and Tibet as well as to the artist's philosophical collaborations with academics at Passau University, Germany, and with spiritual leaders of many faiths, including Judaism, Buddhism, Hinduism, Christianity and Islam. Thus, she has said, her new works may be related to 'a contemplation on the present condition of life', including challenges of ecological destruction and the suffering of the poor and marginalised.[90]

90 Arahmaiani, a Muslim, has spoken often about her fascination with and research into spiritual and religious traditions including:

> the past cultures of Animism, Hinduism, and Buddhism in Indonesia, which left behind many temples—even the largest Buddhist temple in the world, Borobudur … Furthermore, there is the relationship in ancient times between Tibetan Buddhism and local Buddhism in what is now Indonesia (which in the past was of the Mahayana/Tantrayana sect). A monk known by the name Lama Atisha, who became a reformer of the Buddhist religion in Tibet and who founded Kadampa school, once studied for twelve years in the Buddhist university in Sriwijaya (the ancient kingdom in Indonesia), where he received the guidance of a local master by the name of Dharmakirti, who in Tibet is known as Lama Serlingpa.

Arahmaiani, 'Artist's Statement', in *Shadow of the Past*, 2016, accessed 5 October 2021, www.trfineart.com/wp-content/uploads/2016/09/Arahmaiani-2016-Catalog-lr.pdf.

Conclusion: Redefining the Contemporary in Art

The artists discussed in this chapter were part of a post-independence generation of artists in Indonesia who engaged closely with the concept of who Indonesians are and what their nation and society might become in the future as well as with issues of relevance and importance for humanity as a whole. They exemplify art and artists providing new models for cultural, social and political understanding in both local and international contexts referred to in the question posed at the beginning of this chapter and also Preziosi's proposition cited earlier that art is one of the most powerful social instruments 'for the creation and maintenance of the world in which we live'. All have reflected Terry Smith's emphasis on the urgency and, one might add, the contingency of contemporary art practice. All have engaged in world-making. They and other artists from the former 'periphery' not only joined the new global art world in formation in the 1990s but also contributed to reshaping its discourses and redefining contemporary art for a new century in transcultural contexts.

Acknowledgements

The artists whose work is discussed in this chapter and especially Arahmaiani, Dadang Christanto, Heri Dono and FX Harsono, deserve my special thanks along with many other colleagues who have been an important part of my journey exploring Indonesian art, which began with the First Asia Pacific Triennial in the early 1990s. These include my co-curators in 1993 Jim Supangkat, Soedarso SP, David Williams and the late Sanento Yuliman. There are many others who are named in the general acknowledgements to this volume but here I particularly thank Dolorosa Sinaga, Kartika Affandi, Mella Jaarsma, Glen Barclay, Christine Clark, Pat Hoffie, Jen Webb, Astri Wright, Alison Carroll, Jennifer Lindsay, David Elliott and Michelle Antoinette. It has been particularly inspiring to work with my brilliant coeditors, Virginia Hooker and Elly Kent, who have so generously shared with me their profound knowledge of and insights into Indonesian culture.

8

New Order Policies on Art/ Culture and Their Impact on Women's Roles in Visual Arts, 1970s–90s

Alia Swastika

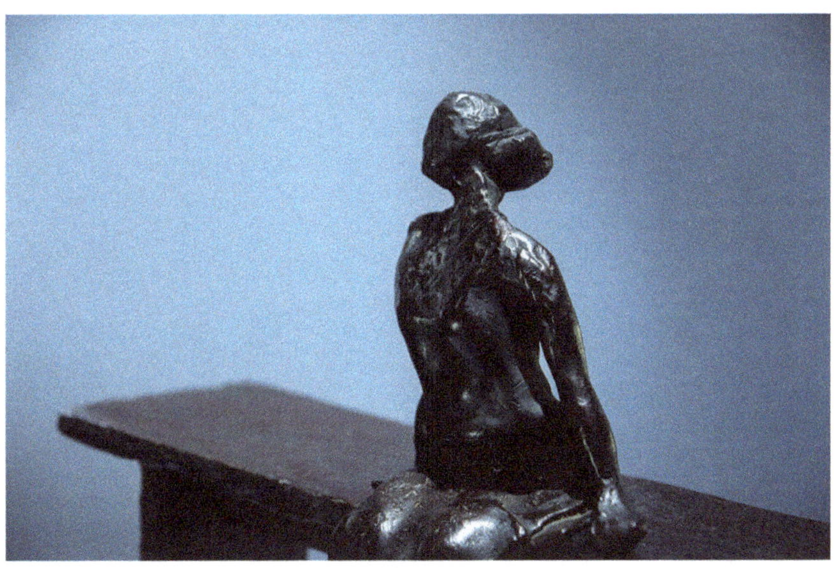

Figure 8.1: Dolorosa Sinaga, *Tak Kunjung Datang* (*They Never Came*), 1992.
Detail view. Bronze. Image courtesy the artist.

The New Order regime in Indonesia, which held power from 1966 to 1998 and is considered the most powerful authority in the history of the nation, established many values and norms that differed from previous periods. One of the most heavily impacted was the role and position of women in society, including in the arts and cultural sector. While reading the hidden history of the Sukarno era, or the Old Order, I found it very interesting to see the ideological shift in women's movements, including the visibility of women (artists) in the sociopolitical context. Many women had actively joined movements and political organisations and some very strong and critical voices had emerged. By contrast, during the New Order it seemed that women's voices were systematically silenced. This has led to the invisibility of women in the (canonical) art history of Indonesia: even now, more than two decades into the reformation era, women artists remain hidden and almost unknown. Rewriting history, in my opinion, is not only thinking about making a new canon, but most importantly documenting the diverse experiences and narratives that formed women artists during that important period of political silencing. Therefore, I am interested in looking at the small narratives—almost biographical—of five women artists from different backgrounds who lived and worked during the New Order, and examining how gender policies during the New Order influenced their artistic practices in one way or another. I studied archival texts (mostly catalogue essays and newspaper/magazines articles) on how women artists were portrayed in the mass media during the early 1970s to early 1990s to gain insight into the broader context of the art scene in general. The five women I studied and interviewed—Siti Adiyati (b. 1949), Hildawati Soemantri (1945–2003), Dyan Anggraini (b. 1957), Dolorosa Sinaga (b. 1953) and Mangku Muriati (b. 1967)—should not be seen as representative of women's art practices of the period; rather, they represent five different stories that enrich the study.

In 1965, at the end of the Old Order, the world of art and culture had changed its ideology and perspectives in reaction to the newly emerging political situation. In the New Order era, Manikebu (Cultural Manifesto) artists marked their victory, mainly due to the dissolution of the Lekra (Institute for the People's Culture), the imprisonment of Lekra's important exponents and the massive exile to Buru Island. The New Order also raised the need for an aesthetic regime that worshipped a kind of obscurity and ambiguity in political matters. That need was easily filled by abstract painting. In his 1978 book *Strategi Kebudayaan* (Strategy of culture),

Ali Murtopo wrote: 'The New Order is a cultural process'.[1] In the context of art, the New Order needed a type of art practice that was not critical of the government and did not interfere with political affairs—art for art's sake. Formalism met this need.

In relation to female artists, the New Order's emphasis on women as mothers and wives influenced how women were represented in various media and the way they represented themselves. During the 1950s and 1960s, one of the most significant women's movements in Indonesia was Gerakan Wanita Indonesia, shortened to Gerwani (Indonesian Women's Movement), which also came under the umbrella of the Indonesian Communist Party, with many progressive female intellectuals and artists among its members. After the dissolution of Gerwani, when communism was banned in Indonesia, women were not only politically domesticated, but also awareness of the body, sexuality and individuality were restricted; hence, related issues became taboo for the majority of artists. Rachmi Diyah, in a study on body politics and power in dance, argues that female dancers during the New Order experienced structural violence on their bodies, mainly due to the loss of opportunity to express resistance.[2]

From my observations, during the 1970s there were several strong female artists, such as Edi Sedyawati, Retno Maruti, Gusmiati Suid and N. H. Dini, who raised themes related to women's position in society, emphasising the tension between tradition and modernity. Questions concerning the position of women occasionally appeared in the form of voices criticising how women were positioned in traditional social structures. The New Order regime strictly limited the agenda of women's organisations to non-political spheres, forming a new structure in which most organisations were attached to the state's bureaucracy, enabling the government to control them. Among the most important organisations of the time were Dharma Wanita, an association of civil servants' wives; Kowani, the Indonesian Women's Coalition; and associations of wives of military members. The government implemented national programs, such as Kesejahteraan Keluarga (Family Prosperity Program) and Dasa Wisma (Ten Households), based on families and their residential areas.

---

1 Ali Murtopo, *Strategi Kebudayaan* (Jakarta: Yayasan Proklamasi, Centre for Strategic and International Studies, 1978), 36.

2 Rachmi Diyah Larasati, 'Lingkaran Tubuh Tari: Ritme dan Kekuasaan' [Dance body circle: Rhythm and power], *Jurnal Perempuan, Perempuan dan Seni Pertunjukan* [Women's journal, women and performance art], ed. Alia Swastika, et al. (Jakarta: Yayasan Jurnal Perempuan and Yayasan Kelola, 2009), 39.

These programs functioned as mechanisms of control, gathering women together every month to learn domestic skills such as cooking, sewing and other household duties. Julia Suryakusuma, one of Indonesia's best-known feminists, called the New Order's gender strategy '*ibuism*' (mother-ism) because its state-sanctioned ideological standpoint emphasised only the roles of women as wives and mothers.[3]

In literature, as in visual art, women's voices were eliminated in male-dominated literary canons, selected through a series of masculine procedures. Rukiah Kertapati is one notable example. Yerry Wirawan, a lecturer in history at Sanata Dharma University, claimed that Rukiah Kertapati was deliberately omitted from the history of Indonesian women and Indonesian modern literary history as she was a member of Lekra.[4]

In fact, the taming of the women's movement not only caused the decline of women's involvement in the sociopolitical arena, but also limited space for women to exhibit their work, compared to that of male artists. The female body was constructed as a machine to strengthen the state's identity where the ruling regime held almost absolute control over what was permissible and what was not. Thus, ideas of 'being female' and 'being an artist' were developed in a highly standardised, narrow field.

Outside the Canon: Discourse and Themes in the Work of Women Artists during the 1970s and 1980s

The Indonesian art scene in the late 1970s and 1980s was fairly dynamic, marked by the birth of many new experiments and interesting encounters with various foreign ideas. In Jakarta, Taman Ismail Marzuki, built in 1974, enabled artists, intellectuals, art audiences and the public to gather and see each other's work, conduct discussions and become part of a growing city. In addition, there were cultural spaces, including Balai Budaya, Bentara Budaya, Goethe Institut and several hotels, that occasionally held art events.

---

3 Julia Suryakusuma, *State Ibuism: The Social Construction of Womanhood in New Order Indonesia* (Depok: Komunitas Bambu, 2011).

4 'Siti Rukiah Kertapati, Sastrawati Era Kemerdekaan yang Terlupakan', BBC Online, 24 November 2018, accessed 21 January 2022, www.bbc.com/indonesia/indonesia-46224526.

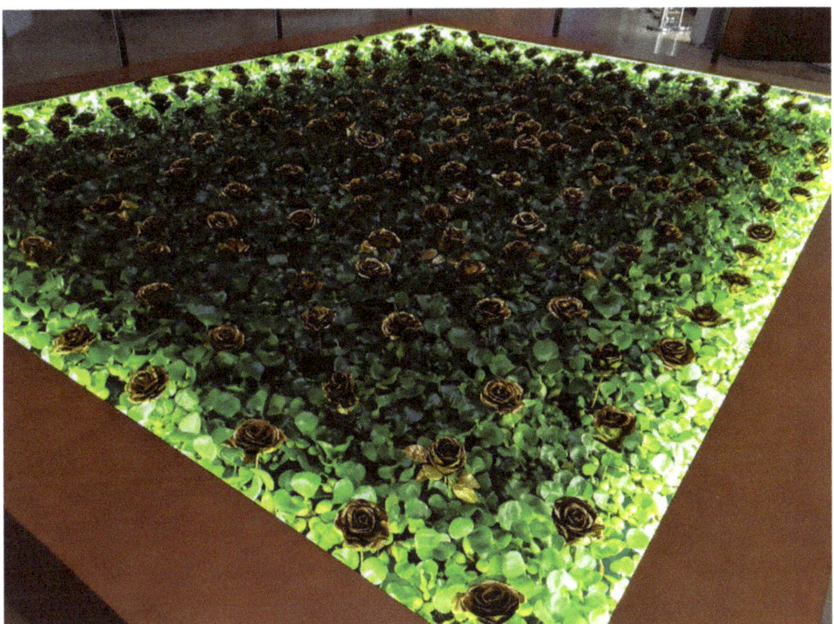

Figure 8.2: Siti Adiyati, *Eceng Gondok Berbunga Emas* (*Water Hyacinth with Golden Roses*), 1979, remade in 2017.

Pond, water hyacinths and plastic flowers, dimensions variable. Collection: the artist. © Siti Adiyati, image with the artist's permission. *Eceng Gondok Berbunga Emas* was originally shown in 1979 in the second Gerakan Seni Rupa Baru (GSRB, New Art Movement Indonesia) exhibition in Taman Ismail Marzuki, re-created for the Jakarta Biennale 2017 and for the exhibition *Awakenings: Art in Society in Asia 1960s–1990s* (2018–19).[5]

In terms of the practice of art creation, there were a number of emerging trends in Indonesian visual art, including those that Gerakan Seni Rupa Baru (GSRB, the Indonesian New Art Movement) explored in several exhibitions and in their manifesto. During the 1960s, the dominant discourse on art turned on the dichotomy between 'the political' and 'the aesthetic', represented by Lekra and Manikebu, respectively. Such debates loosened somewhat after the 1965 incident, as many artists were imprisoned, exiled overseas or were simply missing. In the early 1970s,

5 Editors' note: Seng Yu Jin, senior curator at the Singapore National Gallery, noted the work combined a living plant that is also a harmful weed with artificial roses. He quotes the artist as saying that the work criticised Indonesia's then president Suharto's New Order as 'just an illusion symbolised by the golden rose in the sea of absolute poverty that the *eceng gondok* represents'. Siti Adiyati to Seng Yu Jin, 1 January 2017, quoted in Seng Yu Jin, 'The Re-Materialisation of Everyday Life', National Gallery of Singapore, 13 June 2019, accessed 9 April 2022, www.nationalgallery.sg/magazine/siti-adiyati-re-materialisation-everyday-life.

artists were still trying to understand the period of political transition from the Old Order to the New Order in which political issues only appeared vaguely. The large-scale exhibition Pameran Besar Seni Lukis Indonesia (Major exhibition of Indonesian painting) held in 1974—historically significant because it triggered the birth of the 1974 *Desember Hitam* (Black December) manifesto—was considered by Bambang Bujono to be an exhibition with strong diversity in artistic orientation and style.[6] Nashar, Zaini, Abas Alibasjah and Fadjar Sidik were the main references for artistic ideas. Meanwhile, mainstream exhibitions continued to attract visitors, especially if they displayed the works of maestro artists such as Basuki Abdullah, Affandi and other well-known names of their generation.

The history of visual arts during the colonial period—seen through art writing published in various mass media outlets, in introductory textbooks on Indonesian art history and in notes in some exhibition catalogues—indicates that art was a highly male-dominated scene. There were extremely few female artists mentioned, let alone as primary actors in the developing art discourses. In some sources, as in the important book by Carla Bianpoen, Farah Wardani and Wulan Dirgantoro, artists such as Emiria Soenassa, Mia Bustam and Trijoto Abdullah are mentioned.[7] Yet it is very difficult to find other Indonesian female artists from the colonial period in these texts. This phenomenon is not specific to Indonesia or even Asian countries, as this absence is also notable at the global level. Griselda Pollock underlines the invisibility of women artists in canonical art history texts.

Against the backdrop of this masculine and canon-based history of art, fighting for women's positions means questioning the criteria used to warrant recording an artist or artwork, including critically reassessing 'hobbyist' art practices, arts that are intertwined as a part of women's social functions in certain structures—for example, in *kraton* (palaces) and in traditional ceremonies—and works that represent long traditions of craft, such as batik, weaving, *ikat*, embroidery and glass painting, all of which are mostly performed by women.[8]

6 Bambang Bujono, 'Gado-gado, Ya Biar' [Mixed, yes, let it be], in *Melampaui Citra dan Ingatan* [Beyond image and memory] (Jakarta: Gajah Hidup, 2017), 61–67.

7 C. Bianpoen, F. Wardani and W. Dirgantoro, *Indonesian Women Artists: The Curtain Opens* (Indonesia: Yayasan Senirupa, 2007).

8 Elly Kent, 'Visual Arts and Artists: Indonesia', in *Encyclopedia of Women in Islamic Cultures*, 2019, doi.org/10.1163/1872-5309_ewic_COM_002173.

If we want to question the elimination of women from the art canon, first we need to problematise the very concept of the canon. Generally, canons are understood as comprising works by maestros—masterpieces. However, there are more complex struggles for values in the establishment of a canon. Pollock defines the canon as a 'discursive formation which constitutes the works or thoughts it selects as the product of artistic mastery'.[9] The selection is conducted within existing race and class structures. This discursive formation legitimises white male supremacy.

According to Heidi Arbuckle, the language and structure of the Indonesian art canon (from the colonial period to the contemporary era) adopted Western ideas, including gender exclusion. This makes the role of female artists indefinite in art history. Arbuckle also investigated how the language or terms used in art have perpetuated masculine regimes. For example, the term '*seniman*' is constructed from the incorporation of the words '*seni*' (art) and '*man*' (male), which, in itself, indicates a gender preference.[10] This masculine regime lasted long enough that traces of the likely male-dominated social environment are still found in the Indonesian art scene today. In the late 1970s and 1980s, one of the well-known collectives was Decenta, whose members were all male. Apotik Komik, established in the mid-1990s, also consists of male artists only. Other recent artist collectives have also had exclusive male memberships, such as Mes 56, which restricted its membership to men until 2016.

A number of art exhibitions during the New Order included women artists, but they are not recorded in art history texts, let alone as part of the canon, as they were held in hotels or other commercial spaces. Thus, even when female artists contribute in the public sphere, they are not considered equal to male artists and do not receive the same level of media or critical attention. While some art critics, such as Sanento Yuliman, Bambang Bujono, Kusnadi and Soedarmadji, did write about female artists in this period, especially those who were considered to display interesting artistic ideas, the numbers were insignificant compared to the reviews of work by male artists. Sanento Yuliman conducted careful research on women's involvement in Indonesian visual art for his introduction to the Nuansa exhibition catalogue in 1988, re-presenting Kartini, Emiria Sunassa and

9 Griselda Pollock, *Differencing the Canon: Feminist Desire and the Writing of Art's Histories* (London and New York: Routledge, 1999), 9.

10 Heidi Arbuckle, 'Performing Emiria Sunassa: Reframing the Female Subject in Post-Colonial Indonesia' (PhD diss., University of Melbourne, 2012), 112–14.

Trijoto Abdullah in an important historical context.[11] According to Heidi Arbuckle, Yuliman's major contribution was his insight that gendered differentiations of labour had significantly erased women's roles in the art world.[12]

Yuliman identified an important distinction in art: men, he said, made statues and paintings, and women made crafts and ceramics. He noted that, by the end of the 1980s, men were making work using fabric and ceramics and that they were more commercially successful in this endeavour than women. Arbuckle underlines Yuliman's sociological conclusion—that the problem for female artists in Indonesia was not aesthetics, creativity or ability, but a lack of opportunity and accessibility, and the need to overcome significant social barriers.

In the late 1980s, Carla Bianpoen began paying attention to the works of female artists. Her early writings have become an important source of data on the position of female artists in Indonesia and she continues to publish reviews in *Kompas* and the *Jakarta Post*. Bianpoen's *Indonesian Women Artists*, co-written with Farah Wardani and Wulan Dirgantoro, made an important contribution to the literature on female artists, as did her collection of biographies, fragments of thoughts and artworks of almost 100 female artists.[13]

When distinctions are drawn between 'professional' and 'amateur' artists, presentations or exhibitions of women's artwork were often relegated to the latter category. Bambang Bujono, a journalist who faithfully followed and wrote about the development of Indonesian art in the 1970s–90s, noted that female artists faced limited possibilities.[14] They might be categorised as 'real' artists, hobby artists, Sunday artists or commercial artists. Maria Tjui, from Pariaman, West Sumatra, was considered quite successful in marketing her artworks during this period. Her works were often compared to Affandi's works, especially because she learned from Affandi, even living with his family for some time. To a certain extent, she was widely known as a commercial artist and frequently featured in magazines and other popular media.

---

11 Sanento Yuliman, 'Wanita dan Seni Rupa di Indonesia: Sebuah Catatan untuk Nuansa Indonesia', in *Nuansa Indonesia III* [Indonesian nuances III] (Taman Ismail Marzuki, 1988), 23–30.

12 Arbuckle, 'Performing Emiria Sunassa', 74.

13 Bianpoen, Wardani and Dirgantoro, *Indonesian Women Artists*.

14 Bujono, 'Pertama Memang Nyonya' [Firstly a lady], in *Melampaui Citra dan Ingatan*, 56–60.

There was little recognition of gendered issues in the 1970s and 1980s, and some even denied the existence of gender inequalities. Bambang Bujono stated that, generally, there was no problem of gender representation in these decades. However, in his review of Pameran Besar Seni Lukis Indonesia IV 1981 (Major exhibition of Indonesian painting IV 1981), Tjok Hendro lamented the lack of female artists. According to him, there were only three female artists out of 90 exhibitors—Nunung WS, Sriyani and Titik Setiawati—and all of them came from Jakarta.[15]

At that time, female artists often participated in joint exhibitions with fellow female artists. While this 'short cut' enabled them to overcome the problem of quantity, it also reinforced discrimination, as female artists were effectively limited to exhibiting with other female artists. Moreover, some exhibitions seemed to be organised only to create a joint event for female artists and were not otherwise based on shared ideas. One such event was *Exhibition of 27 Female Painters* from Jakarta, Bandung, Yogyakarta and Semarang, which took place at Balai Seni Rupa Jakarta (now Museum Seni Rupa dan Keramik/Museum of Fine Art and Ceramics) in 1979.

Five years later, *Pameran Seni Rupa Bias 27* (Bias 27 art exhibition) was held at Galeri Cipta, TIM, showcasing works by 27 female artists from Jakarta. The event deliberately gathered staff, teachers and female students who had studied at the Jakarta Institute of Art. Some of the artists participating in this exhibition were Hildawati Soemantri, Farida Srihadi, Ananda Moersyid, Dolorosa Sinaga, Windradiati and Lydia Poetri.

Given that GSRB's artistic experimentations are regarded as having been successful, it is necessary to mention Siti Adiyati and Nanik Mirna, the two female artists of the group. The movement promoted a spirit of experimentation in finding new artistic expressions and members had the freedom to pursue their respective concerns and ideas. Siti Adiyati and Nanik Mirna seemed to have equal positions to other members. Thus, their contribution might be quite different from some aforementioned female artists. The fact that Siti Adiyati and Nanik Mirna were not recorded in the list of female artists compiled by Carla Bianpoen, Farah Wardani and Wulan Dirgantoro is quite intriguing. The general public only started to notice Siti Adiyati and study her important contribution after her participation in the 2019 Biennale in Jakarta.

15 Tjok Hendro, 'Sedang Bertarung Seni Lukis Indonesia di TIM' [Battling for painting at TIM], *Kompas*, 23 December 1980.

Themes of Female Artists' Works, Mid-1970s – Early 1990s

It is interesting that, in many reviews, female artists were mentioned alongside the names of male artists that might have influenced them. For example, Bujono described Umi Dachlan's work as nonfigurative due to the prominent influence of Ahmad Sadali, her mentor (see Figure 1.7), and Ida Hajar's work as Picasso-like, but without any explanation or elaboration on the context or the theme.[16] In another essay, Bujono described Reni Hoegeng's work as embracing minimalism—'a canvas with single background colour, and one or several shapes with one single colour as well'. Later, Bujono praised this choice, stating: 'Some paintings succeeded in presenting quite reasonable beauty of form'.[17] Nunung WS's work *Garis Putih* (White line) prompted a review praising the artist's ability to offer imaginative adventures, weaving between long linear fields that emerge abruptly.[18] These are some examples of how critics often read women's work through their visual preferences instead of trying to describe the thinking behind those lines, colours or others features.

Popular styles during the mid-1970s – early 1990s were landscape painting and painting with decorative elements. In *Pameran 27 Perupa* (Exhibition of 27 artists), held to celebrate the anniversary of Jakarta in 1979, Kustiyah presented two paintings: one portrays a frangipani flower (one of her most frequent subjects of paintings) and the other is a painting titled *Laut Madura* (*Madura Sea*) (see Map 2). Landscape painting was a developing genre in the late 1970s in Indonesia.

Strong media experimentation was demonstrated by Hildawati Soemantri (b. 1945), a female artist working mostly with ceramics. In a striking exhibition in 1976 at Taman Ismail Marzuki (more details are in the later section about her biography and works), Soemantri showed her determination to work with clay. Her experiments and relationship with the medium itself created a strong spiritual element within her works.

16 Bujono, 'Ada Ida ada Haryati', in *Melampaui Citra dan Ingatan*, 129–32.

17 Bujono, 'A.H., I.K., J.S., N.S., P.S., R.H.', in *Melampaui Citra dan Ingatan*, 55.

18 Bambang Bujono, 'Pameran Besar Seni Lukis Indonesia II—Sebuah Catatan Kaki' [Major exhibition of Indonesian painting II—a footnote], *Berita Buana,* 10 January 1977.

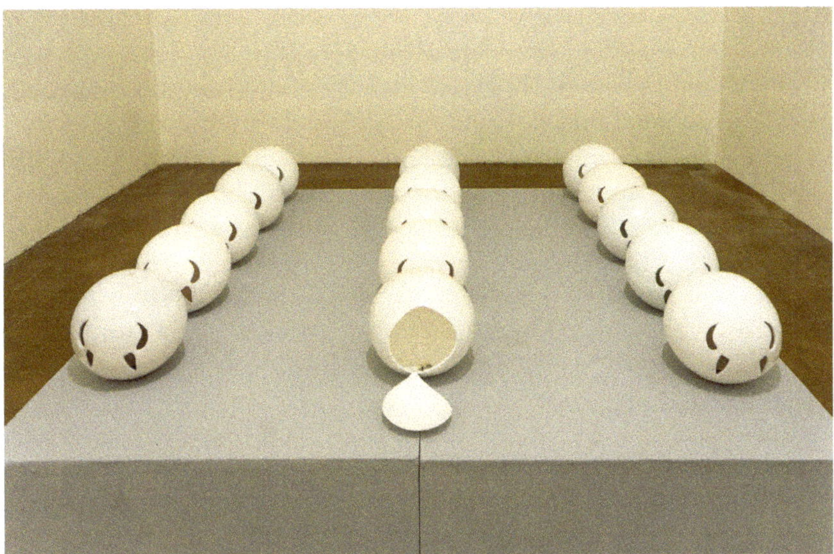

Figure 8.3: Hildawati Soemantri (1945–2003), Untitled, 1978 (re-created in 2019).
29.5 cm (each), glazed stoneware. Reproduction by Purnomo Clay, Yogyakarta. Photograph by Deni Fidinillah, courtesy the Biennale Jogja.

Amid the tendency to be apolitical, female artists determined to keep working and to play a role in the art scene. Meanwhile, among the streams of aesthetic and formalistic ideas, very few female artists worked consistently with dominant trends or themes. At that time, feminism was regarded as merely one among other emerging concepts, such as modernism and existentialism. It did not serve as a mainstream discourse within communities of female artists. A sense of agency was not necessarily presented in an obvious manner within their works. Nevertheless, expressions indicating self-acknowledgement are quite subversive in certain ways.

Images of women questioning issues of identity and relations with traditional structures are present in Astari Rasjid's (b. 1953) paintings. Rasjid stated that she longed for the freedom to express herself the way she wanted to, but the Javanese tradition her parents had taught her ruled out individualistic behaviour. Her sense of individualism was heightened when she lived abroad for several years. Coming back to Indonesia, tensions between individualism and communalism inevitably arose.[19]

19 'Lebih Jauh dengan Astari Rasyid' [Further with Astari Rasyid], *Kompas*, 24 December 2000 (archived with writer).

The notions of self that appeared in the works of Indonesian artists from the mid-1970s to the 1980s were quite different from the ones operating in the Western art scene. In Western art, notions of the self in work by female artists were presented mostly through their relationships to their physical body. Hence, performance art was a popular approach, and the medium was frequently used by female artists of that era. Lucy Lippard notes that one of the fundamental differences between the body art practised by male and female artists at that time was attitude.[20] However, this element might be less obvious to those who opposed feminism or those who did not consciously examine women's ideas or thoughts. Due to being invisible, to 'speak louder' women had to create radical visual images.

Does a female aesthetic exist? What are the issues? In the 1980s, and even today, Indonesian society considered the matter of sex to be taboo. One of the early artists to present issues of sex straightforwardly in the Indonesian art scene was Gusti Ayu Kadek (IGAK) Murniasih (1966–2006). Depicting radical images of the body on her canvases, Murniasih broke a longstanding taboo in Indonesian art. It follows that there are at least two ways that feminist artists can provide new perspectives on the canon and challenge established gender perceptions in the world of art. First, by redefining visual symbols that have already entailed certain connotations of gender; second, by creating radical images to immediately deliver the issues into the centre of a dialogue. Therefore, a strong sense of agency is critical for female artists.

Existential discussions about female artists frequently start with the issue of proportionate quota and end up with questioning whether there are distinctive characteristics in the works of female artists that distinguish them from those of male artists. To take the question deeper, we might ask: is there a feminist art?

Lucy R. Lippard argues that there are certain prominent aspects in the works of female artists that are inaccessible to male artists.[21] These originate in the different political, biological and social experiences of

20 Lucy R. Lippard, *The Pink Glass Swan: Selected Essays on Feminist Art* (New York: New Press, 1995), 101.
21 Ibid., 152.

females. In my opinion, female experiences are deeply personal. At the same time, such experiences are always in tension with the culture that constructs them.

In a society where craftsmanship serves as an essential part of traditional rituals, the notion of artworks as the representation of the individual becomes ambiguous. Within this society, women's ideas and thoughts are anonymised, leading to more biases since the society is, in itself, patriarchal. Correspondingly, the works of female artists, which are highly influenced by traditional legacies, such as making batik, woven fabric and ceramics, are not categorised as representations of thought. Such assumptions are reproduced continuously until women eventually believe that the products of their labour are not art and are unlike what men make. Another consequence coming from this assumption is the stereotypical construction of female art as if it only encompasses limited forms such as painting, fabric, embroidery, handicrafts, etc. This emphasis on labelling women's art as 'craft' can, in a way, be seen as part of the domestication strategy described earlier—the politics of *ibuism* during the New Order period.

While the politics of *ibuism* touched almost every level of society, it is interesting to see how it impacted the works of female artists who practised during that period. Did the themes of their works become less political and less critical? How did they bring women's problems of the time into their work? How did this depoliticising of women change their aesthetic vision or artistic practice, if at all?

I made a small study of five women artists, examining their trajectories, artworks and everyday life practices during the New Order era: Hildawati Soemantri, who made a very significant contribution to the history of ceramic art in Indonesia; Dyan Anggraini and Siti Adiyati, both eminent figures in the Yogyakarta art scene; Mangku Muriati, a painter from Klungkung, Bali, who explores the traditions of Kamasan as her visual language and is also the first priestess in Klungkung Village's temple; and Dolorosa Sinaga, a sculptor who dedicates herself to humanitarian issues. Their stories (or case studies) go some way towards answering some of the fundamental questions mentioned above.

Political Narratives: The Political and the Personal

It is thought-provoking to study artists' attitudes towards the political landscape of the 1980s. It is especially stimulating to see how they responded (or not) to the policies of the New Order and whether they consciously or unconsciously avoided political topics in their works. During the 1980s, global feminism was highly influenced by the concept that 'the personal is political', an argument widely addressed in the works of European and American female artists in response to political regulations that directly put women in unfavourable situations. At the same time, artists such as Doris Salcedo and Valie Export sought to connect their artworks to other political discourses to deliver criticisms of the state and authority. Yet, in Indonesia during this period, a consciousness of what was political in one's personal realm was still undeveloped.

Siti Adiyati, a prominent artist who was a signatory to the *Pernyataan Desember Hitam* (Black December Statement) and GSRB, stated that, during the 1980s, the political was defined as a matter of building critical awareness and enhancing the desire to question the social context. Meanwhile, Dolorosa encountered an appealing discourse shift in regard to the meaning of the political itself. She swayed from interpreting the political as a matter of representation to understanding it as direct engagement—or, to be precise, activism. Among the five interviewees, Dolorosa is the only artist and activist. Hildawati was not interested in directly penetrating the political domain through her art practices. Thus, her works mostly talk about fundamental issues of humanity. Meanwhile, Dyan Anggraini and Mangku Muriati were directly involved in actual political arenas. Dyan worked as a bureaucrat and Muriati serves in a customary institution as the first female priest in the temple of her district, a very rare position in Balinese society. How should we see their political engagement at this point? How could one create meaning by being political in a period in which political trauma and state propaganda on developmentalism were so intense? How do female artists, in particular, raise issues of gender politics in their artworks and everyday life practices?

In general, government policies of the 1980s did not directly affect the thoughts of women of that generation. Most of them grew up during a transition phase in which the remains of the Old Order had been removed and the New Order was just sprouting into a regime. The New Order's propaganda for the ideal image of women had no direct effect on their works, since the art scene they chose to be in offered an open, free space for thinking. Neither did they necessarily criticise propaganda, mainly because they were already conscious of not addressing problems exclusive to women in their art, instead speaking about them within broader social contexts. In a way, this became their strategy: they wanted to be seen in an equal position to men as 'artists' and so avoided being put under the umbrella of 'female artists' by not addressing women's issues in their art. Gender issues were portrayed as part of other social problems, for instance, in relation to religion or poverty, instead of being underlined as separate issues. For example, few female artists openly and critically discussed the domestication of women during the 1980s. Later, in the 1990s, commentary slowly appeared on the state of women as marginalised citizens, suffering from economic and structurally generated difficulties. Subsequently, this became part of women artists' narratives.

Nevertheless, among the five women artists I interviewed, only Dolorosa Sinaga referred to herself as a feminist. Wulan Dirgantoro found a similar tendency in Sinaga's work. Most of the female artists she encountered during her research, particularly those who were active in the late 1990s (post-1998), such as Lakshmi Sitaresmi, Titarubi and Theresia Agustina, refused the feminist label attributed by others to their works.[22]

Indeed, due to different values and perspectives on the world, gender issues were largely 'absent' in Indonesian women artists' practices. With the exception of Dolorosa Sinaga, female artists in Indonesia tended not to present gender problems overtly in their work. Instead, the appearance of such issues was unconscious, accentuating certain perspectives and readings in response to social realities. The sub-narratives of these five artists contain important insights into their awareness of gender issues. First, their awareness of *women's sense of agency*. Most of the artists discussed here are strong people who see themselves both as individuals and as members of society. Their personal lives show varying degrees of independence and self-awareness. Most have created a balanced and equal relationship with their life partners (husbands) and are able to maintain their personal vision within marriage (except Mangku Muriati, who is celibate). In some cases, husbands have become supporters of their artistic

22 Wulan Dirgantoro, *Feminisms and Contemporary Art in Indonesia: Defining Experiences* (Amsterdam: Amsterdam University Press, 2017), doi.org/10.1017/9789048526994.

activities. The dilemma faced by many women of having a career and undertaking domestic duties seems to have been eased through honesty, transparency and respect: the women made it clear from the beginning that their partners needed to respect their vision as women and their artistic work as part of their identity.

All of them take part in activities outside their art practice that connect them to broader sociopolitical issues. Dolorosa is a lecturer and activist. Siti Adiyati has worked at the National Museum and is engaged with underground movements involving environmentalists, farmers and researchers. Mangku Muriati is a priestess and serves in the temple. Dyan Anggraini works in the bureaucracy of the culture sector. Hildawati Soemantri dedicates her life to tertiary education and was the first Indonesian female to be awarded a doctoral degree in art history. These activities have resulted in various achievements that may not be listed in the canon of art history but nevertheless contribute to social change. They deserve to be recognised.

A sense of agency encourages an individual to actively take part in changing or redefining their social reality. The five artists' biographies and artworks imply plural social realities and, hence, point to their distinctive subjective attitudes. Judith Butler defines agency in opposition to authority; it is not something that is merely constructed by authority. A sense of agency becomes critical when one is shaping one's identity in the midst of tense power contestations. Hildawati was one of the most important figures in pushing the Jakarta Art Institute to become a highly regarded art institution while battling well-respected and more senior male colleagues. When she held her first exhibition at Taman Ismail Marzuki in 1974—and in spite of the fact that she was a young woman who had just graduated from art school—she gained attention because her method of working with ceramics represented a significant breakthrough compared to other (male) artists of that generation. Her main installation in that exhibition not only utilised ceramics as a medium for installation (unlike its stereotypical label as craft) but also showed her personal intervention on the whole process, which included destroying and breaking the objects. While her works themselves never clearly captured or articulated a gender problem, her determination to promote ceramic art education was absolute proof of her self-agency as a woman.

In our daily practice, feminism is often positioned as a 'discipline' or 'study'; however, in a more specific context, it might be regarded as a movement, hence its followers are called 'feminists'. These perspectives frequently lead us to a binary opposition between 'being' or 'not being' a feminist. However, if feminism is perceived as a perspective or as embodying values and principles of life, then what matters most is how those values are applied in practice. The contradiction between saying 'I am not a feminist' while taking progressive action for the advancement of women does not, to me, indicate any problem regarding the subjects' feminism. The problem lies not in whether artists demonstrate the appropriate values or not, but in the complexities of interpreting socially constructed values and the label 'feminist' (or feminism). The things they are fighting for are not necessarily acknowledged in the constructed label.

The second crucial sub-narrative that appears is the *notion of women's bodies as a feminist statement.* Siti Adiyati presented women's bodies (mainly the face in the 1970s) as a concept of human existence (related to her interest in notions of space and shadows); her works themselves do not specifically refer to issues around women's bodies. But, in her works at the end of 1990s, some women's bodies appear in the context of questioning identity and the complexity of modern life.

A strong feminist narrative in relation to the representation of women's bodies is visible in Dolorosa Sinaga's works, particularly in the late 1990s. These works affirm the way women's bodies act as an immediate symbol of violence and social repression in society. Her most famous work, *Solidarity* (see Figure 0.4), depicts seven women with different positions and identities holding each other's hands, resisting the controlling system. These gestures represent fighting together and emphasise the sense of solidarity among marginalised women. The bodies are not shown in a realistic style but instead focus on gestures and expressions, thus reducing the possibility of stereotyping. With her artistic decision to make the body more fluid and distorted, Sinaga raises the power and the energy of those women, far from the stereotypical conception of women's bodies.

Dyan Anggraini believes that bodies are representations of humanism. In her early works, from the mid-1980s, the existence of women's bodies in her paintings almost resembles the image of the ideal women as constructed by the state. Women in *kebaya* with noble postures, looking out of windows—these are images that could remind one of the figure of Kartini, the Javanese female heroine who has been constructed and represented by the state and other powerful agencies as the ideal Indonesian woman. Subsequently, men's bodies were sometimes portrayed in Dyan's work to deliver criticism of patriarchal culture, which she later associated specifically with Javanese culture through typical symbols and masks. In this way, the feminist spirit was addressed by criticising the patriarchal system. On one occasion, as expressed in her art, this critique became stronger in response to the bureaucratic system she had to face in her work. Using invitations and formal official letters as a ground, she drew a self-portrait with various expressions that showed the repressed thoughts and initiatives she could not realise in the name of the system.

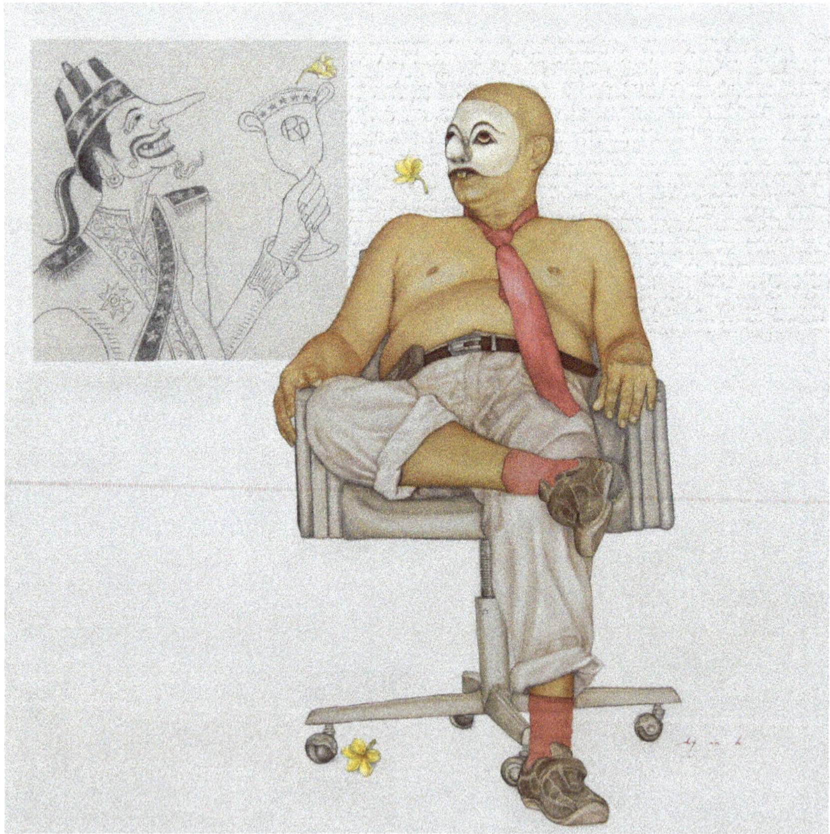

Figure 8.4: Dyan Anggraini (b. 1957), East Java, *Sang Inspektur* (*The Inspector*), 2012.

Oil and pencil on canvas. 150 x 150 cm. Image courtesy the artist.

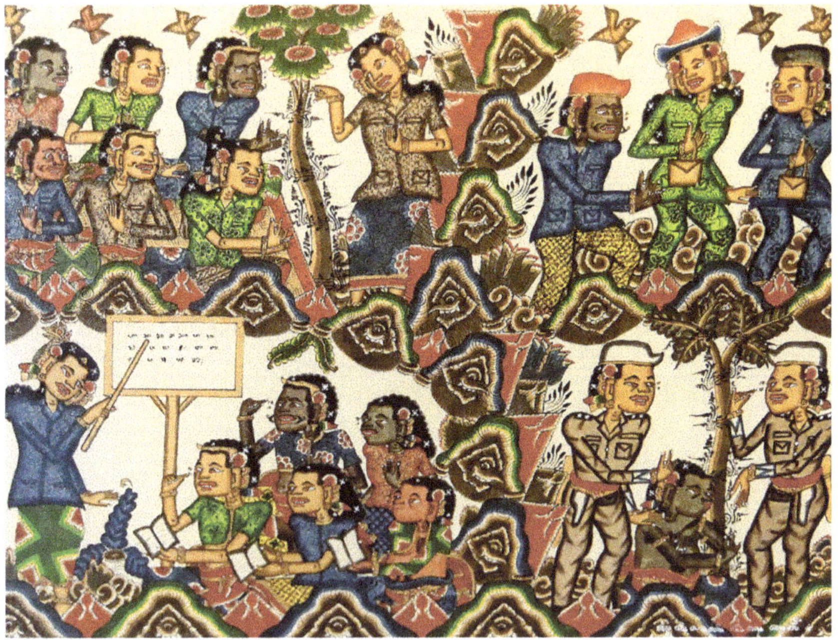

Figure 8.5: Mangku Muriati (b. 1967), Bali, *Wanita Karir* (*Career Women*), detail, 2015.

Image courtesy the author. Permission: the artist.

Mangku Muriati's artworks portray a specific political dimension, as therein she discusses the myths and narratives of Mahabharata, the great Hindu epics that have been adapted in Javanese and Balinese mythologies, and that principally address political issues and authority. Muriati inserted additional female characters into selected narratives from within the Mahabharata epics, which she represented as analogies through which she responded to Indonesia's contemporary political situations. For example, she represented the Suharto dynasty as the Kaurava, one of the dynastic families central to the Mahabharata. To be able to scrutinise Muriati's thoughts behind the narratives appearing in the form of Bali's traditional paintings, it is important to understand her thoughts and ideas as a whole as well as her rare position as a female Balinese priest.

Bodies and self-portraits serve as a powerful metaphor to drag thoughts about politics and authority into more personal domains in the works of artists from the next generation, especially those of Arahmaiani. Her works demonstrate the artist's shift in perspective, from the objective to the subjective. She presents her personal experiences in confronting religion, the state and wider society. Using herself as the subject, she deconstructs society's values and the ways of thinking that preserve the values of patriarchy and masculinity. This could also be underlined in works by IGAK Murniasih, which strongly reflect her trauma around her own body and sexuality.

It is not an easy task to draw conclusions about how the new policies of domestication and *ibuism* influenced the practices and works of women artists during the New Order. The fact that, after Gerwani was banned, there was no organisation that clearly advocated for the role of women in sociopolitical fields, let alone a union of female artists themselves, meant that the spirit of solidarity among women was already less visible, and this prevented women from openly discussing common issues. Women involved themselves in more inclusive organisations, where they had to compete with male peers and where, because of the strong patriarchal culture, men's voices usually took centre stage, leaving women's contributions forgotten, hidden, silenced.

The five women artists discussed here had different ways of critiquing New Order policies in their works. Some looked at class gaps that resulted from rapid economic development, where poor and marginalised groups (including women) became the victims of intense capitalism. Others looked at how the value of tradition was instrumentalised as a tool of political identity instead of being appreciated as part of everyday wisdom. In my opinion, it is not that their practices lacked political acts or ideas, but that the regime limited the political vision of female organisations. Even if some or many of them expressed criticism of the regime, without common actions and unified voices, personal interventions were not taken seriously or echoed as shared solidarity. In the mid-1990s, when some women activists started to create their own organisations, the notion of 'gender issues' started to become evident and this showed the importance of gathering and making coalitions or associations.

To Work on Intergenerational Feminist Ideas

It is quite complicated to create artistic work under a regime in which the notion of political and economic stability is coopted as a slogan to justify the absolute controlling power and domination of the state. In the context of depoliticisation, to be critical of sociopolitical realities meant daring to take risks that threatened one's individual dignity and freedom of expression. In the wake of such oppression, resistance groups emerged among the younger generation, bringing with them calls to terminate the dictatorial regime and support pro-democracy ideas.

Female artists of this era explored more diverse themes, rather than focusing on particular political issues. The concerns they presented were inherently political, highlighting the problems engendered by binary opposition between state/society and individuals, rather than critiquing government policy (e.g. the works of Arahmaiani, Lucia Hartini and IGAK Murniasih).

In the post-1998 generation, concerns related to personal life became an important element in the works of female artists. Female artists put forward a wide range of interwoven issues of subjectivity, identity, body and sociopolitical topics. The invigorating sense of gender and feminism eventually contributed to providing a larger space for female artists to critically discuss the power relations that exist in gender discourses in Indonesia, as well as how political regulations affect women's personal lives.

In turn, after 1998, a more powerful sense of gender among women was directly influenced by the more visible women's movements, highlighting ideas and issues that immediately affected people's lives. The Suara Ibu Peduli (Voice of Concerned Mothers) movement initiated by Karlina Supelli, Gadis Arivia and other exponents, fought for the rights of mothers and children to be able to afford milk, the price of which was prohibitive at that time. In the wake of their public fight for rights and demands for the acceleration of democracy, the issue of equal rights for women has always been included in the reformation agenda. This agenda has been fought for intensively and consistently. During the same period, a publication entitled *Jurnal Perempuan* served as a medium to broadcast women's thoughts, intervening through academic discussions organised on many campuses.[23]

23 On shifting meanings of the term *ibu* and claims regarding the political rights that were erased under the New Order, see Ruth Indiah Rahayu, 'Konsep Ibu Berpolitik Sekarang adalah Sosok yang Melawan' [The concept of the political mother today is a figure of opposition], *Tirto*, 15 July 2020, accessed 21 January 2022, tirto.id/cB85. Movements from 1998 are described in Nur Janti, 'Puncak Kebangkitan (Kembali) Feminisme' [The peak of the (re)revival of feminism], *Historia*, 24 May 2018, accessed 15 July 2020, historia.id/politik/articles/puncak-kebangkitan-kembali-feminisme-vXjR5.

Under the presidency of Gus Dur (Abdurrahman Wahid), an institution was established that functioned as the locus for the Indonesian women's movement. The Komisi Nasional Perempuan (National Commission on the Elimination of Violence against Women) was authorised to advocate for more favourable policies for women and to overcome legal and political disputes on behalf of women.

More attention to the problems of identity, and the rediscovery of personal narrative and its links to global culture, are among the things that gained prominence in artworks produced after 1998. Take, for example, *Boys Don't Cry*, an exhibition at Cemeti Art House in 2002, in which young female artists celebrated their identities as women while critically questioning a range of 'given' social norms. Another initiative was taken by the then all-male art collective Mes 56. They conducted several exhibitions and workshops called *Youth of Today*, in which they invited female artists to join a series of meetings for three months. The artists who showed their works became actively involved in the art scene during the 2000s, creating their own individual works and projects. Some of these young artists, for instance Prilla Tania and Ferial Afiff, played an important role in the dynamics of Indonesian art and went on to represent Indonesia on the global art stage.

The two examples mentioned above suggest how female artists built their collective networks in order to express their thoughts. Conversely, during the early 2000s, female artists also started appearing in more individual domains. Among them were Christine Ay Tjoe, Bunga Jeruk Permata Pekerti, Sekar Jatiningrum, Ayu Arista Murti, Titarubi and Tintin Wulia.

Overall, for the generation of female artists who grew up during the transition between the New Order and Reformasi, tensions between individuality and collectivity, subjectivity and social contexts, and the personal and the political, are fundamental elements of the gender discourses presented in their works. Compared to the third wave of the Western women's movement—which mainly explored subjectivity and personal narratives, and in which women's right as individuals, including sexuality, were central issues—in Indonesia, sensitive issues such as legal abortion sank under the weight of other issues considered more relevant to the local context. Female artists not only challenged patriarchal power through their criticisms of the state, society and religion, but also fought to conduct deeper thinking to relate their notions of self and identity to the more complex narratives of globalisation, identity and capitalism.

By reading the works of female artists who were active during the New Order, the younger generation learned how to negotiate with different state apparatus to create a productive vision for the role of women in society, and, at the same time, to think about the importance of organisation and coalition.

Therefore, for me, feminism also serves as a vast, open space to be constantly deconstructed and redefined, taking into consideration the highly diverse lives practised by individual women. The female artists discussed in this chapter have recorded their experiences and related their practices and thoughts to a broader social context to be continuously re-read and interpreted, in the hope that it might inspire others to move collectively to create a fair and just living space. It is the prerogative of feminist critics and researchers to apply the label of feminism to these artists' contributions and actions, but it is not for them to push artists to embrace that label themselves.

9

After 1965: Historical Violence and Strategies of Representation in Indonesian Visual Arts

Wulan Dirgantoro

Introduction

In the early hours of 30 September 1965, an attempted coup was foiled in Jakarta. General Suharto then assumed control of the armed forces and, in a radio broadcast, stated that he had saved the nation from a 'communist threat'. Suharto and his followers used the spectre of a communist-led takeover as the rationale for protecting the state and instigating or countenancing the mass murder of at least half a million alleged communists and their sympathisers. Hundreds of thousands more were imprisoned or detained. In March 1966, Suharto officially succeeded Sukarno as president and initiated his New Order government (1966–98). During the 32 years of Suharto's regime, the discourse of 'communist threat' became a master narrative—a canon from the state-generated 'potentially endless exegetical discourse'.[1] This narrative established the New Order regime's legitimacy and served an essential

1 James Clifford quoted in Ariel Heryanto, 'Where Communism Never Dies: Violence, Trauma and Narration in the Last Cold War Capitalist Authoritarian State', *International Journal of Cultural Studies* 2, no. 20 (1999): 153, doi.org/10.1177/136787799900200201.

function in the protracted period of political 'stability and order' and economic growth. Further, during the regime's 32 years of power, cultural production largely supported this official narrative by producing and reproducing it through artistic creations such as films, literary works and visual arts.[2]

Suharto's New Order was characterised by the control of all aspects of government, especially their official version of how they came to power. The representation and discussion of the anti-communist killings was especially censored and controlled throughout their long rule. Their version of the 'communist threat' and the language used to describe it had far-reaching consequences, many of which had little to do with historical truths being revealed or concealed.[3] Fifty-five years after the killings, while successive Indonesian governments have attempted to respond to the crimes and human rights violations of the New Order period, the subject is still controversial and highly sensitive, with the result that the representation of the anti-communist killings is fraught with ethical and moral imperatives.[4] The massive scale of the violence is compounded by many Indonesians' collective desire to move on and the instrumentalisation of the topic by the state and mass organisations. This has resulted in ongoing communal resistance to any suggestion that communism might return. These factors make it nearly impossible, and even undesirable, to discuss the violence of 1965–66 in contemporary Indonesia, even within the language of 'logic and evidence'.[5]

---

2 The Indonesian literary world has been seen as an enabling space for stories and narratives about the 1965–66 period to circulate. See, for example, Harry Aveling, ed., *Gestapu: Indonesian Short Stories on the Abortive Coup* (Honolulu: University of Hawai'i, 1975) for an early anthology; more recent ones include Laksmi Pamuntjak, *Amba: Sebuah Novel* [Amba: The question of red] (Jakarta: Gramedia Pustaka Utama, 2012). For an analysis of films, see, for example, Wijaya Herlambang, *Kekerasan Budaya Pasca 1965: Bagaimana Orde Baru Melegitimasi Anti-Komunisme Melalui Sastra dan Film* [Cultural violence after 1965: How the New Order legitimised anti-communism through literature and film] (Tangerang: Marjin Kiri, 2013).

3 Heryanto, 'Where Communism Never Dies', 147–77.

4 See Jacqueline Baker, ed., 'Indonesia Roundtable: *The Act of Killing*', *Critical Asian Studies* 46, no. 1 (2014), doi.org/10.1080/14672715.2014.863601, for the debate surrounding Joshua Oppenheimer's film *The Act of Killing* (2012).

5 Ariel Heryanto, 'The Impossibility of History?', in *Identity and Pleasure: The Politics of Indonesian Screen Culture* (Singapore: Kyoto University and NUS Press, 2014), doi.org/10.2307/j.ctv1qv1rz.9. See also Stephen Miller, 'Zombie Anti-Communism? Democratisation and the Demons of Suharto-Era Politics in Contemporary Indonesia', in *The Indonesian Genocide of 1965: Causes, Dynamics and Legacies*, ed. Katharine McGregor, Jess Melvin and Annie Pohlman (Switzerland: Palgrave Macmillan, 2018), 287–310, doi.org/10.1007/978-3-319-71455-4_15.

Indonesian Visual Arts and the Anti-Communist Killings

Indonesian artists certainly have not remained silent about the anti-communist killings. Even before the fall of the New Order regime in 1998, a small body of artworks already engaged with the subject matter. The works represented a range of responses to the events, from joy to criticism, such as A. D. Pirous's painting *Mentari Setelah September 65* (*The Sun after September 65*) (1968) and Semsar Siahaan's work *Penggalian Kembali* (*The Excavation*) (1993), a site-specific installation shown at Taman Ismail Marzuki during the ninth Jakarta Biennale.[6]

For many contemporary Indonesian artists whose works engage with current political issues, such as environmental destruction, gender critique and human rights violations, testimony often lies at the heart of the artist's message. Artists used powerful visual strategies to represent the hidden mass graves, express stories of forced abduction and give voices to the silenced victims of 1965–66. Artists who gained prominence during the 1990s, such as Dadang Christanto, FX Harsono, Agung Kurniawan, Arahmaiani and Titarubi, highlight the importance of their body of works as forms of testimony and witnessing or, to be more precise, the processes by which the past is remembered and represented in the present through artistic practices.

Testimony through art becomes essential, indeed vital, to fill the gaps where truth and its supporting legal evidence are often called into question. It is also significant because, in the face of campaigns by mass organisations against justice, remembrance and reconciliation for the survivors of the mass killings, Indonesian visual artists and activists' visual strategies become crucial.[7]

---

6 I have discussed elsewhere the possibility of abstract lyricism in Indonesia as a carrier of the trauma from the anti-communist killings. See Wulan Dirgantoro, 'Aesthetics of Silence: Exploring Trauma in Indonesian Art after 1965', in *Ambitious Alignments: New Histories of Southeast Asian Art, 1945–1990*, ed. Stephen Whiteman, Sarena Abdullah, Yvonne Low and Phoebe Scott (Australia: Power Publications and the National Gallery of Singapore, 2018), 199–224. For Siahaan's work see Efix Mulyadi, 'Semangat Kemanusiaan Semsar' [The spirit of Semsar's humanity], accessed 16 January 2020, cemara6galeri.wordpress.com/event-2008/mengenang-semsar/.

7 See, for example, Brita L. Miklouho-Maklai, *Exposing Society's Wounds: Some Aspects of Indonesian Contemporary Art since 1966* (Adelaide: Flinders University Asian Studies Monograph no. 5, 1991); Caroline Turner, 'Indonesia: Art, Freedom, Human Rights and Engagement with the West', in *Art and Social Change: Contemporary Art in Asia and the Pacific*, ed. Caroline Turner (Canberra: Pandanus Books), 196–217. For discussion specifically on artistic responses to 1965–66 events, see Hendro Wiyanto, 'Memberi Makna Pada Ingatan' [Giving meaning to memory], in *Kengerian Tak*

However, given the weight and emphasis placed on one artistic trope to represent a complex historical event whose effects are still being felt across time and generations, some questions remain unresolved: what is made visible, what is concealed and what is obscured by specific kinds of artistic production? Further, how and in what ways do these artistic works continue to unravel some of our assumptions about the role of 1965–66 in the present? In the attempt to answer some of these questions, we need to reposition the role of testimony in Indonesian contemporary art and its impact.

For the current generation of younger scholars in Indonesia, there is a new source of research. This is oral history, particularly those accounts that emerged around and since 2015, the year of the fiftieth commemoration of the mass killings. This was enabled by the emergence of materials that had previously been inaccessible to researchers, the publication of biographies by former political prisoners and the amount of time that had passed since the event.[8]

Most importantly, of the relatively few visual materials from the immediate aftermath of the 30 September event, most were produced and circulated by the perpetrators for propaganda purposes. This includes the infamous film *Pengkhianatan G30S/PKI* (Treachery of G30S/PKI, 1984, directed by Arifin C. Noer) and various military operation images found in Indonesian military museums. The propaganda and subsequent tight military and state control over the visual material concerning one of the worst atrocities in Indonesia's modern history explains why most Indonesian artists place oral history and testimonies from the survivors and witnesses at the heart of their works. They do so in various ways, including reimagining the events based on ethnographic research, creating (counter)-memorial works, or digging deep into their personal and collective memories. For example, inspired by a story about a roving photographer in his hometown who took photographs of alleged communists before they were interrogated, Dadang Christanto adopted the story and developed it into several series of works for the *M I S S I N G* exhibition at Wei-ling Gallery, Kuala Lumpur, Malaysia.

Terucapkan/The Unspeakable Horror, exhibition catalogue (Jakarta: Bentara Budaya, 2002); Badan Ekonomi Kreatif Indonesia (BEKRAF – Indonesian Agency for Creative Economy), 'A Thousand and One Martian Homes', in *Indonesian Pavilion: 1001 Martian Homes—Tintin Wulia*, exhibition catalogue, 57th Venice Biennale (Jakarta: BEKRAF, 2017).

8 Katharine McGregor, Jess Melvin and Annie Pohlman, 'New Interpretations of the Causes, Dynamics and Legacies of the Indonesian Genocide', in *The Indonesian Genocide of 1965: Causes, Dynamics and Legacies*, ed. Katharine McGregor, Jess Melvin and Annie Pohlman (Switzerland: Palgrave Macmillan, 2018), 1–26, doi.org/10.1007/978-3-319-71455-4_1.

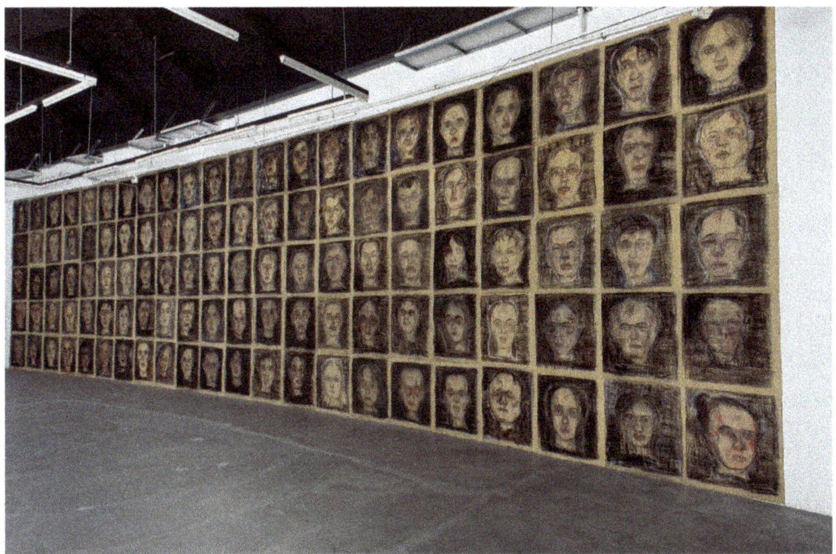

Figure 9.1: Dadang Christanto, *MISSING*, 2018.
Acrylic and charcoal on canvas. Image courtesy Dadang Christanto and Wei-Ling Gallery, Kuala Lumpur.

The exhibition featured several series of works with the drawing series of portraits entitled *MISSING* dominating the exhibition space. The artist explained that the drawings visually referenced work by the French Iranian photojournalist Reza Deghati in documenting displaced children in various refugee camps in the aftermath of the Rwandan genocide (1994).[9] The artist later reflected that he wanted to shift the focus from his narrative to the victims' stories and testimony (Figure 9.1).

The act of referring to factual reality through the use of testimony allows Indonesian visual artists to act as historians but still leaves room for the imaginative evocation of the events of 1965–66 in ways that are unavailable to the historian. For Christanto, the portraits represent an imaginary visual archive, not known individuals, but unrecorded, anonymous victims and survivors. The artist's familiarity with, and use of, photojournalistic visual strategy reveals his ongoing search to make sense of the historical violence that claimed his father when he was only seven years old.

9 For further discussion of this work, see Wulan Dirgantoro, 'From Silence to Speech: Witnessing and Trauma of the Anti-Communist Mass Killings in Indonesian Contemporary Art', in *World Art* 10, no. 2–3 (2020): 301–22, doi.org/10.1080/21500894.2020.1812113.

The emphasis on testimony exemplified by Semsar Siahaan's and Dadang Christanto's bodies of work illustrate the continuing trauma of the 1965–66 events.[10] The trauma represented through the artworks refuses to be historicised and relegated to the past. As Cathy Caruth has argued, to be traumatised is to be possessed by an image or event. It continues to drive towards a compulsion—forms of re-enactment by those who did not experience the original events—in response to the trauma experienced through intergenerational transmission. At the same time, as an aesthetic category, testimony is also composed of bits and pieces of memory that have been overwhelmed by occurrences that have not settled into understanding or remembrance, or events that are in excess of our frames of reference.[11] Given that testimony cannot provide a total understanding of the past, the enterprise of truth telling through works of art seems an impossible task.

Identification: Bystanders and Perpetrators

In the relative absence of a methodology to examine the representation of historical violence and trauma in Indonesian art history, I turn to works by Holocaust studies scholar Ernst van Alphen, who suggests possible ways to examine the complexity surrounding the visual representation of historical traumatic events. Van Alphen alerts us to the tension between the representation of documentation, including archival material and oral testimony, on the one hand, and identification on the other.[12]

In Indonesia's context, so far, artists have responded to the 1965–66 events with a strongly felt need to represent the victims, believing that the role of their artworks is to reveal and amplify the repressed truth. Indeed, the trope of testimony and witnessing in engaging with the anti-communist killings of 1965–66 has recently been perceived as representing a lack of control over the future or, in some cases, an ongoing sense of victimhood.[13]

---

10 For more information about Siahaan's work, see Grace Samboh, 'Consequential Privileges of the Social Artists: Meandering through the Practices of Siti Adiyati Subangun, Semsar Siahaan and Moelyono', *Southeast of Now: Directions in Contemporary and Modern Art in Asia* 4, no. 2 (2020): 205–35, doi.org/10.1353/sen.2020.0010.

11 Cathy Caruth, ed., *Trauma: Explorations in Memory* (Baltimore: The John Hopkins University Press, 1995), 153.

12 Ernst van Alphen, 'Toys and Affect: Identifying with the Perpetrator in Contemporary Holocaust Art', *Australian and New Zealand Journal of Art* 2/3, no. 2/1 (2006): 158–90, doi.org/10.1080/14434318.2002.11432710.

13 Interviews with Agung Kurniawan and LIR Collective, December 2019, Yogyakarta.

More problematically, within the context of the intellectual debate on memory, the widely held view is that remembering is usually a virtue and that forgetting is necessarily a failing. So widespread and emphatic is the current conviction that remembering has both private and public virtue that some theories have emerged that state that even victims of traumatic experiences must be helped to speak the horrifying truth about their past—to 'speak the unspeakable'. In writing about the processes of recovery from trauma, Judith Herman, a renowned clinical psychiatrist, stated that telling the truth about the past is held to be both a personal therapeutic value and a public value of overwhelming importance.[14]

However, as Paul Connerton, a social theorist, points out, forgetting should be considered a strategy to construct a new identity, achieved by constructing newly shared memories drawing on, among other things, a set of tacitly shared silences.[15] In this context, some artists have noted that there is a lack of space to acknowledge silence (or forgetting), resilience and the emotional complexities in the collective memory of 1965–66.

The artists discussed in the following section explore the ambiguity surrounding history, memory and individuals in the context of 1965–66. Awareness of those events has begun to extend to the younger generation, which includes children and grandchildren of survivors, as well as non-family members, who want to recover the truth of what occurred in the past. They seek to understand the experiences of relatives, of family disruption and of trauma. Others outside the family circle wish to comprehend this stain of historical violence that haunts contemporary Indonesian society.

Indonesian artists who are second- and third-generation descendants of the post-1965 survivors are, theoretically, in the position of being unwilling post-facto bystanders. Thus, they may, theoretically at least, choose their forms of identification as bystander, victim or perpetrator. In his work on choice of identification, van Alphen argues that representation in art traditionally uses strategies that promote identification. Yet the reverse is not the case. Identification can be directed outside the realm of representation. He notes: 'Soliciting partial and temporary identification with the perpetrators makes one aware of the ease with which one can slide

14 Judith Herman, *Trauma and Recovery: The Aftermath of Violence, from Domestic Violence to Political Terror* (New York: Basic Books, 1992).
15 Paul Connerton, *The Spirit of Mourning: History, Memory and the Body* (Cambridge: Cambridge University Press, 2011), doi.org/10.1017/CBO9780511984518.

into a measure of complicity'.[16] This could be the case with the historical amnesia surrounding Indonesia's anti-communist killings. In the artworks that have been discussed so far, identification (full or partial) is generally solicited from the position of the victims. For example, Christanto's works discussed above evoke pain to elicit empathy from the audience.

Yet, to address the complexity of the collective memory of 1965–66 and its impact, some Indonesian artists chose to shift the identification away from the victims and direct it instead to bystanders and even perpetrators. For example, the immersive theatre performance *Gejolak Makam Keramat* (*Turmoil at the sacred grave*, 2017), directed by Agung Kurniawan and Irfanuddin Ghozali, engaged the audience as actors and not-so-innocent bystanders. The play involved 13 actors from KIPER (Kiprah Perempuan or Women's Activities), a group of women survivors of the 1965–66 events based in Yogyakarta. In consultation with the actors, the directors constructed the play such that the audience was physically involved—from sitting on the stage alongside the actors to joining in the dialogue. The audience was then given instructions to sing or chant to build a sense of atmosphere. As the directors explained, the play's interactive nature was designed to capture the interest of the younger generation in the audience so that they would want to know more about the anti-communist killings.[17] While the play shifted the focus away from victimhood towards survivor narratives of resilience, it was also able to make visible the role of the community in shaping the perception and reception of the historical violence by soliciting the audience's participation in the play (albeit unwillingly).

Although not quite at the expense of representation, Patriot Mukmin's mixed media work *Reminiscence of 98* (2019) depicts the artist's self-identification with Indonesia's New Order president, Suharto (1921–2008). The video and woven photography work exhibited in Salihara Gallery, Jakarta, further illustrate the complex entanglement between documentation and representation. Mukmin (b. 1987), a graduate from the Faculty of Fine Arts, Design and Craft at the Bandung Institute of Technology, has primarily worked with photography and painting, particularly exploring the formal quality and materiality of the medium.

16 Van Alphen, 'Toys and Affect', 178.

17 Interviews with Agung Kurniawan and Irfanuddin Ghozali, December 2019, Yogyakarta. See also Wulan Dirgantoro and Barbara Hatley, 'Memory on Stage: Affect, Gender and the Performative in 1965–66 Survivor Testimonies', in *Gender, Violence and Power in Indonesia: Across Time and Space*, ed. Katharine McGregor, Ana Dragojlovic and Hannah Loney (New York: Routledge ASAA Women-in-Asia Series, 2020), 101–18, doi.org/10.4324/9781003022992-5.

In 2014, Mukmin began creating a series of works that incorporate images related to the New Order regime, in particular to the 1965–66 mass killings. Mukmin's woven photographs first came to public attention at his solo exhibition *KUP: Titik Silang Kuasa 66–98* (Coup: Crossroads of power 66–98), held 21 May – 25 June 2015 at Lawangwangi Creative Space, Bandung. The exhibition explored the beginning and the end of the New Order regime framed by the artist's partial understanding of Indonesia's political history. According to the artist, as someone who grew up during the late New Order period, his works have been driven by the gaps in his knowledge of history and collective memory in post–New Order Indonesia.[18]

The work *Reminiscence of '98* takes the form of a 58-second stop motion video and a wall work made of several photographs woven together to form two large images. The stop motion video uses short frames from the making of the wall work and is accompanied by two audio files. One is of Suharto reading his resignation speech on the eventful day of 21 May 1998 and the second audio file is a recording of the artist reading the same statement (Figure 9.2).

Mukmin's *Reminiscence of '98*, centred on one historic moment in Indonesia's history, appeared both intimate and jarring. In contrast to the tired and elderly voice of the former president, the artist's voice sounds melancholic even respectful—though it is not clear whether the respect is for the person or the historical moment that he re-created. The large wall work, where we see Mukmin's self-portraits merge with the image of Suharto's final minutes on Indonesia's collective television screens, speaks further of this ambiguity. The work consists of 60 still images from the stop motion video, woven with an iconic image of Suharto reading his resignation speech at the Merdeka Palace. The artist merges the images by measuring and precision cutting each image before carefully weaving them together. We can still discern the artist's individual frames, shot in the act of reading from the front, the side and partial close-ups of his lower face, before they gradually merge into the darker part of the larger image. The result is a tightly woven image that produces a lenticular effect: different images depending on the audience's perspective.

18 Gumilar Ganjar, *KUP: Titik Silang Kuasa '66-'98*, exhibition catalogue (Bandung: Lawangwangi Creative Space, 2015), 10.

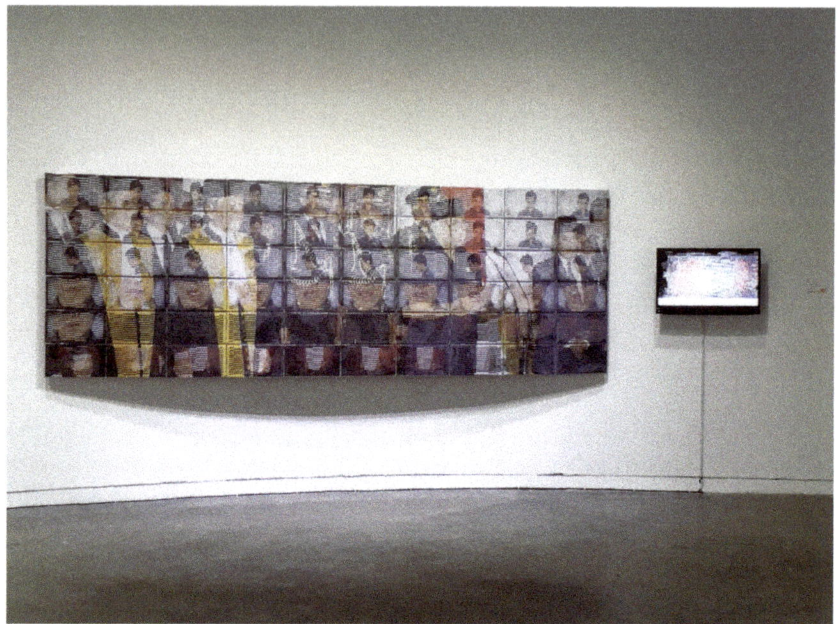

Figure 9.2: Patriot Mukmin (b. 1987), Java, *Reminiscence of '98*, 2019.
Woven photography, single-channel video, variable dimension. Image courtesy the author.

Mukmin was 11 when the speech was televised, the scene seared onto his memory without full comprehension of the context of the momentous event.[19] Suharto's carefully designed long-term technological and economic development plans earned him the name Bapak Pembangunan (Father of Development). Yet, his presidency was also characterised by authoritarianism, rampant corruption, nepotism and gross human rights abuses. He is now held largely responsible for the anti-communist killings and crimes against humanity committed in East Timor, Aceh and Papua during his presidency. His resignation was preceded by weeks of rioting, culminating in looting and a wave of violence against many Chinese Indonesians, including the rape of hundreds of Chinese-Indonesian

19 Tia Agnes, 'Ratusan Kertas Dianyam Jadi Foto Momen 21 Mei 98 ala Patriot Mukmin' [Hundreds of paper woven into a photograph Moment from 21 May 98 according to Patriot Mukmin], accessed 11 February 2022, hot.detik.com/art/d-4397291/ratusan-kertas-dianyam-jadi-foto-momen-21-mei-1998-ala-patriot-mukmin?_ga=2.38258723.128792247.1644541731-139710893.1644541731. The work was part of a group exhibition titled *The Concept of Self: Individuality and Integrity*, 19 January – 3 February 2019, Galeri Salihara, Jakarta.

women in May 1998.[20] Ironically, for many Indonesians who have experienced the democratic and economic uncertainties of the post–New Order (or Reformasi) period, the 32 years of relative stability provided by Suharto's regime are remembered with a degree of nostalgia.[21]

Significantly, Mukmin's work was exhibited at Komunitas Salihara in Jakarta, an independent art and culture space established by some of the most vocal opponents of the New Order regime. The exhibition of a work that depicts the artist's partial identification with the former dictator in such a space is intriguing, but perhaps more instructive of Mukmin's own experience with the New Order regime's end. His video installation appears to focus on the tenuous understanding of the history of the violent past that was beyond the memory of many young Indonesians, but without offering any resolution, as often demanded by artworks dealing with human rights violations or a difficult past.

While there are no fixed 'commandments' as such when representing historical violence in Indonesia, it is implied that the violent events should be treated respectfully, solemnly and in a manner that acknowledges the victims and survivors' rights. The works of Kurniawan, Ghozali and Mukmin discussed here do not fit perfectly into this mould. By shifting modes of representation towards identification with bystanders and perpetrators, their works cross boundaries, perhaps not in terms of their art but rather in their remembrance of the events and the precarity of their witnessing.

The Forensic Imagination

As Indonesian artists began to feel the weight of testimony and witnessing, some artists began their investigation into testimony's materiality by exploring the use of archives, objects and the agency of dead bodies. The following section discusses works by two artists, Rangga Purbaya (b. 1976) and Yaya Sung (b. 1986), to examine recent developments in representing

20 See Edward Aspinall, *Opposing Suharto: Compromise, Resistance and Regime Change in Indonesia* (Stanford: Stanford University Press, 2005), doi.org/10.1515/9780804767316; Jemma Purdey, *Anti-Chinese Violence in Indonesia, 1996–1999* (Honolulu: University of Hawai'i Press, 2006), doi.org/10.1163/9789004486560.

21 Arzia Tivany Wargadiredja, 'Indonesia's New Order Nostalgia Isn't Going Anywhere. Here's Why', *Vice Indonesia*, 20 October 2017, accessed 28 January 2019, www.vice.com/en_asia/article/7x4pq9/indonesias-new-order-nostalgia-isnt-going-anywhere-heres-why.

the anti-communist killings of 1965–66, particularly the use of archives. The affective impact of these strategies is increasingly mobilised, not only in public, media and political representations of violence, but also in the processes of memory formation, memorialisation and musealisation.

In their seminal work *Mengele's Skull: The Advent of Forensic Aesthetics* (2012), Thomas Keenan and Eyal Weizman noted a turn from the era of witnessing towards forensic aesthetics as a new cultural sensibility, ethic and political aesthetic whose implications and influences quickly overflowed the boundaries of their initial forums. The authors moved forensics from the juridical field to how we understand and represent political conflicts, whether in media, political debates, literature, film or the arts.[22] The following discussion on two Indonesian artists' works follows Weizman and the Forensic Architecture group's directions where the intersection between art and forensic methodology opens up a discourse about truth.[23]

Rangga Purbaya (b. 1976) is a graduate from Institut Seni Indonesia (ISI, Indonesian Institute of the Arts), Yogyakarta. Purbaya is also a member of Mes 56, a photography collective based in Yogyakarta. Since 2015, Purbaya has used photography as his primary medium to create four series of works that explore the anti-communist killings of 1965–66. Purbaya's first series deals with his family history: his grandfather, Boentardjo Amaroen Kartowinoto, was seized in 1965, disappeared and is presumed dead. *Stories Left Untold* (2015) is a documentation series using objects belonging to his grandfather and portraits of members of his family. A text accompanies each image to explain the object's origin or, in the case of his family members, their memories of Boentardjo (or lack thereof). The first series is a journalistic impression emphasising personal and familial stories of loss, longing and hope from the different individuals.

The second series, *Investigating Boentardjo* (2016), sees Purbaya assume the role of an archivist. He meticulously collected his grandfather's extant documents from family members—certificates, official documents, diaries and photographs—and displayed them inside two glass vitrines. The artist retraced his grandfather's life through the artefacts to understand

22 Thomas Keenan and Eyal Weizman, *Mengele's Skull: The Advent of Forensic Aesthetics* (Berlin: Sternberg Press, 2012).

23 'Forensic Architecture', accessed 27 March 2020, forensic-architecture.org/. See also Stephenie Young, 'The Forensic Imagination: Evidence, Art and the Post-Yoguslav Document', in *Mapping the 'Forensic Turn'*, ed. Zuzanna Dziuban (Vienna: New Academic Press, 2017), 309–27.

the person as well as his family history.[24] As an intimate look into a past life, however, the installation is clinical in its presentation. The artist places the smaller photographs on the right side of the bigger documents, creating a grid system that allows the audience to 'read' the installation from the official documents to the images on the right, with the images adding further support to the contents of the documents. For example, Boentardjo was a member of Barisan Tani Indonesia (BTI, Indonesian Peasants' Front), a farmers' union linked to the Indonesian Communist Party. The relevant section shows Boentardjo's membership certificate as well as photographs of Boentardjo working with his colleagues.

In the third series, *Letter to the Lost One* (2017), Purbaya shifts the focus from his own narrative to that of others who also lost family members in the violence of 1965–66. The artist invited his friends and collaborators from the *Living 1965/1965 Setiap Hari* collective exhibition to write a letter addressed to their missing family members. He transferred the letters to the walls of Mes 56's space, effectively turning the house into a memorial to the victims. In 2018, Purbaya was invited to Gwangju for an art residency. He exhibited *Letter to the Lost One* there and displayed the letters in a darkened room lit only by UV lighting. In addition, Purbaya also included audience participation in the exhibition by inviting them to contribute to the letter-writing project.

The fourth series, *Landscape of Deception* (2018), comprises 12 photographic images of rural and urban landscapes. Some of the buildings were shot on the exterior or from the street, with one image showing a corridor with doors leading to the adjacent rooms. The buildings are covered or obscured by plants or, in one case, by street vendors. The rural landscapes are more diverse, with images of ponds, beaches, forests, fish farms and caves. In this fourth series, the colour and black and white images are not accompanied by the captions or texts that Purbaya used in his earlier series. The images can be simply seen as depictions of the idyllic countryside or a small town in Indonesia, in the style of salon photography.

24 Rangga Purbaya, 'Investigating Boentardjo', accessed 16 January 2020, www.ranggapurbaya.com/page6.html.

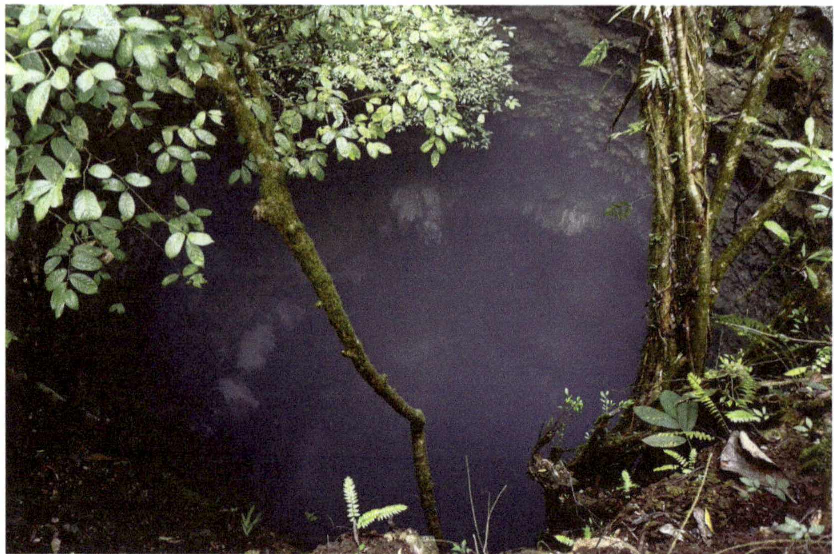

Figure 9.3: Rangga Purbaya (b. 1976), Central Java, *Titik Awal*, 2015.
C-print on paper, 60 x 90 cm. Image courtesy the artist.

Yet, one image from the first series makes a return in *Landscape of Deception*. It is the image of Luweng Grubug, a limestone cave with an opening of a vertical shaft, 50 km south-east of Yogyakarta (Figure 9.3). The tourist attraction is famous for its natural beauty. It has been featured in various local and international nature television programs, but is also alleged to have been one of the killing fields during the 1965–66 violence. Purbaya states that his grandfather is rumoured to have met his death at this site. Suddenly, the idyllic landscapes take on a different meaning. They are, in fact, trauma sites or 'contaminated landscapes'—sites that contain human remains that have not gone through the funerary rites and burials of individuals who die a natural death. These people died under suspicious circumstances and were probably murdered.

Purbaya's four series of works engage deeply with the anti-communist killings of 1965–66. While the series starts with the familial as its subject matter, it develops gradually into an investigation and eventually becomes a memorial. Compared with other works that focus on testimony, Purbaya does not rely on drama to convey his messages, but he still makes the same appeal for truth. The processes of unearthing, displaying and manipulating 'forensically' acquired material, such as the objects and documents that once belonged to his missing, presumed dead, grandfather, elicit a strong emotive response. In addition, Purbaya's use of UV lighting in the second series' iteration in Gwangju recalls the technique used in forensic investigation to reveal unseen or hidden biological traces.

Certainly, the use of objects and photography in contemporary art to examine the relationship between memory and image is not new. Artists from across the globe—such as Doris Salcedo, Christian Boltanski, William Kentridge, Nalini Malani, Nadiah Bamadhaj, Brook Andrew and FX Harsono, whose works often deal with difficult pasts—have used objects and photography as a mnemonic strategy or as a memorialisation of the victims. In this regard, Purbaya follows a long tradition in contemporary art practice of engaging with the complexity of memory, particularly about the aftermath of historical violence. However, his fourth series offers a potentially different path from a conventional representation of historical violence.

The landscape that Purbaya portrayed in the fourth series, according to the artist, is a reflection of his anxiety about 'blurring contexts'. He explains:

> A beautiful location, sometimes storing a completely different history. Behind the subtle and graceful scenery, hidden dark stories, gloomy and heartbreaking, far from their appearance and designation. It could be that the beauty was intentionally made to obscure the dark history, and was carried out by the government or the local community with the aim of diverting the past from us.
>
> One of Indonesia's dark history is Tragedy 65. At that time, hundred million innocent humans were killed and their bodies were thrown away in places far from the crowds and covered by scary stories to avoid people to come. But today the situation has changed. These places also changed. The places were opened as tourist places, inviting people to come. These places turn into stunned, organized and well-maintained space. Far from the grim and gloomy impression which the murder took place. History is no longer discussed. People then forget. And today we don't realize it. In fact, we are often lulled by the elegance of the place, so we never question it again.
>
> It turns out that beauty can also deceive us.[25]

---

25 Rangga Purbaya, 'Landscape of Deception', accessed 16 January 2020, www.ranggapurbaya.com/page8.html. See also 'Sebuah Kamp di Tengah Sungai' [A camp in the middle of the river], *Tempo*, 7 October 2012, 100.

Purbaya's statement records how sites of trauma in Indonesia—sites where the killings occurred—are being rapidly subsumed by relentless urbanisation in the country's most densely populated island, Java. As these trauma sites are built over, the affective aura that was their trademark is lost. Victims, survivors and their families are unable to publicly remember and mourn 'Tragedy 65' in Indonesia and, in the absence of official memorials, natural sites are the only physical places where there are indexical traces of their loved ones. Further, the unmarked graves and killing fields in Indonesia are often protected by animistic, primordial belief systems that identify such places as haunted. Ironically, this prevents the sites from being used for other purposes. Yet, as the artist states, such protection is slowly disappearing.

Despite the pessimism, Purbaya's *Landscape of Deception* series highlights the distinction between monument and memorialisation in the context of Indonesia's historical violence. As a solid and physical site, the monument is constructed out of the need to mark a gravesite as an easily discernible, localised and developed space. Memorials can be understood as something less solid, being movable or temporary. They can even be physical acts including performative actions, such as reading aloud, collective recollection and so on. Purbaya's photographs come to embody the latter in the form of posthumous memorials. The landscape and the buildings no longer serve as a background to human activities. Instead, they become a powerful presence. The vast body of water, including waterfall and waves crashing on the beach, and the vegetation that engulfs the caves and buildings in Purbaya's photographs represent this force.

Because there are very few physical monuments to remember the victims of 1965–66,[26] Purbaya's landscape series becomes a space of remembrance, in particular of places that already exist in the collective memory—that melt inconspicuously into their surroundings, unplanned, pragmatic, vernacular and used by local communities for silent communication, intended for an as yet undetermined future investigator.

---

26 For discussion on monuments and memorialisation, see Ken Setiawan, 'Remembering Suffering and Survival: Sites of Memory in Buru', in *The Indonesian Genocide of 1965: Causes, Dynamics and Legacies*, ed. Katharine McGregor, Jess Melvin and Annie Pohlman (Switzerland: Palgrave Macmillan, 2018), 215–34, doi.org/10.1007/978-3-319-71455-4_11; Katharine McGregor, 'Heads from the North: Transcultural Memorialisation of the 1965 Indonesian Killings at the National Gallery of Australia', in *The Indonesian Genocide of 1965: Causes, Dynamics and Legacies*, ed. Katharine McGregor, Jess Melvin and Annie Pohlman (Switzerland: Palgrave Macmillan, 2018), 235–52, doi.org/10.1007/978-3-319-71455-4_12.

In comparison to Purbaya's trajectory from personal history to posthumous memorialisation through artefacts and landscapes, Yaya Sung's (b. 1986) work directly engages with a critical historical document that exposed one of the biggest myths created by the New Order about a progressive women's group, Gerwani (Gerakan Wanita Indonesia, Indonesian Women's Movement), affiliated with the Indonesian Communist Party. Yaya Sung is a graduate from the visual communication program at Pelita Harapan University in Indonesia. Because of her interest in photography, in 2013 she began to participate in several group exhibitions in Jakarta before eventually joining a program on critical photography practices organised by Mes 56, Yogyakarta. Sung has since expanded her practice into multimedia installation and performance art.

The seven-channel video installation titled *The Future (Lies)* (2018) is part of a group exhibition *#perempuan* (#women) curated by Santy Saptari in Melbourne, Australia (Figure 9.4).

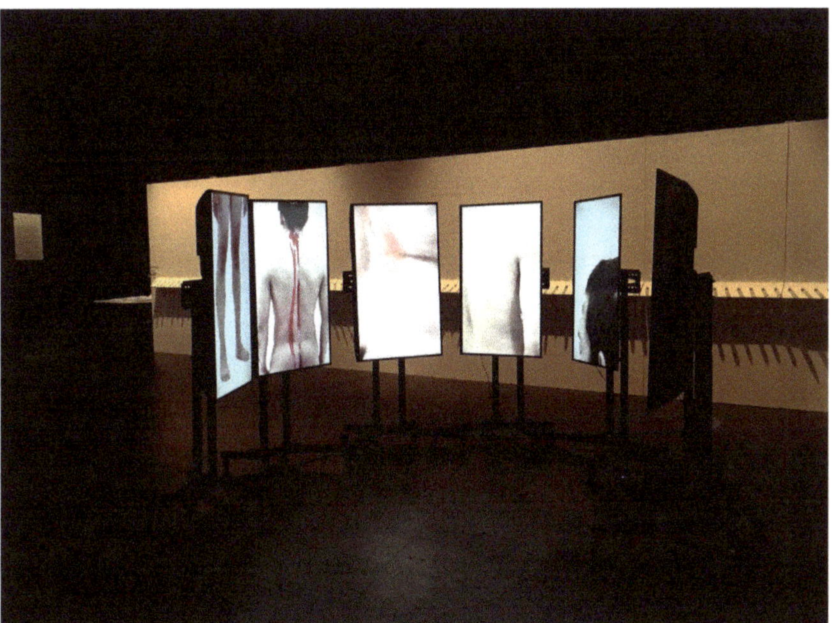

Figure 9.4: Yaya Sung (b. 1986), Jakarta, *The Future (Lies)*, 2018.
Mixed media installation, variable dimension. Image courtesy the author.

The installation consisted of seven flat screen televisions on vertical frames. The screens were arranged in a semicircular formation facing away from the gallery entrance. Positioned slightly apart from the screens, a large portfolio and a pair of white gloves sat on a table. The portfolio was the artist's research journal that also contained copies of archival materials that the artist had consulted for her work.

The main document that Sung referred to was an article entitled 'How Did the Generals Die?' by the late Benedict Anderson, an eminent scholar of Southeast Asia. Anderson analysed and translated into English a forensic report by the medical team that performed the autopsy on the bodies of the six high-ranking Indonesian officers who were killed in the early hours of 30 September 1965. Anderson's analysis highlighted the fact that the bodies showed no signs of torture.[27] The official New Order version luridly described the bodies as being in a mutilated state, with the eyes and genitals particularly disfigured. The New Order version accused the members of Gerwani of desecrating the bodies and this was used as evidence for arresting and torturing members of Gerwani. It is also the basis for ongoing vilification of the Gerwani women as cruel and depraved.[28] Sung's work aims to highlight the findings of the autopsy report that showed that the bodies of the officers were, in fact, intact.[29]

Revealing the agency of the dead is, of course, the basis of forensic science as a discipline. It is a trope, bordering on a cliché, that the remains of the dead can 'bear witness' to what has befallen them.[30] This trope frames forensic evidence collected from the body as a kind of post-mortem testimony. The forensic scientist or archaeologist merely acts as the interlocutor who allows the dead to speak.[31] Sung's seven-channel video installation visualises the figure of a speaking corpse or, rather, seven corpses.

27 Ben Anderson, 'How Did the Generals Die?', in *Indonesia* 43 (April 1987): 112–13, doi.org/10.2307/3351215.

28 See Saskia Wieringa, *Sexual Politics in Indonesia* (UK: Palgrave Macmillan, 2002), doi.org/10.1057/9781403919922; Ita F. Nadia, ed., *Suara Perempuan Korban Tragedi '65* [Voices of women victims of the '65 tragedy] (Yogyakarta: Galang Press, 2008); Annie Pohlman, *Women, Sexual Violence and the Indonesian Killings of 1965–66* (UK: Routledge, 2017).

29 Interview with the artist, January 2019, Jakarta.

30 Layla Renshaw, 'The Forensic Gaze: Reconstituting Bodies and Objects as Evidence', in *Mapping the 'Forensic Turn'*, ed. Zuzanna Dziuban (Vienna: New Academic Press, 2017), 232.

31 Claire Moon, 'Interpreters of the Dead: Forensic Knowledge, Human Remains and the Politics of the Past', *Social and Legal Studies* 22, no. 2 (2013): 149–69, doi.org/10.1177/0964663912463724.

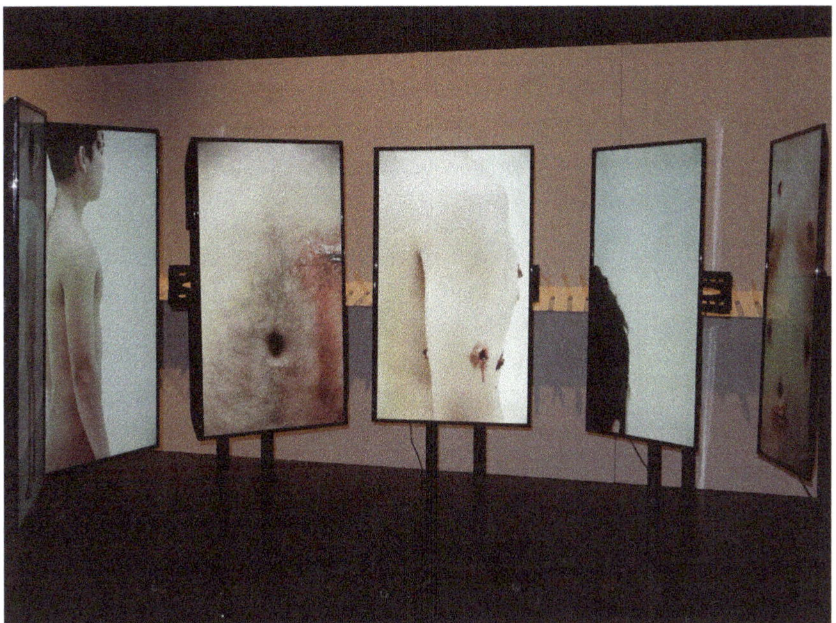

Figure 9.5: Yaya Sung, *The Future (Lies)*, details, 2018.
Mixed media installation, variable dimension. Image courtesy the author.

The videos depict seven rotating naked male bodies, accompanied by mournful music played on a loop.[32] Working with a team of make-up artists, videographers and talents, Sung carefully and meticulously reconstructed the bodies' condition based on the forensic report. Her team vividly re-created bleeding gunshot wounds and bruises that had resulted from blunt trauma injuries (Figure 9.5).[33] In this particular work, ambiguity and nuance are not Sung's primary concern when depicting the impact of 1965–66. In her artist's journal, she states that Gerwani's gender equality and education achievements are still very relevant for contemporary Indonesian women. She feels strongly that her work should speak about the injustices that many Gerwani women experienced during the 1965–66 events.[34] In this context,

32 Sung interviewed and recorded the song by female survivors of 1965–66 events: Pujiati, Sri Sulistiawati, Lestari and Sri Suprapti, who currently live in Waluyo Sejati Abadi Retirement Home in Jakarta. The artist slowed down the tempo of the song to accompany the slow rotation of the bodies. Email to the author, March 2020.

33 Sung explains that the talents were fully informed about the ideas behind the video and most consented to continue, except one who withdrew due to the nudity content. Conversation with the artist, January 2019, Jakarta.

34 Sung continues to make several series of works about Gerwani. In 2019, she exhibited a small series of works titled *Present Measures* at Project Space, 4 April – 3 May 2019, RMIT Melbourne, accessed 1 April 2020, www.intersect.rmit.edu.au/-ps-sr-st-/present-measures.

the bodies in Sung's video provide the viewer with an osteobiographical story of the violence inflicted upon them, thus giving the dead a sense of agency. Based on the artist's belief in the bodies' ability to convey a 'truthful' account of events, namely the details about the circumstances and causes of their death, they are evidence of the lies that the New Order regime constructed about members of Gerwani.

Purbaya and Sung's works share the aim of revealing repressed truths about what happened to individuals during 1965–66. They also utilise a forensic imagination to create a space where third and fourth generation Indonesians can connect with one of Indonesia's darkest periods of history. In their works, the forensic imagination does not follow strict scientific methods, but rather creates a space to present evidence. Yet, the evidence provided by the objects and documents that they employ in their works is not intended to close down discussions or conversations about the truth. On the contrary, the evidence has been chosen to stimulate discussions about the construction of 'truth' during and after the mass killings in contemporary Indonesia.

Conclusion: Challenges of Representation

In the artworks discussed in this chapter, the anti-communist killings of 1965–66 are portrayed through various strategies of representation: installation, drawing, performing arts, photography and multi-channel video work. The trauma of the historical violence still endures in Indonesia's collective memory, largely because there are so few opportunities to mourn the many Indonesians who lost their lives, and because of the lies, censorship and propaganda so successfully maintained during Suharto's New Order regime.

Artistic representations of the anti-communist killings are thus seen as an enabling space to help Indonesians remember and commemorate the events, with varying degrees of reception. Through their works, Indonesian visual artists have positioned themselves alongside the victims and survivors to tell their stories and reveal the truth. This is exemplified in the practices of Dadang Christanto and the late artist–activist Semsar Siahaan, whose works have been exhibited in Indonesia and overseas. Christanto's body of work has been seen as an emblematic representation of the violence of the anti-communist killings and its legacy in contemporary Indonesia. As Christanto delves deep into his personal memory, namely the loss of his father, to speak about human rights abuses more globally, his works, in fact, encapsulate the tension between history and imagination. As artists strive to represent the hard facts of history, they also tend to turn towards figurative strategies to represent the violence. The representation of violence has been argued to be an aestheticisation of suffering and another form of violation of the victims, which some artists have argued has led to the trope of loss and further victimisation.

Other Indonesian artists have chosen a different mode of art-making, turning away from literal representation. The collaborative project and artworks by Kurniawan, Ghozali and Mukmin retain the testimonial framing of their content, despite some artists' distinct disillusionment with the approach. In addition, the discursive role of the witness can be extended into the materiality of the archive and non-human actors, such as seen in the works of Yaya Sung and Rangga Purbaya. In the latter, the reorientation speaks to the political dimension, documenting human rights abuses and the necessity of reconsidering the ethics of secondary witnessing. Images that depict the traces of people, rather than people themselves, have the potential to avoid ethics-based accusations of exploitation and aestheticisation of suffering while retaining emotional and moral impact. Paradoxically, Sung's video installation returns us to the realm of trauma. Trauma's original meaning as a physical wound is reconstructed on the bodies of seven male talents to manifest the high-ranking military officers' violent deaths. Simultaneously, Sung's evidence-based work also potentially evokes psychic trauma that could haunt the audience.

The term 'After 1965' in the title of this chapter speaks of the broader impact of historical violence in Indonesia, not only on history, collective memory and legal aspects but also on the artistic imagination. Nonetheless, art that documents traces of conflict and political violence, can, and does, go beyond merely grappling with the ethics and politics of witnessing. Drawing on identification and forensic imagination theories, as proposed in this chapter, does not diminish the role of testimony in representing the voice of the victims. Instead, it aims to initiate a critical reconsideration of the complex entanglements between testimony, trauma and representation, particularly their divergent modalities and purposes. Indeed, meaningful and imaginative remembering is necessary for a survivor to move beyond crisis, and the process of remembrance is not only an individual but also a social process.

10

From the Oppressed towards a Dark History

FX Harsono
Translated by Elly Kent

Broadly speaking, my art practice can be divided into two parts: one during the New Order, from 1975 to 1998 under the Suharto regime, followed by a minor transition during the Reformasi (Reform) period after the Suharto regime fell, around 1998–2002. During the period since 2003 until today, I have taken as subject matter my own identity as an Indonesian of Chinese descent, a group that has experienced much discrimination. My most recent project was about the history of ethnic Chinese on Java from 1947 to 1949.

During the New Order my focus was on social critique, and I made artworks that challenged the policies of the repressive New Order. During the transition period, I saw enormous change in politics, society and culture. These changes impressed me, especially the freedom of expression, which I had never experienced during the previous regime. But these freedoms also brought up questions about my own identity as an Indonesian of Chinese descent. In Indonesia, ethnic Chinese are still seen as foreigners, even though they came to the archipelago in the seventh century.

Art as a Form of Resistance

In the beginning, in 1975, I took up social and political issues with the intention of experimenting with the search for a national Indonesian identity. Several young artists came together as the Gerakan Seni Rupa Baru Indonesia (Indonesian New Art Movement [GSRBI]) to consider national identity this way.[1] We began with a consciousness that Indonesia, being so geographically and culturally enormous and diverse, struggles to present a cultural identity. Culture that is located in a particular place cannot represent Indonesia more broadly. Meanwhile the political situation was the same across Indonesia, under a government that implemented militaristic and repressive policies. Thus we thought we should address these social and political issues by using them as a representation of Indonesia.

As I became more involved in sociopolitical issues, I became more aware that I could not only look at these as mere inspiration for my art. I could no longer just interpret a situation or condition without becoming involved in that situation myself. I became increasingly involved with NGOs and activists who opposed Suharto's policies.

These interactions gave me a new consciousness that the work of an artist came with a kind of responsibility to society. So, the creation of art could no longer only happen in the studio. Interactions and collaborations between disciplines, with society and research became an inseparable part of my creative process. Consequently I was swept along in the current of resistance to the Suharto regime, and it was quite stressful to oppose those repressive policies.

There were political controls in place to monitor all social activity in order to ensure there was no political activity. This was known as depoliticisation, and affected all areas of life, including, of course, art and education. Artists were afraid to make work with social themes, political opinions, social criticism or even art that depicted the lives of the lower classes and the economic and social problems they faced.

1 Editors' note: this period in Indonesian art's development, and in Harsono's career more specifically, is addressed in a contemporaneously written chapter by Sanento Yuliman and republished in translation in this book and also in Supangkat, Chapter 6 (this volume), and Turner, Chapter 7 (this volume), the latter in relation to Harsono's artworks for GSRB.

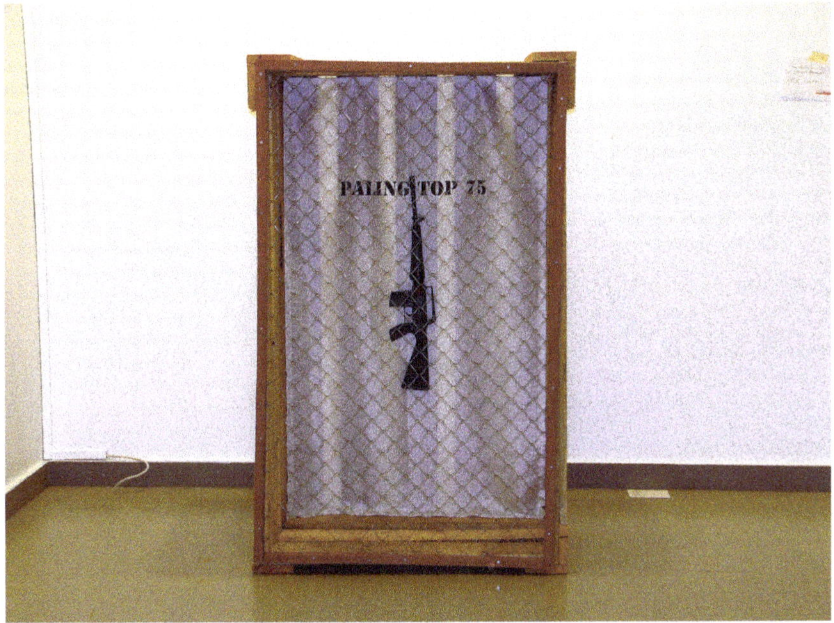

Figure 10.1: FX Harsono, *Paling Top '75* (*Most Popular '75*), 1975.
Plastic gun, textile, wooden crate, wire mesh, 50 x 100 x 157 cm. Exhibited in the first exhibition by GSRBI in 1975. Image courtesy the artist.

In facing this resistance from artists, the government announced restrictive values that could be used to sanction or even gaol artists. This policy was a kind of value system that was termed 'national identity'. There was no clear definition for these values, but the system was government regulated. National identity was used as a parameter for evaluating works that attempted to criticise sociopolitical situations created by the government. National identity could be pulled any which way, like a rubber band.

There were a number of artistic disciplines that were closely monitored by the government, particularly forms of art that were easily understood by society, such as the verbal arts. This included theatre, music and literature. If these kinds of practices expressed criticism it could create a social movement. Hence these were seen as dangerous forms that threatened the government's development program.

It seemed that art was not subject to these restrictions, so long as it was not a poster at a demonstration or a comic book that raised political consciousness, and so long as the artwork was exhibited indoors. Semsar Siahaan took his paintings as a placard to a demonstration. He suffered a broken leg after a soldier stomped on him. But apart from that, usually artwork tends to use a lot of metaphors or symbols that are difficult for the military to understand, so they were not particularly attentive. But intelligence officers did visit my solo exhibition at the National Gallery of Indonesia in 1994, two days in a row. Fortunately, they did not find me there.[2]

Performance art became the new medium, seen as an effective resistance to the government. Interaction and collaboration with activists produced new participatory art forms. Artists began to mingle with the community and collaborate, and community-based art began to appear.

I worked with activists to run workshops for labourers, making alternative media to disseminate information on sociopolitical issues. In 1998, when the May riots erupted in Jakarta, I became a volunteer in a team working with female victims of violence.

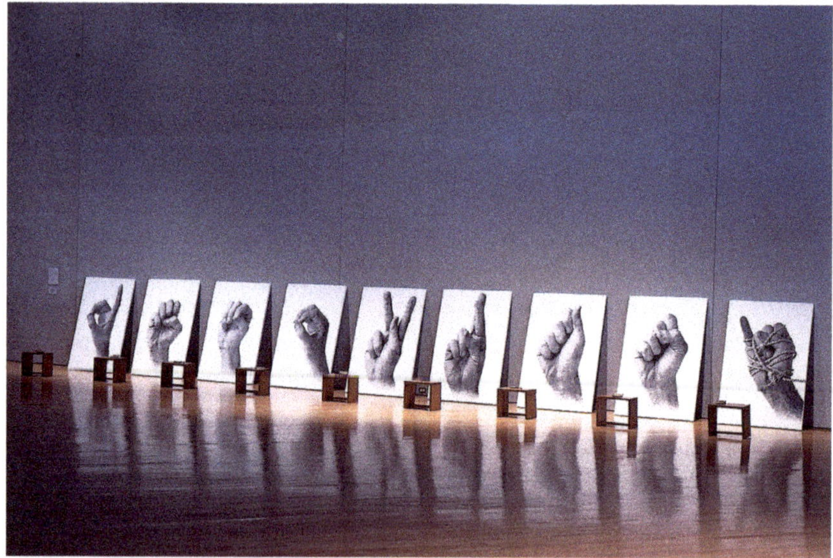

Figure 10.2: FX Harsono, *Voice without a Voice/Sign*, 1993–94.
Photographic screen print on canvas, wooden stool, stamp. Image courtesy the artist.

2 Editors' note: in the full version of this story, recounted in a 2010 article published in the *New York Times*, Harsono describes how these spies are also unable to understand the work because it depicts hands using sign language to spell out DEMOKRASI. Harsono is quoted: '"I know a government spy came to the gallery to see the work, asking questions about the meaning, but I wasn't there, so I got lucky. The person in the gallery lied and told him he didn't know the meaning of the work" he said, laughing'. Sonia Kolesnikov-Jessop, 'FX Harsono's Rebellious, Critical Voice against "Big Power" in Indonesia', *New York Times*, 12 April 2010, accessed 18 March 2021, www.nytimes.com/2010/03/12/arts/12iht-Jessop.html?pagewanted=1&_r=0&sq=fx harsono&st=cse&scp=1.

Research as a Creative Platform

The research I do is not in keeping with methodologies from the social sciences. My research is a mix between anthropology, sociology and ethnography. It is also not intended to seek methodological validation as scientific practice. My research tends to focus on the search for a very subjective 'truth' that I could use as a basis for the creation of artworks. This truth is intended to provide a limitation so that there is no distortion in the interpretation of the problems that might then be transferred to the artwork.

In 1985, when I began to work with NGOs, I gained some understanding of participatory research methodologies. This knowledge was not about research methods, but rather about how we see the community as an entity that is positioned as an equal of the researcher. Participatory methods depart from a place of empathy. Empathy is the basic capital an artist has in meeting ethical issues. Without empathy, the community is just a voiceless object. The artwork also becomes dry. The artist is not the centre, or the most authoritative subject. Artists must in fact learn from society. When we 'go into the field' the distance between artist and community or social group must be reduced through dialogue, interaction, merging and direct, intense engagement.

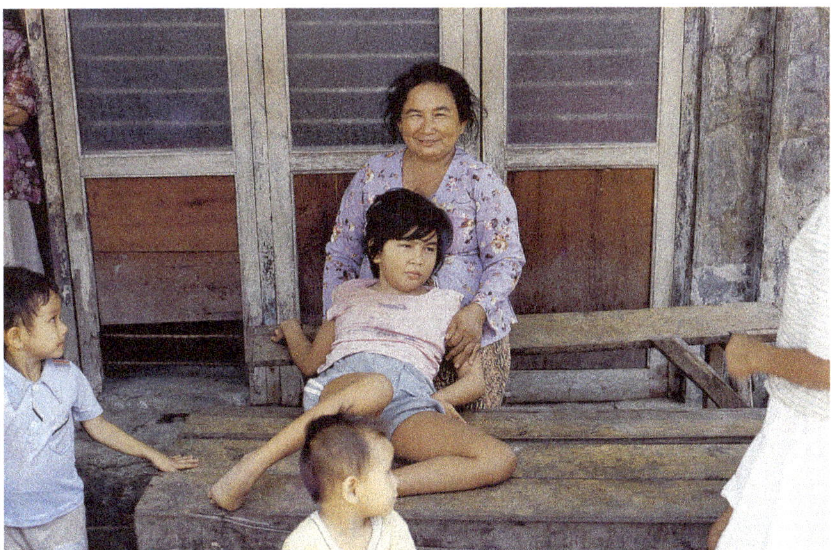

Figure 10.3: FX Harsono, *Korban Merkuri 1 (Mercury Victim 1)*, 1985.
Photographic print, dimensions unknown. Image courtesy the artist.

In my creations I see that reality is no longer subjective or imaginative only, because the issues in society are very real. This transformative and participatory social science made me conscious of breaking down the falsehoods that protected the controlling regime, critically exposing them through 'systematic work' that differs from the working patterns of studio artists.

The Reform Era (Reformasi)

During the New Order era under the Suharto regime, not just anyone could establish a media company. The establishment of a company involved with media and information required permission. This also required tight screening. News was censored. There was no freedom of speech. But after 1998 the political situation changed, and this was a huge contrast with the previous era. Anyone could establish a TV station and print media without any government permissions.

Many things amazed me after the fall of Suharto. Suddenly I could see free speech, people could criticise the government. I had never experienced this during the previous 32 years. Advances in information technology meant information was easily shared through the internet. Computers helped to raise my awareness of digital reproduction, which inevitably became a medium for the creation of artwork. I felt a kind of culture shock.

I tried to look at all of this critically and a number of my works addressed this situation. Behind these amazing shifts, I also saw that change swallows up its own victims. I saw Chinese people fall victim to these changes. When a massive riot broke out in Jakarta around May 1998, most of the victims were Chinese. Hundreds of Chinese-owned shops were burned and looted. Chinese women were raped. At that time, I become a volunteer in a gender-based violence team called 'A Volunteer Team for Women Victims of Violence'. I began to wonder and ask myself, 'who am I?' I began to question my own identity, history and roots. I acknowledged that I was an Indonesian of Chinese descent. But when I looked more closely, what was the culture that I practised in my life as an Indonesian of Chinese descent? I was aware that I knew nothing of Chinese culture, and I also did not understand the Javanese culture I was born into. Then I knew that I was a 'peranakan' [Indonesian-born] Chinese who no longer understood my root culture; I knew that was part of a Chinese diaspora.

Untold History

In my search for my identity I could no longer find it through culture, so I tried to examine my family's history. I began find out who my father was and what he did, and who my mother was. My father was Oh Hok Tjoe, with the Indonesian name Hendro Subagio—a portrait photographer who established the 'Atom' studio in Blitar. But that was all I knew. I couldn't investigate my family history further, because there was so little information.

There was one interesting thing I found in the documentation of the photos my father took. The photo [on which the painting depicted in Figure 10.4 is based] had been kept in the guest room of our family home for decades. The album contained black and white photos of the excavation of the remains of Chinese people killed in 1948 around Blitar, the town where I was born. These photos recorded images of human bones and skulls that had been freshly removed from the ground. On the photo a handwritten caption in white ink indicates the location and date the picture was taken, and the number of victims found.

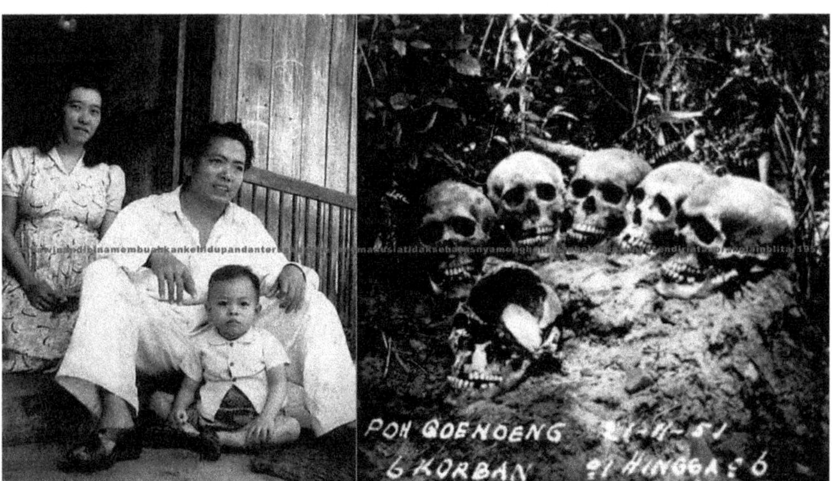

Figure 10.4: FX Harsono, *Preserving Life, Terminating Life* #2, 2009.

Diptych, acrylic and oil on canvas, thread, 200 x 350 cm. Image courtesy the artist. The work depicts the artist with his parents as a child.

The skeletons of these massacre victims were then reinterred in a mass grave in Karangsari village, Blitar. These movements of human remains still often occur, for all sorts of reasons.[3] In Chinese belief systems, the ritual burial of family members and ancestors must be done appropriately, so that the lives of the deceased's descendants now and in the future can be better.

My father and the other volunteers in the group searched for, exhumed and then re-buried the victims that they found. These activities were coordinated by a Chinese community organisation called Cung Hua Tjung Hui, by instruction of the Jakarta Branch. The victims were Chinese people who had been massacred from 1948 to 1949 in Blitar. In a number of texts, the massacre was described as an effect of the Dutch Military Aggression, which was in contravention of the Linggadjati Agreement of 1947. When the Indonesian army used guerrilla tactics and a scorched earth policy in the defence against the Dutch army, the Chinese became the target of violence as a result of political disunity and the actions of opportunists and interlopers who took their chance in an uncertain economic situation.

This research continued until I began to look at the historical stories of Chinese massacres in other periods, and in other places across Java. A number of mass graves of victims can be found in Muntilan, Yogyakarta, Kediri, Nganjuk, Pare, Caruba, Tulungagung, Wonosobo and Purwokerto.[4] This research took place from 2009 to 2018.

One of the artistic strategies that I used in this project was the 'reproduction' of signs that I found during the research. I duplicated these signs directly, then constructed a composition with them, adding my personal interpretations. This method is in fact not new to my artistic journey. Since 1975, I have utilised everyday objects as found objects and then linked them in order to create meaning within the context and issues I want to address.

3 Editors' note: in modern Indonesian society, the act of moving grave sites and human remains also takes place due to decreasing space in city cemeteries. The exhumation of graves happens when land is re-designated as a commercial zone. In addition, the development of cemetery complexes as 'property' in suburban areas has affected an increase in moving graves.

4 Editors' note: these sites are spread between Central and East Java (see Map 2).

Figure 10.5: FX Harsono, *Rewriting on the Tomb*, 2013.
Pastel frottage on cotton fabric. Image courtesy the artist.

This 'duplication' and reproduction method is also obvious in *Rewriting on the Tomb* (2013). I performed this at the sites of mass burials, draping a white cloth over the headstones and then taking rubbings with a red crayon. The result was a frottage of names in Chinese script, cast clearly and in high contrast.

In the Exhibition Space

As well as being a performance and resulting in the creation of an artwork made through frottage, this action was also my pilgrimage to the victims. I titled this event *Berziarah ke Sejarah* (*A Pilgrimage to History*, 2013). Critic and curator Agung Hujatnikajennong said that: 'this configuration created tension between a sense of solemn mourning and the scientific approach of the researcher or historian looking for information'.[5]

Hendro Wiyanto said 'these two works are a sublime effort by Harsono to give a place for "the other" who has been silenced and marginalised'.[6]

5 Agung Hujatnikajennong, 'Kita Ingat Maka Terjadilah: Sejarah dan Ingatan dalam Kesenian FX Harsono' [We remember and so it happened: History and memory in FX Harsono's art], in the exhibition catalogue to Harsono's solo exhibition at Selasar Sunaryo, Bandung 2014.

6 Hendro Wiyanto, 'Kebenaran, Keindahan dan Pencarian FX Harsono' [Truth, beauty and FX Harsono's search], curatorial essay for FX Harsono's solo exhibition *What We Have Here Perceived as Truth, We Shall Someday Encounter as Beauty*, Jogja National Museum, Yogyakarta, 2013 (Yogyakarta: Galeri Canna, 2013), 14.

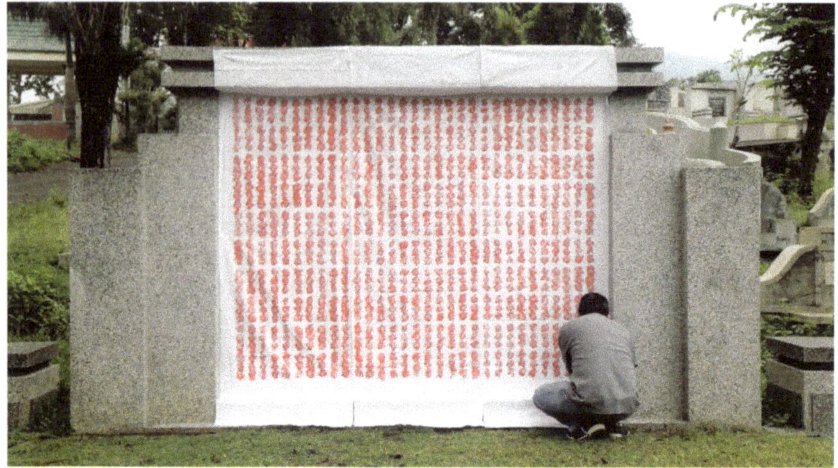

Figure 10.6: FX Harsono, *Berziarah ke Sejarah* (*Pilgrimage to History*), 2013.

Still image from video performance [13:40 minutes]. Image courtesy the artist.

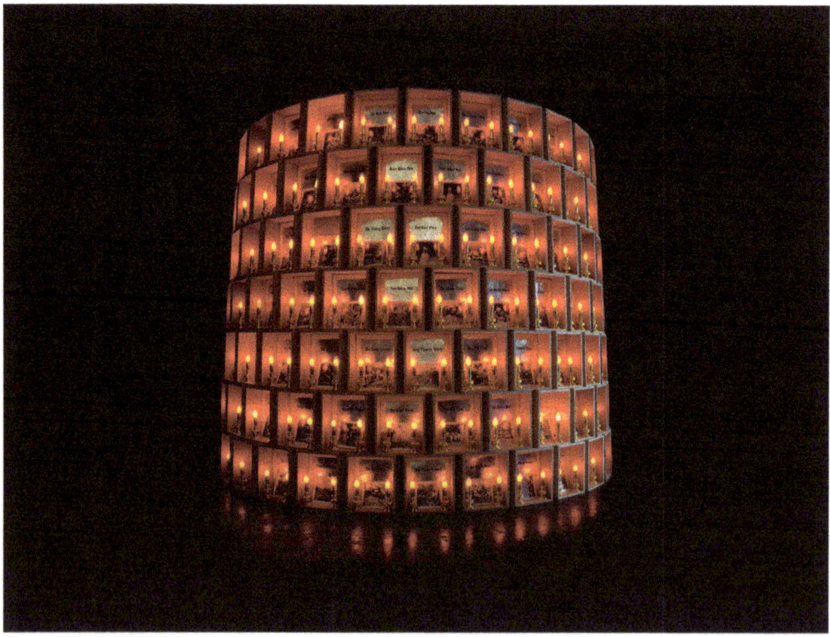

Figure 10.7: FX Harsono, *Monumen Bong Belung* (*Bone Cemetery Monument*), 2011.

Installation with 202 wooden boxes, perspex, electric lamps, paper and photographs, 270 x 270 x 270 cm. Image courtesy the artist.

In presenting my work, I always think that the public is the most important part. That's why I try to think about how to communicate my work. But this does not mean that the aesthetic value is unimportant. For instance, interacting with the public or reproducing signs as an effort to use a language that is easily understood.

Another work is the installation *Monumen Bong Belung* (*Bone Cemetery Monument*, 2011), which was made by arranging wooden boxes in a circle that resembled a chimney. In each box was an electric candle lamp, the Romanised name of each victim and a photograph. These boxes were a representation of the kind of altar Chinese people often have in their homes. The work was intended to rebuild a memorial monument, and to pay respect to the victims.

After seeing and experiencing several incidences of violence directed at ethnic Chinese in Indonesia, particularly the major riots in May 1998 in Jakarta, I felt disappointed, angry and sad. These events combined with the discovery of the photographs and archives of the massacres made me even more keen to ask, why do ethnic Chinese become victims every time there is social change?[7] This question made me then look at the issue differently, in that there was no sense of revenge or anger in taking up the issues of discrimination or massacre. What I hope for this project is that it can remind us all of a dark history that was never recorded, so that dark history does not continue to be forgotten.

Although I have finished the research, I will still produce several more works, a documentary film and a book related to my research and this unwritten history. Aside from this long-term project, I am also delving into the stories of my own history, names and collective memory, or my personal history and its connection to collective history.

7 Editors' note: Harsono has addressed this issue extensively in his artwork and research, with a particular focus on the historical victimisation of Chinese Indonesians featuring in his 2016 exhibition, *Gazing on Identity*, at Arndt Fine Art Gallery at Gillman Barracks, Singapore. See 'Gazing on Identity', Arndt, accessed 21 January 2022, www.arndtfineart.com/website/page_55325?year=2016. For an accompanying research essay that discusses the use of state and social surveillance in repressing Chinese culture in Indonesia, see 'FX Harsono: Gazing on Identity', Arndt, accessed 21 January 2022, www.arndtfineart.com/website/artist_8554_publication?idx=h.

Epilogue: Future Tense

Elly Kent

This volume was conceived in what seems now the relative calm of 2019 and reveals the complex social and political conditions that have underpinned the development of art in Indonesia over a period of more than 70 years. It grew out of a conference at The Australian National University held in conjunction with a retrospective exhibition at the National Gallery of Australia. That exhibition featured art from the period of intense creative, political and social change that has unfolded in Indonesia in the decades after the fall of the autocratic New Order and through the proliferation of public expression that was fostered by Reformasi, as well as recent events that have been characterised by some scholars as 'democratic regression'.[1]

As we moved forward with our plans for the book, the world shifted on enormous and minute scales: nations around the world, including our own, battled months of unprecedented extreme weather events and climate-induced disasters. Barely had the air cleared when the World Health Organization declared a global pandemic that forced the closure of public institutions including our own university. Confined to our territorial borders, and often to our own homes, as millions around the world suffered and died from COVID-19, we have questioned the place of art and art history in such a context. What meaning can we find in our efforts to compile a volume that reveals the complex social and political conditions that have underpinned the development of fine arts in Indonesia, when Indonesians are suffering grief and loss on a scale that defies documentation? What is the purpose of art in times so unpredictable, uncertain and painful? We have persisted through this existential doubt in part because we see that our colleagues, friends and

1 Eve Warburton and Edward Aspinall, 'Explaining Indonesia's Democratic Regression: Structure, Agency and Popular Opinion', *Contemporary Southeast Asia* 41, no. 2 (2019): 255–85, doi.org/10.1355/cs41-2k.

family in Indonesia continue with their own work: creating, expressing and responding to the conditions created by the pandemic; adjusting their lifestyles from peripatetic artworkers to housebound creatives; and maintaining a vigorous and rigorous discourse around what it means to make art and contribute to society in Indonesia and the world.

This discourse in essence encompasses the book's broader themes: the artistic ideologies that underpin a continuous faith in the expressive power of all kinds of art; the particular responsibilities of an artist to their own society; and the issues of identity—religious, gendered, ethnic, regional and more—that have emerged in the art discussed in the preceding pages of this book. It is a living discourse, shifting, changing, resolving and dissolving as the tenacity of the individuals, and their experiences of the world in which they live, are brought to bear. In this Epilogue, we also wanted to capture something of the urgency of this state of play in Indonesian art today.

Art and artists have long held an influential position in Indonesian society—in politics, in movements for social and environmental justice, community development, education, commercial design and contemporary life. As everywhere, Indonesian society is now in unprecedented times. After decades of enormous social change on global and local scales, what role will art and artists play in Indonesia's future? We invited five practitioners from diverse sectors within the theory and practice of Indonesian art to respond to this question in a public forum entitled 'Arts and Artists in Society: Pathways for Indonesian Art in the 21st Century' held, in the spirit and necessity of the times, as a webinar via video link. Through this focused and significant forum, we aimed to identify some starting points to carry forward from this closing chapter into future research and practice.

We identified five key areas for exploration, based on our most recent observations and the long-term issues raised by contributors to the book. These were:

1. curatorial practice and its contribution to intellectual debate on the national and international stage
2. art history/historiography and its contribution to understandings of the role of art in broader Indonesian history
3. artistic and curatorial practice outside of the major centres
4. interdisciplinary collaboration in experimental and research-based art
5. pedagogy and politics in artistic practice and the emergence of new directions within old discourses in Indonesia but also globally.

To gain a deeper understanding of the significance of these issues in Indonesia today and into the future, we invited the five practitioners to reflect on their experiences and to speculate on the possibilities for their fields. Art historian, then at Cornell University, Dr Anissa Rahadiningtyas spoke about art history and collaborative research and practice. Artists I Made Bayak and Karina Roosvita talked about established and emerging areas of art practice. The challenges of curating art beyond the major metropolitan centres were addressed by Arham Rahman, who has worked from inside and outside Sulawesi on projects such as the Makassar Biennale, and by Alia Swastika, who examined the shifting roles of curators on the national and international contemporary art stage.

What emerged from this coalescence of diverse art practitioners was a palpable sense of the continuing, and deepening, intersections between these themes and the themes in earlier chapters of this book. However, it was also clear that there are distinct new pathways—in part engendered by the enormous social and technological shifts that have taken place since this book project began. These are: first, the impact of the largest and longest global pandemic of modern times, coronavirus, and its attendant impacts on mobility and proximity; and, second, shifts in attitudes to human rights, political engagement and ethno-religious visibility in Indonesia since the fall of the New Order in 1998.

Visibility through Practice and Theory: Absences and Erasures

As observed by our discussant Wulan Dirgantoro in her summary of the perspectives offered by the speakers, there was a focus on bringing visibility to the 'absences and erasures' in art practices, art communities and art historiography in Indonesia. The particular phrase 'absences and erasures' emerged from Anissa Rahadiningtyas's examination of the role of religion, in this case Islam, in shaping modernist art practices in Indonesia. It may also remind readers of the important work over recent decades to redress the deliberate erasure of women artists from art history canons, in Indonesia and around the world, as examined by Alia Swastika in Chapter 8 of this book.[2] Dirgantoro extends the scope of this redressing

2 Griselda Pollock, *Differencing the Canon: Feminist Desire and the Writing of Art's Histories* (London: Psychology Press, 1999).

of 'absences and erasures' from the under-examined histories of Islamic art to encompass the 'public and collective memory' of the anti-communist purge in Indonesia in the mid-1960s, and also includes gender and environmental issues that remain unresolved, if not exacerbated, as a consequence of contemporary developments. Explicit in these efforts are movements to decolonisation and decentring, both of art historical canons imposed by Euro-American norms, and also of centralised governance inherited from departing colonial powers in the mid-twentieth century and exploited by the New Order regime. What do these movements mean for ordinary Indonesians, for minority identity groups, for those newly empowered and for those more recently marginalised?

The Expressive Power of Artwork

The expressive power of artwork continues to be directed by many artists to imagining and enacting social change, often through collective action. Relationality—collectivity, interdisciplinarity, responsibility, tension between those who are considered inside and those outside or other—is a strong feature in the challenges and opportunities faced by those working in the arts in Indonesian today. Artist and arts organiser Karina Roosvita presents a diagrammatic reflection of the predominant (not to say exclusive) preoccupation with collaboration, in which she positions interlocking circles of 'writers', 'researchers', 'artists' and 'activists' so that they overlap and create a central, shared space that she labels 'collaboration'.

Rather than undermining the expressive power of art, this collaborative approach is seen to accommodate the kind of multi-perspectival and evidence-based movement needed to address the complex problems that Indonesia, and all nations, are facing today. Dirgantoro notes an:

> ongoing concern and role for art and artists with and in communities, to effect social transformation and positive change, especially related to climate change and gender … these issues cannot be solved by one alone, but instead require a collective movement to effect these changes.[3]

---

3 Unless otherwise stated, all quotations from participants at the webinar come from the recording made of that event: 'Arts and Artists in Society: Pathways for Indonesian Art in the 21st Century', ANU webinar, 11 March 2021.

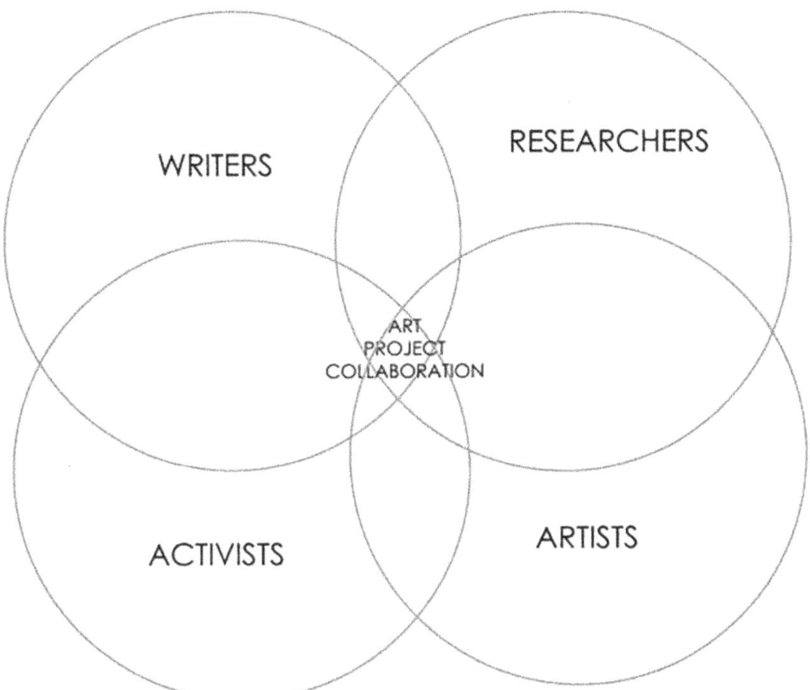

Figure 11.1: Karina Roosvita's diagram of interdisciplinary practice in the twenty-first century.

Image courtesy the artist.

As an example of this approach, Roosvita points to her work on the issue of gender inequality, which she has been addressing since 2010. She emphasises that this is an issue too complex for her to solve by herself, so her projects bring together representatives from each of the four groups defined in her diagram, to seek collective solutions. Interestingly, some of Roosvita's projects dealing with gender have focused on the Indonesian art world, which has in recent years faced its own revelations of internal gender-based violence and harassment, as well as a belated acknowledgement of the vast inequities experienced by women artists and art workers.[4] Workshops facilitated by activists and experts from women's crises centres discuss issues such as 'what defines violence' and how to ensure art spaces are safe spaces for all genders. In addition, discussion groups focused on feminist readings

4 The esteemed 'Koalisi Seni' (Coalition for the Arts) formed an advocacy group in 2021 to specifically address these issues, while a new wave of collectives focused on building an arts scene inclusive of women and non-binary arts workers (e.g. Peretas and Futuwonder) has been gathering momentum since the mid-2010s.

and projects to reveal the experiences of women, LGBTQI+ and non-binary identifying individuals and groups in Indonesia are increasingly frequent on the art world's calendar. It seems certain that as the effects of these endeavours resonate through younger generations of artists, the Indonesian art scene of the future will be a more diverse and inclusive one.

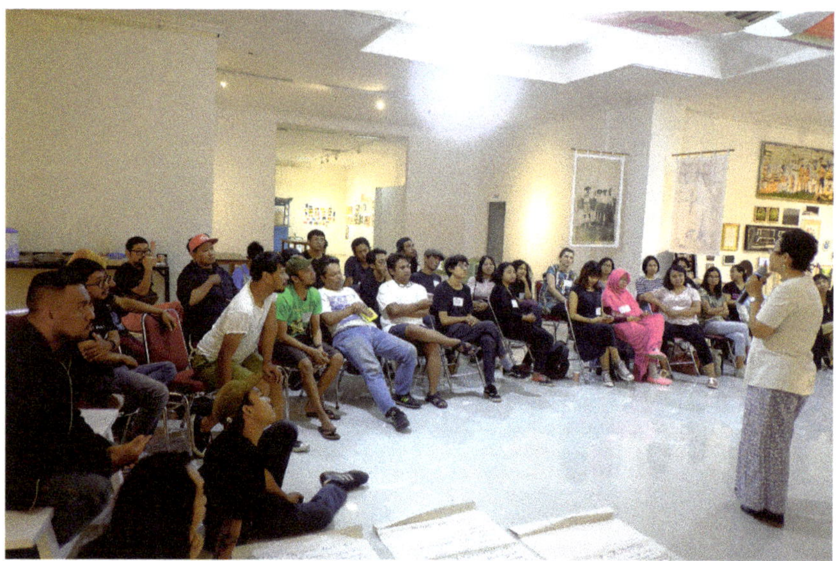

Figure 11.2: Workshop for art practitioners, 'How to Create a Safe Space', held in 2019 in the gallery space at the Indonesian Institute of the Arts, Yogyakarta.

Photograph courtesy Karina Roosvita.

This coalition of practitioners in diverse fields is far from unprecedented. From revolutionary studio cooperatives (*sanggar*) in the 1930s and 1940s, to institutions and forums dedicated to the 'people's culture', to study groups and research collectives, chapters in the book provide examples of how Indonesian artists and curators have invested in collaboration to create work that is both aesthetically sound and a practical way to communicate with the broader public. The drive to work together towards common goals has long also encompassed environmental concerns. As we have seen in the chapters by Turner, Kent and Hooker in this book, the degradation of the natural environment as a result of human exploitation (and in turn, the impact of this damaged landscape on the social environment) has preoccupied many Indonesian artists since the 1970s. One of their responses has been to collaborate with NGOs and movements such as WALHI (Wahana Lingkungan Hidup Indonesia/Indonesian Forum for the Environment), or with other civil society organisations, including religious groups, to effect change. Bayak's work over recent years with the enormous Tolak Reklamasi movement, which opposed a reclamation project in Bali's previously protected Benoa Bay (see Map 2), has seen him work as part of a coalition of musicians, artists, writers and activists in a long-running series of actions. Bayak was an integral part of this movement, contributing performances and artworks, and his involvement also 'fires his creativity'.[5]

From the perspective of form and material, these environmentally conscious practices have often encompassed the use of post-consumer waste as an artistic medium.[6] We can see evidence of both these trends over recent decades in the practice of established artists such as Tisna Sanjaya, FX Harsono, Nindityo Adipurnomo, Moelyono, I Made Bayak, Tita Salina, Irwan Ahmett and many more. But Swastika identifies the recent emergence of a 'new relationship with environment' through eco-friendly studios and 'awareness of the natural aspect of art events' or, in other words, attention to the environmental impact of art-making and public presentation itself, and efforts to mitigate its ill effects.

A few examples of artists currently exploring environmentally friendly art practices include the printmaking collectives *Grafis Minggiran* and *Grafis HuruHara*, as well as contemporary batik artists Nia Fliam and Agus Ismoyo through their Brahma Tirta Sari studio. Textile artists appear to be at the forefront of this movement, with a 2021 project curated by Swastika also exploring traditional, plant-based weaving practices through a collaboration that brought together textile artists Charwei Tsai (Taiwan) and Nency Dwi Ratna (Sumba, Indonesia) (see Map 1). Together they explored the use of natural fibres and dyes, as well as motifs of regeneration, that have been practised for countless generations by Ratna's 'Marapu' ancestors in Eastern Indonesia.[7] Cast into contemporary form, the weavings that resulted from this project, dyed with indigo, turmeric, and morinda leaves and roots, were displayed in an installation titled *Ndewa and Hamanang* (2021), as part of *The Womb & The Diamond* (31 January – 30 May 2021) exhibition at the Live Forever Foundation's Vital Space and the National Taichung Theatre in Taichung City, Taiwan.[8]

5 Elly Kent, *Artists and the People: Ideologies of Art in Indonesia* (Singapore: NUS Press, 2022), 166.

6 Elly Kent, 'Critical Recycling: Post-Consumer Waste as Medium and Meaning in Contemporary Indonesian Art', *Southeast of Now: Directions in Contemporary and Modern Art in Asia* 4, no. 1 (March 2020): 73–98, doi.org/10.1353/sen.2020.0003.

7 Marapu is the ancestral religion primarily practised on the islands of Sumba and Flores in Eastern Indonesia.

8 Further detail and documentation from this collaboration is available in Alia Swastika, 'Charwei Tsai: Collaboration as Method', *Ocula Magazine*, 17 March 2021, accessed 21 January 2022, ocula.com/magazine/insights/charwei-tsai-collaboration-as-method/.

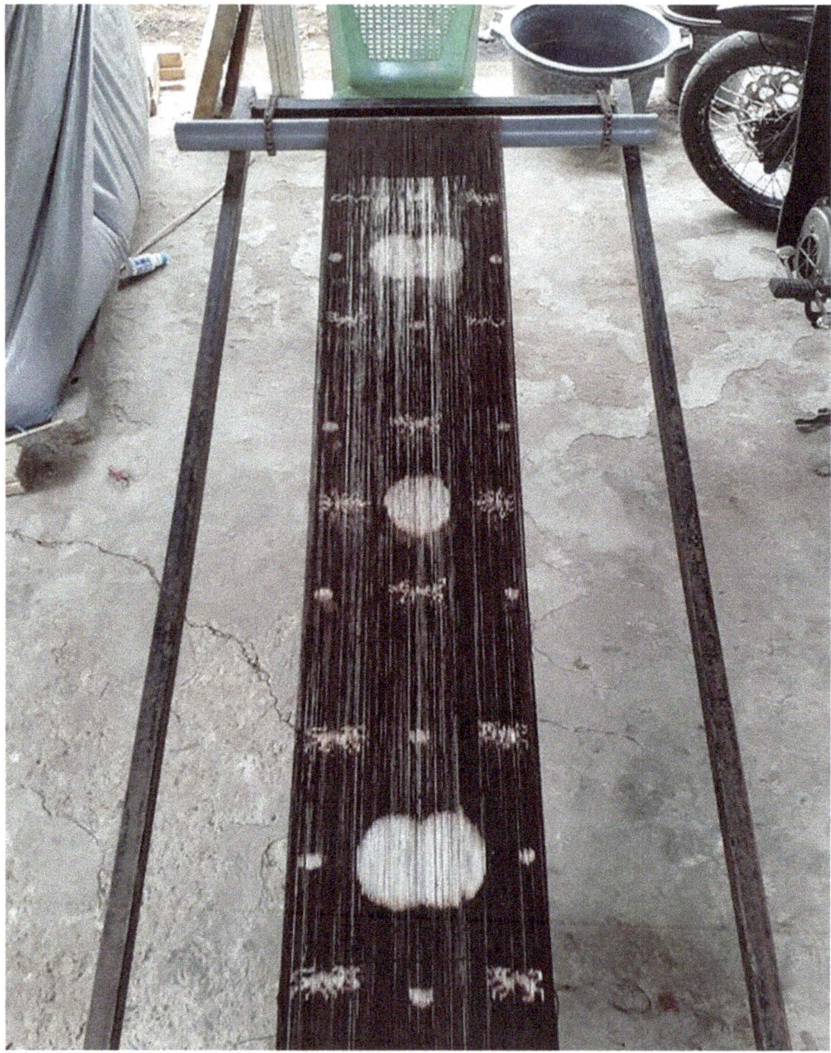

Figure 11.3: Nency Dwi Ratna and Charwei Tsai, work in progress on textiles in Sumba, 2021.

Permission: the artist.

The kernel of these kinds of transnational art projects may well be found in the activities of Indonesia's earliest post-independence artists, who travelled across the globe in the 1950s to represent their newly formed nation[9]

9 Jennifer Lindsay and Maya H. T. Liem, eds, *Heirs to World Culture: Being Indonesian, 1950–1965* (Leiden: Brill, 2012), doi.org/10.26530/OAPEN_403204.

and to satisfy their own intellectual and creative curiosity.[10] But twenty-first century Indonesian curators, artists and institutions are consciously exploiting the disruptive possibilities embedded in deconstructing false binaries between traditional and contemporary practices. Swastika writes: 'Encounters between contemporary artists such as Tsai with younger generations of weavers like Ratna open new possibilities for the future of art, particularly in places like Asia'.[11]

Decolonisation and Decentring

The project of decolonisation and decentring spans the breadth of practices in Indonesia. Transnational collaborations have long been one of the primary approaches to dismantling the colonial structures that have controlled many of the world's subjugated peoples. In Indonesia in 2010, taking as its reference Sukarno's historic Asia–Africa Conference held in Bandung in 1955,[12] the Biennale Jogja is one among many initiatives to reframe postcolonial geographical norms in order to explore relations between the centre and the periphery, between art and society, and between nations with similar historical and geographic contexts. Architect and member of the Biennale Yogyakarta Foundation, Eko Prawoto, wrote in the 2011 Biennale Jogja catalogue:

> Biennale Jogja looks to the future, developing a new perspective while confronting the established conventions for events of this nature … We search for a common platform that would stimulate the growth of diverse perspectives that would bring forth new alternatives to the hegemonic discourse … The equator will become a common platform to 're-read' the world by focusing on the centres in the region around the equatorial belt, with perspectives that are non-centred.[13]

Ten years later Swastika, who was co-curator of the Biennale Jogja Equator #1 and then went on to become director, points out that, in the present day, 'while we are experiencing an intimate relation with

10 Hendro Wiyanto and Maya H. T. Liem, eds, *Dia Datang, Dia Lapar, Dia Pergi* (Yogyakarta: Agung Tobing, 2014).

11 Swastika, 'Charwei Tsai'.

12 See further Jamie Mackie, *Bandung 1955: Non-Alignment and Afro-Asian Solidarity* (Singapore: Editions Didier Millet, 2005).

13 Eko Prawoto, *Biennale Jogja, 10 Years in the Future: An Interview with the Equator* in *Biennale Jogja XI—Equator #1 Shadow Lines: Indonesia Meets India* (Yogyakarta: Yayasan Biennale, 2011), 178–79.

[the] virtual world', the internet may be the main medium of the future. Simultaneously, she says, constraints on geographic mobility bring local communities and community spaces into greater proximity, creating the possibility that 'centred' exhibitions may not play as significant a role as they have before. This search for a common platform to decentre and decolonise continues, not only through subsequent iterations of the Biennale Jogja's equatorial explorations, but also through art projects that take place away from the Java and Bali-centric art centres, such as the Makassar Biennale on Sulawesi, the Jatiwangi Art Factory in rural West Java and, in 2020, a proliferation of online events. Amid the COVID-19 restrictions, many artists focused their practices on projects to support their local communities: for example, artist Anang Saptoto collaborated with farmers to market their produce through social media in the absence of traditional markets, and Tisna Sanjaya distributed personal protective equipment by post to health workers across his region of West Java.[14]

Dirgantoro identified among our presenters a 'deep concern with past practices in institutions and society about the way artistic, cultural and political identity … [is] being written into the history of Indonesian art'. The tensions between the recognition of a singular national identity, and the manifold ethno-religious identities that have been amplified since the fall of the New Order and the rise of the internet in the first two decades of the twenty-first century, remain pertinent. Speaking on the history of modern and contemporary art in Sulawesi, Rahman noted that among the many barriers to the development of robust art discourse in the regions is a sense that those outside (including those who have migrated away) are not welcome to comment on or contribute to the conversation. While this protective instinct is logical in the context of an art world working in resistance to the homogenising effect of globalisation, Rahadiningtyas proposes an important counter position that sees the local and global coming together to challenge older art canons. She stresses the need for projects to explore art history and history at a community level, a proposal that has a precedent in one of Rahman's own projects for the 'Parallel Events' program for the Biennale Jogja XII Equator #2. With his research collective *Colliq Puji*, Rahman conducted research into the history of Arab and Makassan literary traditions. Rahman and his collective were able to work so successfully with the Library and Archival Body for the South Sulawesi Region that they were given permission to take key historical artefacts from Sulawesi to Yogyakarta to exhibit alongside four interpretive artworks.

14 Kent, *Artists and the People*, 1–4.

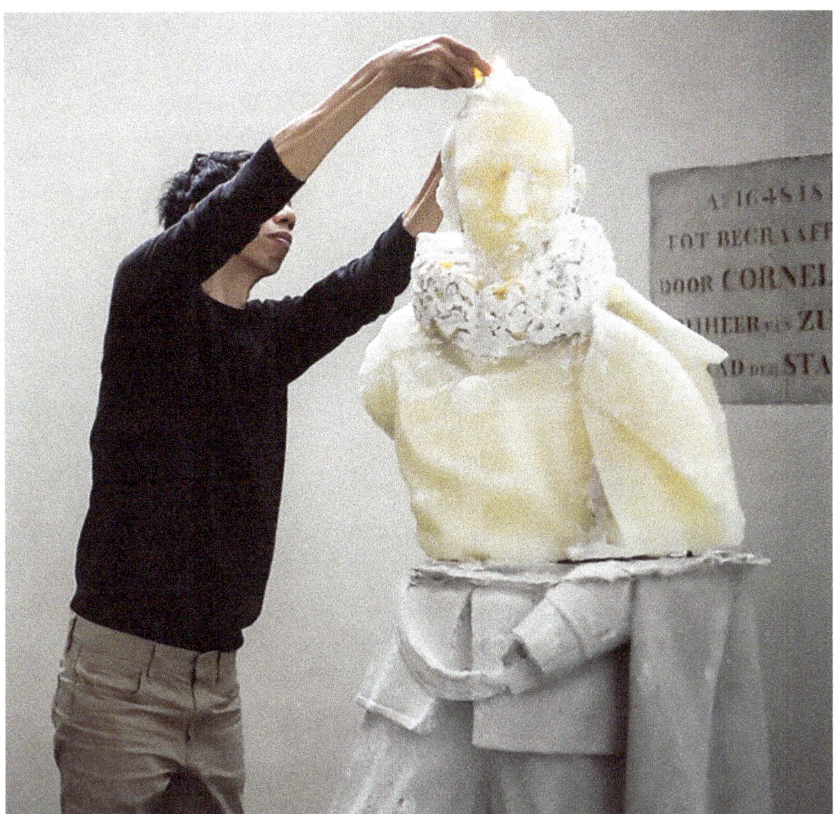

Figure 11.4: Iswanto Hartono, *Monuments*, Europalia Indonesia, Oude Kerk, Amsterdam, 2017.

Wax, fibre-reinforced polymer. Image and permission courtesy the artist.

Within Indonesia, these early efforts ultimately brought peripheral art histories into the centre and succeeded in expanding the audience for contemporary art and art histories there. But subsequent events like the Makassar Biennale (established in 2015), which has a perpetual theme of 'maritime' reflecting the province's cultural and economic history, push the decentring project further, to cultivate communities of scholars and artists who work on their own art histories. In preparation for the 2021 Makassar Biennale, research and writing workshops were held not only across Sulawesi, but also in Flores and West Papua (see Map 3), which lie in provinces virtually unrepresented in the Indonesian art worlds of the past. Facilitated by Director of Makassar Biennale, writer and curator Anwar 'Jimpe' Rachman and others, the workshops are designed to develop arts and cultural discourse as well as practitioner networks.[15]

The decolonisation projects on a more global scale often involve speaking back to art and other histories in colonial centres. Swastika described such an endeavour conducted with artist Iswanto Hartono in Amsterdam, as part of the 2017 Europalia Festival. In this project, Hartono created a wax, life-sized copy of a well-known statue of colonial Dutch figure Jan Pieterszoon Coen—recognised both as the founder of Batavia (now Jakarta) and the 'Butcher of Banda'[16]—which was then transformed into a 'candle' and set alight to melt into nothingness. The original statue occupied a public park in central Jakarta for 70 years until it was removed during the Japanese occupation of Indonesia. Indicative of the complexities of the postcolonial and decolonial imperatives of the twentieth and twenty-first centuries, the park has, since the 1960s, featured the 'West Irian Liberation Monument', which the city government claims was the design of Henk Ngantung, the first post-independence governor of Jakarta and also a former general secretary of Lekra. It was executed in bronze by sculptor Edhi Sunarso.[17] Hartono wrote:

> Street names are changed, monuments are taken down and buildings are destroyed. But the VOC's [Dutch United East India Company's] true legacy—a corrupt system—was not destroyed by purging the monuments. As a matter of fact, the Soeharto era was synonymous [with] corruption.[18]

---

15 'Writing and Research Workshop Sekapur Sirih in Five Cities', Yayasan Makassar Biennale, accessed 26 April 2021, makassarbiennale.org/writing-and-research-workshop-sekapur-sirih-in-five-cities/.

16 In the seventeenth century, Dutch and English trading companies used every tactic to gain a monopoly of the trade in spices that were grown only in Eastern Indonesia, particularly nutmeg and mace on the island of Banda (see Map 1). To prevent the local population engaging in free trade, Coen (in 1621) and others virtually depopulated Banda by deportation, starvation and massacres to ensure they controlled both the growing and selling of spices. See M. C. Ricklefs, *A History of Modern Indonesia since c. 1200* (Houndmills, Basingstoke, Hampshire: Palgrave, 2001), 34. See also Titarubi's artwork on this era in Introduction (Figure 0.6).

17 The annexation of West Irian (now known as West Papua) was conducted under pressure, but minimal supervision, from the UN in the midst of a power vacuum created by the rapid departure of the Dutch colonists. The legitimacy of the conduct of the referendum on the question of whether to join Indonesia or create an independent state has been strongly contested and West Papua remains an uneasy member of the Unitary States of the Republic of Indonesia, vulnerable to exploitation of its vast natural resources and human rights abuse. See 'Pembebasan Irian Jaya, Monumen', Jakarta Go Id, accessed 26 April 2021, web.archive.org/web/20171108100930/http://www.jakarta.go.id/web/encyclopedia/detail/2331/Pembebasan-Irian-Jaya-Monumen.

18 Linawati Sidarto, 'The Burning Memory of Colonialism', *Jakarta Post*, 9 November 2017, accessed 24 April 2021, www.thejakartapost.com/life/2017/11/09/the-burning-memory-of-colonialism.html. Spelling of Suharto/Soeharto as in the original text.

History and Historiography

History and historiography play an increasingly important role in the creation of intellectual and artistic projects and communities. The imperative to decolonisation and decentring is driven by a search for the truth that seems, as in the case described above, to lead inexorably further and further back into history and art history. While revelations about the political context, international involvement, and ongoing impunity and secrecy around perpetrators of the violence of 1965 continue to be unearthed by researchers, artists' relations are often focused on more personal individual and family truths. These personal truths, as Turner discusses in Chapter 7, were the catalyst inspiring the artworks of Dadang Christanto. As FX Harsono has described, at the end of the New Order, artists were finally free to examine the subjugation of their own histories in public, and the search for historical truths in familial archives has been a staple of Indonesian art since that time. Many younger generations of artists are encountering these histories first through the artwork of senior artists, and then through their own explorations.

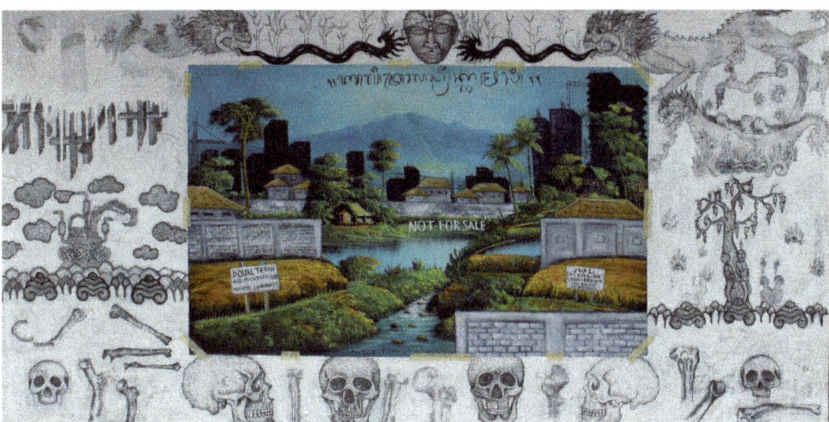

Figure 11.5: I Made 'Bayak' Muliana, *Industry, Hidden History and Legacy the Island of the Gods*, 2014.

Mixed media on plywood. Photograph and permission courtesy the artist.

Bayak's large-scale paintings depicting the links between colonial history, the mass killings of 1965, and the present-day exploitation of Bali's human and natural resources represent creative historiographies that can create a bridge to the 'truth' for younger generations. He says:

> The questions come from my young son, when I was creating the scene of murder during 1965, and he asked a question, a simple question. 'Is this a true story? Or is it imagination?' And I said to him, 'This is true. But soon, if you want to understand it more you can learn more'.

Since the fall of the New Order in 1998, seeing history in new ways has become important in defining new ways of understanding the present and future of Indonesia. Elia Nurvista's re-imaginings of *rijstafel,* a Dutch multi-dish buffet meal of performative excess, led her to further examinations of food politics and the intersection between colonial labour exploitation and the intimate domestic relations as documented in the archives of Dutch museum collections. Zico Albaiquni's large-scale paintings draw on images found in nineteenth- and twentieth-century ethnographic photograph collections, juxtaposed with renditions of Indonesian art historical objects and contemporary visual culture. Through these encounters he explores commonalities across the colonial, capitalist and canonical gaze. Dirgantoro underscores the importance of the archive 'in excavating the past … but also as an archive for building future memory' through curatorial practice.

In Rahadiningtyas's vision for the future of Indonesian art history, she points to opportunities for art historians to develop accessible and inclusive community-based scholarship. Already present in collaborative spaces in Bandung, Yogyakarta, Jakarta and—in part through the work of initiatives like the Indonesian Visual Art Archive (IVAA) *Gudskul* (*ruangrupa*) and the Makassar Biennale—in other cities in Indonesia, these networks expand 'the possibility to produce research, workshops, and programs that focus on comparative modernities'. Rahadiningtyas also proposes:

> initiatives in teaching and writing art history within and outside of institutions or universities—and perhaps, they could be more connected—where students or participants could actively participate in producing low-stakes research and entries, building databases on Wikipedia, or on other digital humanities platforms, of women and other marginalized groups of artists or artistic practices in Indonesia.

Technology and Disruption

Technology and disruption have created opportunities and challenges. In the very recent past, there have been fundamental shifts in the ways that people are connected, and to whom they are connected, facilitated by new technologies and the impact of the pandemic on mobility and proximity. These changes are not sudden but have been underway for several decades. Technology and COVID-19 have accelerated their effects and potential, both positive and negative. The digital humanities are, for many young scholars, their first encounter with archives and history. In Indonesia, as in most Southeast Asian nations, the combination of relatively good mobile coverage, extreme disparity between the rich and the poor, and generally low levels of higher education and digital literacy create a complex environment for the utilisation of digital infrastructure towards positive ends. As Rahadiningtyas notes, technology, especially the internet, is 'one of the tools that can be utilised to foster more collaborative works in terms of building databases'; yet, as Swastika warns, it is still necessary to consider how to mitigate the elitism of access to the internet, and how to 'democratise this infrastructure so that it can be accessed by everyone'. Swastika also emphasises the role that technology can play in promoting greater access to those outside the centre. The global pandemic has forced the gatekeepers of such canonical spaces and institutions to stand aside. She says:

> I've been following many zoom meetings and discussions and I've been hearing so many stories not only happening in Java or the centre of culture here, but we expand, from Papua, from Palu, from Poso, from Aceh—I think this is really being enabled by the technology.

Arts initiatives have pivoted to technology in ways that have arguably facilitated their initial aims with greater openness. The *Inkubator Inisiatif*, launched in 2019 by Karina Roosvita, Lashita Situmorang and Venerdi Handoyo, is an ongoing project to establish an independent platform for knowledge sharing to reach a wider public than many of the existing workshops and study clubs allowed. One of its aims is to encourage and support the emergence of female artists. Established artists Arahmaiani and Mella Jaarsma, as well as curators Grace Samboh and Alia Swastika, have contributed to this effort. In 2021, *Inkubator Inisiatif* offered free online masterclasses for up to 100 participants to share the 'interdisciplinary and intergenerational expertise' of masters and mentors like FX Harsono, Martin Suryajaya and Grace Samboh.

Conclusion

Two key questions emerged from our webinar discussions across different time zones and geographic boundaries. First, artist Tintin Wulia, whose own practice spans continents, drew our attention to the rapidly approaching *Documenta 15*, directed by Jakarta collective *ruangrupa* and asked how Indonesian arts practitioners see newly formed networks within the existing networks they have been weaving between their respective worlds? Second, art historian Wulan Dirgantoro sought to synthesise the past and the future by asking whether artistic practices, despite being a reminder of difficult pasts, could also be a source of hope?

Swastika responded by pointing to a work presented by a group of sociology students, Studio Malya, whose collectively produced artwork featured in the 2019 Jogja Biennale:

> More and more younger generations in Indonesia try to dig into what we call this dark history and try to find their own way to articulate their memory or articulate their interpretation of what they've read in history lessons.

After participating in an art project with women survivors of 1965, organised by Agung Kurniawan, Studio Malya began their own series of interviews with survivors. These were then interpreted in artworks and installations that were presented as a 'new museum' documenting 'historical events and conflict management practices which have long been overlooked due to the existence of dominant narratives/interests'.[19]

Swastika concluded: 'I have so much optimism for this trajectory for art and history, and this will be one of the starting points for creating [the] critical thinking space'.

19 'Studio Malya', Biennale Jogja XV 2019, accessed 26 April 2021, biennalejogja.org/2019/studio-malya/?lang=en.

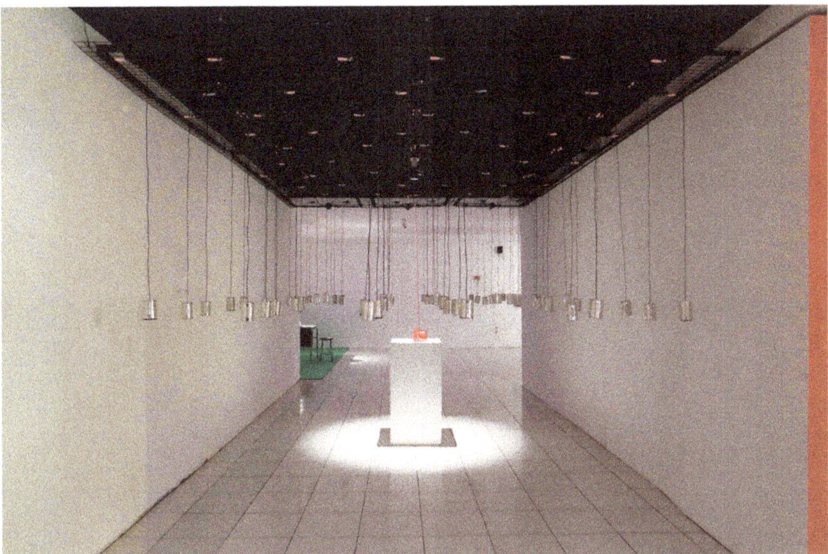

Figure 11.6: Studio Malya, *Have You Heard It Lately?* 2019.
Mixed media, 64 cans, 1 telephone. Installed at a pre-event for the Biennale Jogja XV. Photograph courtesy Studio Malya.

Roosvita responded to Dirgantoro's provocation by referring to Tintin Wulia's own participatory work, *Nous Ne Notons Pas Les Fleurs* (*We Don't Record the Flowers*, 2009–15). She drew attention to the fluidity and flexibility of art like Wulia's to open channels through which to encourage dialogue. In this multi-iteration installation, audiences in various cities in Asia and Europe deconstructed cartographic floral arrangements as they retraced their own migratory routes, all the while monitored by surveillance videos that are then recast in multi-channel video works. Roosvita says:

> When you see artwork like that it will create dialogue [with] the people who come to the exhibition … With my work it's a bit different because I bring the art as like a vehicle and then create like a workshop to address the issue. Both of these ways are actually important for us now.

This optimism about the emergence of a diversity of forms is echoed by Rahadiningtyas in her expectations for the future of art history in Indonesia, as she highlights in her proposal that there is also the possibility to:

> work together with universities in Indonesia to build art history curriculum and syllabi that make use of or highlight the universities' strength as laboratories of artistic and curatorial practice … And building classes to facilitate students' research and collaboration with artists' spaces—artist-led galleries, collaborative research spaces, private collections' and museums such as the Museum MACAN [Modern and Contemporary Art in Nusantara] in Jakarta.[20]

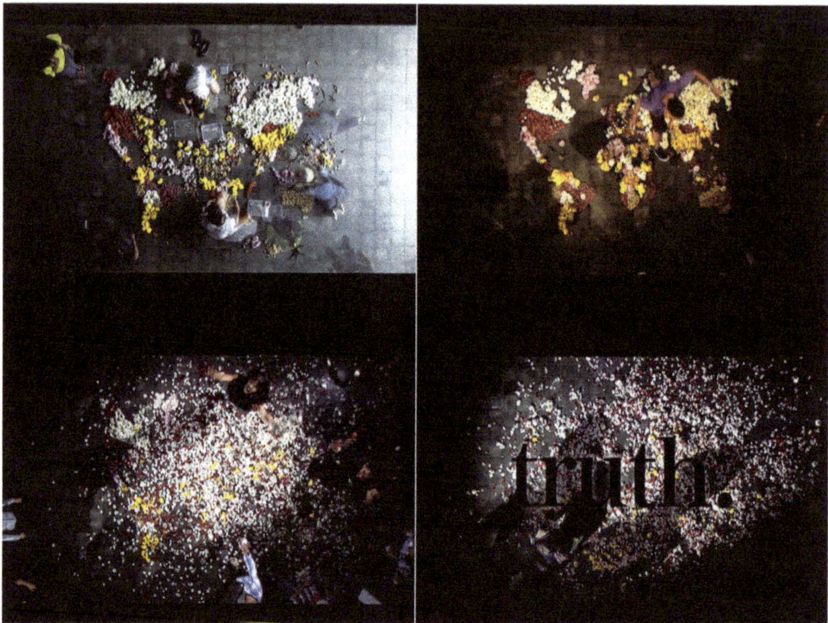

Figure 11.7: Tintin Wulia, *Nous Ne Notons Pas Les Fleurs*, Jakarta, 2010.[21]

Eight-channel video installation (unsynchronised, looped) in the collection of the Singapore Art Museum, from a participatory installation (2009–15). Wulia initiated this work during a residency in India, and has re-created the map of flowers, spice and herbs representing different countries in various locations around the world. Audiences were invited to move components of the map around to reflect their personal histories and journeys, with the shifting boundaries documented on video. Image and permission courtesy the artist.

20 MACAN showcases the international (and Indonesian) art collection of Haryanto Adikoesoemo, and also serves as a centre for new curatorial, exhibition-making and public programming around modern and contemporary art in Jakarta. It opened to the public in 2017.

21 For further information on this work, please see the artist's doctoral dissertation, Tintin Wulia, 'Aleatoric Geopolitics: Art, Chance and Critical Play on the Border' (PhD diss., RMIT University, 2013), researchrepository.rmit.edu.au/esploro/outputs/doctoral/Aleatoric-geopolitics-art-chance-and-critical-play-on-the-border/9921861425001341.

These kinds of activities, well underway outside of formal institutions through organisations like Gudskul, IVAA and KUNCI, can be further enhanced and reach larger audiences by mainstreaming artistic research and practice through universities. Universities also benefit from the integration of more speculative and open forms of research that art practice can facilitate, and the more intimate stories that these practices can bring into focus.

All the participants in the webinar saw hope in more open access to history and memory, and greater opportunities to share these stories with others through exhibitions and collaboration. As Bayak put it: 'So that simple thing I think really brings more hope to the future of art itself, and to the future of knowing the other stories of ourselves'.

APPENDICES

Maps

Robert Cribb

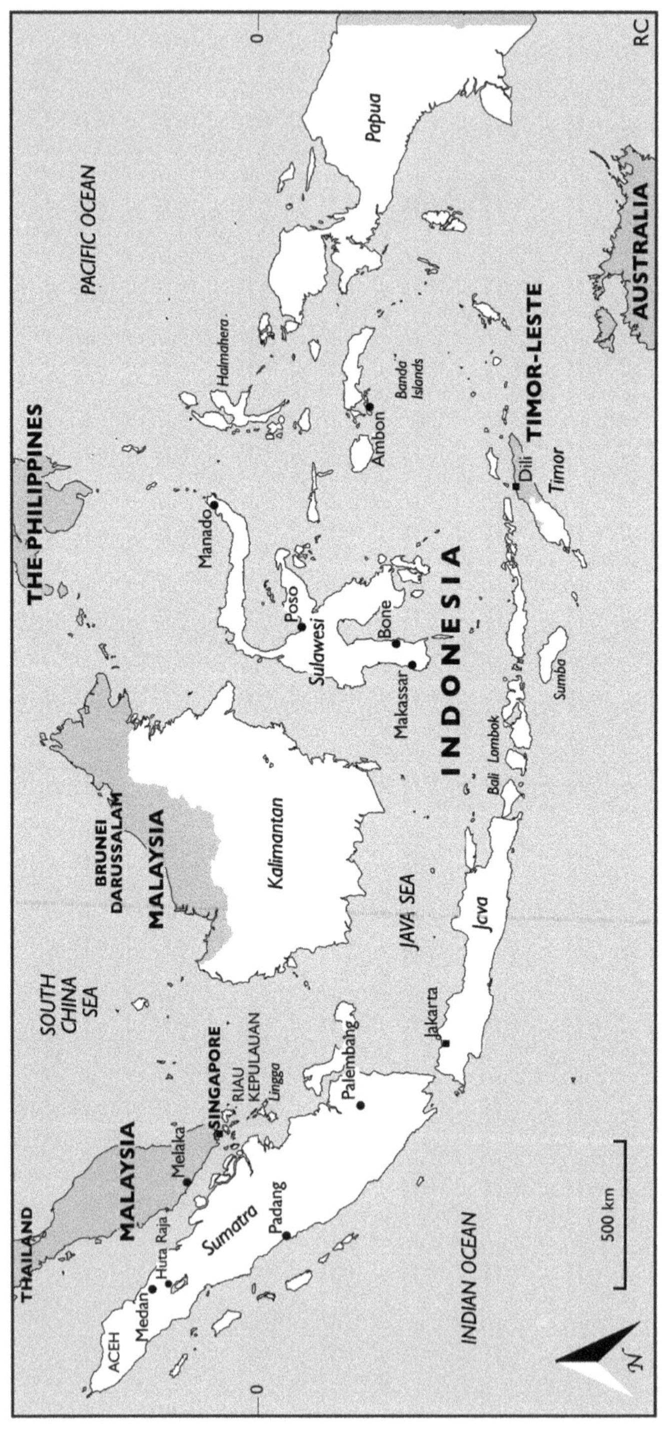

Map 1: The Indonesian archipelago.
Created by Robert Cribb.

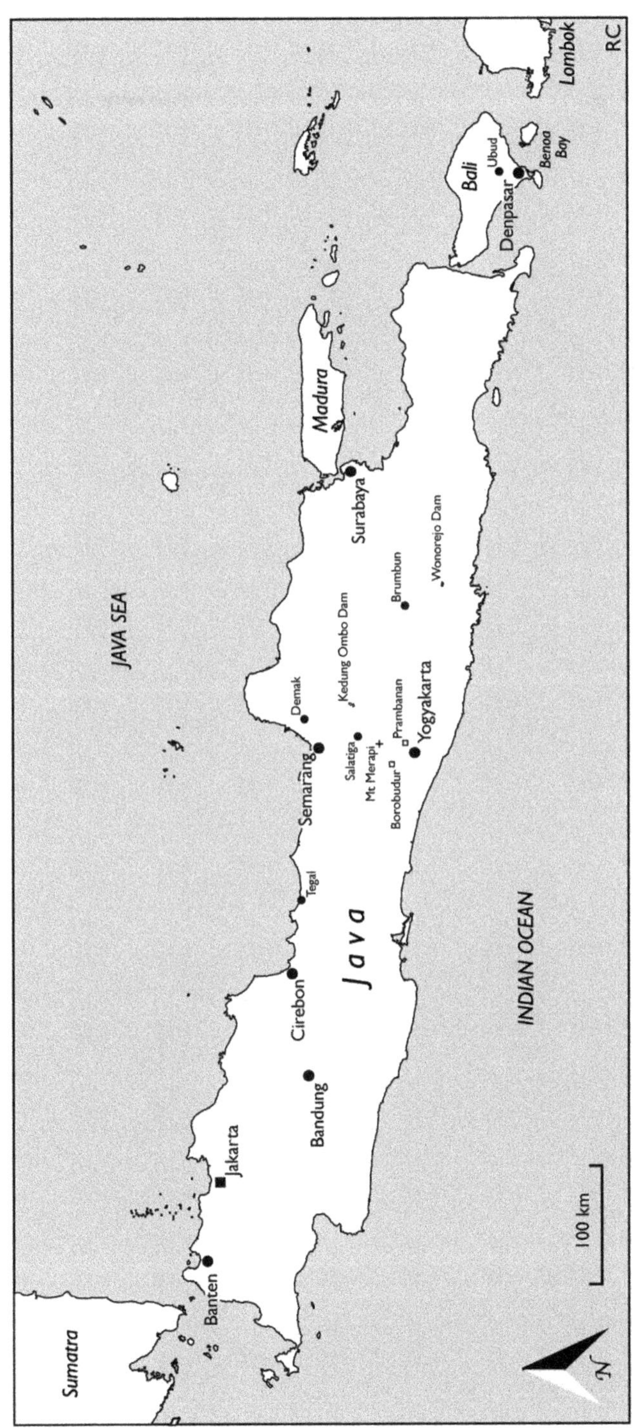

Map 2: Java and Bali.
Created by Robert Cribb.

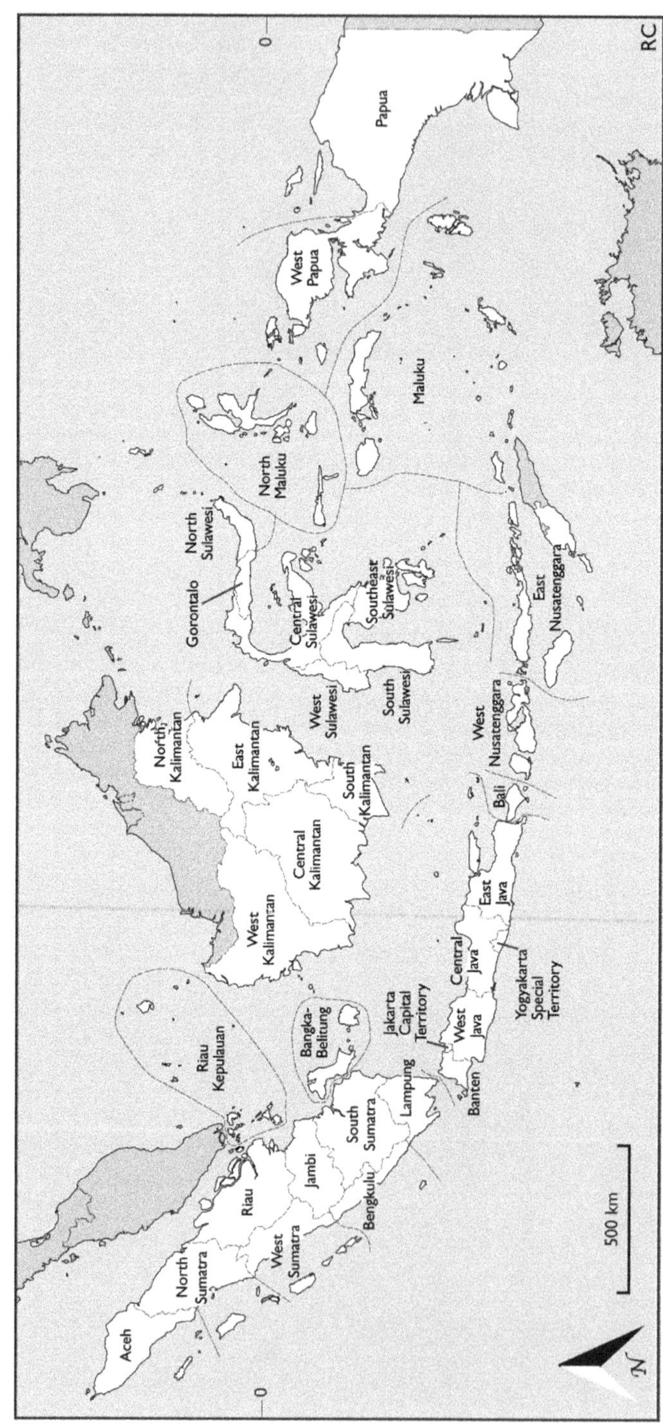

Map 3: Indonesia's provinces, 2022.

Created by Robert Cribb.

Table of Indonesian Modern and Contemporary Artists Illustrated in This Volume

Artists	Chapter	Figure
Nindityo Adipurnomo	Chapter 6	Figure 6.5
Siti Adiyati	Chapters 3, 8	Figures 3.7, 8.2
Affandi	Chapters 1, 3, 6	Figures 1.6, 3.4, 6.2
Irwan Ahmett	Chapter 2	Figure 2.5
Zico Albaiquni	Introduction	Figure 0.1
Dyan Anggraini	Chapter 8	Figure 8.4
Arahmaiani	Chapter 7	Figures 7.7, 7.8, 7.9
Dadang Christanto	Introduction, Chapters 1, 7, 9	Figures 0.9, 1.8, 7.5, 7.6, 9.1
Umi Dachlan	Chapter 1	Figure 1.7
Heri Dono	Chapters 2, 6, 7	Figures 2.2, 2.3, 2.4, 6.6, 7.3, 7.4
FX Harsono	Introduction, Chapters 5, 7, 10	Figures 0.10, 5.1, 5.3, 5.4, 7.1, 7.2, 10.1–10.7 (inclusive)
Iswanto Hartono	Epilogue	Figure 11.4
Yusuf Susilo Hartono	Chapter 1	Figure 1.14
Mella Jaarsma	Introduction, Chapter 6	Figures 0.5, 6.7
Jompet Kuswidananto	Chapter 5	Figure 5.5
Moelyono	Chapter 2	Figure 2.7
Patriot Mukmin	Chapter 9	Figure 9.2
I Made 'Bayak' Muliana	Epilogue	Figure 11.5
Mangku Muriati	Chapter 8	Figure 8.5
Eko Nugroho	Chapter 1	Figure 1.13
Mas Pirngadi	Chapter 3	Figure 3.2
A. D. Pirous	Chapter 4	Figure 4.2

Artists	Chapter	Figure
Rangga Purbaya	Chapter 9	Figure 9.3
Nency Dwi Ratna	Epilogue	Figure 11.3
Karina Roosvita	Epilogue	Figure 11.1
Ahmad Sadali	Introduction, Chapters 3, 4	Figures 0.8, 3.6, 4.1
Raden Saleh	Chapters 1, 3, 6	Figures 1.4, 3.1, 6.1
Tita Salina	Cover, Introduction, Chapter 2	Figures 0.11, 2.5
Tisna Sanjaya	Chapter 4	Figures 4.3, 4.4
Dolorosa Sinaga	Introduction, Chapters 1, 8	Figures 0.4, 1.10, 8.1
Marintan Sirait	Chapter 6	Figure 6.8
Srihadi Soedarsono	Chapter 6	Figure 6.3
Hildawati Soemantri	Chapter 8	Figure 8.3
Studio Malya	Epilogue	Figure 11.6
S. Sudjojono	Introduction, Chapters 2, 3	0.7, 2.6, 3.3
Yaya Sung	Chapter 9	Figure 9.4, 9.5
Dede Eri Supria	Chapter 6	Figure 6.4
Agus Suwage	Introduction, Chapter 1	Figures 0.2, 1.12
Taring Padi Collective	Chapter 1	Figures 1.11
Titarubi	Introduction	Figure 0.6
Tintin Wulia	Epilogue	Figure 11.7
Amri Yahya	Chapter 1	Figure 1.9

Abbreviations and Glossary[1]

Ahmadiyah/ Ahmadi	In Indonesia, Ahmadiyah is considered heretical and a deviant sect of Islam. Its followers, Ahmadis, have been persecuted and, in 2011, even killed. Major Muslim organisations have called for Ahmadiyah and Shi'a sects (see below) to be banned. The government has so far only banned Ahmadi outreach activities.
Angkatan '45	The generation, mostly writers but also artists and other cultural workers, that emerged during the revolution for independence, which was declared in 1945. They issued the *Surat Kepercayaan Gelanggang* in 1950 (see below).
APT	Asia Pacific Triennial of Contemporary Art founded in 1993 at the Queensland Art Gallery | Gallery of Modern Art in Brisbane, Australia; is held every three years and is a major exhibition focusing on contemporary art from Asia and the Pacific.[2]
ASRI	Akademi Seni Rupa Indonesia (Indonesian Academy of Visual Art), part of a larger group of academies. ASRI's campus was in Gampingan, Yogyakarta.
b.	born
bahasa	language
bangsa	people, nation
Bapak, Pak	Mr, Sir, father or a general honorific for an older man
Bhinneka Tunggal Ika	'Unity in diversity' (Indonesia's national motto)

1 Some of the definitions in this section owe much to the Glossary in Greg Fealy and Ronit Ricci, eds, *Contentious Belonging: The Place of Minorities in Indonesia* (Singapore: ISEAS-Yusof Ishak Institute, 2019), xiii–xviii, doi.org/10.1355/9789814843478.

2 See 'The Asia Pacific Triennial of Contemporary Art', QAGOMA, accessed 22 January 2022, www.qagoma.qld.gov.au/about/our-story/apt.

c.	approximately (in reference to time period)
CIVAS	Centre for Indonesian Visual Art Studies Institut Teknologi Bandung (Bandung Institute of Technology)
Darul Islam	A violent Islamist movement that sought to replace the secular nation-state of Indonesia with an Islamic state and rebelled against the Republic of Indonesia (1948–62). Never completely disbanded.
demokrasi	democracy
DPR	Dewan Perwakilan Rakyat (People's Representative Council); often translated as 'parliament' or 'House of Representatives'.
FPI	Front Pembela Islam (Islamic Defenders' Front). Islamic vigilante group formed in 1999 to oppose (often by force) immoral behaviour. Declared illegal in late 2020 and subsequently reconstituted as the Islamic Brotherhood Front.
Gelanggang	Forum: the name of a group of writers and artists formed in 1946 in Jakarta whose publication of the same name carried their debates and ideas about the form and nature of a new national culture for Indonesia.
Gerwani	Gerakan Wanita Indonesia (Indonesian Women's Movement). The group took this name in 1954 as a non-party, national political organisation to improve the position of women. Some members of Gerwani were linked with the Indonesian Communist Party and participated in the attempted coup of 1965 but were falsely accused of desecrating bodies and lewd acts. They suffered vilification, torture and imprisonment after 1965.
Golkar	Golongan Karya (Group of Professionals), the state political party under President Suharto; a political party in the Reformasi period.
gotong royong	Mutual assistance and cooperation; a broad concept of communal responsibility that often takes the form of a specific event similar to a working bee.
GSRB (in early texts, GSRBI)	Gerakan Seni Rupa Baru (New Art Movement) started in 1975; early variation is Gerakan Seni Rupa Baru Indonesia, or the New Indonesian Art Movement.
Guided Democracy	ideology of semi-authoritarianism practised by President Sukarno (1959–65)

Ibu, Bu	Mrs, Madam, mother or a general honorific for an older woman
iman	faith
ISI	Institut Seni Indonesia (Indonesian Institute of the Arts). Encompassing all art forms, traditional and contemporary, performance, visual arts and music. Campuses are located in Yogyakarta, Java, and Denpasar, Bali. The Denpasar visual arts campus was formerly known as STSI, and the Yogyakarta visual arts campus was known as ASRI.
ITB	Institut Teknologi Bandung (Bandung Institute of Technology) founded 1920 and Indonesia's first science and technology university
IVAA	Indonesian Visual Art Archive
JAKKER	People's Art Network, affiliated with the People's Democratic Party (PRD)
JI	Jemaah Islamiyah (Islamic Community), covert jihadist organisation, founded in Malaysia in 1993 and based in Indonesia since 1998
jiwa ketok	'Visible soul', a concept popularised by modernist artist Sudjojono, to describe the importance of the artist's own soul, evident (according to Sudjojono) in the brushstrokes of a painting.
kabupaten	regency/administrative unit below the level of province
kecamatan	administrative level below the level of *kabupaten*
khilafa	Islamic governance; caliphate
LBH Lembaga Bantuan Hukum	Legal Aid Institute
Lekra	Lembaga Kebudayaan Rakyat (Institute for People's Culture, 1950–65)
Manikebu	*Manifesto Kebudayaan* (Cultural Manifesto) of universal humanism declared in 1963
MANIPOL-USDEK	Manifesto Politik-USDEK (political manifesto of the 1945 Constitution, Indonesian-style socialism, guided democracy, guided economy, Indonesian identity); Sukarno's 1959 political manifesto
manusia	human being/humankind
Muhammadiyah	Modernist Islamic mass social organisation founded 1912 in Yogyakarta; current membership approximately 35 million

Mukadimah	manifesto, preface
NGA	National Gallery of Australia
NGO	non-government organisation
NU	Nahdlatul Ulama (Revival of the Religious Scholars); founded in 1926 to promote 'traditionalist Islam'. With a current membership of over 40 million, it is probably the largest Muslim organisation in the world.
Orde Baru	New Order, the term President Suharto gave his government when he took office in 1966 and maintained until he resigned in 1998.
Pancasila	The 'Five Principles' of the national ideology of the Indonesian nation-state: belief in one supreme God, just and civilised humanity, national unity, democracy led by wisdom and prudence through consultation and representation, and social justice.
PDI	Partai Demokrat Indonesia (Indonesian Democratic Party)
Perda Syariah	Peraturan Daerah Syariah (Regional Sharia Regulations)
pesantren	Islamic boarding school or study community
PKI	Partai Komunis Indonesia (Indonesian Communist Party)
PPP	Partai Persatuan Pembangunan (United Development Party)
PRD	Partai Rakyat Demokratik (People's Democratic Party) formed 1996
PRRI-Permesta	Pemerintah Revolusioner Republik Indonesia (Revolutionary Government of the Republic of Indonesia). Permesta (Piagam Perjuangan Semesta Alam/Charter of Universal Struggle). These were linked rebellions against the central government, fought in Sumatra and Sulawesi in the late 1950s.
rakyat	'the people', as opposed to 'the elite', 'the state', 'the leaders' or other figures of authority
Reformasi	'reform' and also 'reformation'; used to refer to the period since 1998 when the Suharto regime was ended
rupiah	Indonesian currency (AUD$1 = approximately Rp. 10,770 at time of publication)
sanggar	artist's studio; small collectives of artists
seni	art

Shi'a Islam	Regarded in Indonesia as a minority sect of Islam within a Sunni majority nation. In some parts of Indonesia, Shi'a Muslims have been harassed, intimidated and forced from their homes.
STB	Theatre Study Club of Bandung
Surat Kepercayaan Gelanggang	Gelanggang statement of beliefs; published 1950 to express the new values and vision for Indonesia's national culture
tauhid (also *tawhid*)	the absolute unity of God
TIM	Taman Ismail Marzuki
turba	From the phrase '*turun ke bawah*' or 'to go down', a term used by leftist artists to describe spending time with 'the people' (usually in villages) to experience their way of life; also a key methodology advocated by the Institute for People's Culture (Lekra).
UNIFEM	United Nations Development Fund for Women. Formed in 1976 to provide financial and technical assistance for women's empowerment and gender equality.
WALHI	Wahana Lingkungan Hidup/Forum for the Environment, established 1980.

Timeline of Selected Indonesian Historical Events[1]

Virginia Hooker

Please see Maps 1, 2 and 3 for locations of places mentioned below.

10,000 BCE	Islands of the Indonesian archipelago form when lower land is covered by water from melting ice, leaving only higher ground above water. Oceans and rivers link, rather than divide, peoples. Colliding tectonic plates create a constant threat of earthquakes and volcanic activity.
400 CE	Inscriptions in Indian scripts record Hindu rulers in East Kalimantan and West Java.
632	After the death of Prophet Muhammad, Islam spreads through the Middle East, North Africa, Spain, India and China.
c. 670	Maritime kingdom of Sriwijaya in southern Sumatra becomes the regional centre for Buddhism and extensive trading networks extend to mainland Southeast Asia and Java.
760–830	Buddhist monument Borobudur constructed in Central Java.
900s	Hindu temple complex of Prambanan constructed in Central Java.

1 This timeline supports and extends the contextual information in Chapter 1. Its entries identify events that have influenced and shaped Indonesia's sociopolitical history and the lives of its inhabitants. Sources consulted include: Greg Fealy and Virginia Hooker, eds and compilers, *Voices of Islam in Southeast Asia: A Contemporary Sourcebook* (Singapore: Institute of Southeast Asian Studies, 2006), xxii–xxix; Ian Chalmers, *Indonesia: An Introduction to Contemporary Traditions* (South Melbourne: Oxford University Press, 2006), 3–7; Jennifer Lindsay and Maya H. T. Liem, eds, *Heirs to World Culture: Being Indonesian 1950–1965* (Leiden: KITLV Press, 2012), 495–99, doi.org/10.26530/OAPEN_403204; M. C. Ricklefs, *A History of Modern Indonesia since c. 1200* (Houndmills, Basingstoke: Palgrave, 2001).

1294–1478	Majapahit, Hindu-Buddhist kingdom in East Java, expands its influence into surrounding regions. Present-day Hindu Bali maintains Balinese–Hindu culture and preserves some of the literature of pre-Islamic Java.
Late 1200s	Muslim gravestones in North Sumatra mark the presence of Muslim communities.
1500s – late 1600s	Land and sea contests between local rulers on both sides of the Melaka straits for control of the east–west trade passing through the straits.
1500s – late 1600s	The sultanate of Aceh in North Sumatra supports Muslim scholars and Islamicate culture. Four Muslim female rulers preside over a golden age of commerce in the mid to late seventeenth century.
1500s – c. 1800	Demak, the first Muslim court in Java, and the coastal Javanese sultanates that follow, develop distinctive syntheses of local, Muslim and regional arts. Courts in Central Java do likewise despite extended periods of warfare against each other and the Dutch.[2]
1600s – late 1700s	British and Dutch formal and informal commercial networks join the contest for access to lucrative regional trade. The Dutch try to enforce a monopoly of the spice trade. In 1600, the English East India Company is formed followed in 1602 by the Dutch United East India Company (VOC).
Mid-1700s–onwards	In the royal courts of Java, distinctive Javanese styles of Islam and Sufism develop; the arts, crafts, dance-drama, shadow theatre, literature and music flourish.
1799	The VOC lacks the capital to maintain its position in the archipelago. The Dutch government is forced to take over the administration of the Netherlands East Indies (NEI).
1811–16	Napoleonic Wars in Europe force the Netherlands to request a British inter-regnum in NEI. Sir Thomas Stamford Raffles does the job. The return of the Dutch in 1816 is not welcomed by all.
1824	Present-day international boundaries between Malaysia and Indonesia established by the Treaty of London negotiated between Britain and the Netherlands.

2 We thank Dr James Bennett for his advice on this complex period of Indonesian history.

1825–30	Pangeran (Prince) Diponegoro (1785–1855) leads a mass uprising against the Dutch fuelled by general anger about taxes and corruption (perpetrated by Europeans, Chinese and the hereditary Javanese aristocracy). After five years of brutal fighting and the deaths of over 200,000 Javanese, 8,000 European and 7,000 local soldiers, Diponegoro opens negotiations with the Dutch who arrest him. He is exiled to Sulawesi where he dies in 1855.
1830 – late 1870s	Dutch impose *cultuurstelsel* (cultivation system) of compulsory delivery to the government of export crops. The resulting revenues make the Dutch and the local Indonesian officials extremely prosperous. In 1860, under the pen-name 'Multatuli' (I bear much), former colonial official Eduard Douwes Dekker publishes the novel *Max Havelaar*, which remains the best-known exposé of the Dutch colonial system and the corruption and cruelty of the local indigenous aristocracy. Just over a century later, in 1976, Dutch film director F. Radermakers, who had prior approval from the Indonesian Ministry of Information, releases his film *Max Havelaar*. In 1977, the Indonesian Censorship Board bans it, claiming that the film creates the impression that colonialism was good and that it was the local Javanese aristocrats who exploited their fellows. Radermakers refuses to make changes to his film and says 'Multatuli's protests [against injustice] are still very topical'.[3]
1851	Raden Saleh (1811–1880), a Javanese aristocrat, returns to Java after 25 years studying and painting in Europe. He was the 'first Indonesian who spoke a number of European languages [and the] first Indonesian who had lived for an extended time in Europe'.[4] Indonesians date the beginning of modern Indonesian art to his works.
1873–1904	The Dutch engage in guerrilla wars with Acehnese forces, including those under female leader Cut Nyak Din (1850–1908). A modus vivendi is achieved but Aceh retains its independent spirit up to the present.[5]

3 Carmel Budiardjo, 'Dutch Film Banned', *Index on Censorship* 7, no. 2 (1978): 52, doi.org/10.1080/03064227808532764.

4 See further Werner Kraus, 'First Steps to Modernity: The Javanese Painter Raden Saleh (1811–1880)', in *Eye of the Beholder: Reception, Audience, and Practice of Modern Asian Art*, ed. John Clark, Maurizio Peleggi and T. K. Sabapathy (Sydney: Wild Peony, 2006), 29–55.

5 For a sensitive, revealing and moving analysis of Aceh's internal and external struggles, see Edward Aspinall, *Islam and Nation: Separatist Rebellion in Aceh* (Stanford, California: Stanford University Press, 2009).

1894 – c. 1912	Either by force (e.g. Lombok 1894, Bone in Sulawesi 1904, Bali in 1908) or by deposition and treaty (e.g. the sultanate of Lingga-Riau in 1912), the Dutch assume control over most of the territory now constituting modern Indonesia.
1901	Several enlightened Dutch colonials, following in the steps of 'Multatuli', persuade the Dutch government that it should take responsibility for the negative effects of the cultivation system and other forms of exploitation of the peoples of the NEI by improving their welfare. In 1901, an enquiry into the people's welfare marks the beginning of the Dutch 'Ethical Policy' aimed at improving the basic education and material conditions of 'the masses'.
Late nineteenth – early twentieth century	In Cairo, Jamal al-Din al-Afghani (1839–1897) and Muhammad Abduh (1849–1905) teach that selected progressive ideas from European thinking (e.g. on education, science, technology, medicine) can be adopted by Muslims who want to participate in the modern world and still remain true to Islam. These ideas spread in Muslim Southeast Asia and, especially, in Indonesia, through publications and religious schools.
1904	Raden Ajeng Kartini, aged 25, dies soon after having her first child. Born into a progressive aristocratic Javanese family, her father encouraged his daughters to attend the local Dutch school, which, as aristocrats, they were entitled to do and could afford.[6] From 1899 until her death, Kartini corresponded in Dutch with the wives of Dutch officials. Her letters provide insights into the visions she and her sisters had for the education of girls. Kartini's concern for the condition of Javanese women and girls is commemorated in her status as a national hero in modern Indonesia. Recently attention has been given to Kartini's interest in and talent for art.[7]
1908	Budi Utomo (The Beautiful Endeavour), a Javanese association for Dutch-educated members of the lesser aristocracy (*priyayi*), is established. It was largely apolitical with members united by cultural, educational and welfare interests. In 1909 it had its highest membership of 10,000 and was eventually dissolved in 1935, but it was the forerunner of a number of 'proto-nationalist' organisations formed by Dutch-educated and/or progressive Muslims that culminated in the pan-Indonesia youth congress of 1928.

6 See further Ricklefs, *A History of Modern Indonesia*, 199–205.

7 See, for example, Enin Supriyanto, 'The Mother of Indonesian Art?', in *Indonesian Women Artists: The Curtain Opens*, ed. Carla Bianpoen, Farah Wardani and Wulan Dirgantoro (Jakarta: Yayasan Seni Rupa Indonesia, 2007), 15–21.

1912 Ahmad Dahlan establishes the modernist Muslim social organisation 'Muhammadiyah' in Yogyakarta. Currently Indonesia's second largest Muslim organisation with branches in every province and extremely active women's groups, it runs hospitals, kindergartens, schools and universities.

1926 Nahdlatul Ulama (Revival of the Religious Scholars) is formed by Muslim religious teachers (*kyai*) in East Java who did not support the 'modernist' approach to Islam promoted by members of Muhammadiyah. Known as NU, this movement currently claims around 40 million members, has very enterprising women's wings, runs traditional religious boarding schools and colleges known as *pesantren*, and cares for orphans, the very poor and the graves of individuals revered as 'saints'.[8] Although originally founded in opposition to Muhammadiyah, shared interests in human rights, engaging fully with the contemporary world and its issues from an Islamic perspective, and concern about the growth of extremist interpretations of Islam, have recently brought the two organisations closer together to cooperate for the common good.

1928 In October, many ethnically based associations of young people, known as 'Young Bataks', 'Young Javanese' and so on, hold a pan-Indonesia congress in Batavia (Jakarta). By 28 October, they have agreed to place nationalism ahead of their ethnic loyalties and they swear a Youth Pledge (*Sumpah Pemuda*) that continues to be made each year on 28 October: 'One land, Indonesia; one nation, Indonesia, one language, Indonesian'. This commitment to a national unity of place, nation and language differentiates Indonesia from other postcolonial nations, such as India, which remain deeply divided by religions, ethnicities and languages.

1929 The collapse of the US stock market that initiated the Great Depression seriously affects the prices of Indonesia's exports with cascade effects on patterns of employment and availability of work.[9] Muslim welfare organisations support many of the needy.

8 The following highly readable and informative study of selected saints is recommended: George Quinn, *The Bandit Saints of Java* (Leicestershire: Monsoon Books Ltd, 2019).

9 See Ricklefs, *A History of Modern Indonesia*, 234–35.

1930s–40	A period of competing nationalist movements whose leaders, including Sukarno (1901–1970), were being exiled or imprisoned by the Dutch who granted no concessions to nationalist demands for a parliament for Indonesians. Beyond Indonesia, major changes were occurring: Hitler came to power in Germany in 1933; in 1937, the Sino-Japanese War broke out; in May 1940, Hitler invaded the Netherlands, whose government reassembled in exile in London and declared martial law in Indonesia.
1941	Japan attacks Pearl Harbor in Hawaii, lands military forces in mainland Southeast Asia and starts the Pacific War.
1942	Japan's army occupies Sumatra and Java and its navy occupies the islands of the eastern archipelago.
1942–44	Indonesians observe an Eastern power supplant a European one and intern non-Indonesians. They also see the Japanese subject Indonesians to forced labour and send thousands of Indonesians to mainland Southeast Asia to work on Japanese projects. Japanese control of food and natural resources for their war effort compounds the deprivations Indonesians suffered during the Depression. The Malay language (Bahasa Indonesia) is strengthened as Indonesia's language of unity when the Japanese use it for administration and mass communication and Indonesia's nationalist leaders take the opportunity to further their own aims. In an attempt to win the support of these leaders, Japan promises independence to Indonesia but does not name a date.
1945	In August, the US drops atomic bombs on Japan, which surrenders. Two days later, on 17 August, Sukarno proclaims Indonesia's independence on what later becomes its national day. Revolutionary excitement, especially among young Indonesians, is expressed in art, literature, journals and newspapers. This generation of activist artists and writers is known as 'Angkatan 45' (the generation of '45). The general situation across Indonesia is poverty stricken, chaotic and dangerous with the Japanese military still in control of some regions, British forces trying to accept Japanese surrenders, the Dutch wanting to reoccupy 'their' colony and Indonesian nationalists fighting for their newly proclaimed independence.[10]

10 The complexities and violence of this period of revolutionary struggle are described in Ricklefs, *A History of Modern Indonesia*, 261–86. They include a communist uprising in Madiun in 1948 when at least 8,000 people were killed, and an attempt to establish an Islamic state during the Darul Islam rebellion, which ended only when its leader, Kartosoewirjo, was executed in 1962.

1946 – December 1949	Despite at least two formal agreements with the Dutch to end hostilities in the struggle for control of Indonesia, protracted armed struggles continue. Only on 27 December 1949, after intervention from the United Nations, do the Netherlands agree to transfer sovereignty to Indonesia. The Netherlands retains sovereignty over West Irian (now Papua) whose status will be determined separately.
1948	ASRI (Indonesian Academy of Fine Arts) established in Yogyakarta. Its name later changed to ISI (Indonesian Institute of Fine Arts).
18 February 1950	*Surat Kepercayaan Gelanggang* (Gelanggang statement of beliefs) setting out a vision for Indonesia's new, independent and inspiring national culture is signed and published in October 1950.
17 August 1950	Lekra (Lembaga Kebudayaan Rakyat/People's Institute of Culture) established.[11]
1950	Art Department established at Institute of Technology Bandung. It is later called the Faculty of Visual Art and Design.
1955	In April in Bandung, Sukarno hosts the first Asia–Africa Conference attended by the heads of 29 newly independent nations. In September, Indonesia holds its first general elections.
1957–59	The linked rebellions of the Revolutionary Government of the Republic of Indonesia (PRRI) in Sulawesi and West Sumatra are fought against the central government.
1959	In June–July Sukarno dissolves the Constituent Assembly that had been unable to agree whether Pancasila or Islam should be Indonesia's national ideology. By Presidential Decree, he returns to the 1945 Constitution and establishes his 'Guided Democracy' regime giving himself full executive powers. He presents a political manifesto that is known by its acronym MANIPOL-USDEK.
1961–63	Sukarno uses military force against the Dutch in Irian. The UN withdraws authority for Irian from the Dutch and entrusts it to Indonesia, creating long-term issues for all involved.

11 The first and still best account in English of Lekra is Keith Foulcher, *Social Commitment in Literature and the Arts: The Indonesian 'Institute of People's Culture' 1950–1965* (Monash University: Centre of Southeast Asian Studies, 1986).

1960–65	During this period, Indonesia sends official state-sponsored cultural missions and arts visits to the following countries and events (in order of visits): Honolulu, Japan, Hong Kong, the Philippines, Singapore; USSR, PRC; North Korea, North Vietnam; Pakistan; New York World Fair, the Netherlands, France; Cambodia and Japan; PRC, North Korea, Japan.[12]
1963	Lekra sponsors a cultural delegation to PRC, North Vietnam and North Korea.[13]
	In April, Sukarno announces hostilities towards Malaysia in a policy known as Konfrontasi.
	On 17 August, *Manifesto Kebudayaan* (*Manikebu*/cultural manifesto) of universal humanism published by intellectuals opposed to the ideologies of Lekra.
1964	On 8 May, *Manifesto Kebudayaan* (*Manikebu*) is banned and its supporters reviled.
1965	In May in Jakarta, the Indonesian Communist Party (PKI) stages lavish public celebrations of its forty-fifth anniversary. There is increasing disquiet within and outside Indonesia about Sukarno's tilt to the left, authoritarian behaviour and poverty-stricken nation.
	On 1 October, General Suharto (1921–2008), with military backing, takes control of Jakarta after an alleged coup attempt. On 9 October, parliament impeaches Sukarno.[14]
1966	Sukarno, under house arrest, signs over presidential power to General Suharto, who becomes Indonesia's second president (1966–98).
October 1965 – February 1966	At least half a million Indonesians murdered in mass executions because of real or suspected association with the Communist Party and leftist organisations.

12 This information gathered from Lindsay and Liem, *Heirs to World Culture*, 497–99.

13 Ibid., 498.

14 For more details of these events, see David Jenkins, *Young Soeharto: The Making of a Soldier, 1921–1945* (Singapore: ISEAS-Yusof Ishak Institute, 2021), xxiii–xxiv, doi.org/10.1355/9789814881012. The book is the first in a trilogy that will describe 'the rise to power of one of Asia's most brutal, most durable, most avaricious and most successful dictators' (p. xxviii).

October 1965 – 1969	Indonesia-wide operations to identify and detain individuals with real or suspected connection with leftist organisations, including prominent intellectuals, artists and writers. Exiled, imprisoned, held without trial until the late 1970s or later, their families were permanently stigmatised and discriminated against. All references to these events are forbidden and censored. The killings, atrocities and imprisonments are only able to be discussed openly after Suharto's resignation in 1998.
1966–67	President Suharto bans the PKI and Lekra. He restores relations with Malaysia, the UN and the World Bank.
1968–69	Suharto declares his government the 'New Order' with development as its theme. He becomes known as 'Bapak Pembangunan' (Father of Development) and plans the nation's future for the next 25 years through five, five-year plans known as 'Repelita' (Rencana Pembangunan Lima Tahun/Five-Year Development Plan). All aspects of government are tightly controlled and regulated to create a modern, technology-driven nation. The military has a new 'dual function' as protector of security (including policing) as well as supporting civil administration.
1973–74	An unexpected boom in world oil prices lifts the New Order economy. But appropriation of land for industrial estates, exploitation of cheap labour and massive concessions to Chinese conglomerates provoke reactions.
1974	Anti-government riots in Jakarta in January, given the acronym MALARI (Malapetaka Limabelas Januari/Disaster of 15 January) signal organised resistance to the authoritarian nature of the New Order's policies and their implementation. They also reveal the New Order's determination to crush opposition to their policies.
1975	Portugal withdraws from Timor, which declares its independence. Indonesia invades in December. In May 1976, Indonesia declares East Timor to be its twenty-eighth province and East Timorese resistance begins.
1980	Prominent Indonesians sign 'The Petition of Fifty', criticising the policies of the Suharto regime. Their careers are ended and they are socially ostracised.
1984	At Tanjung Priok (Jakarta's port area), armed forces massacre scores of Muslims protesting against New Order policies.

mid-1980s–ongoing	The negative effects of industrialisation (pollution of waterways), deforestation (catastrophic mud-slips that bury villages in the wet season), mono-cultures (particularly oil palm plantations), pesticides that destroy the natural balances of eco-systems, forest fires that ignite subterranean peat beds and practices such as over-fishing cause serious concern to many Indonesian professional and non-professional groups. Although long-term solutions are not firmly in place, monitoring and remediation have begun despite pushback from groups with vested interests. On the plus side, Indonesia now has a substantial middle class (although distribution of wealth is an ongoing economic and social issue); basic health services have been extended to villages and there are more midwives trained to support mothers and babies; primary education is compulsory and increasing numbers continue to secondary and tertiary education; satellite communications and access to the internet are widespread; and transport, especially by air, is relatively affordable, although safety standards have been criticised by international bodies.
1991	A peaceful demonstration in Dili, capital of East Timor, is fired on by the Indonesian military. The protesters try to shelter behind graves in the Santa Cruz cemetery, where over 90 are gunned down. Courageous camera people capture the horror, which is broadcast internationally.
9 May 1993	Marsinah, a worker at a watch factory in East Java, leads a strike for a minimum wage and improved conditions. The military are called in and Marsinah disappears. Her mutilated body is found in nearby fields with signs of rape and torture. During this year, the government bans several major newspapers including the weekly magazine *Tempo*.
1996	Wiji Thukul, poet, arts worker and activist, disappears. His body has never been found and he is believed to have been killed during a purge by Indonesian military that left 14 people missing, presumed murdered. He had been head of the People's Art Network, a body affiliated with the opposition party's People's Democratic Party (PRD). He worked with children from the poorest areas in Central Java and his poetry was openly critical of Suharto's regime.

1997 In July, the Asian Economic Crisis hits Indonesia hard and the value of the national currency (rupiah) collapses. Despite this, Suharto's adult children maintain their corrupt business activities and increase their massive wealth, causing widespread criticism and contempt. The acronym coined to describe the activities of the Suharto family and their cronies 'KKN' (*korupsi, kolusi dan nepotisme*) is widely and openly used.

1998 In March, Suharto is re-elected by parliament for a seventh term as president, with B. J. Habibie as his vice-president. The economic crisis is out of control and mass protests increase.

On 12 May, four Trisakti University student protesters are killed by armed forces, igniting the worst urban riots and rapes in Indonesian history between 13 and 15 May. Suharto comes under increasing pressure to resign.

On 21 May, Suharto resigns and is replaced by Bacharuddin Jusuf Habibie (1936–2019) as Indonesia's third president. He initiates many reforms, including a democratic general election in 1999. He also enables East Timor to vote on whether it will remain part of Indonesia or become autonomous. His government introduces greater freedoms for trade unions and the press, which had laboured under New Order censorship for several decades.

Suharto's zero-tolerance policy of public criticism and protest suppressed civil society organisations, but, in the post-Suharto period known as Reformasi (reform or reformation), they re-surface and flourish, notably human rights and environmental groups.[15]

1998–ongoing The transition from New Order authoritarianism to democracy through the process of reform has involved the strengthening of 'guardian' institutions such as the National Human Rights Commission (Komnas HAM) and the introduction of new institutions such as the Corruption Eradication Commission and the Office of the Ombudsman. An ongoing process of judicial reform is also in process.[16]

---

15 A balanced and considered evaluation of writings about the New Order from its inception is Henk Schulte Nordholt and Gerry van Klinken, 'Introduction', in *Renegotiating Boundaries: Local Politics in Post-Suharto Indonesia*, ed. Henk Schulte Nordholt and Gerry van Klinken (Leiden: KITLV Press, 2007), 1–30, doi.org/10.1163/9789004260436_002.

16 For an assessment of these reforms and examples of their implementation, see Tim Lindsey and Helen Pausacker, eds, *Religion, Law and Intolerance in Indonesia* (London and New York: Routledge, 2016), doi.org/10.4324/9781315657356.

1999 In January, President Habibie, to the anger of Indonesia's military that had lost lives fighting in Timor, announces that East Timor will have an act of free choice. On 4 September, when a 78.5 per cent victory for the pro-independence option was announced, a widespread, well-planned campaign of murder, destruction and violence was carried out by militias backed by the Indonesian military. A few days' later, Indonesia was forced to allow an Australian-led peacekeeping force into East Timor.[17]

Habibie also appoints a committee to advise on the drafting of regional autonomy legislation. The legislation includes popularly elected local parliaments and devolution of a fixed share of locally generated revenues.

The second democratic election since 1955 consolidates the Reformasi period and sees the decline of Suharto's Golkar party.

1999–2001 K. H. Abdurrahman Wahid (1940–2009) elected Indonesia's fourth president but impeached in 2001 and replaced by his vice-president, Megawati Sukarnoputri, daughter of the first president, Sukarno.

2001 On 23 July 2001, Megawati Sukarnoputri (b. 1947) succeeds Abdurrahman Wahid as Indonesia's fifth president (2001–04).

The implementation of Habibie's decentralisation laws begins in 2001. The central government maintains authority for external defence, foreign policy, fiscal policy, judicial matters and religious affairs.

In a major shift, governors, mayors and district administrators are elected locally, not appointed from Jakarta.

The effects of decentralisation are still being assessed. The increase in local revenues was insufficient to meet the needs of education and health, resulting in increased local taxes that burden the less well-off. Cultural identity politics increased in some areas to the detriment of minority groups. On the other hand, the 'invention' of tradition has enriched some forms of artistic practice.[18] (See Map 3 for current boundaries of Indonesia's provinces.)

---

17 See accounts of this period in Chris Manning and Peter van Diermen, eds, *Indonesia in Transition: Social Aspects of Reformasi and Crisis* (Singapore: ISEAS Institute of Southeast Asian Studies, 2000), passim and especially Part II, 87–142.

18 For some of the pros and cons of decentralisation and the phenomenon known as *pemekaran* (flowering or blossoming of existing administrative units by subdivision), see Nordholt and van Klinken, 'Introduction', 15–23.

2000	In mid-2000, members of a radical Islamic movement known in Indonesia as JI (Jemaah Islamiyah), founded by two former members of Darul Islam and intent on establishing an Islamic state, begins a campaign of bomb attacks on churches in Indonesian cities. Nineteen Indonesians are killed.
2002, 2005	On 12 October 2002, suicide-bombers from JI attack two nightclubs in Bali, killing 212 people. A second bombing in Bali on 1 October 2005 kills 21 people. Indonesia's mainstream Muslim organisations condemn the violence of JI and other radical Islamic radical groups, such as Laskar Jihad (Holy War Fighters) and Front Pembela Islam (Islamic Defenders Front).
2003	Martial law is declared in Aceh to 'eradicate' GAM (Gerakan Aceh Merdeka/Free Aceh Movement), a secessionist movement operating in Aceh since 1976.
2004	After extensive public education about the meaning and process of democratic elections, a series of successfully held elections result in a new legislature and a new president, Susilo Bambang Yudhoyono (known as SBY) (b. 1949), who held office for the maximum two terms between 2004 and 2014.
	On 26 December, the Sumatra-Andaman undersea earthquake measuring 9 on the Richter scale, 30 km below sea level, occurs 160 km off the west coast of Aceh, causing a horrendous three-wave tsunami. Over 167,000 individuals in Aceh are estimated to have perished, with over 500,000 being displaced and all the population of northern Aceh suffering severe trauma. Aceh receives massive national and international disaster relief and rebuilding assistance.
2005	An international peace process between GAM representatives and the Indonesian government makes progress and a memorandum of understanding is signed in August in Helsinki as the basis for self-government for Aceh within the Republic of Indonesia.
2006	On 27 May, an undersea earthquake, magnitude 6.3 on the Richter scale, occurs 25 km south of Yogyakarta, Central Java. One of the deadliest earthquakes in Java in historic times, it causes over 5,700 deaths, injures over 200,000 and displaces over 600,000 people. More than 154,000 homes are destroyed. As in Aceh, disaster relief teams come from across Indonesia as well as from overseas.

In July, the Indonesian Parliament passes the *Law for the Government of Aceh* (replacing the special autonomy law), and Aceh holds its first elections in December. Since the beginning of the secessionist movement in 1976, between 12,000 and 20,000 Acehnese have been killed.[19]

2011 From the mid-2000s, reports of attacks on Ahmadis and Shi'a Muslims increase. In 2011, three Ahmadis are killed while police look on. Research by Indonesia's Ministry of Religion indicates that training local leaders to act as peacemakers and to resolve religious disputes before they escalate is the most effective way to avoid inter-religious violence.

2014 Joko Widodo (known as Jokowi) (b. 1961) is elected as Indonesia's seventh president and re-elected in 2019. His first presidential term focuses on initiating large infrastructure projects, such as ports, roads, bridges and railways. He also gradually reduces fuel subsidies and strengthens the economy.

2016–17 The governor of Jakarta, Chinese-Christian Ahok (full name Basuki Tjahaja Purnama) is accused of insulting the Quran under a 1965 Blasphemy Law. He is tried, convicted and sentenced to two years in gaol.[20]

2018 On 6 August, on the island of Lombok, a 6.9 Richter scale earthquake, followed by mudslides, kills more than 450 people and causes widespread damage and homelessness.

2019–21 On 28 September 2019, in Central Sulawesi, a 7.5 earthquake and tsunami, followed by soil liquefaction and mud flows, kills at least 4,340 people, with over 10,000 injured and more than 70,000 houses destroyed.

Indonesia's improved economic situation under presidents SBY and Jokowi has strengthened the middle class in numbers and complexity. There are increasing numbers of cosmopolitan, tertiary educated, urban-middle-class Indonesians who are devout, conservative Muslims. Their attitudes to the role of Islam in politics and on the public expression of Islam in their daily lives are not yet fully understood but are of critical interest to researchers and others who are analysing the apparent growth of literalist, conservative Islam in Indonesia.

19 See Aspinall, *Islam and Nation*, 2, 220–47.

20 For this case and recent research on intolerance and discrimination against minorities, see Greg Fealy and Ronit Ricci, eds, *Contentious Belonging: The Place of Minorities in Indonesia* (Singapore: ISEAS-Yusof Ishak Institute, 2019), doi.org/10.1355/9789814843478.

The influence of Muslim preachers in urban and rural mosques remains strong as shown by their role in generating criticism and condemnation of Jakarta's Governor Ahok, resulting in his trial for blasphemy.

The COVID-19 virus(es) that spread rapidly in Indonesia highlights the divide between the super-rich, who are able to access private hospital treatment; the rich, who are allocated beds in hospitals that are apparently full; ordinary Indonesians, who are brought to public clinics for treatment and, if lucky, find spaces in tents outside the hospitals; and the poor, who die where they have lived.[21]

The pandemic showcases the strength and dedication of Indonesia's civil society, which organised groups to run emergency ambulance services, improvised personal protective equipment and masks, located oxygen and administered it, and cared for individuals and their families in community-based centres. Whether earthquakes, tsunamis, landslips, floods or pandemics, Indonesia's civil society organisations provide the basis for the survival of its people, particularly the very poor.

21 World Health Organization statistics for COVID-19 in Indonesia from 3 January 2020 to 19 November 2021 are 4,252,705 confirmed cases and 143,714 deaths, although the actual numbers are believed to be much higher. See World Health Organization, COVID-19 figures for Indonesia, accessed 20 November 2021, covid19.who.int/region/searo/country/id.

Art Historiographical Introduction to Important Sources and Selected Further Reading on Modern and Contemporary Asian Art

Caroline Turner

The references below are mainly English language sources and some critical sources in Indonesian. The focus is on publications in English that examine Indonesian modern and contemporary art, but an extended set of readings on Southeast Asian and Asian modern and contemporary art more broadly is also provided. For a more detailed discussion of Indonesian art historiography, see the Introduction to this volume and essays throughout this book.

Indonesian art history today is inevitably part of the larger art historiography still being written on Southeast Asian, Asian and global art histories. National art histories were dominant and are still important but regional art histories and attempts to develop a new global art history are increasingly widening the focus of research and writing. Chaitanya Sambrani has indicated that sophisticated traditions of art historical scholarship already existed in many Asian nations, but were largely confined to national boundaries until recent times.[1] Yet there were historical artistic connections between Asian nations in art, as Sambrani

1 Chaitanya Sambrani, 'An Experiment in Connectivity: From the "West Heavens" to the "Middle Kingdom"', in *Contemporary Asian Art and Exhibitions: Connectivities and World-Making*, ed. Michelle Antoinette and Caroline Turner (Canberra: ANU Press, 2014), 89–107, doi.org/10.22459/CAAE.11.2014. See also John Clark, *Modern Asian Art* (Honolulu: University of Hawai'i Press, 1998).

and Singaporean scholar T. K. Sabapathy have noted.[2] There are many issues to be explored within this larger framework of regional art, including questions of overlapping and parallel art histories, especially in relation to modern art, as addressed by speakers at John Clark's groundbreaking 1991 conference, a project of the Humanities Research Centre at The Australian National University, entitled 'Modernism and Post-Modernism in Asian Art'. This was the first such international conference outside Asia to address the history and current developments in Asian modern art. While much debate has focused on modern and contemporary art, it has long been realised by scholars that there is a need to link historical, modern and contemporary art histories in Asia.

There have been connections and exchanges in the Asian region through the centuries. T. K. Sabapathy has commented in relation to Southeast Asia (but his comments can also be applied to the whole region of Asia and to art and culture): 'Movements of peoples, languages, technologies, and belief systems across boundaries and seas within South-East Asia have been continuous over the millennia'.[3]

In the postcolonial world that emerged at the end of World War II, the Asian region developed its own exhibitions and forums for art.[4] It is now accepted that exhibitions are important sites for art historical formation and that the role of art museums, both public and private, has also been critical in the new art histories under construction in Asia.[5] In the last 30 years, biennales, of which there are now a significant number in Asia, have become key sites for audiences to view contemporary art across the Asian region. Selected key biennales are listed below.

The 1990s, in particular, witnessed a rethinking of cultural frameworks, including the previous domination by Europe and North America of modern and contemporary art debates—often referred to at the time

2 Sambrani, 'An Experiment in Connectivity', notes links between India and Japan. See also T.K. Sabapathy, 'Developing Regionalist Perspectives in South-East Asian Art Historiography', *Second Asia-Pacific Triennial* (Brisbane: Queensland Art Gallery, 1996), 13–17; T.K. Sabapathy, ed., *Modernity and Beyond: Themes in Southeast Asian Art* (Singapore: Singapore Art Museum, 1996); Caroline Turner, 'Introduction Part 1', in Antoinette and Turner, *Contemporary Asian Art and Exhibitions*, 1–22.

3 Sabapathy, 'Developing Regionalist Perspectives', 17. An early example he cites was the connections between Indonesia and Cambodia and the influence of Borobudur on Angkor Wat.

4 For a discussion of these developments, see Caroline Turner and Jen Webb, 'Frameworks and Contexts', in *Art and Human Rights: Contemporary Asian Contexts* (Manchester: Manchester University Press, 2016), 1–35, doi.org/10.7765/9781526100719.00005.

5 See Turner, 'Introduction Part 1'.

as the 'Euro-American paradigm'. For a discussion of this issue, and the beginnings of a more global art history, see the discussion and references in Chapter 7 (this volume).

One of the critical questions is whether a new global art history can be written. John Clark points to 'the still largely absent discourse of a worlded art history that takes account of Asia'.[6] But, increasingly, those writing on global art today, such as Hans Belting and Terry Smith, are including art from Asia as well as Africa, South America and art from other areas that used to be considered on the 'periphery' of the art world. Smith makes the convincing point that contemporary art is no longer one kind of art, but is 'becoming—perhaps for the first time in history—truly an art of the world', meaning it comes from the whole world.[7] The selection of the Indonesian group *ruangrupa* to curate the 2022 iteration of one of the postwar world's most influential contemporary art exhibitions, *Documenta* in Germany, is another indication of a substantial change in the art world, although the exhibition proved controversial.[8]

New definitions of the 'modern' and the 'contemporary' in Asian art remain a source of debate in conferences and symposia, exhibitions and publications in the region and beyond.[9] This is a complex task, as Philippines' curator Patrick Flores notes in a foreword, 'An Art History to be Named', to John Clark's monumental new book, *The Asian Modern*.[10]

Some Key Bibliographies

For Indonesian art, see resources listed in the Introduction and more generally throughout this volume. See also the bibliography in Elly Kent's new book, *Artists and the People: Ideologies of Art in Indonesia*

6 John Clark, 'The Worlding of the Asian Modern', in Antoinette and Turner, *Contemporary Asian Art and Exhibitions,* 67–88, 67.

7 Terry Smith, 'Currents of World-Making in Contemporary Art', *World Art* 1, no. 2 (2011): 171–88, 188, doi.org/10.1080/21500894.2011.602712. See Chapter 7 (this volume) for discussion of these issues.

8 See Wulan Dirgantoro and Elly Kent, 'We Need to Talk! Art, Offence and Politics in Documenta 15', *New Mandala*, 29 June 2022, accessed 11 September 2022, newmandala.org/we-need-to-talk-art-offence-and-politics-in-documenta-15/.

9 Japan has been an early leader in these debates and more recently Singapore. In the Australian context, the conferences held in 1993, 1996 and 1999 in association with the Asia Pacific Triennial exhibitions were also important early platforms for connecting to Asian discourses.

10 See foreword by Patrick Flores in John Clark, *The Asian Modern* (Singapore: National Gallery Singapore, 2021), 3–6.

(Singapore: NUS Press, 2022), and the Indonesian Visual Art Archive.[11] Astri Wright's comprehensive framing of Indonesian art historiography includes references on classical and traditional art as well as modern and contemporary art. The bibliography from Wright's 1994 book, *Soul, Spirit, and Mountain: Preoccupations of Contemporary Indonesian Painters*,[12] is now available online. See also the chapter by Wright, 'The Arc of My Field Is a Rainbow with an Expanding Twist and All Kinds of Creatures Dancing: The Growing Inclusivity of Indonesian Art History' in Eric Tagliacozzo's edited collection, *Producing Indonesia: The State of the Field of Indonesian Studies* (Ithaca NY: Cornell University Press Southeast Asia Program Publications at Cornell University, 2014).[13]

The majority of authors in this book place the subject of their chapters in the context of the literature on that subject. Some chapters have extensive bibliographical references to politics, society and history as well as art. See, for example, Introduction, Chapters 1, 2, 7 and 9.

On Asia, see, in particular, the bibliographies in the John Clark Archive at the Asia Art Archive Hong Kong.[14]

Archives, Collections and Resources

The Galeri Nasional Indonesia[15] and the new Museum MACAN (Modern and Contemporary Art in Nusantara)[16] have major collections of Indonesian art. The Claire Holt Archive at Cornell University in the US is a significant source for Indonesian art.[17] The Asia Art Archive based

11 Indonesian Visual Art Archive, 'Home', accessed 22 January 2022, archive.ivaa-online.org/.

12 Astri Wright, *Soul, Spirit, and Mountain: Preoccupations of Contemporary Indonesian Painters* (Kuala Lumpur and New York: Oxford University Press, 1994), 256–65. See 'Modern and Contemporary Indonesian Art Bibliography (1994)', accessed 25 January 2022, www.artdesigncafe.com/modern-contemporary-indonesian-art-bibliography-1994.

13 Also available online, see Eric Tagliacozzo, ed., *Producing Indonesia: The State of the Field of Indonesian Studies* (Ithaca NY: Cornell University Press, 2014), accessed 25 January 2022, www.jstor.org/stable/10.7591/j.ctt20d87jt.

14 'John Clark Archive', Asia Art Archive, accessed 25 January 2022. aaa.org.hk/en/collections/search/archive/john-clark-archive.

15 Galeri Nasional Indonesia, 'Home', accessed 25 January 2022, galeri-nasional.or.id/.

16 Museum MACAN, 'Home', accessed 22 January 2022, www.museummacan.org/.

17 Cornell University Library, 'The Claire Holt Papers', accessed 22 January 2022, rmc.library.cornell.edu/holt/.

in Hong Kong is a critical source of resource material on modern and contemporary Asian art.[18] Also see the previously mentioned Indonesian Visual Art Archive.[19]

Japan was an early leader in bringing Asian artists together in the postwar world and the Japan Foundation Asia Art Archive[20] provides extensive resources on exhibitions and conferences of great interest in the history of Asian modern and contemporary art. The Queensland Art Gallery | Gallery of Modern Art, Brisbane, Australia, has an extensive collection of art and an archive on that art from different parts of Asia collected from the Asia Pacific Triennial exhibitions since the early 1990s, which it has begun digitising.[21] The Fukuoka Asian Art Museum in Japan[22] has been collecting for even longer and also has a superb collection, while the National Gallery Singapore[23]and Singapore Art Museum[24] are collecting and documenting Southeast Asian art in-depth. Singapore has been a key force in intra-Asian art and cultural exchange. Southeast Asian art exchanges grew out of ASEAN exhibitions and Singapore also has strong links with East Asia.

The list of sources that follows contains scholarly publications and important recent doctoral dissertations; names of influential regional art institutions; art exhibition catalogues from critical exhibitions; and websites for archival and research resources in Asian art, both within art museums and institutions, and also from independent research collectives.

Museums in Asia have played a vital role in initiating new exchanges, exhibitions and scholarship. The hundreds of new museums and art institutions that now exist or are in planning across Asia have rich resources, providing significant infrastructure and with the potential to be shapers of culture through art networks and exhibitions across the region. For example, networks were developed by the Japan Foundation through its Asia Center in Tokyo for exhibitions and conferences in the 1990s. ASEAN has provided opportunities for exchange. The Singapore Art

18 Asia Art Archive, 'Home', accessed 22 January 2022, aaa.org.hk/en.

19 Indonesian Visual Art Archive, 'Home', accessed 22 January 2022, archive.ivaa-online.org/.

20 'Japan Foundation Asia Art Archive', Japan Foundation, accessed 22 January 2022, www.jpf.go.jp/e/publish/asia_exhibition_history/index.html.

21 Queensland Art Gallery | Gallery of Modern Art, 'Library: Asian and Pacific Art', accessed 22 January 2022, www.qagoma.qld.gov.au/learn/research/library.

22 Fukuoka Asian Art Museum, 'Home', accessed 22 January 2022, faam.city.fukuoka.lg.jp/en/.

23 Singapore National Gallery Singapore, 'Home', accessed 25 January 2022, www.nationalgallery.sg/.

24 Singapore Art Museum, 'Home', accessed 25 January 2022, www.singaporeartmuseum.sg/.

Museum has, since 1996, been a centre for Southeast Asian contemporary art, complemented by the National Gallery, Singapore, from 2015. A crucial source of knowledge about contemporary Asian art is the many biennales that have emerged in Asia. For a listing of Asian biennales and world biennales, see the Biennial Foundation's extensive web listing.[25] In Indonesia, for example, the Jakarta- and Yogyakarta-based biennales have played a central role in Indonesian contemporary art. The Jakarta Biennale grew out of the *Grand Exhibition of Indonesian Painting* (Pameran Besar Seni Lukis Indonesia) at the Jakarta Arts Centre, Taman Ismail Marzuki (1968). The name was changed to the Jakarta Biennale (painting) in 1975, then Biennale Fine Arts in 1993. The Biennale Jogja began in 1988 but was restructured in 2011. For Asian biennales, see the listing of world biennales below.

Key Exhibitions Exploring Similarities and Differences in Asian Art

- *Asian Modernism: Diverse Developments in Indonesia, the Philippines and Thailand*, Japan Foundation, Tokyo, 1995
- *The Birth of Modern Art in Southeast Asia: Artists and Movements*, Fukuoka Art Museum, 1997
- *Visions and Enchantment: Southeast Asian Paintings*, exhibition catalogue, Singapore Art Museum in Association with Christie's Singapore, 2000
- *Negotiating Home, History and Nation: Two Decades of Contemporary Art in Southeast Asia 1991–2011*, exhibition catalogue, Singapore Art Museum, 2011
- *SUNSHOWER: Contemporary Art from Southeast Asia 1980s to Now*, National Art Center, Tokyo, Mori Art Museum, and the Japan Foundation Asia Center, 2017
- *Awakenings: Art in Society in Asia 1960s–1990s,* National Gallery Singapore, National Museum of Modern Art, Tokyo, National Museum of Modern and Contemporary Art, Korea, the Japan Foundation Asia Center, 2019

25 See 'Directory of Biennials', Biennial Foundation, accessed 22 January 2022, www.biennialfoundation.org/network/biennial-map/.

Biennales (by Starting Year)

Early biennales in Asia included:

- Tokyo Biennale (1952–70; revived in a different form in 2020)[26]
- Indian Triennial (1968)
- Jakarta Biennale (1975, changed form in 1993)
- Bangladesh Biennale (1981)
- Biennale Jogja (1988, changed form in 2011).

The Fukuoka Art Museum initiated recurring exhibitions of contemporary Asian art from the late 1970s.

Important biennales and triennales in the last decade of the twentieth century and the early twenty-first century included:

- Asia Pacific Triennial, Queensland Art Gallery, Brisbane (1993)
- Gwangju Biennale (1995)
- Shanghai Biennale (1996)
- Taipei Biennale (1998)
- Fukuoka Triennale (1999)
- Yokohama Triennale (2001)
- Busan Biennale (2002)
- Guangzhou Triennial (2002)
- Beijing Biennale (2003)
- Singapore Biennale (2006)
- Kochi-Muziris Biennale (2012)
- Bangkok Biennale (2018).

A World Biennial Forum in Gwangju, South Korea, in 2012 had representatives from all over Asia and there are now at least 150 biennales worldwide, many of them in Asia.[27]

---

26 See 'Why Tokyo Biennale? Visions for 2020', Tokyo Art Beat, accessed 25 January 2022, www.tokyoartbeat.com/event/2018/460E.en. The website states:

> The Japan International Art Exhibition (Tokyo Biennale) was an international exhibition that went on in the Tokyo Metropolitan Art Museum during the post-war reconstruction period. Within its continuous years of exhibition, the 10th running in 1970 carrying the theme, 'Between man and matter' left a profound trace in the history of Japanese art.

27 See 'Directory of Biennials'.

Selected Further Reading on Modern and Contemporary Asian Art[28]

Adipurnomo, Nindityo, Priyambudi Sulistiyanto and Moelyono. *Retak Wajah Anak-Anak Bendungan* [Disintegrating faces of the children of the dam]. Yogyakarta: Cemeti Art House, 2011.

Antoinette, Michelle. 'Deterritorializing Aesthetics: International Art and its New Cosmopolitanisms, from an Indonesian Perspective'. In *Cosmopatriots: On Distant Belongings and Close Encounters*, edited by Edwin Jurriëns and Jeroen de Kloet, 205–33. Amsterdam: Rodopi, 2007. doi.org/10.1163/9789401205559_011.

Antoinette, Michelle. *Reworlding Art History: Encounters with Contemporary Southeast Asian Art after 1990*. Amsterdam & New York: Rodopi, 2014. doi.org/10.1163/9789401211963.

Antoinette, Michelle and Caroline Turner, eds. *Contemporary Asian Art and Exhibitions: Connectivities and World-Making*. Canberra: ANU Press, 2014. doi.org/10.22459/CAAE.11.2014.

Arbuckle, Heidi. 'Performing Emiria Sunassa: Reframing the Female Subject in Post/colonial Indonesia'. PhD diss., University of Melbourne, 2011.

Art Asia Pacific (1993–).

Asia Art Archive. 'Home'. Accessed 22 January 2022. aaa.org.hk/en.

Asia Pacific Triennial of Contemporary Art. Catalogues of the First, Second, Third, Fourth, Fifth, Sixth, Seventh, Eighth, Ninth and Tenth *Asia Pacific Triennial of Contemporary Art*. Brisbane: Queensland Art Gallery | Gallery of Modern Art, 1993–2021.

Asia Pacific Triennial of Contemporary Art, Caroline Turner and Rhana Devenport, eds. *Present Encounters: Papers from the Conference of the Second Asia-Pacific Triennial of Contemporary Art, 1996*. Brisbane: Queensland Art Gallery, 1996.

Awakenings: Art in Society in Asia 1960s–1990s. Exhibition catalogue. National Gallery Singapore, National Museum of Modern Art, Tokyo, National Museum of Modern and Contemporary Art, Korea, the Japan Foundation Asia Center, 2019.

28 See also references in the individual essays in this volume.

Babington, Jaklyn and Carol Cains. *Contemporary Worlds: Indonesia.* Exhibition catalogue. Canberra: National Gallery of Australia, 2019.

Badham, Marnie. *Cultural Development, Community Arts and Creative Empowerment.* Yogyakarta, Indonesia: Indonesian Visual Arts Archive KUNCI, 2014.

'Bandung Artist Collection'. Cornell University Library. Accessed 22 January 2022. digital.library.cornell.edu/collections/bandung?fbclid=IwAR2BEqxK6sAH7c-29cuvt-dmUTvbh0ZUX3jKnN2q7OFY-X7951WQX1zFTq0ni.

Belting, Hans. *Art History after Modernism.* Chicago: University of Chicago Press, 2003.

Belting, Hans and Andrea Buddensieg. *The Global Art World: Audiences, Markets and Museums.* Ostfildern: Hatje Cantz, 2009.

Belting, Hans, Andrea Buddensieg and Peter Weibel, eds. *The Global Contemporary and the Rise of New Art Worlds.* Cambridge, Mass.: MIT Press Ltd, 2013.

Bennett, James. *Crescent Moon: Islamic Art and Civilisation in Southeast Asia Bulan Sabit: Seni dan Peradaban Islam di Asia Tenggara.* Adelaide: Art Gallery of South Australia; Canberra: National Gallery of Australia, 2005.

Bennett, James. 'Making Art in Early Modern Java (16th–19th century): A New Reading'. PhD diss., University of Adelaide, 2021.

Bianpoen, Carla, Farah Wardani and Wulan Dirgantoro. *Indonesian Women Artists: The Curtain Opens.* Jakarta: Yayasan Senirupa Indonesia, c. 2007.

Bollansee, Marc and Enin Supriyanto. *Indonesian Contemporary Art Now.* Singapore: SNP Editions, 2007.

Burhan, M. A., J. Suyono and U. Hartati. *Masterpieces of the Indonesia National Gallery.* Jakarta: Galeri Nasional Indonesia, 2012.

Campbell, Siobhan. 'Women, Tradition and Art History in Bali'. *Southeast of Now: Directions in Contemporary and Modern Art in Asia* 3, no. 1 (2019): 77–101. doi.org/10.1353/sen.2019.0004.

Carroll, Alison. 'An Examination of the Significance of Soviet Socialist Realist Art and Practice in the Asia Pacific Region'. PhD diss., University of Melbourne, 2016.

Carroll, Alison. *The Revolutionary Century: Art in Asia 1900–2000.* South Yarra: Macmillan Australia, 2010.

Cemeti Institute for Art and Society. 'Home'. Accessed 22 January 2022. cemeti.art/.

Chiu, Melissa and Benjamin Genocchio, eds. *Contemporary Art in Asia: A Critical Reader*. Cambridge, Mass.; London, England: MIT Press, 2011.

Clark, Christine. 'Distinctive Voices: Artist-Initiated Spaces and Projects'. In *Art and Social Change: Contemporary Art in Asia and the Pacific*, edited by Caroline Turner, 554–68. Canberra: Pandanus Press, 2005.

Clark, Christine and Caroline Turner. 'Cross-Cultural Exchanges and Interconnections from the 1980s and 1990s: ARX and the APT'. *Australian and New Zealand Journal of Art* 16, no. 2 (2016): 167–84. doi.org/10.1080/14434318.2016.1240649.

Clark, Christine, Elly Kent, Viviana Mejia Montoya, Weng Choy Lee, Hendro Wiyanto and Adeline Ooi. *Beyond the Self: Contemporary Portraiture from Asia*. Canberra: National Portrait Gallery, 2012.

Clark, John. *The Asian Modern*. Singapore: National Gallery Singapore, 2021.

Clark, John. *Asian Modernities: Chinese and Thai Art Compared, 1980 to 1999*. Sydney: Power Publications, 2010.

Clark, John. 'Bibliographies, Timelines and Notes'. John Clark Archive, Asia Art Archive. Accessed 22 January 2022. aaa.org.hk/en/collections/search/archive/john-clark-archive-bibliographies-timelines-and-notes.

Clark, John. *Modern Asian Art*. Sydney: Craftsman House G+B Arts International, 1998.

Clark, John, ed. *Modernity in Asian Art*. University of Sydney East Asian Series, no. 7. Sydney: Wild Peony, 1993. (Authors on Indonesia: Anthony Forge, Astri Wright and Helena Spanjaard.)

Clark, John. 'Negotiating Change in Recent Southeast Asian Art'. *Southeast of Now: Directions in Contemporary and Modern Art in Asia* 2, no 1 (March 2018): 43–92. doi.org/10.1353/sen.2018.0002.

Clark, John. 'The Worlding of the Asian Modern'. In *Contemporary Asian Art and Exhibitions: Connectivities and World-Making*, edited by Michelle Antoinette and Caroline Turner, 67–88. Canberra: ANU Press, 2014. doi.org/10.22459/CAAE.11.2014.04.

Clark, John, Maurizio Peleggi and T. K. Sabapathy, eds. *Eye of the Beholder: Reception, Audience, and Practice of Modern Asian Art*. University of Sydney East Asian Series, no. 15. Sydney: Wild Peony, 2006.

Cornell University Library. 'The Claire Holt Papers'. Accessed 22 January 2022. rmc.library.cornell.edu/holt/.

Count 10 Before You Say Asia. Asian Art after Postmodernism. International Symposium 2008 Report. Tokyo Japan Foundation, 2009.

Cox, Matthew. 'The Javanese Self in Portraiture from 1880-1955'. PhD diss., University of Sydney, 2015.

Crossing Boundaries: Bali: A Window to Twentieth Century Indonesian Art. Exhibition catalogue. Asia Society Austral/Asia Centre, 2002.

Desai, Vishakha, ed. *Asian Art History in the Twenty-First Century.* Williamstown, Mass.: Sterling and Francine Clark Institute, 2007.

'Directory of Biennials'. Biennial Foundation. Accessed 22 January 2022. www.biennialfoundation.org/network/biennial-map/.

Dirgantoro, Wulan. 'Aesthetics of Silence: Exploring Trauma in Indonesian Art after 1965'. In *Ambitious Alignments: New Histories of Southeast Asian Art, 1945–1990*, edited by Stephen Whiteman, Sarena Abdullah, Yvonne Low and Phoebe Scott, 199–224. Australia: Power Publications and the National Gallery of Singapore, 2018.

Dirgantoro, Wulan. 'Arts: Visual Arts and Artists: Indonesia'. *Encyclopedia of Women & Islamic Cultures.* General Editor Suad Joseph. Brill Online, 2012. EWIC-contributors. Accessed 22 January 2022. referenceworks.brillonline.com/entries/encyclopedia-of-women-and-islamic-cultures/arts-visual-arts-and-artists-indonesia-EWICCOM_001420.

Dirgantoro, Wulan. *Feminisms and Indonesian Contemporary Art: Defining Experiences.* Amsterdam: Amsterdam University Press, 2017. doi.org/10.1017/9789048526994.

Dysart, Dynah and Hannah Fink, eds. *Asian Women Artists.* Sydney: Craftsman House, 1996.

Elliott, David. *Art & Trousers: Tradition and Modernity in Contemporary Asian Art.* Hong Kong: Artasiapacific, 2021.

Ewington, Julie. 'Between the Cracks: Art and Method in Southeast Asia'. *Art Asia Pacific* 3, no. 4 (1996): 57–63.

Fischer, Joseph. *Modern Indonesian Art: Three Generations of Tradition and Change 1945–1990.* Jakarta: KIAS Festival of Indonesia: 1990.

Flores, Patrick D. *Past Peripheral: Curation in Southeast Asia.* Singapore: NUS Museum, National University of Singapore, 2008, 2009.

Fontein, Jan, R. Soekmono and Edi Sedyawati. *The Sculpture of Indonesia.* Washington: National Gallery of Art and New York: Harry N. Abrams, 1990.

4A Centre for Contemporary Asian Art. 'About 4a'. Accessed 22 January 2022. www.4a.com.au/about-4a/.

Foulcher, Keith. *Social Commitment in Literature and the Arts: 'The Indonesian Institute of People's Culture' 1950–1965.* Monash University, Centre of Southeast Asian Studies, 1986. Published in Indonesian in 2000 as *Komitmen Sosial dalam Sastera dan Seni: Sejarah LEKRA 1950–1965.*

Fukuoka Asian Art Museum. Catalogues of Asian Art exhibitions, Fukuoka Art Museum, late 1970s–1999 and catalogues of the Fukuoka Asian Art Triennale, Fukuoka, from 1999–ongoing. Fukuoka Asian Art Museum, Japan.

Fukuoka Asian Art Museum. 'Home'. Accessed 22 January 2022. faam.city.fukuoka.lg.jp/en/.

Furuichi, Yasuko, ed. *Alternatives 2005: Contemporary Art Spaces in Asia.* Kyoto & Tokyo: Tankosha Publishing Co., 2004.

Furuichi, Yasuko. *Asian Contemporary Art Reconsidered.* Tokyo: Japan Foundation Asia Center, 1998.

Galeri Nasional Indonesia. 'Home'. Accessed 22 January 2022. www.galeri-nasional.or.id.

Gao, Minglu, et al. *Inside Out: New Chinese Art.* Exhibition catalogue. Berkeley: University of California Press, 1998.

Gardner, Anthony and Charles Green. *Biennials, Triennials, and Documenta: The Exhibitions that Created Contemporary Art.* Hoboken, New Jersey: Wiley-Blackwell, 2016.

Geertz, Hildred. *Images of Power: Balinese Paintings Made for Gregory Bateson and Margaret Mead.* Honolulu: University of Hawai'i Press, 1994.

Geertz, Hildred and Christopher Hill. *Survival and Change: Three Generations of Balinese Painters.* Canberra: Pandanus Books, 2006.

George, Kenneth M. *Picturing Islam: Art and Ethics in a Muslim Lifeworld.* Chichester, West Sussex, UK; Malden, Mass.: Wiley-Blackwell, 2010. doi.org/10.1002/9781444318265.

George, Kenneth M. 'Some Things That Have Happened to the Sun after September 1965: Politics and the Interpretation of an Indonesian Painting'. *Comparative Studies in Society and History* 39, no. 4 (1997): 603–34. doi.org/10.1017/S001041750002082X.

Girard-Geslan, Maud, ed. *Indonesian Gold: Treasures from the National Museum, Jakarta.* Published in association with an exhibition held at the Queensland Art Gallery from 26 March – 16 May 1999 and at the Art Gallery of New South Wales from 3 June to 1 August 1999.

Gladston, Paul. *Contemporary Chinese Art: A Critical History.* London: Reaktion; and Chicago: University of Chicago Press, 2014.

Guillermo, Alice. *Image to Meaning.* Ateneo de Manila University Press, 2001.

Guillermo, Alice. *Protest/Revolutionary Art in the Philippines 1970–1990.* Quezon City: University of the Philippines Press, 2001.

'Gwangju Biennale'. Biennale Foundation. Accessed 22 January 2022. www.biennialfoundation.org/biennials/gwangju-biennale/.

Harsono, FX. 'Tema Kerakyatan dalam Seni Lukis Indonesia, Sejak Persagi hingga Kini'. MA diss., Jakarta Art Institute.

Hasan, Asikin, Agung Kurniawan, Aminuddin T. Siregar, Amanda Katherine Rath, Christine Clark, Anusapati, Hong Djien Oei, et al. *Exploring Vacuum: 1988–2003, 15 Years Cemeti Art House*, edited by S. Situmorang, Elly Kent, Mella Jaarsma and Nindityo Adipurnomo. Yogyakarta: Cemeti Art House, 2003.

Hashmi, Salima. *Hanging Fire: Contemporary Art from Pakistan.* New York: Asia Society, 2009.

Hashmi, Salima. *Unveiling the Visible: Lives and Works of Women Artists of Pakistan.* Lahore: Sang-i-Meel Publications, 2002.

Heryanto, Ariel. 'The Impossibility of History?'. In *Identity and Pleasure: The Politics of Indonesian Screen Culture*, 106–32. Singapore: Kyoto University and NUS Press, 2014. doi.org/10.2307/j.ctv1qv1rz.9.

Hjorth, Larissa, Natalie King and Mami Kataoka, eds. *Art in the Asia-Pacific: Intimate Publics.* New York & London: Routledge, 2014. doi.org/10.4324/9781315858104.

Hoffie, Pat. 'A New Tide Turning: Australia in the Region, 1993–2003'. In *Art and Social Change: Contemporary Art in Asia and the Pacific*, edited by Caroline Turner, 516–41. Canberra: Pandanus Books, 2005.

Holt, Claire. *Art in Indonesia: Continuities and Change.* Ithaca, NY: Cornell University Press, 1967.

Hooker, Virginia. '"By the Pen!": Spreading *'ilm* in Indonesia through Qur'anic calligraphy'. In *'Ilm: Science, Religion and Art in Islam*, edited by Samer Akkach, 81–97. University of Adelaide Press, South Australia, 2019. doi.org/10.20851/ilm-1-05.

Hooker, Virginia Matheson, ed. *Culture and Society in New Order Indonesia.* Kuala Lumpur: Oxford University Press, 1993.

Hooker, Virginia Matheson. 'Expression: Creativity despite Restraint'. In *Indonesia beyond Suharto: Polity, Economy, Society, Transition*, edited by Donald K. Emmerson, 265–68. Armonk, New York: M.E. Sharpe, 1999.

Hooker, Virginia. 'Seeing with the "Eyes of the Heart": *Dhikr, Fikr* and Insight in Indonesian Islamic Art'. In *Nazar: Vision, Belief and Perception in Islamic Cultures*, edited by Samer Akkach, 88–119. Leiden: Brill, 2022. doi.org/10.1163/9789004499485_006.

Hou, Hanru and Hans–Ulrich Obrist, eds. *Cities on the Move.* Exhibition catalogue. Ostfildern–Ruit: Gerd Hatje, 1997.

Huangfu, Binghui, ed. *Text and Subtext: Contemporary Art and Asian Woman.* Singapore: Earl Lu Gallery, 2000.

Hujatnikajennong, Agung. 'The Contemporary Turns: Indonesian Contemporary Art of the 1980s'. In *Negotiating Home, History and Nation: Two Decades of Contemporary Art in Southeast Asia 1991–2001*, edited by Iola Lenzi, 85–90. Singapore: Singapore Art Museum, 2011.

Hujatnikajennong, Agung and Charles Esche. *Art Turns. World Turns.* Jakarta: Museum Macan, 2017.

Indonesian Visual Art Archive. 'Home'. Accessed 22 January 2022. archive.ivaa-online.org/.

Indonesische Moderne Kunst, Indonesian Modern Art, Indonesian Painting since 1945. Amsterdam: Gate Foundation,1993.

Ingham, Susan. 'Going Global: Indonesian Visual Art in the 1990s'. Accessed 22 January 2022. www.reformasiart.com/.

Isabella, Brigitta. 'The Politics of Friendship: Modern Art in Indonesia's Cultural Diplomacy, 1950–65'. In *Ambitious Alignments: New Histories of Southeast Asian Art, 1945–1990*, edited by Stephen H. Whiteman, Sarena Abdullah, Yvonne Low and Phoebe Scott, 83–105. Singapore: Power Publications and National Gallery Singapore, 2018.

Jaarsma, Mella. 'The Search for Stable Ground in Indonesia's Art Scene'. In *Concept Context Contestation: Art and the Collective in Southeast Asia*, edited by Iola Lenzi, 184–85. Bangkok: Bangkok Art and Cultural Centre, 2014.

'Japan Foundation Asian Art Archive'. Japan Foundation. Accessed 22 January 2022. www.jpf.go.jp/e/publish/asia_exhibition_history/index.html.

Japan Foundation. *Under Construction*. Tokyo: The Japan Foundation Asia Center and Tokyo Opera City Cultural Foundation, 2002.

Jessup, Helen Ibbitson. *Court Arts of Indonesia*. New York, NY: Asia Society Galleries, H. N. Abrams, 1990.

Jurriëns, Edwin. 'Gendering the Environmental Artivism: *Ekofeminisme* and *Unjuk Rasa* of Arahmaiani's Art'. *Southeast of Now: Directions in Contemporary and Modern Art in Asia* 4, no. 2 (2020): 3–38. doi.org/10.1353/sen.2020.0006.

Jurriëns, Edwin. 'Urban Transition through Indonesian Art: From the Generation of '66 to the Millennials'. *World Art* 11, no. 2 (2021): 229–54. doi.org/10.1080/21500894.2021.1893806.

Jurriëns, Edwin and Jeroen de Kloet, eds. *Cosmopatriots: On Distant Belongings and Close Encounters*. Amsterdam and New York: Rodopi, 2007. doi.org/10.1163/9789401205559.

Kam, Garrett, ed. *Modern Indonesian Art: From Raden Saleh to the Present Day*. Bali, Indonesia: Koes Artbooks, 2006.

Kapur, Geeta. *When Was Modernism: Essays on Contemporary Cultural Practice in India*. New Delhi: Tulika, 2000.

Kee, Joan. 'What Is Feminist about Contemporary Asian Women's Art?'. In *Global Feminisms: New Directions in Contemporary Art*, edited by Maura Reilly and Linda Nochlin, 107–22. London: Merrell Publishers Ltd., 2007.

Kent, Elly. *Artists and the People: Ideologies of Art in Indonesia*. Singapore: NUS Press, 2022.

Kent, Ellen. 'Critical Recycling: Post-Consumer Waste as Medium and Meaning in Contemporary Indonesian Art'. *Southeast of Now: Directions in Contemporary and Modern Art in Asia* 4, no. 1 (March 2020): 73–98. doi.org/10.1353/sen.2020.0003.

Kent, Ellen. 'Entanglement: Individual and Participatory Art Practice in Indonesia'. PhD diss., The Australian National University, 2016.

Kent, Ellen. 'Looking for Indonesia in Contemporary Art'. In *Contemporary Worlds: Indonesia*, edited by Jaklyn Babington and Carol Cains, 23–26. Canberra: National Gallery of Australia, 2019.

Kent, Elly. 'Visual Arts and Artists: Indonesia'. *Encyclopedia of Women & Islamic Cultures*. General Editor Suad Joseph. Brill Online, 2019. Accessed 22 January 2022. referenceworks.brillonline.com/entries/encyclopedia-of-women-and-islamic-cultures/arts-visual-arts-and-artists-indonesia-COM_002173?s.num=2&s.f.s2_parent=s.f.book.encyclopedia-of-women-and-islamic-cultures&s.q=Kent.

Kent, Elly and F. Prasetyo. '"SIASAT"—Artistic Tactics for Transgression on State Authority'. In *Paririmbon Jatiwangi,* edited by Grace Samboh. Majalengka: Yayasan Daun Salambar, 2016.

Khairuddin, Nur Hanim, Beverly Yong, Yap Sau Bin and Simon Soon, eds. *Narratives in Malaysian Art, Vol. 4: Perspectives*. RogueArt, 2019.

Kim, Youngna. *Modern and Contemporary Art in Korea: Tradition, Modernity and Identity*. Elizabeth, New Jersey: Hollym Corporation, 2005.

Knol, Meta, Remco Raben and Kitty Zijlmans, eds. *Beyond the Dutch: Indonesia, the Netherlands and the Visual Arts, from 1900 until Now*. Amsterdam: KIT Publishers; Utrecht: Centraal Museum, 2009.

Kraus, Werner. 'First Steps to Modernity: The Javanese Painter Raden Saleh (1811–1880)'. In *Eye of the Beholder: Reception, Audience, and Practice of Modern Asian Art,* edited by John Clark, Maurizzio Peleggi and T.K. Sabapathy, 29–55. University of Sydney: Wild Peony, 2006.

Kraus, Werner. 'Raden Saleh's Interpretation of the *Arrest of Diponegoro*: An Example of Indonesian "Proto-Nationalist" Modernism'. *Archipel* 69 (2005): 259–94. doi.org/10.3406/arch.2005.3934.

Kusnadi. 'Basic Foundations of Contemporary Indonesian Art'. *ASEAN Art Exhibition: Third ASEAN Exhibition of Painting and Photography*. Manila, 1984.

Kuss, Alexandra and Rizki Zaelani. *Awas! Recent Art from Indonesia*. Yogyakarta: Cemeti Art Foundation, 2002.

Kwok, Kian Chow. *Channels & Confluences: A History of Singapore Art*. Singapore Art Museum, 1995.

Lenzi, Iola, ed. *Concept Context Contestation: Art and the Collective in Southeast Asia*. Bangkok: Bangkok Art and Cultural Centre, 2014.

Lenzi, Iola. 'The Contemporary Turn in Hanoi, Vietnam, 1989–2002: Vu Dan Tan, Nguyen Van Cuong, Salon Natasha, and doi moi-in-art'. PhD diss., Nanyang Technological University, Singapore, 2020.

Lenzi, Iola ed. *Negotiating Home, History and Nation: Two Decades of Contemporary Art in Southeast Asia 1991–2011.* Singapore Art Museum, 2011.

Lindsay, Jennifer and Maya H.T. Liem, eds. *Heirs to World Culture: Being Indonesian, 1950–1965.* Leiden: Brill, 2012. doi.org/10.26530/OAPEN_403204.

Low, Yvonne. 'Women Artists: Becoming Professional in Singapore, Malaya and Indonesia'. PhD diss., University of Sydney, 2015.

Low, Yvonne, Roger Nelson and Clare Veal. 'Editorial Introduction: Gender in Southeast Asian Art Histories'. *Southeast of Now: Directions in Contemporary and Modern Art in Asia* 3, no. 1 (March 2019): 1–11. doi.org/10.1353/sen.2019.0000.

MAAP-Media Art Asia Pacific. 'About'. Accessed 22 January 2022. www.maap.org.au/about-maap/.

Maxwell, Robyn. *Textiles of Southeast Asia: Tradition, Trade, and Transformation.* Melbourne: Oxford University Press, 1990.

McIntyre, Sophie. *Imagining Taiwan: The Role of Art in Taiwan's Quest for Identity.* Modern Asian Art and Visual Culture. The Netherlands: Brill, 2018.

Meskimmon, Marsha. *Transnational Feminisms, Transversal Politics and Art Entanglements and Intersections.* Abingdon: Routledge, 2020. doi.org/10.4324/9780429507830.

Miklouho-Maklai, Brita. *Exposing Society's Wounds, Some Aspects of Contemporary Art since 1966.* Adelaide: Flinders University of South Australia, 1991.

Mohamad, Goenawan. 'Indonesia's Asia'. *Asia in Transition: Representation and Identity.* The Japan Foundation 30th Anniversary International Symposium. Tokyo: Japan Foundation, 2002.

Munroe, Alexandra, ed. *Scream against the Sky: Japanese Art after 1945.* New York: Harry N. Abrams, Inc., 1994.

Museum MACAN (Modern and Contemporary Art in Nusantara). 'Home'. Accessed 22 January 2022. www.museummacan.org/.

Nadarajan, Gunalan, Russell Storer and Eugene Tan. *Contemporary Art in Singapore.* Institute of Contemporary Arts Singapore, 2007.

Nakamura, Fuyubi, Morgan Perkins and Olivier Krischer, eds. *Asia through Art and Anthropology: Cultural Translation Across Borders*. London; New York: Bloomsbury Academic, 2013.

Nelson, Roger. *Modern Art of Southeast Asia: Introductions from A to Z*. Singapore: National Gallery Singapore, 2019.

Piyadasa, Redza. 'Modern Malaysian Art, 1945–1991: A Historical Overview'. In *Tradition and Change: Contemporary Art of Asia and the Pacific*, edited by Caroline Turner, 58–71. Brisbane: University of Queensland Press, 1993.

Poshyananda, Apinan. *Contemporary Art in Asia: Traditions/Tensions*. New York: Asia Society Galleries, 1996.

Poshyananda, Apinan. *Modern Art in Thailand: Nineteenth and Twentieth Centuries*. Oxford University Press, 1992.

Queensland Art Gallery | Gallery of Modern Art. 'Library: Asian and Pacific Art'. Accessed 22 January 2022, www.qagoma.qld.gov.au/learn/research/library.

Rahadiningtyas, Anissa. 'Islam and Art in the Makings of the Modern in Indonesia'. PhD diss., Cornell University, 2021.

Rahman, Arham. 'Post-1989 Indonesia: Investigating the Position of Our Art in the Era of Globalised Art'. Accessed 2 November 2020. www.academia.edu/21592067/Post_1989_Indonesia_Investigating_the_Position_of_Our_Art_in_the_Era_of_Globalised_Art.

Rath, Amanda Katherine. 'Contextualizing "Contemporary Art": Propositions of Critical Artistic Practice in Seni Rupa Kontemporer in Indonesia'. PhD diss., Cornell University, 2011.

Rath, Amanda Katherine. *Taboo and Transgression in Contemporary Indonesian Art*. Herbert F. Johnson Museum of Art, Cornell University, 2005.

Roberts, Claire. *New Art from China: Post-Mao Product*. Exhibition catalogue. Sydney: Art Gallery of NSW, 1992.

Robinson, Kathryn. *Asian and Pacific Cosmopolitans: Self and Subject in Motion*. UK: Palgrave Macmillan, 2007. doi.org/10.1057/9780230592049.

Sabapathy, T. K. 'Developing Regionalist Perspectives in South-East Asian Art Historiography'. In *The Second Asia-Pacific Triennial of Contemporary Art*, 13–17. Brisbane: Queensland Art Gallery, 1996.

Sabapathy, T. K. *Intersecting Histories: Contemporary Turns in Southeast Asian Art*. Nanyang Technological University, 2012.

Sabapathy, T. K. ed. *Modernity and Beyond: Themes in Southeast Asian Art.* Singapore: Singapore Art Museum, 1996.

Sabapathy, T. K. *Vision and Idea: ReLooking Modern Malaysian Art.* Kuala Lumpur: National Art Gallery, 1994.

Sabapathy, T. K. *Writing the Modern: Selected Texts on Art & Art History in Singapore, Malaysia & Southeast Asia*, edited by Ahmad Mashadi, Susie Lingham, Peter Schoppert and Joyce Toh. Singapore: Singapore Art Museum, 2018.

Sabapathy, T. K., Patrick D. Flores and Niranjan Rajah, eds. *36 Ideas from Asia: Contemporary South-East Asian Art.* Singapore Art Museum, 2002.

Saidon, Hasnul J. and Beverly Yong. *Between Generations: 50 Years across Modern Art in Malaysia.* Kuala Lumpur and Penang: University of Malaysia, Valentine Willie Fine Art and Universiti Sains Malaysia, 2007.

Samboh, Grace. 'Consequential Privileges of the Social Artists: Meandering through the Practices of Siti Adiyati Subangun, Semsar Siahaan and Moelyono'. *Southeast of Now* 4, no. 2 (October 2020): 205–35. doi.org/10.1353/sen.2020.0010.

Sambrani, Chaitanya. 'Achipelagic Cosmopolitanism: A Prehistory of Contemporary art in Indonesia'. In *Contemporary Worlds: Indonesia*, edited by Jaklyn Babington and Carol Cains, 15–20. Canberra: National Gallery of Australia, 2019.

Sambrani, Chaitanya, ed. *Edge of Desire: Recent Art in India.* London: Philip Wilson Publishers, 2005.

Scott, Phoebe. 'Forming and Reforming the Artist: Modernity, Agency and the Discourse of Art in North Vietnam, 1925–1954'. PhD diss., University of Sydney, 2012.

Shioda, Junichi, Osamu Fukunaga and Yasuko Furuichi. *Art in Southeast Asia 1997: Glimpses into the Future.* Exhibition catalogue. Tokyo: Museum of Contemporary Art & Hiroshima: 1997.

Sidharta, Amir. 'Indonesia Art during the Revolutionary War'. Lecture Stedelijk Museum, 7 October 2019. Accessed 16 March 2022. www.stedelijk.nl/en/digdeeper/indonesian-art-during-revolutionary-war.

Sidharta, Amir. 'Indonesian Views of Raden Saleh'. Accessed 25 January 2022. www.academia.edu/37630216/Indonesian_Views_of_Raden_Saleh.

Sidharta, Amir, et al. *S. Sudjojono: Visible Soul.* Jakarta: Museum S. Sudjojono, 2006.

Singapore Art Museum. 'Home'. Accessed 25 January 2022. www.singaporeartmuseum.sg/.

Singapore Biennale. [Catalogues]. 2006–continuing.

Singapore National Gallery Singapore. 'Home'. Accessed 25 January 2022. www.nationalgallery.sg/.

Smith, Terry. *What Is Contemporary Art?* Chicago: University of Chicago Press, 2009.

Smith, Terry, Okwui Enwezor and Nancy Condee, eds. *Antimonies of Art and Culture: Modernity, Postmodernity, Contemporaneity*. Durham, NC: Duke University Press, 2009. doi.org/10.2307/j.ctv11hpm3c.

Soebadio, Haryati, ed. *Pusaka: Art of Indonesia: From the Collections of the National Museum of the Republic of Indonesia*. Singapore: Archipelago Press, 1992.

Soedarmadji, Jean Henry Damais. *Majapahit Terracotta: The Soedarmadji Jean Henry Damais Collection*. Indonesia: Bab Publishing, 2012.

Soon, Simon. 'What is Left of Art? The Spatio-Visual Practice of Political Art in Indonesia, Singapore, Thailand, and the Philippines, 1950s–1970s'. PhD diss., University of Sydney, 2015.

Southeast of Now: Directions in Contemporary and Modern Art in Asia. Journal. Singapore: National University of Singapore. Accessed 25 January 2022. muse.jhu.edu/journal/716.

Spanjaard, Helena. *Artists and Their Inspiration: A Guide through Indonesian Art, 1930–2015*. LM publishers, 2016 (first published in Dutch).

Spanjaard, Helena. *Modern Indonesian Painting*. Translated by S. Wessing. Sotheby's, 2003. (A revision of her 1998 dissertation in Dutch, 'Het ideaal van een moderne Indonesische schilderkunst, 1900–1995, de creatie van een nationale culturele identiteit'.)

Spielmann, Yvonne. *Contemporary Indonesian Art: Artists, Art Spaces and Collectors*. National University of Singapore Press, 2017. (German edition first published in 2015.)

S. Sudjojono Center. 'Home'. Accessed 25 January 2022. ssudjojonocenter.com/.

Storer, Russell. *Between Worlds: Raden Saleh and Juan Luna*. Singapore: National Gallery Singapore, 2017.

Strassler, Karen. *Demanding Images: Democracy, Mediation, and the Image-Event in Indonesia*. Durham, NC: Duke University Press, 2020. doi.org/10.2307/j.ctv11qdxrf.

Sudjojono [Soedjojono], S. 'Kesenian, Seniman dan Masyarakat'. In *Seni Loekis, Kesenian dan Seniman*. Yogyakarta: Penerbit Indonesia Sekarang, 1946.

Sudjojono [Soedjojono], S. 'Seni Loekis di Indonesia, Sekarang dan Jang Akan Datang'. In *Seni Loekis, Kesenian dan Seniman*. Yogyakarta: Penerbit Indonesia Sekarang, 1946.

Sudjojono [Soedjojono], S. *Seni Loekis, Kesenian dan Seniman*. Yogyakarta: Penerbit Indonesia Sekarang, 1946.

Sudjojono, Sindudarsono. '"We Know Where We Will Be Taking Indonesian Art", 1948'. *Southeast of Now: Directions in Contemporary and Modern Art in Asia* 1, no. 2 (October 2017): 159–64. Translated Isabella Brigitta. (Originally published in 1948.) doi.org/10.1353/sen.2017.0017.

Sullivan, Michael. *The Meeting of Eastern and Western Art*. Berkeley: University of California Press, 1989. doi.org/10.1525/9780520324084.

S*UNSHOWER: Contemporary Art from Southeast Asia 1980s to Now*. National Art Center. Tokyo: Mori Art Museum and the Japan Foundation Asia Center, 2017.

Supangkat, Jim. 'A Brief History of Indonesian Modern Art'. In *Tradition and Change: Contemporary Art of Asia and the Pacific,* edited by Caroline Turner, 47–57. Brisbane: University of Queensland Press, 1993.

Supangkat, Jim. 'Art and Politics in Indonesia'. In *Art and Social Change: Contemporary Art in Asia and the Pacific*, edited by Caroline Turner, 218–28. Canberra: Pandanus Press, 2005.

Supangkat, Jim, ed. *Gerakan Seni Rupa Baru Indonesia*. Jakarta: Gramedia, 1979.

Supangkat, Jim. *Indonesian Modern Art and Beyond*. Jakarta: Yayasan Seni Rupa Indonesia/The Indonesian Fine Arts Foundation, in cooperation with Museum Universitas Pelita Harapan & Edwin's Gallery, 1997.

Supangkat, Jim. 'Multiculturalism/Multimodernism'. In *Contemporary Art in Asia: Traditions/Tensions*, edited by Apinan Poshyananda, 70–81. New York: Asia Society Galleries, 1996.

Supangkat, Jim. 'Two Forms of Indonesian Art'. In *Modern Indonesian Art: Three Generations of Tradition and Change*, edited by Joseph Fischer, 158–62. Jakarta: Panitia Pameran KIAS; New York: Festival of Indonesia, 1990.

Supangkat, Jim, Irma Damajanti and Elly Kent. *The World and I: Heri Dono's Art Odyssey*. Jakarta: ArtOne, 2014.

Supangkat, Jim and Landung Rusyanto Simatupang. *Outlet: Yogya Dalam Peta Seni Rupa Kontemporer Indonesia*. Yogyakarta: Yayasan Seni Cemeti, 2000.

Supangkat, Jim, Sanento Yuliman, Arief Budiman, Emmanuel Subangun and Soejtipto Wirosardjono. *Seni Rupa Baru Proyek 1: Pasaraya Dunia Fantasi*. Jakarta: Percetakan Gramedia, 1987.

Supartono, A. and S. Karsono, eds. *Dolorosa Sinaga: Body, Form, Matter – Analysis, Artistic Genealogy, and Archive*. Jakarta, Indonesia: Jakarta Art Institute Press, 2020.

Suprianto, Enin. 'The Mother of Indonesian Art'. In *Contemporary Worlds: Indonesia*, edited by Jaklyn Babington and Carol Cains, 33–40. Canberra: National Gallery of Australia, 2019.

Swastika, Alia. 'Aktivisme Sebagai Medium Seni'. 2016. Accessed 25 January 2022. www.academia.edu/23732416/Aktivisme_sebagai_Medium_Seni.

Swastika, Alia. 'Biennale Sebagai Ruang Wacana: Penciptaan, Pembacaan dan Gagasan Tentang Publik'. *Skripta* 1, no. 1 (2014): 5–15.

Swastika, Alia. *Manifesto: The New Aesthetic of Seven Indonesian Artists*. Singapore: Institute of Contemporary Arts Singapore, 2010.

Swastika, Alia. *Membaca Praktik Negosiasi Seniman Perempuan dan Politik Gender Orde Baru* [Reading the negotiation practices of women artists and gender politics in the New Order]. Jakarta: Tan Kinira Books, 2019.

Swastika, Alia. *The Past The Forgotten Time*. Exhibition. Amsterdam, Jakarta, Semarang, Shanghai, Singapore, 2007–08.

Swastika, Alia. 'The Private and the Public Body in the Works of Indonesian Women Artists'. In *Contemporary Worlds: Indonesia*, edited by Jaklyn Babington and Carol Cains, 44–50. Canberra: National Gallery of Australia, 2019.

Tatehata, Akira, Tsutomu Mizusawa and Junichi Shioda, eds. *Asian Modernism – Diverse Development in Indonesia, the Philippines, and Thailand*. Tokyo: The Japan Foundation Asia Center, 1995.

Tatehata, Akira, et al. *Asian Cubism*. Tokyo: Museum of Modern Art, 2005.

Taylor, Nora Annesley. *Painters in Hanoi: An Ethnography of Vietnamese Art*. Honolulu: University of Hawai'i Press, 2009. doi.org/10.1515/9780824845100.

Taylor, Nora A. and Boreth Ly, eds. *Modern and Contemporary Southeast Asian Art: An Anthology*. New York: Cornell University, 2012.

Teh, David. 'Regionality and Contemporaneity'. *World Art* 10, no. 2–3 (2020): 351–70. doi.org/10.1080/21500894.2020.1802331.

Teh, David. *Thai Art: Currencies of the Contemporary*. Cambridge Mass: MIT Press, 2017.

Tomii, Reiko. *Radicalism in the Wilderness: International Contemporaneity and 1960s Art in Japan*. Cambridge MA: The MIT Press, 2016.

Turner, Caroline, ed. *Art and Social Change: Contemporary Art in Asia and the Pacific*. Canberra: Pandanus Books, 2005.

Turner, Caroline. 'Cultural Transformations in the Asia-Pacific: The Asia-Pacific Triennial and the Fukuoka Triennale Compared'. In *Eye of the Beholder: Reception, Audiences and Practice of Modern Asian Art*, edited by John Clark, Maurizo Peleggi and T.K. Sabapathy, 221–43. The University of Sydney East Asian Series, no. 15. Sydney: Wild Peony, 2006.

Turner, Caroline. 'Indonesia: Art, Freedom, Human Rights and Engagement with the West'. In *Art and Social Change: Contemporary Art in Asia and the Pacific*, edited by Caroline Turner, 196–217. Canberra: Pandanus Books.

Turner, Caroline, ed. *Tradition and Change: Contemporary Art of Asia and the Pacific*. St Lucia: University of Queensland Press, 1993.

Turner, Caroline and Morris Low, eds. *Beyond the Future: Papers from the Conference of the Third Asia-Pacific Triennial of Contemporary Art, 1999*. Brisbane: Queensland Art Gallery, 1999.

Turner, Caroline and Jen Webb. *Art and Human Rights: Contemporary Asian Contexts*. Manchester: Manchester University Press, 2016.

Universes in Universe. 'Home'. Accessed 17 March 2022. universes.art/en/.

Ushiroshoji, Masahiro. *The Birth of Modern Art in Southeast Asia: Artists and Movements*. Fukuoka: Fukuoka Art Museum, 1997.

Ushiroshoji, Masahiro. *New Generation of Asian Art*. Fukuoka Art Museum, 1997.

Veal, Clare. 'Thainess Framed: Photography and Thai Identity, 1946–2010'. PhD diss., University of Sydney, 2016.

Vickers, Adrian. *Balinese Art: Paintings and Drawings of Bali 1800–2010*. Singapore: Tuttle Publishing, 2012.

Vickers, Adrian. 'Balinese Modernism'. In *Charting Thoughts: Essays on Art in Southeast Asia*, edited by Low Sze Wee, Patrick D Flores, 120–29. Singapore: National Gallery Singapore, 2017. doi.org/10.2307/j.ctv13xpr6k.12.

Vickers, Adrian. 'Bali's Place in Indonesian Art'. In *Crossing Boundaries – Bali: A Window to 20th Century Indonesian Art*. Melbourne: Asia Society AustralAsia Centre, 2002.

Vickers, Adrian. 'History and Art History in Southeast Asia'. Accessed 11 September 2022. www.newmandala.org/history-and-art-history-in-southeast-asia/.

Vickers, Adrian. *A History of Modern Indonesia*. New York: Cambridge University Press, 2012. doi.org/10.1017/CBO9781139094665.

Vickers, Adrian. 'A Hundred Years of Indonesian Art'. Seminar ISEAS-Yusof Ishak Institute Singapore 2017. Accessed 25 January 2022. www.iseas.edu.sg/media/event-highlights/indonesian-art-in-1976-a-hundred-years-of-indonesian-art/.

Wardani, Farah. 'The Japan Factor: Great Asianism & The Birth of Indonesian Modern Art (1942–1945)'. Paper delivered at CAA Conference 2013. Accessed 25 January 2022. www.academia.edu/2919490/Paper_THE_JAPAN_FACTOR_Great_Asianism_and_The_Birth_of_Indonesian_Modern_Art_1942_1945_?auto=download.

Wee, Wan-ling, C. J. '"We Asians"? Modernity, Visual Art Exhibitions, and East Asia'. *Boundary 2* 37, no. 1 (2010): 91–126. doi.org/10.1215/01903659-2009-038.

Whiteman, Stephen H., Sarena Abdullah, Yvonne Low and Phoebe Scott. *Ambitious Alignments: New Histories of Southeast Asian Art, 1945–1990*. Sydney and Singapore: Power Publications and National Gallery Singapore, 2018.

Wiyanto, Hendro. 'Memberi Makna Pada Ingatan' [Giving meaning to memory]. In *Kengerian Tak Terucapkan/The Unspeakable Horror*. Exhibition catalogue. Jakarta: Bentara.

Wiyanto, Hendro. *What We Have Here Perceived as Truth, We Shall Some Day Encounter as Beauty: A Solo Show by FX Harsono*. Jakarta: Indonesia Galeri Canna, 2013.

Wiyanto, Hendro, Seng Yu Jin and Tan Siuli. *Repetition/Position: FX Harsono*. Magelang: Langgeng Art Foundation. 2010.

Wright, Astri. 'The Arc of My Field Is a Rainbow with an Expanding Twist and All Kinds of Creatures Dancing: The Growing Inclusivity of Indonesian Art History'. In *Producing Indonesia*, edited by Eric Tagliacozzo. Ithaca NY: Southeast Asia Program, 2014. Accessed 25 January 2022. www.academia.edu/12176189/Astri_Wright_The_Arc_of_my_Field_is_a_Rainbow_with_an_Expanding_Twist_and_all_kinds_of_Creatures_Dancing_The_Growing_Inclusivity_of_Indonesian_Art_History_in_Eric_Tagliacozzo_Ed._Producing_Indonesia_2014.

Wright, Astri. *Soul, Spirit, and Mountain: Preoccupations of Contemporary Indonesian Painters*. Kuala Lumpur; New York: Oxford University Press, 1994.

Wright, Astri. 'Titik Pertama, Titik Utama—First Dot, Main Dot: Creating and Connecting in Modern/Indigenous Javanese/Global Batik Art'. In *Modern and Contemporary Southeast Asian Art: An Anthology*, edited by Nora A. Taylor and Boreth Ly, 1–39. Ithaca, NY: Southeast Asia Program, Cornell University, 2012.

Wright, Astri and Agus T. Dermawan. *Hendra Gunawan: A Great Modern Indonesian Painter*. Jakarta: Ciputra Foundation, 2001.

Wu Hung, ed. *Chinese Art at the Crossroads: Between Past and Future, Between East and West*. Hong Kong: INIVA and New Art Media, Hong Kong, 2001.

Wulia, Tintin. 'Aleatoric Geopolitics: Art, Chance and Critical Play on the Border'. PhD diss., RMIT University, 2013.

Yuliman, Sanento. 'Dua Seni Rupa'. Paper for the Simposium Nasional Seni Rupa, at the Dewan Kesenian Surabaya, 1984. In *Dua Seni Rupa: Sepilihan Tulisan Sanento Yuliman*, edited by Hasan Asikin. Jakarta: Yayasan Kalam, 2001.

Yuliman, Sanento. 'Genèse de la Peinture Indonésienne contemporaine: Le rôle de S. Sudjojono' [The origins of contemporary Indonesian art: S. Sudjojono's role]. PhD diss., École des Hautes Études en Sciences Sociales, Paris, 1981.

Yuliman, Sanento. 'Perspektif Baru' [A new perspective]. In *Gerakan Seni Rupa Baru Indonesia*, edited by Jim Supangkat, 96–98. Jakarta: PT Gramedia, 1979.

Yuliman, Sanento. 'S. Sudjojono'. In *S. Sudjojono 1913–1986*. Retrospective. Jakarta Duta Fine Arts Gallery, 1986.

Yuliman, Sanento and Jim Supangkat. 'Seni Rupa Sehari-Hari Menentang Elitisme'. In *Seni Rupa Baru Proyek 1 Pasar Raya Dunia Fantasi*, edited by Jim Supangkat. Jakarta: Gramedia, 1987.

Zaelani, Rizki. 'Contemporary Art in Indonesia: Beware! After the Big Chance'. In *Awas! Recent Art from Indonesia*. Yogyakarta: Cemeti Art Foundation, 2002.

Zhang, Lansheng. 'The Spirit of Individualism: Avant-Garde Art in Shanghai 1979–1989'. PhD diss., The Australian National University, 2020.

Author Biographies

Wulan Dirgantoro is a lecturer in art history and curatorship in the School of Culture and Communication at the University of Melbourne, where she was previously a McKenzie Postdoctoral Fellow. Her research interests are gender and feminism, and trauma and memory, in Indonesian modern and contemporary art. Her publications include *Feminisms and Contemporary Art in Indonesia: Defining Experiences* (Amsterdam University Press, 2017) and 'Aesthetics of Silence: Exploring Trauma in Indonesian Painting 1970–1980' in *Ambitious Alignments: New Histories of Southeast Asian Art 1945–1990* (Power Publication and the National Gallery of Singapore, 2018). She has also contributed to various art publications in Asia, Australia and UK on Indonesian modern and contemporary art. Prior to her current role, she was a lecturer at the MA Asian Art Histories program at LASALLE College of the Arts, Singapore (2014–16), research fellow of Art Histories and Aesthetic Practices 2016/2017 (Forum Transregionale Studien) and visiting fellow at the Institute for Cultural Inquiry, Berlin.

FX Harsono is one of Indonesia's most distinguished and internationally respected artists. He studied painting and worked as a graphic designer in Jakarta. During the 1970s he was a founding member of Gerakan Seni Rupa Baru (New Art Movement) and the Desember Hitam (Black December) movement. During the New Order of President Suharto (1966–98) his art utilised compelling symbols to indicate the silencing of dissent and was concerned with issues of justice and injustice, democracy, the destruction of the environment and human rights. For his commitment to social justice he was awarded the international Joseph Balestier Award for Freedom of Art in 2015. In the post-Reformasi era, after the fall of the Suharto government, Harsono's work has become more self-referential. He has engaged in a social research project, working directly with the Chinese-Indonesian community of his ancestry, documenting their stories on film. In 2010, the Singapore Art Museum held a major retrospective of his works from the 1970s to the present day. He was a keynote speaker at the conference 'Contemporary Worlds: Indonesian Art', held at The Australian National University in 2019.

Virginia Hooker, AM, FAHA, is professor emerita and a fellow in the Department of Political and Social Change, ANU College of Asia and the Pacific, The Australian National University. Her current research concerns Islam-themed art in Southeast Asia. She was a member of the board of the Australian Government's Australia–Indonesia Institute from 2002 to 2010. Among her publications are 'Art for Allah's Sake' (*Inside Indonesia* 101, 2010); 'Reflections of the Soul' (*Inside Indonesia* 112, 2013); 'Mindful of Allah: Islam and the Visual Arts in Indonesia and Malaysia' (*Artlink* 33, no. 1, 2013); 'When Laws are Not Enough: Ethics, Aesthetics, and Intra-Religious Pluralism in Contemporary Indonesia', in *Pluralism, Transnationalism and Culture in Asian Law*, edited by Gary F. Bell (ISEAS: Singapore, 2017); and '"By the Pen!": Spreading *'ilm* in Indonesia through Quranic Calligraphy', in *'Ilm: Science, Religion and Art in Islam*, edited by Samer Akkach (University of Adelaide Press, 2019).

Elly Kent is a lecturer in Indonesian studies at UNSW Canberra. Between 2019 and 2022 she was, variously, the editor of *New Mandala*, the deputy director of the ANU Indonesia Institute and a visiting fellow at the Centre for Art History and Art Theory, ANU College of Arts and Social Sciences, The Australian National University. Elly has published widely on artists and art practices in Indonesia and has worked extensively as a translator for arts organisations there, as well as lecturing on Indonesian art and design through the Australian Consortium for In-Country Indonesian Studies. Her book *Artists and the People: Ideologies of Art in Indonesia* (NUS Press, 2022) examines why so many artists in the world's largest archipelagic nation choose, in their art practices, to work directly with people. Elly is an alumna of the Endeavour Award: Prime Minister's Australia–Asia Postgraduate Award, won the 4A Centre for Contemporary Asian Art's Emerging Artist Award in 2012 and sits on the management committee of the Asian Arts Society of Australia.

T. K. Sabapathy is one of the most respected and highly regarded art historians in Southeast Asia, and Singapore awarded him a Cultural Medallion, in recognition of his contribution to art and culture. As an historian, curator, critic and adviser he has influenced artistic opinion and shaped knowledge of visual art in Southeast Asia for over 40 years. While his early work engaged with the Hindu-Buddhist traditions of the region, he is best known for his ardent advocacy of modernist and contemporary art. His work, which exemplifies careful fieldwork and connections with artists and art institutions across Southeast Asia and beyond, has played a seminal role in the awareness of contemporary Asian art outside the region. In addition to being a prolific writer and curator, he continues to teach histories of Asian art and architecture at the National University of Singapore. His most recent book is *Writing the Modern: Selected Texts on Art and Art History in Singapore, Malaysia and Southeast Asia* (NUS Press, 2018). He has been a frequent visitor to The Australian National University and was a keynote speaker at 'Contemporary Worlds: Indonesian Art' (2019).

Jim Supangkat was born in Makassar, Indonesia, in 1948. He entered the Faculty of Fine Art and Design, Bandung Institute of Technology, in 1970. In 1975 he was a key founder of the Gerakan Seni Rupa Baru (Indonesian New Art Movement), which is regarded as a critical movement in contemporary art in Indonesian. In 1992, Supangkat decided to give up his work as a lecturer and artist and become a curator. In that role his work was highly influential in introducing Indonesian contemporary art to international audiences. He has also initiated international contemporary art exhibitions in Indonesia such as Contemporary Art of the Non-Aligned Countries (1995), CP Biennale I (2003) and CP Biennale II (2005). As an independent curator, he has been involved in many major Asian contemporary art exhibitions, including the Asia Pacific Triennial exhibitions in Australia. He has written several important books on Indonesian art and published numerous essays, for example, with the exhibition catalogue for *Traditions/Tensions* in New York in 1996. He is considered Indonesia's most eminent curator. In 1997, he received the prestigious Prince Claus Award (the Netherlands).

Alia Swastika is a Jakarta-based curator and writer. She graduated from the Communication Department, Gadjah Mada University, Yogyakarta. In 2000, she joined the KUNCI Cultural Studies Center to promote cultural studies discourses in Indonesia. She has worked as a freelance curator, writer and program director with Ark Galerie in Yogyakarta, Indonesia. In 2005, she joined a staff exchange program at the UfaFabrik, Berlin, Germany, and went on to complete a curatorial residency with BizArt, Shanghai, in 2008. She was a research fellow at the National Art Gallery, Singapore, supported by the Singapore International Foundation; curated the Jogja Biennale XI (Indonesia, 2011), *Shadow Lines: Indonesia Meets India*; and was co-artistic director of the ninth Gwangju Biennale,

ROUNDTABLE (Korea, 2012). She has curated major international group exhibitions including *The Past—the Forgotten Time* (Amsterdam, Jakarta, Semarang, Shanghai, Singapore, 2007–08) and *Manifesto: The New Aesthetic of Seven Indonesian Artists* (Institute of Contemporary Arts Singapore, 2010), as well as solo exhibitions for Eko Nugroho, Tintin Wulia, Wimo Ambala Bayang and Jompet Kuswidananto. Her most recent publication is in Indonesian with the translated title *Reading the Negotiation Practices of Women Artists and Gender Politics in the New Order* (Jakarta, 2019).

Caroline Turner, AM, FRSA, is an honorary senior research fellow and associate professor in the Research School of Humanities and the Arts, ANU College of Arts and Social Sciences, The Australian National University. She was deputy director of the Humanities Research Centre, ANU, from 2000 to 2006. As a senior museum professional and deputy director of the Queensland Art Gallery from 1982 to 1999, she played a key role in the gallery's international programs and was also co-founder and project director for the Queensland Art Gallery's first three Asia Pacific Triennial exhibitions in the 1990s (a continuing project that has won international acclaim). She was also a member of the board of the Australian Government's Australia–Indonesia Institute in the same decade. She has also served as deputy director of the ANU Indonesia Institute. She has published extensively on contemporary Asian art and her 1993 edited collection of essays *Tradition and Change: Contemporary Art of Asia and the Pacific* (Queensland University Press) was the first publication in English to survey the emerging modern and contemporary art of the Asia Pacific region. Her most recent publication (with Jen Webb) is *Art and Human Rights: Contemporary Asian Contexts* (Manchester University Press, 2016).

Sanento Yuliman (1941–1992) was an eminent art historian, critic and theorist whose work continues to make important contributions to the development of art discourses of, in and about Indonesia. Born in Central Java just before the Japanese occupation, Yuliman took up studies in the painting studio in the Bandung Institute of Art's (ITB) fine art faculty in 1960. From 1966, while still a student, he contributed cartoons to various publications including *Mahasiswa Indonesia* (Indonesian student) and *Mimbar Demokrasi* (Democratic Forum), and in 1968 published his first, award-winning poems in the literary journal *Horison*. Yuliman's final undergraduate thesis (on criticism of painting) won the Hamid Bouchouareb Award from ITB that year. In 1975, he joined Gerakan Seni

Rupa Baru Indonesia (Indonesian New Art Movement) as a writer and conceptor. In 1976, he travelled to France and took up doctoral studies at the École des Hautes Études en Sciences Sociales, Paris. His doctoral dissertation, 'The Origins of Contemporary Indonesian Art: S. Sudjojono's Role', was completed under the supervision of Denys Lombard in 1981. From 1984 Yuliman regularly published in *Tempo,* amassing hundreds of reviews, opinion pieces, treatises and artist profiles. He was awarded the Adam Malik Award for best art critic and, in 1990, was involved in the formation of the Yayasan Seni Rupa Indonesia (Foundation for Indonesian Art). He was selected as curator for the First Asia Pacific Triennial at the Queensland Art Gallery, Brisbane, Australia, but died suddenly on 14 May 1992, before the exhibition opened.

www.ingramcontent.com/pod-product-compliance
Lightning Source LLC
LaVergne TN
LVHW052349100826
845147LV00013B/798